IN CASE OF ACCIDENT

In case of accident notify the laboratory instructor in

FIRE

Burning Clothing. Prevent the person from running and fanning the flames. Rolling the person on the floor will help extinguish the flames and prevent inhalation of the flames. If a safety shower is nearby hold the person under the shower until flames are extinguished and chemicals washed away. Do not use a fire blanket if a shower is nearby. The blanket does not cool and smoldering continues. Remove contaminated clothing. Wrap the person in a blanket to avoid shock. Get prompt medical attention.

Do not, under any circumstances, use a carbon tetrachloride (toxic) fire extinguisher and be very careful using a CO_2 extinguisher (the person may smother).

Burning Reagents. Extinguish all nearby burners and remove combustible material and solvents. Small fires in flasks and beakers can be extinguished by covering the container with a fiberglass-wire gauze square, a big beaker, or a watch glass. Use a dry chemical or carbon dioxide fire extinguisher directed at the base of the flames. **Do not use water.**

Burns, Either Thermal or Chemical. Flush the burned area with cold water for at least 15 min. Resume if pain returns. Wash off chemicals with a mild detergent and water. Current practice recommends that no neutralizing chemicals, unguents, creams, lotions, or salves be applied. If chemicals are spilled on a person over a large area quickly remove the contaminated clothing while under the safety shower. Seconds count, and time should not be wasted because of modesty. Get prompt medical attention.

CHEMICALS IN THE EYE: Flush the eye with copious amounts of water for 15 min using an eyewash fountain or bottle or by placing the injured person face up on the floor and pouring water in the open eye. Hold the eye open to wash behind the eyelids. After 15 min of washing obtain prompt medical attention, regardless of the severity of the injury.

CUTS: Minor Cuts. This type of cut is most common in the organic laboratory and usually arises from broken glass. Wash the cut, remove any pieces of glass, and apply pressure to stop the bleeding. Get medical attention.

Major Cuts. If blood is spurting place a pad directly on the wound, apply firm pressure, wrap the injured to avoid shock, and get **immediate** medical attention. Never use a tourniquet.

POISONS: Call 800 information (1-800-555-1212) for the telephone number of the nearest Poison Control Center, which is usually also an 800 number.

---

[1]Adapted from *Safety in Academic Chemistry Laboratories*, prepared by the American Chemical Society Committee on Chemical Safety, March 1996.

MACROSCALE AND MICROSCALE
ORGANIC EXPERIMENTS

ABBREVIATED FOURTH EDITION

KENNETH L. WILLIAMSON
Mount Holyoke College

Houghton Mifflin
Boston   New York

Publisher: Charles Hartford
Executive Editor: Richard Stratton
Development Editor: Rita Lombard
Editorial Assistant: Rosemary Mack
Senior Project Editor: Kathryn Dinovo
Cover Design Manager: Diana Coe
Senior Manufacturing Coordinator: Marie Barnes
Senior Marketing Manager: Katherine Greig
Marketing Associate: Alexandra Shaw

Custom Publishing Editor: Gina Montoya
Custom Publishing Production Manager: Kathleen McCourt
Project Manager: Kayla Whittet

This work was produced by Houghton Mifflin Custom Publishing and contains material not subject to Houghton Mifflin Company editorial review. The author is responsible for editing, accuracy, and content.

Cover Designer: Joel Gendron
Cover Image: GettyOne

Printed in the United States of America.

ISBN: 0-618-35741-6
N02258

3 4 5 6 7 8 9 – PP – 04

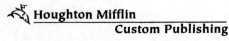

Houghton Mifflin
Custom Publishing

222 Berkeley Street • Boston, MA 02116

Address all correspondence and order information to the above address.

Contents

Preface   xi

1   Introduction   1

2   Laboratory Safety and Waste Disposal   25

Techniques

3   Crystallization   38

4   Melting Points, Boiling Points, and Refractive Indices   65

5   Distillation   80

6   Steam Distillation   98

7   Vacuum Distillation and Sublimation   110

8   Extraction of Acids and Bases and the Isolation of Caffeine from Coffee, Tea, and Cola Syrup   126

9   Thin-Layer Chromatography: Analysis of Analgesics and Isolation of Lycopene from Tomato Paste   156

10   Column Chromatography: Acetylferrocene, Cholesteryl Acetate, and Fluorenone   171

11   Alkenes from Alcohols: Analysis of a Mixture by Gas Chromatography   184

12   Infrared Spectroscopy   194

13   Nuclear Magnetic Resonance Spectroscopy   216

14   Ultraviolet Spectroscopy and Mass Spectrometry   235

38   Grignard Synthesis of Triphenylmethanol and Benzoic Acid   461

39   The Wittig and Wittig–Horner Reactions   479

Reactions of Carboxylic Acids, Esters, and Amines

40   Esterification and Hydrolysis   486

70   Qualitative Organic Analysis   762

71   Searching the Chemical Literature   799

Index   806

Preface

Innovation and exploration have always been the hallmarks of *Macroscale and Microscale Organic Experiments*. We are proud to have been part of a movement toward the increased use of microscale experiments in the undergraduate organic laboratory course. In preparing the fourth edition, we have attempted to build on the strengths of previous editions while continuing to add innovative new techniques, features, and experiments.

New to This Edition

Ease of use characterizes this Fourth Edition of *Macroscale and Microscale Organic Experiments*. A short preface to selected procedures has been added entitled "In this experiment. . . ." This précis gives an overall view of the experimental work to be carried out without the detail that may obscure the end result. You will also find a CD inside the back cover, another addition intended to make the organic chemistry laboratory a pleasant experience.

Student CD-Rom

Throughout the text in the left margin adjacent to the experimental procedures you will find numbers and letters that are keyed to the CD. The numbers refer to photographs that amplify the figures that illustrate apparatus and techniques. The letters refer to short videos of techniques that are more easily shown in motion than in a static drawing or photograph. There are no chemical formulas or numerical data on the CD. It is intended solely to augment the descriptions and drawings in the text.

Several complete experiments are presented as videos on the CD. The "Synthesis of Ferrocene," for example, illustrates in 3 minutes the operations needed for this complex experiment, an experiment that requires a minimum of 90 minutes in the laboratory.

Innovative Techniques from Previous Editions

Innovations from the second edition of this text have proved to be just as valuable as when first introduced. Among the two most important are the use of *t*-butyl methyl ether in place of diethyl ether and the use of anhydrous calcium chloride pellets as a drying agent. *t*-Butyl methyl ether is one of the most common and cheapest solvents being produced because it has replaced tetraethyl lead as an antiknock additive and as an oxygenate, added to reduce pollution, in gasoline. Not only is it cheaper than diethyl ether, it does not easily form peroxides and therefore can be stored more than 30 days after the container is opened; it has a higher boiling point (55°C) than diethyl ether and is therefore somewhat less flammable; and it forms a 4% azeotrope with water, so as it is removed it also removes the last traces of water from a solution. All in all it should become the solvent of choice, replacing diethyl ether in all applications except the Grignard reaction.

We continue to be very enthusiastic about the use of anhydrous calcium chloride pellets as a drying agent, an innovation introduced in the second edition. These pellets do not fracture and powder and so are ideally suited to drying microscale quantities of solutions where the solvent can simply be drawn off with a Pasteur pipette, making conventional filtration unnecessary.

The chapter on computational chemistry and molecular mechanics is an introduction to a tool that, like spectroscopy, can give new insight into the structure of organic molecules. Procedures for the application of this tool are given to no fewer than 20 experiments.

Chemistry students are very enthusiastic about the synthesis of a fluorescer using the Wittig reaction and the synthesis of a Cyalume in order to make their own light sticks. The use of the Multifiber Fabric in the experiment on dyes and dyeing, Norit decolorizing charcoal in the form of pellets, the microscale cracking of dicyclopentadiene, and the multistep syntheses starting with the benzoin condensation of benzaldehyde, benzyne experiments, and tetraphenylcyclopentadienone are among the innovative experiments that have appeared in previous editions of this text, which dates to 1935 when Louis Fieser was the author. Remember, you saw it first in Williamson.

The "Biomimetic Synthesis of Pseudopellitierene" following the classic work of Robert Robinson is a relatively new experiment, as is the "Conversion of Camphene to Camphor."

Waste Disposal and Safety

The section at the end of every experiment entitled "Cleaning Up" has been written with the intent of focusing students' attention on not just the desired product from a reaction but also on all of the other substances produced in a typical organic reaction.

As one of the coauthors of the first edition of *Prudent Practices for the Disposal of Chemicals from Laboratories,* I have continued to follow closely the rapidly evolving regulatory climate and changes in laboratory safety rules and regulations. The safety information in this text is about as current as possible, but this is a rapidly changing area of chemistry; local rules and regulations must be known and adhered to.

Supplements

Instructor's Guide

The *Instructor's Guide* is an important adjunct to this text. It contains discussions about the time needed to carry out each experiment and assessment of the relative difficulty of each experiment, problems that might be encountered, answers to end-of-chapter questions, a list of chemicals and apparatus required for each experiment—both per student and per 24-student laboratory—sources of supply for unusual items, and a discussion of hardware and software needed for running calculational chemistry and molecular mechanics experimentation. Note especially comments regarding the transfer hydrogenation experiment in Chapter 25.

Desk copies of this *Instructor's Guide* are available by contacting your local Houghton Mifflin sales representative.

Web Site

Please visit our Web site at *www.hmco.com* for resource information intended to support users of this lab manual.

Molecular Drawing and Visualization Programs

A free chemical drawing program is available from MDL (Molecular Design Limited) at http://mdli.com/downloads/isis.draw/isisdraw.html and from the same company a molecular visualization program is available at http://www.mdlchime.com/chime

Acknowledgments

I would like to acknowledge the help of many classes of Chemistry 302 at Mount Holyoke College in developing and refining the experiments in this text, as well as the contributions sent to me by students and faculty at many institutions. I am also indebted to the chemistry departments at MIT where I taught in 1996 and 1997 and at Caltech where I taught in 2000.

I also wish to express my thanks to various people at Houghton Mifflin: Richard Stratton, Executive Editor; Rita Lombard, Developmental Editor; and Kathryn Dinovo, Senior Production Editor; to Becky Dodson, Senior Project Editor at Elm Street Publishing Services; and to the reviewers of this text: Jane Wissinger Cornille, Ph.D. (University of Minnesota), Michelle Dose (Hardin-Simmons University), Tracy A. Halmi (Penn State Erie, The Behrend College), Frederick A. Luzzio (University of Louisville), Vimala A. Majeti (Xavier University), Sandra L. Omstead (Augsburg College), Kerri Scott (University of Mississippi), and Stanislaw Skonieczny (University of Toronto). I also wish to thank Peter Samal at UMASS Amherst for providing laboratory facilities and to Barry Snider at Brandeis University for very valuable comments on the transfer hydrogenation experiment.

And finally I wish to acknowledge the enduring legacy of Mary Fieser who passed away in 1997. This great chemist and author was a perceptive critic and constant inspiration.

KENNETH L. WILLIAMSON

ORGANIC EXPERIMENTS AND WASTE DISPOSAL

An unusual feature of this book is the advice at the end of each experiment on how to dispose of its chemical waste. Waste disposal thus becomes part of the experiment, which is not considered finished until the waste products are appropriately taken care of. This is a valuable addition to the book for several reasons.

Although chemical waste from laboratories is less than 0.1% of that generated in the United States, its disposal is nevertheless subject to many of the same federal, state, and local regulations as is chemical waste from industry. Accordingly, there are both strong ethical and legal reasons for proper disposal of laboratory wastes. These reasons are backed up by a financial concern, because the cost of waste disposal can become a significant part of the cost of operating a laboratory.

There is yet another reason to include instructions for waste disposal in a teaching laboratory. Students will someday be among those conducting and regulating waste disposal operations and voting on appropriations for them. Learning the principles and methods of sound waste disposal early in their careers will benefit them and society later.

The basics of waste disposal are easy to grasp. Some innocuous water-soluble wastes are flushed down the drain with a large proportion of water. Common inorganic acids and bases are neutralized and flushed down the drain. Containers are provided for several classes of solvents, for example, combustible solvents and halogenated solvents. (The containers are subsequently removed for suitable disposal by licensed waste handlers.) Some toxic substances can be oxidized or reduced to innocuous substances that can then be flushed down the drain; for example, hydrazines, mercaptans, and inorganic cyanides can be thus oxidized by sodium hypochlorite solution, widely available as household bleach. Dilute solutions of highly toxic cations are expensive to dispose of because of their bulk; precipitation of the cation by a suitable reagent followed by its separation greatly reduces its bulk and cost. These and many other procedures can be found throughout this book.

One other principle of waste control lies at the heart of this book. Microscale experimentation, by minimizing the scale of chemical operations, also minimizes the volume of waste. Chromatography procedures to separate and purify products, spectroscopy methods to identify and characterize products, and well-designed small-scale equipment enable one to conduct experiments today on a tenth to a thousandth the scale commonly in use a generation ago.

Chemists often provide great detail in their directions for preparing chemicals so that the synthesis can be repeated, but they seldom say much about how to dispose of the hazardous byproducts. Yet the proper disposal of a chemical's byproducts is as important as its proper preparation. Dr. Williamson sets a good example by providing explicit directions for such disposal.

Blaine C. McKusick

CHAPTER

1 *Introduction*

PRELAB EXERCISE: Study the glassware diagrams and be prepared to identify the reaction tube, fractionating column, distilling head, addition port, and Hirsch funnel.

Welcome to the organic chemistry laboratory! This laboratory manual presents a unique approach for carrying out organic experiments—they can be conducted on either a microscale or a macroscale. The latter was the traditional way of teaching the principles of experimental organic chemistry and is the basis for all the experiments in this book, a book that traces its history to 1934 when Louis Fieser was its author. Most teaching institutions are equipped to carry out macroscale experiments. Instructors are familiar with these techniques and experiments, and much research in industry and academe is carried out on this scale. These experiments typically involve the use of a few grams of *starting material,* the chief reagent used in the reaction. In recent years the trend has been to carry out these so-called macroscale experiments on a smaller scale, so that they might well now be called miniscale experiments.

For reasons primarily of safety and cost, there is a growing trend toward carrying out work in the laboratory on a microscale, a scale one-tenth to one-thousandth of that previously used. Using smaller quantities of chemicals exposes the laboratory worker to smaller amounts of toxic, flammable, explosive, carcinogenic, and teratogenic material. Microscale experiments can be carried out more rapidly than macroscale experiments because of rapid heat transfer, rapid filtration, and rapid drying. Since the apparatus advocated by the author is inexpensive, more than one reaction may be set up at once. The cost of chemicals is, of course, greatly reduced. A principal advantage of microscale experimentation is that the quantity of waste is reduced by one-tenth to one-thousandth of that formerly produced.

To allow maximum flexibility in the conduct of organic experiments, this book presents procedures for the vast majority of the experiments on both the microscale and the macroscale. As will be seen, some of the equipment and techniques differ. A careful reading of the two procedures will indicate which changes and precautions must be employed in going from one scale to the other.

Synthesis and structure determination

Synthesis and structure determination are two major concerns of the organic chemist, and both are dealt with in this book. The rational synthesis of an organic

1

compound, whether it involves the transformation of one functional group into another or a carbon–carbon bond-forming reaction, starts with a *reaction*.

Organic reactions usually take place in the liquid phase and are *homogeneous* in that the reactants are entirely in one phase. The reactants can be solids and/or liquids dissolved in an appropriate solvent to mediate the reaction. Some reactions are *heterogeneous*—that is, one of the reactants is in the solid phase—and thus require stirring or shaking to bring the reactants in contact with one another. A few heterogeneous reactions involve the reaction of a gas, such as oxygen, carbon dioxide, or hydrogen, with material in solution. Examples of all of these are found in this book's experiments.

An *exothermic* organic reaction evolves heat. If it is highly exothermic with a low activation energy, one reactant is added slowly to the other and heat is removed by external cooling. Most organic reactions are, however, mildly *endothermic,* which means the reaction mixture must be heated to overcome the activation barrier and to increase the rate of the reaction. A very useful rule of thumb is that *the rate of an organic reaction doubles with a 10°C rise of temperature.* The late Louis Fieser, an outstanding organic chemist and professor at Harvard University, introduced the idea of changing the traditional solvents of many reactions to high-boiling solvents in order to reduce reaction times. Throughout this book we will use solvents such as triethylene glycol, with a boiling point (bp) of 290°C, to replace ethanol (bp 78°C) and triethylene glycol dimethyl ether (bp 222°C) to replace dimethoxyethane (bp 85°C). The use of these high-boiling solvents can greatly increase the rates of many reactions.

Effect of temperature

Running an organic reaction is usually the easiest part of a synthesis. The challenge lies in isolating and purifying the product from the reaction because organic reactions seldom give quantitative yields of one pure substance.

"Working up the reaction"
Chapter 3: Crystallization
Chapter 7: Vacuum Distillation
and Sublimation

In some cases the solvent and concentrations of reactants are chosen so that, after the reaction mixture has been cooled, the product will *crystallize*. It is then collected by *filtration,* and the crystals are washed with an appropriate solvent. If sufficiently pure at that point, the product is dried and collected; otherwise, it is purified by the process of recrystallization or, less commonly, by *sublimation.*

Chapter 8: Extraction of Acids
and Bases

If the product of reaction does not crystallize from the reaction mixture, it is often isolated by the process of *extraction.* This involves adding a solvent to the reaction mixture that dissolves the product and is immiscible with the solvent used in the reaction. Shaking the mixture causes the product to dissolve in the extracting solvent, after which the two layers of liquid are separated and the product isolated from the extraction solvent.

Chapter 5: Distillation
Chapter 6: Steam Distillation

If the product is a liquid, it is isolated by *distillation,* usually after extraction. Occasionally the product can be isolated by the process of *steam distillation* from the reaction mixture.

Organic reactions are usually carried out by dissolving the reactants in a solvent and then heating the mixture to boiling. To keep the solvent from boiling away, the vapor is condensed to a liquid, which is allowed to run back into the boiling solvent.

Cool part
of tube

Refluxing liquid
(Air condenser)

Sand

Heated
area

Boiling
liquid

Boiling
chip

Electric
flask heater

Wet pipe
cleaner

(a)

(b)

FIG. 1.1 (a) Reaction tube being heated on a hot sand bath in a flask heater. The area of the tube exposed to heat is small. The liquid boils and condenses on the cool upper portion of the tube, which functions as an air condenser. (b) The condensing area can be increased by adding the distilling column as an air condenser.

1, 2, A   On a microscale, reactions are carried out in a *reaction tube* (Fig. 1.1a). The mass of the reaction tube is so small that a milliliter of nitrobenzene (bp 210°C) will boil in 10 s and a milliliter of benzene (mp 5°C) will crystallize in the same period of time. Cooling is effected by simply shaking the tube in a small beaker of ice water and heating by immersing the reaction tube to the appropriate depth in an electrically heated sand bath. On a larger scale, heat transfer is not quite as fast because of the smaller ratio of surface area to volume in a round-bottomed flask. Cooling is again conducted using an ice bath, but heating is sometimes done on a steam bath for low-boiling liquids. Higher temperatures require electric *heating mantles* or *flask heaters*.

2, A   For microscale heating, a *sand bath* in an electric 100-mL flask heater filled with sand is a versatile heat source (Fig. 1.1a). The relatively poor heat conduction of sand results in a very large temperature difference between the top of the sand and the bottom. Thus, depending on the immersion depth in the sand, a similarly wide temperature range will be found in the reaction tube. Because the area of the tube exposed to heat is fairly small, it is difficult to transfer enough heat to the contents of the tube to cause solvents to boil away. The reaction tube is 100 mm long so that the upper part of the tube can function as an efficient *air condenser* (Fig. 1.1a), since the area of glass is large and the volume of vapor is comparatively small. The air condenser can be made even longer by attaching the empty *distilling column* to the reaction tube using the *connector with support rod* (Fig. 1.1b). The black connector is made of Viton, which is resistant to high-boiling aromatic solvents. The cream-colored connector is made of Santoprene, which is resistant to all but high-boiling aromatic solvents. Solvents such as water and ethanol are boiled and, as the hot vapor ascends to the upper part of the tube, these condense and run back down the tube. This process is called *refluxing* and is the most common method for conducting a reaction at a constant temperature, the boiling point of the solvent. For very low-boiling solvents such as diethyl ether (bp 35°C), a pipe cleaner dampened with water makes an efficient cooling device. A water-cooled condenser is also available (Fig. 1.2) but is seldom needed.

On a larger scale, the same electric flask heater or a sand bath on a hot plate can be used to heat a flask that is connected via a *standard-taper ground glass joint* to a water-cooled *reflux condenser,* where the water flows in a jacket around the central tube. The high heat capacity of water makes it possible to remove the large amount of heat put into the larger volume of refluxing vapor (Fig. 1.3).

B

FIG. 1.2 Refluxing solvent in a 5-mL round-bottomed flask fitted with a water-cooled condenser.

FIG. 1.3 Reflux apparatus for larger reactions. Liquid boils in the flask and condenses on cold inner surface of the water-cooled condenser.

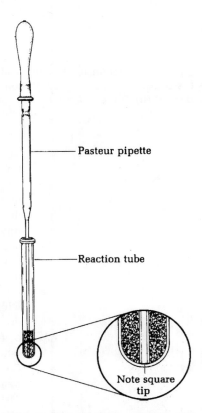

FIG. 1.4 Filtration using the Pasteur pipette and reaction tube.

Chapter 10: Thin-Layer
Chromatography

                                    A, G

Filter paper,
12 mm dia.

Polyethylene
filter disk (frit),
10 mm dia.

Hirsch
funnel

To aspirator

25-mL Filter
flask

FIG. 1.5 Hirsch funnel with an integral adapter, polyethylene frit, and 25-mL filter flask.

                                    F

                                   11

                                   I

                                   22

                                27, M
Chapter 11: Column
Chromatography

Chapter 8:
Extraction   12, 13, V, W

It is worth noting that the reaction tube (Fig. 1.1a) functions as both flask and reflux condenser and is completely equivalent in function to the macroscale standard-taper flask and reflux condenser of Fig. 1.3 but costs about 1/40th as much.

The progress of a reaction can be followed by withdrawing tiny samples at intervals and analyzing them by *thin-layer chromatography*. If the product of a reaction crystallizes from the reaction mixture on cooling, it is isolated by *filtration*. On a microscale, this can be done in several ways. If the crystals are large enough and in the reaction tube, this is accomplished by inserting a *Pasteur pipette* to the bottom of the tube while expelling the air and withdrawing the solvent (Fig. 1.4). Highly effective filtration occurs between the square tip of the pipette and the bottom of the tube. This method of filtration has several advantages over the alternatives. The mixture of crystals and solvent can be kept on ice during the entire process. This minimizes the solubility of the crystals in the solvent. There are no transfer losses of material because an external filtration device is not used. This technique allows several recrystallizations to be carried out in the same tube with final drying of the product under vacuum. Knowing the *tare* (the weight of the empty tube) allows the weight of the product to be determined without removing it from the tube. In this manner a compound can be synthesized, purified by crystallization, and dried without ever leaving the reaction tube. After removal of material for analysis, the compound in the tube can then be used for the next reaction. This technique is used in many of this book's microscale experiments. When the crystals are dry, they are easily removed from the reaction tube. When they are wet, it is difficult to scrape them out. If the crystals are in more than about 2 mL of solvent, they can be isolated by filtration on the *Hirsch funnel*. The one that is in the microscale kit of apparatus is particularly easy to use because the funnel fits into the *filter flask* with no adapter, and is equipped with a *polyethylene frit* for removal of the crystals (Fig. 1.5). The Wilfilter is especially good for collecting small quantities of crystals (Fig. 1.6).

Macroscale quantities of material are crystallized in *Erlenmeyer flasks*; the crystals are collected in porcelain or plastic *Büchner funnels* fitted with pieces of filter paper in the bottom of the funnel. A *filter adapter* (*Filtervac*) is used to form a vacuum-tight seal between the flask and funnel (Fig. 1.7).

Many solids can be purified by the process of *sublimation*. The solid is heated and the vapor of the solid condenses on a cold surface to form crystals in an apparatus constructed from a *centrifuge tube* fitted with a rubber adapter (a *Pluro stopper*) and pushed into a *filter flask* (Fig. 1.8). Caffeine can be purified in this manner. This is primarily a microscale technique, although sublimers holding several grams of solid are available.

Mixtures of solids and, occasionally, of liquids can be separated and purified by *column chromatography*. The *chromatography column* for both microscale and macroscale work is very similar (Fig. 1.9).

Often the product of a reaction will not crystallize. It may be a liquid, it may be a mixture of compounds, or it may be too soluble in the solvent being used. In this case, an immiscible solvent is added, the two layers are shaken to effect *extraction,* and after the layers separate, one layer is

Crystals

Wilfilter

Filtrate

FIG. 1.6 Hirsch funnel with an integral adapter, polyethylene frit, and 25-mL filter flask.

Büchner funnel

Filtervac

FIG. 1.7 Suction filter assembly.

removed. On a microscale, this can be done with a Pasteur pipette, and the process repeated if necessary. A tall, thin column of liquid such as that produced in the reaction tube makes it easy to remove one layer selectively. This is far more difficult to do in the usual test tube because the height/diameter ratio is too small.

The chromatography column in the apparatus kit is also a *micro separatory funnel* (Fig. 1.10b). Remember to remove the frit at the column base of the micro Büchner funnel and to close the valve before adding liquid.

On a larger scale, a *separatory funnel* is used for extraction (Fig. 1.10a). The mixture can be shaken in the funnel and then the lower layer removed through the

15-mL Centrifuge tube, to be filled with ice

Adapter (Pluro stopper)

To vacuum

25-mL Filter flask

Material to be sublimed

Sublimate

Heat source

FIG. 1.8 Small-scale sublimation apparatus.

FIG. 1.10 (a) Separatory funnel with Teflon stopcock. (b) Microscale separatory funnel. Remove the polyethylene frit from the micro Büchner funnel before using.

FIG. 1.9 Chromatography column consisting of funnel, tube, base fitted with a polyethylene frit, and Leur valve.

Chapter 5: Distillation

 17, B

18

stopcock after the stopper is removed. These funnels are available in sizes from 10 to 5000 mL. The microscale version is seen in Fig. 1.10(b).

Some of the compounds to be synthesized in these experiments are liquids. On a very small scale, the best way to separate and purify a mixture of liquids is by *gas chromatography,* but this technique is limited to less than 100 mg of material on the usual gas chromatograph. For larger quantities of material, *distillation* is used. For this purpose, small distilling flasks are used. These flasks have a large surface area to allow sufficient heat input to cause the liquid to vaporize rapidly so that it can be distilled and then condensed for collection in a *receiver.* The apparatus (Fig. 1.11) consists of a *distilling flask, distilling adapter* (which also functions as an air condenser on a microscale), a *thermometer adapter, thermometer,* and on a macroscale a water-cooled *condenser* and *distilling adapter* (Fig. 1.12). *Fractional distillation* is carried out using a small, packed *fractionating column* (Fig. 1.13). The apparatus is very similar on both a microscale and macroscale. On a microscale, 2 to 4 mL of a liquid can be fractionally distilled, and 1 mL or more can be simply distilled. The usual scale in these experiments for macroscale distillation is about 25 mL. The individual components for microscale experimentation are shown in Fig. 1.14 and for macroscale work in Fig. 1.15.

Chapter 6: Steam Distillation   **L**   Some liquids with a relatively high vapor pressure can be isolated and purified by *steam distillation,* a process in which the organic compound codistills with water at a temperature below the boiling point of water. The microscale and macroscale apparatus for this process are shown in Chapter 6 on steam distillation.

Other apparatus commonly used in the organic laboratory are shown in this chapter (Fig. 1.16).

Check In

Your first duty will be to check in to your assigned desk. The identity of much of the apparatus should already be apparent from the preceding outline of the experimental processes used in the organic laboratory.

FIG. 1.11 Small-scale simple distillation apparatus.

FIG. 1.12 Apparatus for simple distillation.

FIG. 1.13 Microscale fractional distillation apparatus. (a) 5-mL round-bottomed flask. (b) Elastomeric connector [Santoprene (white) or Viton (black)]. (c) Fractionating column packed with copper sponge. (d) Distilling head and air condenser. (e) Thermometer adapter (Santoprene). (f) Receiver (1-dram vial).

CAUTION: Notify your instructor immediately if you break a thermometer. Mercury is very toxic.

Check to see that your thermometer reads about 22–25°C (20°C = 68°F), normal room temperature. Examine the mercury column to see if the thread is broken—that the mercury column is continuous from the bulb up. Replace any flasks that have star-shaped cracks. Remember that apparatus with graduations and porcelain apparatus are expensive. Erlenmeyer flasks, beakers, and test tubes are, by comparison, fairly cheap.

FIG. 1.14 Microscale apparatus kit.

(a) Pipette (1 mL), graduated in 1/1000ths.

(b) Chromatography column (glass) with polypropylene funnel and 20-μm polyethylene frit in base, which doubles as a micro Büchner funnel. The column, base, and stopcock are also used as a separatory funnel.

(c) Thermometer adapter (Santoprene).

(d) Connector only (Viton).

(e) Magnetic stirring bars (4 × 12 mm) in distillation receiver vial.

(f) Hirsch funnel (polypropylene) with 20-μm fritted polyethylene disk.

(g) Stopcock for chromatography column and separatory funnel.

(h) Claisen adapter/distillation head with air condenser.

(i) Filter flask, 25 mL.

(j) Distillation head, 105° connecting adapter.

(k) Rubber septa/sleeve stoppers, 8 mm.

(l) Syringe (polypropylene).

(m) Connector (Santoprene) with support rod.

(n) Centrifuge tube (15 mL)/ sublimation receiver, with cap.

(o) Distillation column/air condenser.

(p) Reaction tube, calibrated, 10 × 100 mm.

(q) Erlenmeyer flasks, 10 mL.

(r) Long-necked flask, 5 mL.

(s) Short-necked flask, 5 mL.

(t) Filter adapter (Santoprene) for sublimation apparatus.

(u) Tubing (polyethylene), 1/16-in. diameter.

(v) Spatula (stainless steel) with scoop end.

FIG. 1.15 Macroscale apparatus kit with 14/20 standard-taper ground-glass joints.

(a) Polyacetal Keck clamps, size 14.
(b) Hex-head glass stopper, 14/20 standard taper.
(c) Hirsch funnel (polypropylene) with 20-μm fritted polyethylene disk.
(d) Filter adapter (Santoprene) for sublimation apparatus.
(e) Distilling head with O-ring thermometer adapter.
(f) Vacuum adapter.
(g) Centrifuge tube (15 mL)/ sublimation receiver.
(h) Filter flask, 25 mL.
(i) Claisen adapter.
(j) Water-jacketed condenser.
(k) Chromatography column (glass) with polypropylene funnel and 20-μm polyethylene frit in base, which doubles as a micro Büchner funnel.
(l) Stopcock for chromatography column.
(m) Separatory funnel, 125 mL.
(n) Pear-shaped flask, 100 mL.
(o) Pear-shaped flask, 50 mL.
(p) Conical flask (15 mL) with side arm for inlet tube.
(q) Distilling column/air condenser.
(r) Conical reaction vial (5 mL)/distillation receiver.

FIG. 1.16   Miscellaneous apparatus. (a) 1.0 ± 0.01 mL graduated pipette. (b) Septum. (c) 1.0-mL syringe with blunt needle. (d) Calibrated Pasteur pipette. (e) Pipette pump. (f) Glass scorer. (g) Filtervac. (h) Set of neoprene adapters.

Washing and Drying Laboratory Equipment

Clean apparatus immediately.

More experiments are ruined by damp or wet apparatus than for any other reason. Water is your enemy in the organic laboratory.

Considerable time may be saved by cleaning each piece of equipment soon after use, for you will know at that point which contaminant is present and be able to select the proper method for removal. A residue is easier to remove before it has dried and hardened. A small amount of organic residue can usually be dissolved with a few milliliters of an appropriate organic solvent. Acetone (bp 56.1°C) has great solvent power and is often effective, but it is extremely

Pinhole

(i) Hirsch funnel with perforated plate in place. (j) Thermometer adapter.
(k) Powder funnel. (l) Polyethylene wash bottle. (m) Single-pan electronic
balance with automatic zeroing and digital readout, 100 g ± 0.001 g
capacity. (n) Electric flask heater. (o) Solid-state control for electric flask heater.
(p) Stainless steel spatula. (q) Stirring bar. (r) Keck clamp. (s) Wilfilter.

flammable and somewhat expensive. Because it is miscible with water and
vaporizes readily, it is easy to remove from the vessel. Cleaning after an operation may often be carried out while another experiment is in process.

Both ethanol and acetone are
very flammable.

A *polyethylene bottle* [Fig. 1.16(l)] is a convenient wash bottle for acetone.
The name, symbol, or formula of a solvent can be written on a bottle with a
Magic Marker or wax pencil. For crystallizations, extractions, and quick cleaning of apparatus, it is convenient to have a bottle for each frequently used
solvent—95% ethanol, ligroin, dichloromethane, and ether. A pinhole opposite

the spout, which is covered with the finger when in use, will prevent the spout from dribbling the solvent. For microscale work, these solvents are best dispensed from 25- or 50-mL bottles with an attached test tube containing a graduated (1 mL) polypropylene pipette (Fig. 1.17).

Pasteur pipettes (Fig. 1.18) are very useful for transferring small quantities of liquid, adding reagents dropwise, and carrying out crystallizations. Surprisingly, the acetone used to wash out a dirty Pasteur pipette usually costs more than the pipette itself. Discard used Pasteur pipettes in the special container for waste glass.

Sometimes a flask will not be clean after a washing with detergent and acetone. At that point try an abrasive household cleaner.

Wash acetone goes in the organic solvents waste container.

To dry a piece of apparatus rapidly, rinse with a few millimeters of acetone and invert over a beaker to drain. **Do not use compressed air,** which contains droplets of oil, water, and particles of rust. Instead, draw a slow stream of air through the apparatus using the suction of your water aspirator.

Insertion of a glass tube into a rubber connector or adapter or hose is easy if the glass is lubricated with a very small drop of glycerol. Grasp the tube very close to the end to be inserted; if it is grasped at a distance, especially at the bend, the pressure applied for insertion may break the tube and result in a serious cut.

If a glass tube or thermometer should become stuck to a rubber connector, it can be removed by painting on glycerol and forcing the pointed tip of an 18-cm spatula between the rubber and glass. Another method is to select a cork borer that fits snugly over the glass tube, moisten it with glycerol, and slowly work it through the connector. If the stuck object is valuable, such as a thermometer, the best policy is to cut the rubber with a sharp knife.

FIG. 1.17 Recrystallization solvent bottle and dispenser.

Heat Source

A 10°C rise in temperature will approximately double the rate of an organic reaction. The processes of distillation, sublimation, and crystallization all require heat, which is most conveniently and safely applied from an electrically heated sand bath. A flask heater (Fig. 1.16n, o) is two-thirds filled with sand, the temperature of which depends on the setting of the controller. This heater is small in diameter, giving good access to small apparatus, and the air above the heater is not hot. It is possible to hold a reaction tube containing refluxing solvents in the fingers of the hand. Because sand is a fairly poor conductor of heat, there is a very large variation in temperature in the sand bath depending on its depth. The temperature of a flask can be regulated by piling up or removing sand from near the flask with a spatula. The heater is easily capable of producing temperatures in excess of 300°C; therefore, never leave the controller at its maximum setting. Ordinarily, it is set at 20% of maximum. Because the flask heater can provide high temperatures, microscale equipment need not include a Bunsen burner, but on a macroscale, this has been a common way to heat reaction mixtures in the teaching laboratory. If at all possible, for safety reasons, use an electric flask heater. When the solvent boils

Turn on the Thermowell about 20 minutes before you intend to use it. The sand heats slowly.

CAUTION: Never put a mercury thermometer in a sand bath! It will break, releasing highly toxic mercury vapor.

—— 2.0 mL

—— 1.5 mL

—— 1.0 mL

—— 0.75 mL

—— 0.50 mL

—— 0.25 mL

—— 0.10 mL

—— 0.05 mL

FIG. 1.18 Approximate calibration of Kimble 9″ Pasteur pipette.

below 90°C, the most common method for heating macroscale flasks is the *steam bath*.

A Petri dish containing sand and heated on a hot plate is not recommended for microscale experiments. It is too easy to burn oneself on the hot plate; too much heat wells up from the sand, so air condensers do not function well; the glass dishes break from thermal shock; and the ceramic coating on some hot plates chips and comes off.

Transfer of a Solid

A plastic funnel that fits the top of the reaction tube is most convenient for the transfer of solids to a reaction tube or to small Erlenmeyer flasks for microscale experiments (Fig. 1.19). It is also the top of the chromatography column (Fig. 1.9). A special spatula with a scoop end is used to remove solid material from the reaction tube (Fig. 1.16p). On a large scale, a powder funnel is useful for adding solids to a flask (Fig. 1.16k). A funnel can also be fashioned from a sheet of weighing paper.

Weighing and Measuring

The single-pan electronic balance (Fig. 1.16m) capable of weighing to ±0.001 g and having a capacity of 100 g is the single most important instrument making small-scale organic experiments possible. Most of the quantitative measurements made in microscale experiments will use this balance. Weighing is a pleasure with these balances. For larger-scale experiments, a balance of such high accuracy is not necessary. Although the top-loading digital balances are the easiest to use, a triple-beam balance will work just as well. There should be one top-loading scale for every 12 students.

A container such as a reaction tube standing in a beaker or flask is placed on the pan. At the touch of a bar, the digital readout registers zero, and the desired quantity of the reagent can be added to the reaction tube as the weight is measured periodically to the nearest milligram. Even liquids are weighed when accuracy is needed. It is much easier to weigh a liquid to ±0.001 g than it is to measure it volumetrically to ±0.001 mL.

It is often convenient to weigh reagents on glossy weighing paper and then transfer the chemical to the reaction container. The success of an experiment often depends on using just the right amount of starting materials and reagents. Inexperienced workers might think that if one milliliter of a reagent will do the job, then two milliliters will do the job twice as well. Such assumptions are usually erroneous.

Liquids can be measured by either volume or weight according to the relationship

$$\text{Volume (mL)} = \frac{\text{weight (g)}}{\text{density (g/mL)}}$$

Never pipette by mouth!

FIG. 1.19 Funnel for addition of solids and liquids to a reaction tube.

Tare = weight of empty container

The laboratory notebook:
 What you did.
 How you did it.
 What you observed.
 Your conclusions.

Modern Erlenmeyer flasks and beakers have approximate volume calibrations fused into the glass, but these are *very* approximate. Better graduations are found on the microscale *reaction tube*. Somewhat more accurate volumetric measurements are made in the 10-mL graduated cylinders. For volumes less than 4 mL, use a graduated pipette. **Never** apply suction to a pipette by mouth. The pipette can be fitted with a small rubber bulb. A Pasteur pipette can be converted into a calibrated pipette with the addition of a plastic syringe body (Fig. 1.16d). Also see the calibration marks for a 9-in. Pasteur pipette in Fig. 1.18. You will find among your equipment a 1-mL pipette, calibrated in hundredths of a milliliter (Fig. 1.16a). Determine whether it is designed to *deliver* 1 mL or *contain* 1 mL between the top and bottom calibration marks. For our purposes, the latter is the better pipette.

Because the viscosity, surface tension, vapor pressure, and wetting characteristics of organic liquids are different from those of water, the so-called automatic pipette (designed for aqueous solutions) gives poor accuracy in measuring organic liquids. *Syringes* (Fig. 1.16c) and *pipette pumps* (Fig. 1.20), on the other hand, are quite useful, and frequent use will be made of them. Do not use a syringe that is equipped with a metal needle to measure corrosive reagents. Several reactions that require especially dry or oxygen-free atmospheres will be run in sealed systems. Reagents can be added to the system via syringe through a rubber *septum* (Fig. 1.16b).

Careful measurements of weights and volumes take more time than less accurate measurements. Think carefully about which measurements need to be made with accuracy and which do not.

Tares

The tare of a container is its weight when empty. Throughout this laboratory course it will be necessary to know the tares of containers so that the weights of the compounds within can be calculated. If identifying marks can be placed on the containers (e.g., with a diamond stylus) you may want to record tares for frequently used containers in your laboratory notebook.

To be strictly correct we should use the word *mass* instead of *weight,* because gravitational acceleration is not constant at all places on earth. But electronic balances record weights, unlike two-pan or triple-beam balances, which record masses.

The Laboratory Notebook

A complete, accurate record is an essential part of laboratory work. Failure to keep such a record means laboratory labor lost. An adequate record includes the procedure (what was done), observations (what happened), and conclusions (what the results mean).

Never record anything on scraps of paper. Use a lined, 8.5″ × 11″ paper-bound notebook, and record all data in ink. Allow space at the front for a table of contents, number the pages throughout, and date each day's work. Reserve the left-hand page for calculations and numerical data, and use the right-hand

2-mL Pipette pump

1-mL Pipette graduated to ± 0.01 mL

Reaction tube

FIG. 1.20 Use of a pipette pump to measure liquids to ±0.01 mL.

page for notes. Never record **anything** on scraps of paper to be recorded later in the notebook. Do not erase, remove, or obliterate notes; simply draw a single line through incorrect entries.

The notebook should contain a statement or title for each experiment and its purpose, followed by balanced equations for all principal and side reactions and, where relevant, mechanisms of the reactions. Consult your textbook for supplementary information on the class of compounds or type of reaction involved. Give a reference to the procedure used; do not copy verbatim the procedure in the laboratory manual. Make particular note of safety precautions and the procedures for cleaning up at the end of the experiment.

Before coming to the lab to do preparative experiments, prepare a table (in your notebook) of reagents to be used and the products expected, with their physical properties. Use the molar ratios of reactions from your table to determine the limiting reagent, and then calculate the theoretical yield (in grams) of the desired product. Begin each experiment on a new page.

Include an outline of the procedure and the method of purification of the product in a flow sheet if this is the best way to organize the experiment (for example, an extraction; *see* Chapter 8). The flow sheet should list all possible products, by-products, unused reagents, solvents, and so on that are expected to appear in the crude reaction mixture. On the flow sheet diagram indicate how each of these is removed (e.g., by extraction, various washing procedures, distillation, or crystallization). With this information entered in your notebook before coming to the laboratory, you will be ready to carry out the experiments with the utmost efficiency. Plan your time before the laboratory period. Often two or three experiments can be run simultaneously.

When working in the laboratory, record everything you do and everything you observe **as it happens.** The recorded observations constitute the most important part of the laboratory record, since they form the basis for the conclusions you will draw at the end of each experiment. One way to do this is in a narrative form. Alternatively, the procedure can be written in outline form on the left-hand side of the page and the observations recorded on the right-hand side.

In some colleges and universities, you will be expected to have all the relevant information about the running of an experiment entered in your notebook *before coming to the laboratory* so that your textbook will not be needed when you are conducting experiments. In industrial laboratories, your notebook may be designed so that carbon copies of all entries are kept. These are signed and dated by your supervisor and removed from your notebook each day. Your notebook becomes a legal document in case you make a discovery worth hundreds of millions of dollars!

Record the physical properties of the product from your experiment, the yield in grams, and the percent yield. Analyze your results. When things did not turn out as expected, explain why. When your record of an experiment is complete, another chemist should be able to understand your account and determine what you did, how you did it, and what conclusions you reached. That is, from the information in your notebook, a chemist should be able to repeat your work.

Preparing a Laboratory Record

Use the following steps to prepare your laboratory record. The letters correspond to the completed laboratory records that appear at the end of this chapter. Because your laboratory notebook is so important, two examples, written in alternative forms, are presented.

A. Number each page. Allow space at the front of the notebook for a table of contents. Use a hardbound, lined notebook, and keep all notes in ink.

B. Date each entry.

C. Give a short title to the experiment, and enter it in the table of contents.

D. State the purpose of the experiment.

E. Write balanced equation(s) for the reaction(s).

F. Give a reference to the source of the experimental procedure.

G. Prepare a table of quantities and physical constants. Look up the needed data in the *Handbook of Chemistry and Physics*.

H. Write equation(s) for the principal side reaction(s).

I. Write out the procedure with just enough information so that you can follow it easily. Do not merely copy the procedure from the text. Note any hazards and safety precautions. A highly experienced chemist might write a procedure in a formal report as follows: "Dibenzalacetone was prepared by condensing at room temperature 1 mmol acetone with 2 mmol benzaldehyde in 1.6 mL of 95% ethanol to which was added 2 mL of aqueous 3 *M* sodium hydroxide solution. After 30 min the product was collected and crystallized from 70% ethanol to give 0.17 g (73%) of flat yellow plates of dibenzalacetone, mp 110.5–111.5°C." Note that in this formal report, no jargon (e.g., EtOH for 95% ethanol, FCHO for benzaldehyde) is used and that the names of reagents are written out (sodium hydroxide, not NaOH). In this report the details of measuring, washing, drying, crystallizing, collecting the product, and so on are assumed to be understood by the reader.

J. Don't forget to note how to dispose of the byproducts from the experiment using the "Cleaning Up" section of the experimental procedure.

K. Record what you do as you do it. These observations are the most important part of the experiment. Note that conclusions do not appear among these observations.

L. Calculate the theoretical yield in grams. The experiment calls for exactly 2 mmol fluorobenzaldehyde and 1 mmol acetone, which will produce 1 mmol of product. The equation for the experiment also indicates that the product will be formed from exactly a 2:1 ratio of the reactants. Experiments are often designed to have one reactant in great excess. In this experiment, a very slight excess of fluorobenzaldehyde was used inadvertently, so acetone becomes the limiting reagent.

M. Once the product is obtained, dried, and weighed, calculate the ratio of product actually isolated to the amount theoretically possible. Express this ratio as the percent yield.

N. Write out the mechanism of the reaction. If it is not given in the text of the experiment, look it up in your lecture text.

O. Draw conclusions from the observations. Write this part of the report in narrative form in complete English sentences. This part of the report can, of course, be written after leaving the laboratory.

P. Analyze TLC, IR, and NMR spectra if they are a part of the experiments. Rationalize observed versus reported melting points.

Q. Answer assigned questions from the end of the experiment.

R. This page presents an alternative method for entering the experimental procedure and observations in the notebook. Before coming to the laboratory, enter the procedure in outline form on the left side of the page. Then enter observations in brief form on the right side of the page as the experiment is carried out. Draw a single line through any words incorrectly entered. Do not erase or obliterate entries in the notebook, and never remove pages from the notebook.

Two samples of completed laboratory records follow. An alternative method for recording procedure, cleaning up, and observations is given on p. 24. The other parts of the report are the same.

(A)   p. 35
(B)   Sept. 23, 2004

(C)   **DIFLUORODIBENZALACETONE**

(D)   *Purpose:*   To observe and carry out an aldol condensation reaction.

(E)

4-Fluorobenzaldehyde   Acetone   **4,4′-Difluorodibenzalacetone**

(F)   *Reference:*   Williamson, *Macroscale and Microscale Organic Experiments,* p. 792.

Table of Quantities and Physical Constants   (G)

Substance	Mol wt	G/mol Used or Produced	Mol Needed (from eq.)	Density	mp	bp	Solubility
4-Fluorobenzaldehyde	124.11	0.248/0.002	0.002	1.157		181°C	Slightly soluble in H_2O; soluble in ethanol, diethyl ether, acetone
Acetone	58.08	0.058/0.001	0.001	0.790		56°C	Soluble in H_2O, ethanol, diethyl ether, acetone
4,4′-Difluoro-dibenzalacetone	270.34	0.273/0.001			167°C		Insoluble in H_2O; slightly soluble in ethanol, diethyl ether, acetone
4-Fluorobenzalacetone	164.19					54°C	Insoluble in H_2O; slightly soluble in ethanol, diethyl ether, acetone
Sodium hydroxide	40.01						Soluble in H_2O; insoluble in ethanol, diethyl ether, acetone

(H)   *Side Reactions:*   No important side reactions, but if excess acetone is used, product will be contaminated with 4-fluorobenzalacetone.

p. 36

Ⓘ   *Procedure:*   To a reaction tube, add 0.248 g (0.002 mole) of benzaldehyde and then 1.6 mL of an ethanol solution that contains 0.58 mg of acetone. Mix the solution and observe it for 1 min. Remove sample for TLC. Then add 2 mL of 3 *M* NaOH(*aq*). Cap the tube with a septum and shake it at intervals over a 30-min period. Collect product on Hirsch funnel, wash crystals thoroughly with water, press as dry as possible, determine crude weight, and save sample for mp. Recrystallize product from 70% ethanol in a 10-mL Erlenmeyer flask. Cool solution slowly, scratch or add seed crystal, cool in ice, and collect product on Hirsch. Wash crystals with a few drops of ice-cold ethanol. Run TLC on silica gel plates using hexane to elute, develop in iodine chamber. Run NMR spectrum in deuterochloroform and IR spectrum as a mull.

Ⓙ   *Cleaning Up:*   Neutralize filtrate with HCl and flush solution down the drain. Put recrystallization filtrate in organic solvents container.

Ⓚ   *Observations:*   Into a reaction tube, 0.250 g of 4-fluorobenzaldehyde was weighed (0.248 called for). Using the 1.00-mL graduated pipette and pipette pump, 1.61 mL of the stock ethanol solution containing 0.58 mg of acetone was added (16 mL called for). The contents of the tube were mixed by flicking the tube, and then a drop of the reaction mixture was removed and diluted with 1 mL of hexane for later TLC. The water-clear solution did not change in appearance during 1 min.

Then about 2 mL of 3 *M* NaOH(*aq*) was added using graduations on side of reaction tube. The tube was capped with a septum and shaken. The clear solution changed to a light yellow color immediately and got slightly warm. Then after about 50 sec, the entire solution became opaque. Then yellow oily drops collected on sides and bottom of tube. Shaken every 5 min for ½ hr. The oily drops crystallized, and more crystals formed. At the end of 30 min, the opaque solution became clear, and yellow crystals had formed. Tube filled with crystals.

Product was collected on 12-mm filter paper on a Hirsch funnel; transfer of material to funnel was completed using the filtrate to wash out the tube. Crystals were washed with about 15 mL of water. The filtrate was slightly cloudy and yellow. It was poured into a beaker for later disposal. The crude product was pressed as dry as possible with a cork. Wt (damp) 270 mg. Sample saved for mp.

Recrystallized from about 50 mL of 70% ethanol on sand bath. Almost forgot to add boiling stick! Clear, yellow solution cooled slowly by wrapping tube in cotton. A seed crystal from Julie added to start crystallization. After about 25 min, flask was placed in ice bath for 15 min, then product was collected on Hirsch funnel (filter paper), washed with a few drops of ice-cold solvent, pressed dry and then spread out on paper to dry. Wt 0.19 mg. Very nice flat, yellow crystals, mp 179.5–180.5°C. The crude material before recrystallization had mp 177.5–179°C.

TLC on silica gel using hexane to elute gave only one spot, R_f 0.23, for the starting material and only one spot for the product, R_f 0.66. See attached plate.

The NMR spectrum that was run on the Bruker in deuterochloroform containing TMS showed a complex group of peaks centered at about 7 ppm with an integrated value of 17.19 and a sharp, clear quartet of peaks centered at 6.5 ppm with an integral of 8.62. The coupling constant of the AB quartet was 7.2 Hz. See attached spectrum.

The IR spectrum, run as a Nujol mull on the Mattson FT IR, showed intense peaks at 1590 and 1655 cm^{-1}, as well as small peaks at 3050, 3060, and 3072 cm^{-1}. See attached spectrum.

Cleaning Up: Recrystallization filtrate put in organic solvents container. First filtrate neutralized with HCl and poured down the drain.

Ⓛ *Theoretical Yield Calculations:*

$$0.250 \text{ g fluorobenzaldehyde used } \frac{0.250 \text{ g}}{124.11 \text{ g/mole}} = 0.00201 \text{ mole}$$

$$0.058 \text{ g of acetone used } \frac{0.058 \text{ g}}{58.08 \text{ g/mole}} = 0.001 \text{ mole}$$

The moles needed (from equation) are 2 mmol of the benzaldehyde and 1 mmol of acetone. Therefore, acetone is the limiting reagent, and 1.00 mmol of product should result. The MW of the product is 270.34 g/mol.

$$0.001 \text{ mol} \times 270.34 \text{ g/mol}$$
$$= 0.270 \text{ g, theoretical yield of difluorodibenzalacetone}$$

Ⓜ *Percent Yield of Product:*

$$\frac{0.19 \text{ g}}{0.270 \text{ g}} \times 100 = 70\%$$

Ⓝ *The Mechanism of the Reaction:*

p. 38

$$\text{CH}_3\overset{\overset{\displaystyle O}{\|}}{\text{C}}\!-\!\overset{\overset{\displaystyle H}{|}}{\underset{\underset{\displaystyle H}{|}}{\text{C}}}\!-\!\overset{\overset{\displaystyle H}{|}}{\underset{\underset{\displaystyle OH}{|}}{\text{C}}}\!-\!\!\!\!\left\langle \bigcirc \right\rangle\!\!\!-\!\text{F} \longrightarrow \text{CH}_3\overset{\overset{\displaystyle O}{\|}}{\text{C}}\!-\!\text{C}\!=\!\overset{\overset{\displaystyle H}{|}}{\underset{\underset{\displaystyle H}{|}}{\text{C}}}\!-\!\!\!\!\left\langle \bigcirc \right\rangle\!\!\!-\!\text{F} + \text{H}_2\text{O} + \text{OH}^-$$

⊙ *Discussion and Conclusions:* Mixing the fluorobenzaldehyde, acetone, and ethanol gave no apparent reaction because the solution did not change in appearance, but less than a minute after adding the NaOH, a yellow oil appeared and the reaction mixture got slightly warm, indicating that a reaction was taking place. The mechanism given in the text (above) indicates that hydroxide ion is a catalyst for the reaction, confirmed by this observation. The reaction takes place spontaneously at room temperature. The reaction was judged to be complete when the liquid surrounding the crystals became clear (it was opaque) and the amount of crystals in the tube did not appear to change. This took 30 min. The crude product was collected and washed with water. Forgot to cool it in ice before filtering it off. The crude product weighed more than the theoretical because it must still have been damp. However, this amount of crude material indicates that the reaction probably went pretty well to completion. The crude product was recrystallized from 5 mL of 70% ethanol. This was probably too much, since it dissolved very rapidly in that amount. This and the fact that the reaction mixture was not cooled in ice probably accounts for the relatively low 70% yield. Probably could have obtained second crop of crystals by concentrating filtrate. It turned very cloudy when water was added to it.

Theoretically, it is possible for this reaction to give three different products (*cis, cis-; cis, trans-;* and *trans, trans-*isomers). Because the mp of the crude and recrystallized products were close to each other and rather sharp, and because the TLC of the product gave only one spot, it is presumed that the product is just one of these three possible isomers. The NMR spectrum shows a sharp quartet of peaks from the vinyl protons, which also indicates only one isomer. Since the coupling constant observed is 7.2 Hz, the protons must be *cis* to each other. Therefore, the product is the *cis, cis-*isomer.

Ⓟ   The infrared spectrum shows two strong peaks at 1590 and 1655 cm^{-1}, indicative of an α-β-unsaturated ketone. The small peaks at 3050, 3060, and 3072 cm^{-1} are consistent with aromatic and vinyl protons. The yellow color indicates that the molecule must have a long conjugated system.

The fact that the TLC of the starting material showed only one peak is probably due to the evaporation of the acetone from the TLC plate. The spot with R_f 0.23 must be from the 4-fluorobenzaldehyde.

Ⓠ   Answers to assigned questions are written at the end of the report.

An alternative method for recording procedures, cleaning up, and observations:

p. 36

Ⓡ	Sept. 23, 2004 Procedure	Sept. 24, 2004 Observations
	Weigh 0.248 g of 4-fluorobenz-aldehyde into reaction tube.	Actually used 0.250 g.
	Add 1.6 mL of ethanol stock soln that contains 0.58 g of acetone.	Actually used 1.61 mL.
	Mix, observe for 1 min.	Nothing seems to happen. Water clear soln.
	Add 2 mL of 3 M NaOH(*aq*).	Clear, then faintly yellow but clear, then after about 50 sec, the entire soln very suddenly turned opaque. Got slightly warm. Light yellow color.
	Cap tube with septum; shake at 5-min intervals for 30 min.	Oily drops separate on sides and bottom of tube. These crystallized; more crystals formed. Tube became filled with crystals. Liquid around crystals became clear.
	Filter on Hirsch funnel.	Filtered (filter paper) on Hirsch.
	Wash crystals with much water.	Washed with about 150 mL of H_2O. Transfer of crystals done using filtrate.
	Press dry.	Crystals pressed dry with cork.
	Weigh crude.	Crude (damp) wt 0.27 g.
	Save sample for mp.	Crude mp 177.5−179°C.
	Recrystallize from 70% ethanol; wash with a few drops of ice-cold solvent.	Used about 50 mL of 70% EtOH. Too much. Dissolved very rapidly.
	Dry product.	Dried on paper for 30 min.
	Weigh.	Wt 0.19 g.
	Take mp.	Mp 179.5−180.5°C.
	Run IR as mull.	Done.
	Run NMR in $CDCl_3$.	Done.
	Neutralize first filtrate with HCl, pour down drain.	Done.
	Org. filtrate in waste organic bottle.	Done.

CHAPTER
2
Laboratory Safety and Waste Disposal

PRELAB EXERCISE: Read this chapter carefully. Locate the emergency eyewash station, safety shower, and fire extinguisher in your laboratory. Check your safety glasses or goggles for size and transparency. Learn which reactions must be carried out in the hood. Learn to use your laboratory fire extinguisher; learn how to summon help and how to put out a clothing fire. Learn first aid procedures for acid and alkali spills on the skin. Learn how to tell if your laboratory hood is working properly. Learn which operations under reduced pressure require special precautions. Check to see that compressed gas cylinders in your lab are firmly fastened to benches or walls. Learn the procedures for properly disposing of solid and liquid waste in your laboratory.

Small-scale organic experiments are much safer to conduct than their counterparts run on a scale 10 to 100 times larger. However, on either a microscale or a macroscale, the organic chemistry laboratory is an excellent place to learn and practice safety. Commonsense procedures practiced here also apply to other laboratories as well as to the shop, kitchen, and studio.

General laboratory safety information—particularly applicable to this organic chemistry laboratory course—is presented in this chapter. It is not comprehensive. Throughout this text you will find specific cautions and safety information presented as margin notes printed in red. For a brief and thorough discussion of the topics in this chapter you should read the first 35 pages of *Safety in Academic Chemistry Laboratories,* American Chemical Society, Washington, DC, 6th ed., except for the admonition regarding contact lenses (see below).

Important General Rules

Know the safety rules of your particular laboratory. Know the locations of emergency eyewashes and safety showers. Never eat, drink, or smoke in the laboratory. Don't work alone. Perform no unauthorized experiments, and don't distract your fellow workers; horseplay has no place in the laboratory.

Eye protection

Eye protection is extremely important. Safety glasses of some type must be worn at all times. It has recently been determined "that contact lenses can be worn in most work environments provided the same approved eye protection is worn as required of other workers in the area" (*Chemical and Engineering News,* June 1, 1998, p. 6).

FIG. 2.1 Chemical splash goggles.

Ordinary prescription eyeglasses don't offer adequate protection. Laboratory safety glasses should be of plastic or tempered glass. If you do not have such glasses, wear goggles that afford protection from splashes and objects coming from the side as well as from the front. If plastic safety glasses are permitted in your laboratory, they should have side shields (Fig. 2.1).

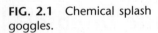

Dress sensibly.

Dress sensibly in the laboratory. Wear shoes, not sandals or cloth-top sneakers. Confine long hair and loose clothes. Don't wear shorts. Don't use mouth suction to fill a pipette, and wash your hands before leaving the laboratory. Don't use a solvent to remove chemicals from skin. This will only hasten the absorption of the chemical through the skin.

Working with Flammable Substances

Relative flammability of organic solvents.

Flammable substances are the most common hazard of the organic laboratory; two factors can make this laboratory much safer than its predecessor: (1) making the scale of the experiments as small as possible and (2) not using burners. Diethyl ether (bp 35°C), the most flammable substance you will usually work with in this course, has an ignition temperature of 160°C, which means that a hot plate at that temperature will cause it to burn. For comparison, *n*-hexane (bp 69°C), a constituent of gasoline, has an ignition temperature of 225°C. The flash points of these organic liquids—that is, the temperatures at which they will catch fire if exposed to a flame or spark—are below −20°C. These are very flammable liquids; however, if you are careful, they are not difficult to work with. Except for water, almost all of the liquids you will use in the laboratory are flammable.

FIG. 2.2 Solvent safety can.

Bulk solvents should be stored in and dispensed from *safety cans* (Fig. 2.2). These and other liquids will burn in the presence of the proper amount of their flammable vapors, oxygen, and a source of ignition (most commonly a flame or spark). It is usually difficult to remove oxygen from a fire, although it is possible to put out a fire in a beaker or a flask by simply covering the vessel with a flat object, thus cutting off the supply of air. Your lab notebook might do in an emergency. The best prevention is to pay close attention to sources of ignition—open flames, sparks, and hot surfaces. Remember the vapors of flammable liquids are **always** heavier than air and thus will travel along bench tops, down drain troughs, and remain in sinks. For this reason all flames within the vicinity of a flammable liquid must be extinguished. Adequate ventilation is one of the best ways to prevent flammable vapors from accumulating. Work in an exhaust hood when manipulating large quantities of flammable liquids.

Flammable vapors travel along bench tops.

Should a person's clothing catch fire with a safety shower close at hand, shove the person under it. Otherwise, push down the person and roll him or her

FIG. 2.3 Carbon dioxide fire extinguisher.

over to extinguish the flames. It is extremely important to prevent the victim from running or standing because the greatest harm comes from breathing the hot vapors that rise past the mouth. The safety shower might then be used to extinguish glowing cloth that is no longer aflame. A so-called fire blanket should not be used because it tends to funnel flames past the victim's mouth, and clothing continues to char beneath it. It is, however, useful for retaining warmth to ward off shock after the flames are extinguished.

An organic chemistry laboratory should be equipped with a carbon dioxide or dry chemical (monoammonium phosphate) *fire extinguisher* (Fig. 2.3). To use this type of extinguisher, lift it from its support, pull the ring to break the seal, raise the horn, aim it at the base of the fire, and squeeze the handle. Do not hold on to the horn because it will become extremely cold. Do not replace the extinguisher; report the incident so the extinguisher can be refilled.

When disposing of certain chemicals, be alert for the possibility of *spontaneous combustion*. This may occur in oily rags; organic materials exposed to strong oxidizing agents such as nitric acid, permanganate ion, and peroxides; alkali metals such as sodium; or very finely divided metals such as zinc dust and platinum catalysts. Fires sometimes start when these chemicals are left in contact with filter paper.

Working with Hazardous Chemicals

If you do not know the properties of a chemical you will be working with, it is wise to regard the chemical as hazardous. The *flammability* of organic substances poses the most serious hazard in the organic laboratory. There is the possibility that storage containers in the laboratory may contribute to a fire. Large quantities of organic solvents should not be stored in glass bottles. Use safety cans. Do not store chemicals on the floor.

Flammable vapors plus air in a confined space are explosive.

A flammable liquid can often be vaporized to form, with air, a mixture that is *explosive* in a confined space. The beginning chemist is sometimes surprised to learn that diethyl ether is more likely to cause a laboratory fire or explosion than a worker's accidental anesthesia. The chances of being confined in a laboratory with a concentration of ether high enough to cause loss of consciousness are extremely small, but a spark in such a room would probably eradicate the building.

The probability of forming an explosive mixture of volatile organic liquids with air is far greater than that of producing an explosive solid or liquid. The chief functional groups that render compounds explosive are the *peroxide, acetylide, azide, diazonium, nitroso, nitro,* and *ozonide* groups (Fig. 2.4). Not all members of these groups are equally sensitive to shock or heat. You would find it difficult to detonate trinitrotoluene (TNT) in the laboratory, but nitroglycerine is treacherously explosive. Peroxides present special problems that are dealt with below.

Safety goggles must be worn at all times.

You will need to contend with the corrosiveness of many of the reagents you will handle. The danger here is principally to the eyes. Proper eye protection is *mandatory,* and even small-scale experiments can be hazardous to the eyes. It takes only a single drop of a corrosive reagent to do lasting damage.

$$R-O-O-R \qquad R-C\equiv C-Metal$$

Peroxide   **Acetylide**

$$R-N=N=N \qquad R-NO_2$$

Azide   **Nitro**

FIG. 2.4 Functional groups that can be explosive in some compounds.

$$R-N=O \qquad R-\overset{+}{N}\equiv N$$

Nitroso   **Diazonium salts**   **Ozonide**

Handling concentrated acids and alkalis, dehydrating agents, and oxidizing agents calls for commonsense care to avoid spills and splashes and to avoid breathing the often corrosive vapors.

Certain organic chemicals present problems with acute toxicity from short-duration exposure and chronic toxicity from long-term or repeated exposure. Exposure can come about through ingestion, contact with the skin, or, most commonly, inhalation. Currently, great attention is being focused on chemicals that are teratogens (chemicals that often have no effect on a pregnant woman but cause abnormalities in a fetus), mutagens (chemicals causing changes in the structure of the DNA, which can lead to mutations in offspring), and carcinogens (cancer-causing chemicals). Small-scale experiments reduce these hazards greatly but do not eliminate them.

Peroxides

Ethers form explosive peroxides.

Certain functional groups can make an organic molecule become sensitive to heat and shock, such that it will explode. Chemists work with these functional groups only when there are no good alternatives. One of these functional groups, the *peroxide* group, is particularly insidious because it can form spontaneously when oxygen and light are present (Fig. 2.5). Ethers, especially *cyclic ethers*

Tetrahydrofuran   **Diisopropyl ether**   **Dioxane**   **Benzylic compounds**   **Ketones**

FIG. 2.5 Some compounds that form peroxides.

Cyclohexene   **Vinyl acetate**   **Allylic compounds**   **Aldehydes**

and those made from primary or secondary alcohols (such as tetrahydrofuran, diethyl ether, and diisopropyl ether), form peroxides. Other compounds that form peroxides are *aldehydes, alkenes* that have allylic hydrogen atoms (such as cyclohexene), compounds having benzylic hydrogens on a tertiary carbon atom (such as isopropyl benzene), and vinyl compounds (such as vinyl acetate). Peroxides are low-power explosives but are extremely sensitive to shock, sparks, light, heat, friction, and impact. The greatest danger from peroxide impurities comes when the peroxide-forming compound is distilled. The peroxide has a higher boiling point than the parent compound and remains in the distilling flask as a residue that can become overheated and explode. This is one reason why it is considered very poor practice to distill anything to dryness.

Don't distill to dryness.

Detection of Peroxides	Removal of Peroxides
To a solution of 0.01 g of sodium iodide in 0.1 mL of glacial acetic acid, add 0.1 mL of the liquid suspected of containing a peroxide. If the mixture turns brown, a high concentration of peroxide is present; if it turns yellow, a low concentration of peroxide is present.	Pouring the solvent through a column of activated alumina will remove peroxides and dry the solvent simultaneously. Do not allow the column to dry out while in use. When the alumina column is no longer effective, wash the column with 5% aqueous ferrous sulfate, and discard it as nonhazardous waste.

Problems with peroxide formation are especially critical for ethers. Ethers form peroxides readily and, because they are frequently used as solvents, they are often used in quantity and then removed to leave reaction products. Cans of diethyl ether should be dated when opened and if not used within one month should be treated for peroxides or disposed of.

t-Butyl methyl ether with a primary carbon on one side of the oxygen and a tertiary carbon on the other does not form peroxides easily. It is highly desirable to use this in place of diethyl ether for extraction. See sidebar in Chapter 8.

You may have occasion to use *30% hydrogen peroxide*. This material causes severe burns if it contacts the skin and decomposes violently if contaminated with metals or their salts. Be particularly careful not to contaminate the reagent bottle.

Working with Corrosive Substances

Handle strong acids, alkalis, dehydrating agents, and oxidizing agents carefully so as to avoid contact with the skin and eyes and to avoid breathing the corrosive vapors that attack the respiratory tract. All strong concentrated acids attack the skin and eyes. *Concentrated sulfuric acid* is both a dehydrating agent and a strong acid and will cause very severe burns. *Nitric acid* and *chromic acid* (used in cleaning solutions) also cause bad burns. *Hydrofluoric acid* is especially harmful, causing deep, painful, and slow-healing wounds. It should be used only after thorough instruction.

Add H_2SO_4, P_2O_5, CaO, and NaOH to water, not the reverse.

Sodium, potassium, and *ammonium hydroxides* are common bases you will encounter. The first two are extremely damaging to the eye, and ammonium hydroxide is a severe bronchial irritant. Like sulfuric acid, *sodium hydroxide, phosphorous pentoxide,* and *calcium oxide* are powerful dehydrating agents. Their great affinity for water will cause burns to the skin. Because they release a great deal of heat when they react with water, to avoid spattering they should always be added to water rather than water being added to them. That is, the heavier substance should always be added to the lighter one so that rapid mixing results as a consequence of the law of gravity.

You will receive special instruction when it comes time to handle *metallic sodium, lithium aluminum hydride,* and *sodium hydride,* substances that can react explosively with water.

$HClO_4$ perchloric acid

Among the strong oxidizing agents, *perchloric acid* is probably the most hazardous. It can form heavy metal and organic *perchlorates* that are *explosive,* and it can react explosively if it comes in contact with organic compounds.

Should one of these substances get on the skin or in the eyes, wash the affected area with very large quantities of water, using the safety shower and/or eyewash foundation (Fig. 2.6). Do not attempt to neutralize the reagent chemically. Remove contaminated clothing so that thorough washing can take place. Take care to wash the reagent from under the fingernails.

Wipe up spilled hydroxide pellets rapidly.

When you are using very small quantities of these reagents, no particular safety equipment is needed except for *safety glasses*. Take care not to let the reagents, such as sulfuric acid, run down the outside of a bottle or flask and come in contact with the fingers. Wipe up spills immediately with a very damp sponge, especially in the area around the balances. Pellets of sodium and potassium hydroxide are very hygroscopic and will dissolve in the water they pick up from the air; they should therefore be wiped up very quickly. When working with larger quantities of these corrosive chemicals, wear protective gloves; with still larger quantities, use a face mask, gloves, and a neoprene apron. The corrosive vapors can be avoided by carrying out work in a good exhaust hood.

Do not use the plastic syringe with the metal needle to dispense corrosive inorganic reagents, such as concentrated acids or bases.

Working with Toxic Substances

Many chemicals have very specific toxic effects. They interfere with the body's metabolism in a known way. For example, the cyanide ion combines irreversibly with hemoglobin to form cyanometmyoglobin, which can no longer carry oxygen. Aniline acts in the same way. Carbon tetrachloride and other halogenated compounds can cause liver and kidney failure. Carcinogenic and mutagenic substances deserve special attention because of their long-term insidious effects. The ability of certain carcinogens to cause cancer is very great; for example, special precautions are needed when handling aflatoxin B_1. In other cases, such as with dioxane, the hazard is so low that no special precautions are needed beyond reasonable normal care in the laboratory.

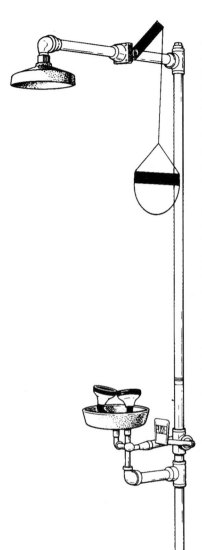

FIG. 2.6 Emergency shower and eyewash station.

Women of childbearing age should be careful when handling any substance of unknown properties. Certain substances are highly suspect teratogens and will cause abnormalities in an embryo or fetus. Among these are benzene, toluene, xylene, aniline, nitrobenzene, phenol, formaldehyde, dimethylformamide (DMF), dimethyl sulfoxide (DMSO), polychlorinated biphenyls (PCBs), estradiol, hydrogen sulfide, carbon disulfide, carbon monoxide, nitrites, nitrous oxide, organolead and mercury compounds, and the notorious sedative thalidomide. Some of these substances will be used in subsequent experiments. Use care. Of course, the leading known cause of embryotoxic effects is ethyl alcohol in the form of maternal alcoholism. The amount of ethanol vapor inhaled in the laboratory or absorbed through the skin is so minute it is unlikely to have these morbid effects.

It is impossible to avoid handling every known or suspected toxic substance, so it is wise to know what measures should be taken. Because the eating of food or the consumption of beverages in the laboratory is strictly forbidden and because one should never taste material in the laboratory, the possibility of poisoning by mouth is remote. Be more careful than your predecessors—the hallucinogenic properties of LSD and **all** artificial sweeteners were discovered by accident. The two most important measures to be taken, then, are (1) avoiding skin contact by wearing the *proper* type of protective gloves (see next section) and (2) avoiding inhalation by working in a good exhaust hood.

Many of the chemicals used in this course will be unfamiliar to you. Their properties can be looked up in reference books, a very useful one being the *Aldrich Catalog Handbook of Fine Chemicals*. Note that 1,4-dichlorobenzene is listed as a "toxic irritant" and naphthalene is listed as an "irritant." Both are used as moth balls. Camphor, used in vaporizers, is classified as a "flammable solid irritant." Salicylic acid, which we will use to synthesize aspirin (Chapter 41) is listed as "moisture-sensitive toxic." Aspirin (acetylsalicylic acid) is classified as an "irritant." Caffeine, which we will isolate from tea or cola syrup (Chapter 8), is classified as "toxic." Substances not so familiar to you—1-naphthol and benzoic acid—are classified respectively as "toxic irritant" and "irritant." To put things in some perspective, nicotine is classified as "highly toxic." Pay attention to these health warnings. In laboratory quantities, common chemicals can be hazardous. Wash your hands carefully after coming in contact with laboratory chemicals. Consult Margaret-Ann Armour, *Hazardous Laboratory Chemicals Disposal Guide,* Lewis Publishers, Inc., 1996,[1] for information on truly hazardous chemicals.

Because you have not had previous experience working with organic chemicals, most of the experiments you will carry out in this course will not involve the use of known carcinogens, although you will work routinely with flammable, corrosive, and toxic substances. A few experiments involve the use of substances that are suspected of being carcinogenic, such as hydrazine. If you pay proper attention to the rules of safety, you should find working with these substances no more hazardous than working with ammonia or nitric acid. The single, short-duration exposure you might receive from a suspected carcinogen, should an accident occur, would probably have no long-term consequences. The

---

1. Free copies of this 2,860-page catalog can be obtained from http://www.sigma-aldrich.com.

reason for taking the precautions noted in each experiment is to learn, from the beginning, good safety habits.

Gloves

Be aware that "protective gloves" in the organic laboratory may not offer much protection. Polyethylene and latex rubber gloves are very permeable to many organic liquids. An undetected pinhole may bring with it long-term contact with reagents. Disposable polyvinyl chloride (PVC) gloves offer reasonable protection from contact with aqueous solutions of acids, bases, and dyes, but no one type of glove is useful as protection against all reagents. It is for this reason that no less than 25 different types of chemically resistant gloves are available from laboratory supply houses.

It is probably safer not to wear gloves and immediately wash your hands with soap and water after accidental contact with any harmful reagent or solvent than to wear inappropriate or defective gloves. See the *Instructor's Guide* for further information in this regard.

Using the Laboratory Hood

Modern practice dictates that in laboratories where workers spend most of their time working with chemicals, there should be one exhaust hood for every two people. This precaution is often not possible in a beginning organic chemistry laboratory, however. In this course you will find that for some experiments the hood must be used and for others it is advisable; in these instances, it may be necessary to schedule experimental work around access to the hoods. However, many experiments formerly carried out in the hood can now be carried out at the desk because the concentration of vapors will be minimal when working at a microscale.

The hood offers a number of advantages when working with toxic and flammable substances. Not only does it draw off the toxic and flammable fumes, it also affords an excellent physical barrier on all four sides of a reacting system when the sash is pulled down. And should a chemical spill occur, it is nicely contained within the hood.

Keep the hood sash closed.

It is your responsibility each time you use a hood to see that it is working properly. You should find some type of indicating device that will give you this information on the hood itself. A simple propeller on a cork works well. The hood is a backup device. Don't use it alone to dispose of chemicals by evaporation; use an aspirator tube or carry out a distillation. Toxic and flammable fumes should be trapped or condensed in some way and disposed of in the prescribed manner. The sash should be pulled down unless you are actually carrying out manipulations on the experimental apparatus. The water, gas, and electrical controls should be on the outside of the hood so it is not necessary to open the hood to adjust them. The ability of the hood to remove vapors is greatly enhanced if the apparatus is kept as close to the back of the hood as possible. Everything should be at least 15 cm back from the hood sash. Chemicals should not be stored permanently in the hood but should be removed to ventilated storage areas. If the hood is cluttered with chemicals, you will not achieve a good, smooth air flow or have adequate room for experiments.

Working at Reduced Pressure

Implosion

Whenever a vessel or system is evacuated, an implosion could result from atmospheric pressure on the empty vessel. It makes little difference whether the vacuum is perfect or just 10 mm Hg; the pressure difference is almost the same (760 versus 750 mm Hg). An implosion may occur if there is a star crack in the flask, or if the flask is scratched or etched. Only with heavy-walled flasks specifically designed for vacuum filtration is the use of a safety shield (Fig. 2.7) ordinarily unnecessary. The chances of implosion of the apparatus used for microscale experiments are remote.

Dewar flasks (thermos bottles) are often found in the laboratory without shielding. These should be wrapped with friction tape or covered with plastic net to prevent the glass from flying about in case of an implosion (Fig. 2.8). Similarly, vacuum desiccators should be wrapped with tape before being evacuated.

Working with Compressed Gas Cylinders

Many reactions are carried out under an inert atmosphere so that the reactants and/or products will not react with oxygen or moisture in the air. Nitrogen and argon are the inert gases most frequently used. Oxygen is widely used both as a reactant and to provide a hot flame for glassblowing and welding. It is used in the oxidative coupling of alkynes (Chapter 24). Helium is the carrier gas used in gas chromatography. Other gases commonly used in the laboratory are ammonia, often used as a solvent; chlorine, used for chlorination reactions; acetylene, used in combination with oxygen for welding; and hydrogen, used for high- and low-pressure hydrogenation reactions.

The following rule applies to all compressed gases: Compressed gas cylinders should be firmly secured at all times. For temporary use, a clamp that attaches to the laboratory bench top and has a belt for the cylinder will suffice (Fig. 2.9). Eyebolts and chains should be used to secure cylinders in permanent installations.

A variety of outlet threads are used on gas cylinders to prevent incompatible gases from becoming mixed because of an interchange of connections. Both right- and left-handed external and internal threads are used. Left-handed nuts are notched to differentiate them from right-handed nuts. Right-handed threads are used on nonfuel and oxidizing gases, and left-handed threads are used on fuel gases, such as hydrogen.

Cylinders come equipped with caps that should be left in place during storage and transportation. These caps can be removed by hand. Under these caps is a hand wheel valve. It can be opened by turning the wheel counterclockwise; however, because most compressed gases in full cylinders are under very high pressure (commonly up to 3000 lb/in.^{2}), a pressure regulator must be attached

FIG. 2.7   Safety shield.

Always clamp gas cylinders.

FIG. 2.8   Dewar flask with safety net in place.

FIG. 2.9 Gas cylinder clamp.

FIG. 2.10 Gas pressure regulator. Turn two-flanged diaphragm valve clockwise to increase outlet pressure.

FIG. 2.11 Gas cylinder cart.

Clockwise movement of diaphragm valve handle increases pressure.

to the cylinder. This pressure regulator is almost always of the diaphragm type and has two gauges, one indicating the pressure in the cylinder, the other the outlet pressure (Fig. 2.10). On the outlet, low-pressure side of the regulator is located a small needle valve and then the outlet connector. After connecting the regulator to the cylinder, unscrew the diaphragm valve (turn it counterclockwise) before opening the hand wheel valve on the top of the cylinder. This valve should be opened only as far as necessary. For most gas flow rates in the laboratory, this will be a very small amount. The gas flow and/or pressure is increased by turning the two-flanged diaphragm valve **clockwise.** When the apparatus is not being used, turn off the hand wheel valve (clockwise) on the top of the cylinder (Fig. 2.9). Before removing the regulator from the cylinder, reduce the flow or pressure to zero. Cylinders should never be emptied to zero pressure and left with the valve open because the residual contents will become contaminated with air. Empty cylinders should be labeled "empty," and their valves should be closed, capped, and returned to the storage area, separated from full cylinders. Gas cylinders should never be dragged or rolled from place to place but should be fastened into and moved in a cart designed for the purpose (Fig. 2.11). The cap should be in place whenever the cylinder is moved.

Odoriferous Chemicals

Some organic chemicals just smell bad. Among these are the thiols (organic derivatives of hydrogen sulfide), isonitriles, many amines (for example, cadaverine), and butyric acid. Washing apparatus and, if necessary, hands in a solution of a quaternary ammonium salt may solve the problem. These compounds apparently complex with many odoriferous substances allowing them to be rinsed away. Commercial products (Zephiran, Roccal, San-O-Fec, and others) are available at pet and farm supply stores.

Waste Disposal—Cleaning Up

Spilled solids should simply be swept up and placed in the appropriate solid waste container. This should be done promptly, because many solids are hygroscopic and become difficult if not impossible to sweep up in a short time. This is particularly true of sodium hydroxide and potassium hydroxide.

Clean up spills rapidly.

Spilled acids should be neutralized. Use sodium carbonate or, for larger spills, cement or limestone. For bases use sodium bisulfate. If the spilled material is highly volatile, clear the area and allow it to evaporate, provided there is no chance of igniting flammable vapors. Other liquids can be taken up into such absorbents as vermiculite, diatomaceous earth, dry sand, kitty litter, or paper towels. Be particularly careful in wiping up spills with paper towels. If a strong oxidizer is present, the towels can later ignite. Bits of sodium metal will also cause paper towels to ignite. Sodium metal is best destroyed with *n*-butyl alcohol. Unless you are sure the spilled liquid is not toxic, wear gloves when using paper towels or a sponge to remove the liquid.

Mercury requires special measures—see instructor.

Cleaning Up   In the not-too-distant past it was common practice to wash all unwanted liquids from the organic laboratory down the drain and to place all solid waste in the trash basket. Never a wise practice it is now, for environmental reasons, no longer allowed by law.

Waste containers:
Nonhazardous solid waste
Organic solvents
Halogenated organic solvents
Hazardous waste (various types)

Organic reactions usually employ a solvent and often involve the use of a strong acid, a strong base, an oxidant, a reductant, or a catalyst. None of these should be washed down the drain or placed in the wastebasket. We will place the material we finally classify as waste in containers labeled for nonhazardous solid waste, organic solvents, halogenated organic solvents, and hazardous wastes of various types.

Nonhazardous waste encompasses such solids as paper, corks, sand, alumina, and sodium sulfate. These will ultimately end up in a sanitary landfill (the local dump). Any chemicals that are leached by rainwater from this landfill must not be harmful to the environment. In the *organic solvents* container are placed the solvents that are used for recrystallization and for running reactions, cleaning apparatus, etc. These solvents can contain dissolved, solid, nonhazardous organic solids. This solution will go to an incinerator where it will be burned. If the solvent is halogenated (e.g., dichloromethane) or contains halogenated material, it must go in the *halogenated organic solvents* container. Ultimately, this will go to a special incinerator equipped with a scrubber to remove HCl from the combustion gases. The final container is for various *hazardous wastes*. Because hazardous wastes are often incompatible (oxidants with reductants, cyanides with acids, etc.), several different containers may be provided in the laboratory for these—for example, phosphorus compounds, heavy metal hydroxides, mercury salts, and so on.

Some hazardous wastes are concentrated nitric acid, platinum catalysts, sodium hydrosulfite (a reducing agent), and Cr^{6+} (an oxidizing agent). To dispose of small quantities of a hazardous waste (e.g., concentrated sulfuric acid), the material must be packed carefully in bottles and placed in a 55-gallon drum called a lab pack, to which an inert packing material is added. The lab pack is carefully documented and hauled off to a site where such waste is disposed of by a bonded, licensed, and heavily regulated waste disposal company. Formerly, many hazardous wastes were disposed of by burial in a "secure landfill." The kinds of hazardous waste that can be thus disposed of have become extremely limited in recent years, and much of the waste undergoes various kinds of treatment at the disposal site (e.g., neutralization, incineration, reduction) to put it in a form that can be safely buried in a secure landfill or flushed to a sewer. There are relatively few places for approved disposal of hazardous waste. For example, there are none in New England, so most hazardous waste from this area is trucked to South Carolina! The charge to small generators of waste is usually based on the volume of waste. So, 1000 mL of a 2% cyanide solution would cost far more to dispose of than 20 g of solid cyanide, even though the total amount of this poisonous substance is the same. It now costs far more to dispose of most hazardous chemicals than it does to purchase them new.

Waste disposal is very expensive.

American law states that a material is not a waste until the laboratory worker declares it a waste. So—for pedagogical and practical reasons—we would like you to regard the chemical treatment of the byproducts of each reaction in this text as a part of the experiment.

The law: A waste is not a waste until the laboratory worker declares it a waste.

In the section titled "Cleaning Up" at the end of each experiment, the goal is to reduce the volume of hazardous waste, to convert hazardous waste to less hazardous waste, or to convert it to nonhazardous waste. The simplest example is concentrated sulfuric acid. As a byproduct from a reaction, it is obviously hazardous. But after careful dilution with water and neutralization with sodium carbonate, the sulfuric acid becomes a dilute solution of sodium sulfate, which in almost every locale can be flushed down the drain with a large excess of water. Anything flushed down the drain must be accompanied by a large excess of Cr^{6+} can be reduced, and reductants such as hydrosulfite can be oxidized (by hypochlorite [household bleach]). Dilute solutions of heavy metal ions can be precipitated as their insoluble sulfides or hydroxides. The precipitate may still be a hazardous waste, but it will have a much smaller volume.

Cleaning up: reducing the volume of hazardous waste or converting hazardous waste to less hazardous or nonhazardous waste

One type of hazardous waste is unique: a harmless solid that is damp with an organic solvent. Alumina from a chromatography column and calcium chloride used to dry an ether solution are examples. Being solids, they obviously can't go in the organic solvents container, and being flammable they can't go in the nonhazardous waste container. A solution to this problem is to spread the solid out in the hood to let the solvent evaporate. You can then place the solid in the nonhazardous waste container. The saving in waste disposal costs by this operation is enormous.

Disposing of solids wet with organic solvents: alumina and anhydrous calcium chloride pellets

Our goal in "Cleaning Up" is to make you more aware of *all* aspects of an experiment. Waste disposal is now an extremely important aspect. Check to be sure the procedure you use is permitted by law in your location. Three sources of information have been used as the basis of the procedures at the end of each experiment: the *Aldrich Catalog Handbook of Fine Chemicals,* which gives brief disposal procedures for every chemical in their catalog; *Prudent Practices in the Laboratory: Handling and Disposal of Chemicals,* National Academy Press, Washington, DC, 1995; and *Hazardous Laboratory Chemicals Disposal Guide,* M.-A. Armour, Lewis Publishers, Inc., 1996. The last title should be on the bookshelf of every laboratory. This 464-page book gives detailed information about hundreds of hazardous substances, including their physical properties, hazardous reactions, physiological properties and health hazards, spillage disposal, and waste disposal. Many of the treatment procedures in "Cleaning Up" are adaptations of these procedures. *Destruction of Hazardous Chemicals in the Laboratory,* G. Lunn and E. B. Sansone, Wiley, New York, NY, 1994, complements this book.

The area of waste disposal is changing rapidly. Many levels of laws apply—local, state, and federal. What may be permissible to wash down the drain or evaporate in the hood in one jurisdiction may be illegal in another, so before carrying out this part of the experiment check with your college or university waste disposal officer.

Questions

1. Write a balanced equation for the reaction between iodide ion, a peroxide, and hydrogen ion. What causes the orange or brown color?

2. Why does the horn of the carbon dioxide fire extinguisher become cold when the extinguisher is used?

3. Why is water *not* used to extinguish most fires in an organic laboratory?

CHAPTER

3   *Crystallization*

PRELAB EXERCISE: Write an expanded outline for the seven-step process of crystallization.

Crystallization: the most important purification method for solids, especially for small-scale experiments

On both a large and small scale, *crystallization* is the most important method for the purification of solid organic compounds. A crystalline organic substance is made up of a three-dimensional array of molecules held together primarily by van der Waals forces. These intramolecular attractions are fairly weak; most organic solids melt in the range of room temperature to 250°C.

Crystals can be grown from the molten state just as water is frozen into ice, but it is not easy to remove impurities from crystals made in this way. Thus most purifications in the laboratory involve dissolving the material to be purified in the appropriate hot solvent. As the solvent cools, the solution becomes saturated with respect to the substance, which then crystallizes. As the perfectly regular array of a crystal is formed, foreign molecules are excluded, and the crystal is thus one pure substance. Soluble impurities remain in solution because they are not concentrated enough to saturate the solution. The crystals are collected by *filtration,* the crystals are washed with cold solvent to remove the adhering impurities, and then the crystals are dried. This process is carried out on an enormous scale in the commercial purification of sugar.

In the organic laboratory, crystallization is usually the most rapid and convenient method for purifying the products of a reaction. Initially you will be told which solvent to use to crystallize a given substance and how much of it to use; later on you will judge how much solvent is needed; the choice of both the solvent and its volume will ultimately be left to you. It takes both experience and knowledge to choose the correct solvent for a given purification.

The Seven Steps of Crystallization

IN THIS EXPERIMENT you will carry out the most important laboratory operation of organic chemistry—crystallization. The process of crystallization can be broken into seven discrete steps: (1) choosing the solvent and solvent pairs; (2) dissolving the solute; (3) decolorizing the solution; use of pelletized Norit; (4) filtering suspended solids; (5) crystallizing the solute; (6) collecting and washing the crystals; and (7) drying the product.

The process of crystallization involves dissolving the impure substance in an appropriate hot solvent, removing some impurities by decolorizing and/or filtering the hot solution, allowing the substance to crystallize as the temperature of the solution falls, removing the crystallization solvent, and drying the resulting purified crystals.

How crystallization starts

Crystallization is initiated at a point of nucleation—a seed crystal, a speck of dust, or a scratch on the wall of the test tube if the solution is supersaturated with respect to the substance being crystallized (the solute). Supersaturation will occur if a hot, saturated solution cools and crystals do not form. Large crystals, which are easy to isolate, are formed by nucleation and then slow cooling of the hot solution.

1. Choosing the Solvent and Solvent Pairs

Similia similibus solvuntur   **A**

In choosing the solvent the chemist is guided by the dictum "like dissolves like." Even the nonchemist knows that oil and water do not mix and that sugar and salt dissolve in water but not in oil. Hydrocarbon solvents such as hexane will dissolve hydrocarbons and other nonpolar compounds, and hydroxylic solvents such as water and ethanol will dissolve polar compounds. Often it is difficult to decide, simply by looking at the structure of a molecule, just how polar or nonpolar it is and which solvent would be best. Therefore, the solvent is often chosen by experimentation.

The ideal solvent

The best crystallization solvent (and none is ideal) will dissolve the solute when the solution is hot but not when the solution is cold; it will either not dissolve the impurities at all or it will dissolve them very well (so they won't crystallize out along with the solute); it will not react with the solute; and it will be nonflammable, nontoxic, inexpensive, and very volatile (so it can be removed from the crystals).

Miscible: capable of being mixed

Some common solvents and their properties are presented in Table 3.1 in order of decreasing polarity of the solvent. Solvents adjacent to each other in the list will dissolve in each other; that is, they are miscible with each other, and each solvent will, in general, dissolve substances that are similar to it in chemical structure. These solvents are used both for crystallization and as solvents in which reactions are carried out.

Procedure

C   **Choosing a Solvent.**   To choose a solvent for crystallization, place a few crystals of the impure solute in a small test tube or centrifuge tube, and add a very small drop of the solvent. Allow it to flow down the side of the tube and onto the crystals. If the crystals dissolve instantly at room temperature, that solvent cannot be used for crystallization because too much of the solute will remain in solution at low temperatures. If the crystals do not dissolve at room temperature, warm the tube on the hot sand bath, and observe the crystals. If they do not go into solution, add a drop more solvent. If the crystals go into solution at the boiling point of the solvent and then crystallize when the tube is cooled, you have found a good crystallization solvent. If not, remove the solvent by evaporation, and try a different solvent. In this trial-and-error process it

TABLE 3.1 Crystallization Solvents

Solvent	Boiling Point (°C)	Remarks
Water (H_2O)	100	The solvent of choice because it is cheap, nonflammable, and nontoxic and will dissolve a large variety of polar organic molecules. Its high boiling point and high heat of vaporization make it difficult to remove from crystals.
Acetic acid (CH_3COOH)	118	Will react with alcohols and amines. Difficult to remove from crystals. Not a common solvent for recrystallizations, although used as a solvent when carrying out oxidation reactions.
Dimethyl sulfoxide (DMSO), methyl sulfoxide (CH_3SOCH_3)	189	Also not a commonly used solvent for crystallization, but used for reactions.
Methanol (CH_3OH)	64	A very good solvent, used often for crystallization. Will dissolve molecules of higher polarity than will the other alcohols.
95% Ethanol (CH_3CH_2OH)	78	One of the most commonly used crystallization solvents. Its high boiling point makes it a better solvent for the less polar molecules than methanol. Evaporates readily from the crystals. Esters may undergo interchange of alcohol groups on recrystallization.
Acetone (CH_3COCH_3)	56	An excellent solvent, but its low boiling point means there is not much difference in solubility of a compound at its boiling point and at room temperature.
2-Butanone, methyl ethyl ketone, MEK ($CH_3COCH_2CH_3$)	80	An excellent solvent with many of the most desirable properties of a good crystallization solvent.
Ethyl acetate ($CH_3COOC_2H_5$)	78	Another excellent solvent that has about the right combination of moderately high boiling point and yet the volatility needed to remove it from crystals.
Dichloromethane, methylene chloride (CH_2Cl_2)	40	Although a common extraction solvent, dichloromethane boils too low to make it a good crystallization solvent. It is useful in a solvent pair with ligroin.

(continued)

is easiest to try low-boiling solvents first, because they can be removed most easily. Occasionally no single satisfactory solvent can be found, so mixed solvents, or *solvent pairs,* are used.

Solvent Pairs.   To use a mixed solvent, dissolve the crystals in the better solvent, and add the poorer solvent to the hot solution until it becomes cloudy and

TABLE 3.2 Solvent Pairs

Acetic acid–water	Ethyl acetate–cyclohexane
Ethanol–water	Acetone–ligroin
Acetone–water	Ethyl acetate–ligroin
Dioxane–water	*t*-Butyl methyl ether–ligroin
Acetone–ethanol	Dichloromethane–ligroin
Ethanol–*t*-butyl methyl ether	Toluene–ligroin

TABLE 3.1   *continued*

Solvent	Boiling Point (°C)	Remarks
Diethyl ether, ether ($CH_3CH_2OCH_2CH_3$)	35	Its boiling point is too low for crystallization, although it is an extremely good solvent and fairly inert. Used in solvent pair with ligroin.
Methyl *t*-butyl ether ($CH_3OC(CH_3)_3$)	52	A relatively new solvent that is very inexpensive because of its large-scale use as an antiknock agent and oxygenate in gasoline. Does not easily form peroxides, and is less volatile than diethyl ether, but has the same solvent characteristics. See sidebar in Chapter 8.
Dioxane ($C_4H_8O_2$)	101	A very good solvent, not too difficult to remove from crystals; a mild carcinogen, forms peroxides.
Toluene ($C_6H_5CH_3$)	111	An excellent solvent that has replaced the formerly widely used benzene (a weak carcinogen) for crystallization of aryl compounds. Because of its boiling point it is not easily removed from crystals.
Pentane (C_5H_{12})	36	A widely used solvent for nonpolar substances. Not often used alone for crystallization, but good in combination with a number of other solvents as part of a solvent pair.
Hexane (C_6H_{14})	69	Frequently used to crystallize nonpolar substances. It is inert and has the correct balance between boiling point and volatility. Often used as part of a solvent pair. See ligroin.
Cyclohexane (C_6H_{12})	81	Similar in all respects to hexane. See ligroin.
Petroleum ether	30–60	A mixture of hydrocarbons of which pentane is a chief component. Used interchangeably with pentane because it is cheap. Unlike diethyl ether or *t*-butyl methyl ether, it is not an ether in the modern chemical sense.
Ligroin	60–90	A mixture of hydrocarbons with the properties of hexane and cyclohexane. A very commonly used crystallization solvent. Also sold as "hexanes."

Note: The solvents in this table are listed in decreasing order of polarity. Adjacent solvents in the list will in general be miscible with each other.

the solution is saturated with the solute. The two solvents must, of course, be miscible with each other. Some useful solvent pairs are given in Table 3.2.

2. Dissolving the Solute

Microscale Procedure

D   Once a crystallization solvent has been found, the impure crystals are placed in a reaction tube, solvent is added dropwise, the crystals are stirred with a microspatula or a small glass rod, and the tube is warmed on a steam bath or sand bath with the addition of more solvent until the crystals dissolve. A solution of this type can become *superheated*; that is, heated above its boiling point without actually boiling. When boiling does suddenly occur, it can happen with almost explosive violence. To prevent this from happening, a *wood applicator stick* can be added to the solution (Fig. 3.1). Air trapped in the wood comes out of the stick and forms the nuclei on which even boiling can occur. Porous

Prevention of bumping

Wood applicator stick

Cool at this point

Air condenser

Boiling solvent

Temperature controlled by depth in sand

FIG. 3.1 The reaction tube being used for crystallization. The wood applicator stick ("boiling stick") promotes even boiling and is easier to remove than a boiling chip. The Thermowell sand is cool on top and hotter down deeper, so it provides a range of temperatures. The reaction tube is long and narrow; it can be held in the hand while the solvent refluxes. Do not use a boiling stick in place of a boiling chip in a reaction.

Do not use wood boiling   **2**
sticks in place of boiling chips
in a reaction. Use them only
for crystallization.

porcelain *boiling chips* work in the same way. Never add a boiling chip or boiling stick to a hot solution, since it may be superheated and boil over.

To remove solid impurities (insoluble byproducts of reaction, lint, dust, etc.), it is necessary to dilute the solution with excess solvent (the better solvent if a solvent mixture is being used), carry out the filtration near room temperature, and then evaporate the solvent to a point at which the hot solution is once more saturated with respect to the solute so that crystallization can take place in the usual way. This is described in Step 4. You will find that this step is usually not necessary in most experiments.

Care must be exercised to use the correct amount of solvent. Observe the mixture carefully as solvent is being added. Allow sufficient time for the boiling solvent to dissolve the solute, and note the rate at which most of the material dissolves. When you believe most of the material has been dissolved, stop adding solvent. There is the possibility that your sample is contaminated with a small quantity of an insoluble impurity that never will dissolve. To hasten the solution process, crush large crystals with a stirring rod, taking care not

Don't use too much solvent.

to break the tube. On a microscale, there is a tendency to use too much solvent so that on cooling the hot solution little or no material crystallizes. This is not a hopeless situation. The remedy is to evaporate some of the solvent and repeat the cooling process. Inspect the hot solution. If it contains no undissolved impurities and is not colored from impurities, you can simply let it cool, allowing the solute to crystallize (Step 5), and then collect the crystals

(Step 6). On the other hand, if the solution is colored, it must be treated with activated (decolorizing) charcoal and then filtered before crystallization (Step 3). If it contains solid impurities, it must be filtered before crystallization takes place (Step 4).

Macroscale Procedure

I   Place the substance to be crystallized in an Erlenmeyer flask (never use a beaker), add enough solvent to cover the crystals, and then heat the flask on a steam bath (if the solvent boils below 90°C) or a hot plate until the solvent boils. Stir the mixture or, better, swirl it (Fig. 3.2) to promote dissolution. Add solvent gradually, keeping it at the boil, until all of the solute dissolves. Addition of a boiling stick or a boiling chip to the solution once most of the solid is gone will promote even boiling. It is not difficult to superheat the solution; that is, heat it above the boiling point with no boiling taking place. Once the solution does boil it does so with explosive violence. Never add a boiling chip or boiling stick to a hot solution. A glass rod with a flattened end can sometimes be of use in crushing large particles of solute to speed up the dissolving process. Be sure no flames are nearby when working with flammable solvents.

Be careful not to add too much solvent. Note how rapidly most of the material dissolves, and then stop adding solvent when you suspect that almost all of the desired material has dissolved. It is best to err on the side of too little solvent rather than too much. Undissolved material noted at this point could be an insoluble impurity that never will dissolve. Allow the solvent to boil, and if no further material dissolves, proceed to Step 4 to remove suspended solids from the solution by filtration, or if the solution is colored, go to Step 3 to carry out the decolorization process. If the solution is clear, proceed to Step 5, Crystallizing the Solute.

FIG. 3.2   Swirling of a solution to mix contents and help dissolve material to be crystallized.

MICROSCALE AND MACROSCALE

E

Activated charcoal = decolorizing carbon = Norit

3. Decolorizing the Solution; Use of Pelletized Norit

The vast majority of pure organic chemicals are colorless or a light shade of yellow and consequently this step is not often required. Occasionally a chemical reaction will produce high molecular weight by-products that are highly colored. The impurities can be adsorbed onto the surface of activated charcoal by simply boiling the solution with charcoal. Activated charcoal has an extremely large surface area per gram (several hundred square meters) and can bind a large number of molecules to this surface. On a commercial scale, the impurities in brown sugar are adsorbed onto charcoal in the process of refining sugar.

In the past, laboratory manuals have advocated the use of finely powdered activated charcoal for removal of colored impurities. This has two drawbacks. Because the charcoal is so finely divided it can only be separated from the solution by filtration through paper, and even then some of the finer particles pass through the filter paper. And the presence of the charcoal completely obscures the color of the solution, so that adding the correct amount of charcoal is mostly a matter of luck. If too little charcoal is added, the solution will

Pelletized Norit (also called active carbon, activated charcoal, decolorizing carbon)

still be colored after filtration, making repetition necessary; if too much is added, it will absorb some of the product in addition to the impurities. We have found that charcoal extruded as short cylindrical pieces measuring about 0.8 × 3 mm made by the Norit Company solves both of these problems. It works just as well as the finely divided powder, and it does not obscure the color of the solution. It can be added in small portions until the solution is decolorized and the size of the pieces makes it easy to remove them from the solution.[1]

Add a small amount (0.1% of the solute weight is sufficient) of pelletized Norit to the colored solution and then boil the solution for a few minutes. Be careful not to add the charcoal pieces to a superheated solution; the charcoal functions like hundreds of boiling chips and will cause the solution to boil over. Remove the Norit by filtration as described in Step 4.

4. Filtering Suspended Solids

The filtration of a hot, saturated solution to remove solid impurities or charcoal can be performed in a number of ways. Processes include gravity filtration, pressure filtration, decantation, or removal of the solvent using a Pasteur pipette. Vacuum filtration is not used because the hot solvent will cool during the process and the product will crystallize in the filter. This can be one of the most vexing operations in the laboratory if, during the process of filtration, the desired compound crystallizes. Test the solution or a small portion of it before filtration to ensure that no crystals form at room temperature. Like decolorization with charcoal the removal of solid impurities by filtration is usually not necessary.

Microscale Procedure

G   **(A) Removal of Solution with a Pasteur Pipette.**   If the solid impurities are large in size, they can be removed by filtration of the liquid through the small space between the square end of a Pasteur pipette and the bottom of a reaction tube (Fig. 3.3). Expel air from the pipette as it is being pushed to the bottom of the tube. Use a small additional quantity of solvent to rinse the tube and pipette. Anhydrous calcium chloride, a drying agent, is removed easily in this way. Removal of very fine material, such as traces of charcoal, is facilitated by filtration of the solution through a small piece of filter paper (3 mm²) placed in the reaction tube. This process is even easier if the filter paper is the thick variety, such as that from which Soxhlet extraction thimbles are made.[2]

5   **(B) Filtration in a Pasteur Pipette.**   To filter 0.1 to 2 mL of a solution, dilute the solution with enough solvent so that the solute will not crystallize out

1. Available from Aldrich Chemical Co., P.O. Box 2060, Milwaukee, WI 53201. Catalog number 32942-8 as Norit RO 0.8. This form of Norit is an extrudate 0.8 mm dia. It has a surface area of 1000 m²/g, a total pore volume of 1.1 mL/g.

2. J.L. Belletire and N.O. Mahmoodi, *J. Chem. Ed.* **66:**964, 1989.

FIG. 3.3 Filtration using the Pasteur pipette and reaction tube.

FIG. 3.4 Filtration of a solution in a Pasteur pipette.

FIG. 3.5 Pressure filtration apparatus. Solution to be filtered is added through the aperture, which is closed by a finger as pressure is applied.

at room temperature. Prepare a filter pipette by pushing a tiny bit of cotton into a Pasteur pipette, put the solution to be filtered into this filter pipette using another Pasteur pipette, and then force the liquid through the filter using air pressure from a pipette bulb (Fig. 3.4). Fresh solvent should be added to rinse the pipette and cotton. The filtered solution is then concentrated by evaporation. One problem encountered with this method is using too much cotton packed too tightly in the pipette so that the solution cannot be forced through it. To remove very fine impurities, such as traces of decolorizing charcoal, a 3- to 4-mm layer of Celite filter aid can be added to the top of the cotton.

(C) Removal of Fine Impurities by Centrifugation.

To remove fine solid impurities from up to 4 mL of solution, dilute the solution with enough solvent so that the solute will not crystallize out at room temperature. Counterbalance the reaction tube, and centrifuge for about two min at high speed in a laboratory centrifuge. The clear supernatant can be decanted (poured off) from the solid on the bottom of the tube. Alternatively, with care, the solution can be removed with a Pasteur pipette, leaving the solid behind.

(D) Pressure Filtration with a Micro Büchner Funnel.

H

The technique applicable to volumes from 0.1 to 5 mL is the use of the *micro Büchner funnel*. It is made of polyethylene and is fitted with a porous *polyethylene frit* 6 mm in diameter. This funnel fits in the bottom of an inexpensive disposable polyethylene pipette in which a hole is cut (Fig. 3.5). The solution to be filtered is placed in the pipette using a Pasteur pipette. The thumb covers the hole in the plastic pipette, and pressure is applied to filter the solution. It is good practice to place a 6-mm-diameter piece of filter paper over the frit, which would otherwise become clogged with insoluble material.

Use filter paper on top of frit.

Using the chromatography column for pressure filtration

The glass chromatography column can be used in the same way. A piece of filter paper is placed over the frit. The solution to be filtered is placed in the chromatography column, and pressure is applied to the solution using a pipette bulb. In both procedures, dilute the solution to be filtered so that it does not crystallize out in the apparatus and use a small amount of clean solvent to rinse the apparatus. The filtered solution is then concentrated by evaporation.

Macroscale Procedure

Decant: to pour off. A fast, easy separation procedure

(A) Decantation.

On a large scale, it is often possible to pour off (decant) the hot solution leaving the insoluble material behind. This is especially easy if the solid is granular like sodium sulfate. The solid remaining in the flask and the inside of the flask should be rinsed with a few milliliters of the solvent in order to recover as much of the product as possible.

(B) Gravity Filtration.

The most common method for the removal of insoluble solid material is gravity filtration through a fluted filter paper (Fig. 3.6). This is the method of choice for the removal of finely divided charcoal, dust, lint, and so on. The following equipment is needed for this process: three Erlenmeyer flasks on a steam bath or hot plate—one to contain the solution to be filtered, one to contain a few milliliters of solvent and a stemless funnel, and the third to contain several milliliters of the crystallizing solvent to be used for rinsing purposes—a fluted piece of filter paper, a towel for holding the hot flask and drying out the stemless funnel, and boiling chips for all solutions.

A piece of filter paper is fluted as shown in Fig. 3.7 and is then placed in a stemless funnel. Appropriate sizes of Erlenmeyer flasks, stemless funnels, and filter paper are shown in Fig. 3.8. The funnel is stemless so that the saturated solution being filtered will not have a chance to cool and clog the stem with crystals. The filter paper should fit entirely inside the rim of the funnel; it is fluted to allow rapid filtration. Test to see that the funnel is stable in the neck of the Erlenmeyer flask. If it is not, support it with a ring attached to a ring stand. A few milliliters of solvent and a boiling chip should be placed in the

FIG. 3.6 Gravity filtration of hot solution through fluted filter paper.

FIG. 3.8   Assemblies for gravity filtration. Stemless funnels have diameters of 2.5, 4.2, 5.0 and 6.0 cm.

FIG. 3.7   Fluting a filter paper.

Be aware that the vapors of low-boiling solvents can ignite on an electric hot plate.

flask into which the solution is to be filtered. This solvent is brought to a boil on the steam bath or hot plate along with the solution to be filtered.

The solution to be filtered should be saturated with the solute at the boiling point. Note the volume, and then add 10% more solvent. The resulting slightly dilute solution is not as likely to crystallize out in the funnel in the process of filtration. Bring the solution to be filtered to a boil, grasp the flask in a towel, and pour the solution into the filter paper in the stemless funnel (Fig. 3.6).

The funnel should be warm in order to prevent crystallization from occurring in the funnel. This can be accomplished in two ways: (1) Invert the funnel over a steam bath for a few seconds, then pick up the funnel with a towel, wipe it perfectly dry, place it on top of the Erlenmeyer flask, and add the fluted filter paper; or (2) place the stemless funnel in the neck of the Erlenmeyer flask and allow the solvent to reflux into the funnel, thereby warming it.

Pour the solution to be filtered at a steady rate into the fluted filter paper. Check to see whether crystallization is occurring in the filter. If it does, add boiling solvent (from the third Erlenmeyer flask heated on the steam bath or hot plate) until the crystals dissolve, dilute the solution being filtered, and carry on. Rinse the flask that contained the solution to be filtered with a few milliliters of boiling solvent, and rinse the fluted filter paper with this same solvent.

Because the filtrate has been diluted in order to prevent it from crystallizing during the filtration process, the excess solvent must now be removed by boiling the solution. This process can be speeded up somewhat by blowing a slow current of air into the flask in the hood or using an aspirator tube to pull vapors into the aspirator (Figs. 3.9 and 3.10). However, the fastest method is to heat the solvent in the filter flask on the sand bath while the flask is connected to the water aspirator. The vacuum is controlled with the thumb (Fig. 3.11).[3] If

---

3. D.W. Mayo, R.M. Pike, and S.M. Butcher, *Microscale Organic Laboratory* (New York: Wiley, 1986), p. 97.

FIG. 3.9 Aspirator tube in use. A boiling stick may be necessary to promote boiling.

FIG. 3.11 Evaporation of a solvent under a vacuum.

FIG. 3.10 Tube being used to remove solvent vapors.

your thumb is not large enough, put a one-holed rubber stopper into the Hirsch funnel or the filter flask and again control the vacuum with the thumb. If the vacuum is not controlled, the solution may boil over and go out the vacuum hose.

5. Crystallizing the Solute

On both a macroscale and a microscale, the crystallization process should normally start from a solution that is saturated with the solute at the boiling point. If it has been necessary to remove impurities or charcoal by filtration, the solution has been diluted. To concentrate the solution, simply boil off the solvent under an aspirator tube as shown in Fig. 3.9 (macroscale) or blow off solvent using a gentle stream of air or, better, nitrogen in the hood as shown in Fig. 3.10 (microscale). Be sure to have a boiling chip (macroscale) or a boiling stick (microscale) in the solution during this process, but do not forget to remove it before initiating crystallization.

A saturated solution

Add a seed crystal.

Slow cooling is important.

Once it has been ascertained that the hot solution is saturated with the compound just below the boiling point of the solvent, it is allowed to cool slowly to room temperature. Crystallization should begin immediately. If it does not, add a seed crystal or scratch the inside of the tube with a glass rod at the liquid–air interface. Crystallization must start on some nucleation center. A minute crystal of the desired compound saved from the crude material will suffice. If a seed crystal is not available, crystallization can be started on the rough surface of a fresh scratch on the inside of the container.

D
H
Once it is ascertained that crystallization has started, the solution must be cooled slowly without disturbing the container so that large crystals can form. On a microscale, it is best to allow the reaction tube to cool in a beaker filled with cotton or paper towels, which act as insulation so cooling takes place slowly. Even insulated in this manner, the small reaction tube will cool to room temperature within a few minutes. Slow cooling will guarantee the formation of large crystals, which are easily separated by filtration and easily washed free of adhering impure solvent. On a small scale, it is difficult to obtain crystals that are too large and occlude impurities. Once the tube has cooled to room temperature without disturbance, it can be cooled in ice to maximize the amount of product that comes out of solution. The crystals are then separated from the *mother liquor* (the *filtrate*) by filtration.

On a macroscale, the Erlenmeyer flask is set atop a cork ring or other insulator and allowed to cool spontaneously to room temperature. If the flask is moved during crystallization, many nuclei will form and the crystals will be small and have a large surface area. They will not be so easy to filter and wash clean of mother liquor. Once crystallization ceases at room temperature, the flask should be placed in ice to cool further. Take care to clamp the flask in the ice bath so that it does not tip over.

6. Collecting and Washing the Crystals

Once crystallization is complete, the crystals must be separated from the ice-cold mother liquor, washed with ice-cold solvent, and dried.

Microscale Procedure

G
(A) Filtration Using the Pasteur Pipette The most important filtration technique to be used in microscale organic experiments employs the Pasteur pipette (Fig. 3.12). About 70% of the crystalline products from the experiments in this text can be isolated in this way. The others will be isolated by filtration on the Hirsch funnel.

The ice-cold crystalline mixture is stirred with the Pasteur pipette and, while air is being expelled from the pipette, forced to the bottom of the reaction tube. The bulb is released, and the solvent is drawn into the pipette through the very small space between the square tip of the pipette and the curved bottom of the reaction tube. When all the solvent has been withdrawn, it is expelled into another reaction tube. It is sometimes useful to rap the tube containing the

FIG. 3.13 label text:

To aspirator

Glass tube

Thermometer
adapter

Reaction tube

Beaker
of warm
water

Crystals to
be dried

FIG. 3.13 Drying crystals under reduced pressure in a reaction tube.

Filter paper,
12 mm dia.

Polyethylene
filter disk (frit),
10 mm dia.

Hirsch
funnel

To aspirator

25-mL Filter
flask

FIG. 3.14 Hirsch funnel used for vacuum filtration. This unique design has a removable and replaceable 20-µm polyethylene frit. No adapter is needed because there is a vacuum-tight fit to the filter flask. Always use a piece of filter paper.

Pasteur pipette

Reaction tube

Note square
tip

FIG. 3.12 Filtration using the Pasteur pipette and reaction tube.

the tube containing the wet crystals against a hard surface to pack them so that more solvent can be removed. The tube is returned to the ice bath, and a few drops of cold solvent are added to the crystals. The mixture is stirred to wash the crystals, and the solvent is again removed. This process can be repeated as many times as necessary. Volatile solvents can be removed from the damp crystals under vacuum (Fig. 3.13). Alternatively, the last traces of solvent can be removed by centrifugation using the Wilfilter (Fig. 3.15).

F   **(B) Filtration Using the Hirsch Funnel.**   When the volume of material to be filtered is larger than 1.5 mL, collect the material on the Hirsch funnel.

The Hirsch funnel in the Williamson/Kontes kit is unique. It is made of polypropylene and has an integral molded stopper that fits the 25-mL filter flask. It comes fitted with a 20-µm polyethylene fritted disk, which is not meant to be disposable, although it costs only about twice as much as an 11-cm piece of filter paper (Fig. 3.14). While products can be collected directly on this disk, it is good practice to place an 11- or 12-mm-diameter piece of no. 1 filter paper on the disk. In this way the frit will not become clogged with insoluble impurities. The disk of filter paper can be cut with a cork borer or leather punch. A piece of filter paper *must* be used on the old-style porcelain Hirsch funnels.

Clamp the clean, dry 25-mL filter flask in an ice bath to prevent it from falling over, and place the Hirsch funnel with filter paper in the flask. Wet the filter paper with the solvent used in the crystallization, turn on the water aspirator (see below), and ascertain that the filter paper is pulled down onto the frit. Pour and scrape the crystals and mother liquor onto the Hirsch funnel and, as soon as the liquid is gone from the crystals, break the vacuum at the filter flask by removing the rubber hose. The filtrate can be used to rinse out the container that held the crystals. Again, break the vacuum as soon as all the liquid has disappeared from the crystals; this prevents impurities from drying on the crystals. The reason for cooling the filter flask is to keep the mother liquor cold so that it will not dissolve the crystals on the Hirsch funnel when the filtrate is used to wash crystals from the container onto the funnel. With a very few drops of ice-cold solvent, rinse the crystallization flask. This container should still be ice cold. Place the ice-cold solvent on the crystals, and then reapply the vacuum. As soon as the liquid is pulled from the crystals, break the vacuum. Repeat this washing process as many times as necessary to remove colored material or other impurities from the crystals. In some cases, only one very small wash will be needed. After the crystals have been washed with ice-cold solvent, the vacuum can be left on to dry the crystals. Sometimes it is useful to press solvent from the crystals using a cork.

Break the vacuum, add a very small quantity of ice-cold wash solvent, reapply vacuum.

11   **(C) Filtration with the Wilfilter (Replacing the Craig Tube).** The isolation of less than 100 mg of recrystallized material from a reaction tube (or any other container) is not easy. If the amount of solvent is large enough (a milliliter or more) the material can be recovered by filtration on the Hirsch funnel. But when the volume of liquid is less than a milliliter, much product is left in the tube during the transfer to the Hirsch filter. The solvent can be removed with a Pasteur pipette pressed against the bottom of the tube, a very effective filtration technique, but scraping the damp crystals from the reaction tube results in major losses. If the solvent is relatively low-boiling, it can be evaporated by connecting the tube to a water aspirator (Fig. 3.13). Once the crystals are dry they are easily scraped from the tube with little or no loss. But some solvents—and water is the principal culprit—are not easily removed by evaporation. And even when removal of the solvent under vacuum is not terribly difficult, it takes time.

We have invented a filtration device that circumvents these problems: the Wilfilter. After crystallization has ceased most of the solvent is removed from the crystals using a Pasteur pipette in the usual way (Fig. 3.12). Then the polypropylene Wilfilter is placed on the top of the reaction tube followed by a 15-mL polypropylene centrifuge tube (Fig. 3.15). The assembly is inverted and placed in a centrifuge such as the International Clinical Centrifuge that holds 12 15-mL tubes. The assembly, properly counterbalanced, is centrifuged for about a minute at top speed. The centrifuge tube is removed from the centrifuge, and the reaction tube is then removed from the centrifuge tube. The three fingers on the Wilfilter keep it attached to the reaction tube. The filtrate is left in the centrifuge tube.

(a)   (b)

FIG. 3.15 The Wilfilter filtration apparatus. Filtration occurs between the flat face of the polypropylene Wilfilter and the top of reaction tube.

Filtration with the Wilfilter occurs between the top surface of the reaction tube and the flat surface of the Wilfilter. Liquid will pass through that space during centrifugation; crystals will not. The crystals will be found on the top of the Wilfilter and inside the reaction tube. The very large centrifugal forces remove all the liquid, so the crystals will be virtually dry and thus easily removed from the reaction tube by shaking or scraping with the metal spatula.

The Wilfilter replaces an older device known as the Craig tube (Fig. 3.16), which consists of an outer tube of 1-, 2-, or 3-mL capacity with an inner plunger made of Teflon (expensive) or glass (fragile). The material to be crystallized is transferred to the outer tube and crystallized in the usual way. The inner plunger is added, and a wire hanger is fashioned so that the assembly can be removed from the centrifuge tube without the plunger falling off. Filtration in this device occurs through the rough surface that has been ground into the shoulder of the outer tube.

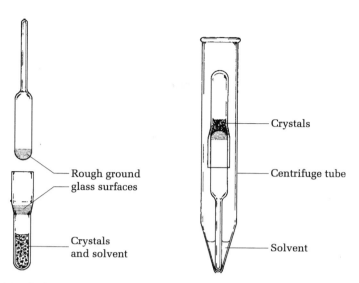

FIG. 3.16   Craig tube filtration apparatus. Filtration occurs between the rough ground glass surfaces when the apparatus is centrifuged.

FIG. 3.17   Microscale Hirsch filtration assembly. The Hirsch funnel gives a vacuum-tight seal to the 105° adapter.

The Wilfilter possesses several advantages: a special recrystallization device is not needed, no transfers of material are needed, it is not as limited in capacity (which is 4.5 mL), and its cost is one-fifth that of the Craig tube assembly.

(D) Filtration into a Reaction Tube on the Hirsch Funnel.   If it is desired to have the filtrate in a reaction tube instead of spread all over the bottom of the 25-mL filter flask, then the process described above can be carried out in the apparatus shown in Fig. 3.17. The vacuum hose is connected to the side arm using the thermometer adapter and a short length of glass tubing. Evaporate the filtrate in the reaction tube to collect a second crop of crystals.

(E) Filtration into a Reaction Tube on the Micro Büchner Funnel. If the quantity of material being collected is very small, the bottom of the chromatography column is a micro Büchner funnel, which can be fitted into the top of the thermometer adapter as shown in Fig. 3.18. Again, it is good practice to cover the frit with a piece of 6-mm filter paper (cut with a cork borer).

(F) The Micro Büchner Funnel in an Enclosed Filtration Apparatus.   In the apparatus shown in Fig. 3.19, crystallization is carried out in the upper reaction tube in the normal way. The apparatus is then turned upside down, the crystals shaken down onto the micro Büchner funnel, and a vacuum applied through the side arm. In this apparatus, crystals can be collected in an oxygen-free atmosphere. This resembles a Schlenk tube.

FIG. 3.18 Filtration using the microscale Büchner funnel.

FIG. 3.19 Schlenk-type filtration apparatus. The apparatus is inverted to carry out the filtration.

 Macroscale Apparatus

F **Filtration on the Hirsch Funnel and the Büchner Funnel.**   If the quantity of material is small (<2 g), the Hirsch funnel can be used in exactly the way described above. For larger quantities, the Büchner funnel is used. Properly matched Büchner funnels, filter paper, and flasks are shown in Fig. 3.20. The Hirsch funnel shown in the figure has a 5-cm bottom plate to accept 3.3-cm paper.

FIG. 3.20 Matching filter assemblies. The 6.0-cm polypropylene Büchner funnel (right) resists breakage and can be disassembled for cleaning.

Clamp

Thin-walled tubing

Two-hole rubber stopper

Splashgon

Heavy-walled tubing

500-mL Filter flask

25-mL
Filter flask

FIG. 3.21   Aspirator, filter trap, and funnel. Clamp small filter flask to prevent its turning over.

Clamp the filter flask.

Place a piece of filter paper in the bottom of the Büchner funnel. Wet it with solvent, and be sure it lies flat so that crystals cannot escape around the edge and under the filter paper. Then, with the vacuum off, pour the cold slurry of crystals into the center of the filter paper. Apply the vacuum; as soon as the liquid disappears from the crystals break the vacuum to the flask by disconnecting the hose. Rinse the Erlenmeyer flask with cold solvent. Add this to the crystals, and reapply the vacuum just until the liquid disappears from the crystals. Repeat this process as many times as necessary, then leave the vacuum on to dry the crystals.

The Water Aspirator and Trap.   The most common way to produce a vacuum in the organic laboratory for filtration purposes is by employing a *water aspirator*. Air is entrained efficiently in the water rushing through the aspirator so that it will produce a vacuum roughly equal to the vapor pressure of the water going through it (17 torr at 20°C, 5 torr at 4°C). A check valve is built into the aspirator, but even so when the water is turned off it will often back up into the evacuated system. For this reason a *trap* is always installed in the line (Fig. 3.21). *The water passing through the aspirator should always be turned on full force.* The system can be opened to the atmosphere by removing the hose from the small filter flask or by opening the screw clamp on the trap. Open the system, then turn off the water to avoid having water sucked back into the filter trap. Thin rubber

Use a trap.

tubing on the top of the trap will collapse and bend over when a good vacuum is established. You will, in time, learn to hear the difference in the sound of an aspirator when it is pulling a vacuum and when it is working on an open system.

Collecting a Second Crop of Crystals.   Regardless of the method used to collect the crystals on either a macroscale or a microscale, the filtrate and washings can be combined and evaporated to the point of saturation to obtain a second crop of crystals—hence the necessity for having a clean receptacle for the filtrate. This second crop will increase the overall yield, but the crystals will not usually be as pure as the first crop.

7. Drying the Product

D *Microscale Procedure*

If possible, dry the product in the reaction tube after removal of the solvent using a Pasteur pipette. This can be done simply by connecting the tube to the water aspirator. If the tube is clamped in a beaker of hot water, the solvent will evaporate more rapidly under vacuum, but take care not to melt the product (Fig. 3.13). Water, which requires a high heat of vaporization, is difficult to remove this way. Scrape the product out onto a watch glass and allow it to dry to constant weight, which will indicate that all the solvent has been removed. If the product is collected on the Hirsch funnel or the Wilfilter, the last trace of solvent can be removed by squeezing the crystals between sheets of filter paper before drying them on the watch glass.

Macroscale Procedure

Once the crystals have been washed on the Hirsch funnel or the Büchner funnel, press them down with a clean cork or other flat object and allow air to pass through them until they are substantially dry. Final drying can be done under reduced pressure (Fig. 3.22). The crystals can then be turned out of the funnel and squeezed between sheets of filter paper to remove the last trace of solvent before final drying on a watch glass.

Experiments

1. Solubility Tests

C   To test the solubility of a solid, transfer an amount roughly estimated to be about 10 mg (the amount that forms a symmetrical mound on the end of a stainless steel spatula) into a reaction tube and add about 0.25 mL of solvent from a calibrated dropper or pipette. Stir with a fire-polished stirring rod (4-mm), break up any lumps, and determine if the solid is readily soluble at room temperature.

FIG. 3.22 Drying a solid by reduced air pressure.

Test Compounds:

OH

OH

Resorcinol

Anthracene

O   OH

C

Benzoic acid

$SO_3^- Na^+$

NH_2

4-Amino-1-naphthalenesulfonic acid, sodium salt

 MICROSCALE AND MACROSCALE

If the substance is readily soluble at room temperature in methanol, ethanol, acetone, or acetic acid, add a few drops of water from a wash bottle to see if a solid precipitates. If it does, heat the mixture, adjust the composition of the solvent pair to produce a hot solution saturated at the boiling point, let the solution stand undisturbed, and note the character of the crystals that form. If the substance fails to dissolve in a given solvent at room temperature, heat the suspension and observe if solution occurs. If the solvent is flammable, heat the test tube on the steam bath or in a small beaker of water kept warm on the steam bath or a hot plate. If the solid dissolves completely, it can be declared readily soluble in the hot solvent; if some but not all dissolves, it is said to be moderately soluble, and further small amounts of solvent should then be added until solution is complete. When a substance has been dissolved in hot solvent, cool the solution by holding the flask under the tap and, if necessary, induce crystallization by rubbing the walls of the tube with a stirring rod to make sure that the concentration permits crystallization. Then reheat to dissolve the solid, let the solution stand undisturbed, and inspect the character of the ultimate crystals.

Make solubility tests on the test compounds shown to the left in each of the solvents listed below. Note the degree of solubility in the solvents—cold and hot—and suggest suitable solvents, solvent pairs, or other expedients for crystallization of each substance. Record the crystal form, at least to the extent of distinguishing between needles (pointed crystals), plates (flat and thin), and prisms. How do your observations conform to the generalization that like dissolves like?

Solvents:
Water—hydroxylic, ionic
Toluene—an aromatic hydrocarbon
Ligroin—a mixture of aliphatic hydrocarbons

Cleaning Up[4]   Place organic solvents and solutions of the compounds in the organic solvents container. Dilute the aqueous solutions with water, and flush down the drain.

2. Crystallization of Pure Phthalic Acid, Naphthalene, and Anthracene

COOH

COOH

Phthalic acid   **Naphthalene**   **Anthracene**

The process of crystallization can be observed readily using phthalic acid. In the reference book *The Handbook of Chemistry and Physics,* in the table

4. For this and all other "Cleaning Up" sections, see Chapter 2 for a complete discussion of waste disposal procedures.

"Physical Constants of Organic Compounds," the entry for phthalic acid gives the following solubility data (in grams of solute per 100 mL of solvent). The superscripts refer to temperature in °C:

Water	Alcohol	Ether, etc.
0.54^{14}	11.71^{18}	0.69^{15} eth., i. chl.
18^{99}		

The large difference in solubility in water as a function of temperature suggests this as the solvent of choice. The solubility in alcohol is high at room temperature. Ether is difficult to use because it is so volatile; the compound is insoluble in chloroform (i. chl.).

Microscale Procedure for Phthalic Acid

D

Set the heater control to about 20% of the maximum.

Crystallize 60 mg (0.060 g) of phthalic acid from the minimum volume of water, using the above data to calculate the required volume. First, turn on the electrically heated sand bath. Add the solid to a 10 × 100 mm reaction tube, and then, using a Pasteur pipette, add water dropwise. Use the calibration marks found in Chaper 1 (*see* Fig. 1.18) to measure the volume of water in the pipette and the reaction tube. Add a boiling stick (a wooden applicator stick) to facilitate even boiling and prevent bumping. After a portion of the water has been added, gently heat the solution to boiling on a hot sand bath in the electric heater. The deeper the tube is placed in the sand, the hotter it will be. As soon as boiling begins, continue to add water dropwise until all the solid just dissolves. Cork the tube and clamp it as it cools, and observe the phenomenon of crystallization.

Alternate procedure: Dry the crystals under vacuum in a steam bath in the reaction tube.

After the tube reaches room temperature, cool it in ice, stir the crystals with a Pasteur pipette, and expel the air from the pipette as the tip is pushed to the bottom of the tube. When the tip is firmly and squarely seated in the bottom of the tube, release the bulb and withdraw the water. Rap the tube sharply on a wood surface to compress the crystals and remove as much of the water as possible with the pipette. Then cool the tube in ice and add a few drops of ice-cold ethanol to the tube in order to remove water from the crystals. Connect the tube to a water aspirator and warm it in a beaker of hot water (Fig. 3.13). Once all the solvent is removed, using the stainless steel spatula, scrape the crystals onto a piece of filter paper, fold the paper over the crystals, and squeeze out excess water before allowing the crystals to dry to constant weight. Weigh the dry crystals, and calculate the percent recovery of product.

Microscale Procedure for Naphthalene and Anthracene

These compounds can also be isolated using the Wilfilter.

Following the procedure outlined above, crystallize 40 mg of naphthalene from 80% aqueous methanol or 10 mg of anthracene from ethanol. You may find it more convenient to use a hot water bath to heat these low-boiling alcohols. These are more typical of compounds to be crystallized in later experiments in that they are soluble in organic solvents. It will be much easier to remove these solvents from the crystals under vacuum than it is to remove water from phthalic acid. You will seldom have occasion to crystallize less than 30 mg of a solid in these experiments.

Cleaning Up   Dilute the aqueous filtrate with water, and flush the solution down the drain. Phthalic acid is not considered toxic to the environment. Methanol and ethanol filtrates go into the organic solvents container.

Macroscale Procedure

I   Using the above data to calculate the required volume, crystallize 1.0 g of phthalic acid from the minimum volume of water. Add the solid to the smallest practical Erlenmeyer flask and then, using a Pasteur pipette, add water dropwise from a full 10-mL graduated cylinder. A boiling stick (a stick of wood) facilitates even boiling and will prevent bumping. After a portion of the water has been added, gently heat the solution to boiling on a hot plate. As soon as boiling begins, continue to add water dropwise until all the solid dissolves. Place the flask on a cork ring or other insulator, and allow it to cool undisturbed to room temperature, during which time the crystallization process can be observed. Slow cooling favors large crystals. Then cool the flask in an ice bath, decant (pour off) the mother liquor (the liquid remaining with the crystals), and remove the last traces of liquid with a Pasteur pipette. Scrape the crystals onto a filter paper using a stainless steel spatula, squeeze the crystals between sheets of filter paper to remove traces of moisture, and allow the crystals to dry. Alternatively, the crystals can be collected on a Hirsch funnel. Compare the calculated volume of water to the volume of water actually used to dissolve the acid. Calculate the percent recovery of dry, recrystallized phthalic acid.

Cleaning Up   Dilute the filtrate with water, and flush the solution down the drain. Phthalic acid is not considered toxic to the environment.

 MICROSCALE

3. Decolorizing a Solution with Decolorizing Charcoal

 E   Into a reaction tube place 1.0 mL of a solution of methylene blue dye that has been made up at a concentration of 10 mg per 100 mL of water. Add to the tube about 10 or 12 pieces of decolorizing charcoal, shake, and observe the color over a period of 1–2 min. Heat the contents of the tube to boiling (reflux), and observe the color by holding the tube in front of a piece of white paper from time to time. How rapidly is the color removed? If the color is not removed in a minute or so, add more charcoal pellets.

Decolorizing using pelletized Norit

Cleaning Up   Place the Norit in the nonhazardous solid waste container.

MACROSCALE

4. Decolorization of Brown Sugar (Sucrose, $C_{12}H_{22}O_{11}$)

Raw sugar is refined commercially with the aid of decolorizing charcoal. The clarified solution is seeded generously with small sugar crystals and excess water removed under vacuum to facilitate crystallization. The pure white crystalline product is collected by centrifugation. Brown sugar is partially refined sugar and can be decolorized easily using charcoal.

In a 50-mL Erlenmeyer flask, dissolve 15 g of dark brown sugar in 30 mL of water by heating and stirring. Pour half the solution into another 50-mL flask. Heat one of the solutions nearly to the boiling point, allow it to cool slightly, and add to it 250 mg (0.25 g) of decolorizing charcoal (Norit pellets). Bring the solution back to near the boiling point for 2 min; then filter the hot solution into an Erlenmeyer flask through a fluted filter paper held in a previously heated funnel. Treat the other half of the sugar solution in exactly the same way, but use only 50 mg of decolorizing charcoal. In collaboration with a fellow student, try heating the solutions for only 15 s after addition of the charcoal. Compare your results.

Cleaning Up   Decant (pour off) the aqueous layer. Place the Norit in the non-hazardous solid waste container. The sugar solution can be flushed down the drain.

MICROSCALE

5. Crystallization of Benzoic Acid from Water and a Solvent Pair

Benzoic acid

Crystallize 50 mg of benzoic acid from water in the same way phthalic acid was crystallized. Then in a dry reaction tube dissolve another 50-mg sample of benzoic acid in the minimum volume of hot methanol, and add water to the hot solution dropwise. When the hot solution becomes cloudy and crystallization has begun, allow the tube to cool slowly to room temperature; then cool it in ice and collect the crystals. Compare crystallization in water to that in the solvent pair.

Cleaning Up   The aqueous solution, after dilution with water, can be flushed down the drain.

MACROSCALE

6. Recrystallization of Naphthalene from a Mixed Solvent

Phthalic acid   Naphthalene

Do not try to grasp Erlenmeyer flasks with a test tube holder.

Add 2.0 g of impure naphthalene[5] to a 50-mL Erlenmeyer flask along with 3 mL of methanol and a boiling stick to promote even boiling. Heat the mixture to boiling over a steam bath or hot plate, and then add methanol dropwise until the naphthalene just dissolves when the solvent is boiling. The total volume of methanol should be 4 mL. Remove the flask from the heat, and cool it rapidly in an ice bath. Note that the contents of the flask set to a solid mass, which would be impossible to handle. Add enough methanol to bring the total volume to 25 mL, heat the solution to the boiling point, remove the flask from the heat, allow it to cool slightly, and add 30 mg of decolorizing charcoal pellets to remove the colored impurity in the solution. Heat the solution to the boiling point for 2 min; if the color is not gone, add more Norit and boil again, then

5. A mixture of 100 g of naphthalene, 0.3 g of a dye such as congo red, and perhaps sand, magnesium, sulfate, dust, etc.

Support the funnel in a ring stand.

— Filtervac

FIG. 3.23 Suction filter assembly clamped to provide firm support. The funnel must be pressed down on the Filtervac to establish reduced pressure in the flask.

filter through a fluted filter paper in a previously warmed stemless funnel into a 50-mL Erlenmeyer flask. Sometimes filtration is slow because the funnel fits so snugly into the mouth of the flask that a back pressure develops. If you note that raising the funnel increases the flow of filtrate, fold a small strip of paper two or three times and insert it between the funnel and flask. Wash the used flask with 2 mL of hot methanol, and use this liquid to wash the filter paper, transferring the solvent with a Pasteur pipette in a succession of drops around the upper rim of the filter paper. When the filtration is complete, the volume of methanol should be 15 mL. If it is not, evaporate the excess methanol.

Because the filtrate is far from being saturated with naphthalene at this point, it will not yield crystals on cooling; however, the solubility of naphthalene in methanol can be greatly reduced by addition of water. Heat the solution to the boiling point and add water dropwise from a 10-mL graduated cylinder using a Pasteur pipette (or use a precalibrated pipette). After each addition of water the solution will turn cloudy for an instant. Swirl the contents of the flask, and heat to redissolve any precipitated naphthalene. After the addition of 3.5 mL of water the solution will almost be saturated with naphthalene at the boiling point of the solvent. Remove the flask from the heat, and place it on a cork ring or other insulating surface to cool, without being disturbed, to room temperature.

Immerse the flask in an ice bath along with another flask containing methanol and water in the ratio of 30:7. This cold solvent will be used for washing the crystals. The cold crystallization mixture is collected by vacuum filtration on a small Büchner funnel (50-mm) (Fig. 3.23). The water flowing through the aspirator should always be turned on full force. In collecting the product by suction filtration, use a spatula to dislodge crystals and ease them out of the flask. If crystals still remain in the flask, some filtrate can be poured back into the crystallization flask as a rinse for washing as often as desired because it is saturated with solute. To free the crystals from contaminating mother liquor, break the suction, pour a few milliliters of the fresh cold solvent mixture into the Büchner funnel, and immediately reapply suction. Repeat this process until the crystals and the filtrate are free of color. Press the crystals with a clean cork to eliminate excess solvent, pull air through the filter cake for a few minutes, and then put the large flat platelike crystals out on a filter paper to dry. The yield of pure white crystalline naphthalene should be about 1.6 g. The mother liquor contains about 0.25 g, and about 0.15 g is retained in the charcoal and on the filter paper.

Cleaning Up   Place the Norit in the nonhazardous solid waste container. The methanol filtrate and washings are placed in the organic solvents container.

 7. Purification of an Unknown

Bear in mind the seven-step crystallization procedure:

1. Choose the solvent.
2. Dissolve the solute.
3. Decolorize the solution (if necessary).

4. Filter suspended solids (if necessary).
5. Crystallize the solute.
6. Collect and wash the crystals.
7. Dry the product.

You are to purify an unknown provided by the instructor, 2.0 g if working on a macroscale and 100 mg on a microscale. Conduct tests for solubility and ability to crystallize in several organic solvents, solvent pairs, and water. Conserve your unknown by using very small quantities for solubility tests. If only a drop or two of solvent is used, the solvent can be evaporated by heating the test tube on the steam bath or sand bath, and the residue can be used for another test. If decolorization is necessary dilute the solution before filtration. It is very difficult to filter a hot, saturated solution from decolorizing carbon without crystallization occuring in the filtration apparatus. Evaporate the decolorized solution to the point of saturation and proceed with the crystallization. Submit as much pure product as possible with evidence of its purity (i.e., the melting point). From the posted list identify the unknown. If an authentic sample is available your identification can be verified by a mixed melting point determination (*see* Chapter 4).

Cleaning Up　　Place decolorizing charcoal, if used, and filter paper in the non-hazardous solid waste container. Put organic solvents in the organic solvents container, and flush aqueous solutions down the drain.

Crystallization Problems and Their Solutions

Induction of Crystallization

Seeding

Scratching

Occasionally a sample will not crystallize from solution on cooling, even though the solution is saturated with the solute at elevated temperature. The easiest method for inducing crystallization is to add to the supersaturated solution a seed crystal that has been saved from the crude material (if it was crystalline before recrystallization was attempted). In a probably apocryphal tale, the great sugar chemist Emil Fischer merely had to wave his beard over a recalcitrant solution and the appropriate seed crystals would drop out, causing crystallization to occur. In the absence of seed crystals, crystallization can often be induced by scratching the inside of the flask with a stirring rod at the air/liquid interface. One theory holds that part of the freshly scratched glass surface has angles and planes corresponding to the crystal structure, and crystals start growing on these spots. Crystallization is often very slow to begin. Placing the sample in a refrigerator overnight will bring success. Other expedients are to change the solvent (usually to a poorer one) and to place the sample in an open container where slow evaporation and dust from the air may help induce crystallization.

Oils and "Oiling Out"

J　　Some saturated solutions—especially those containing water—when cooled deposit not crystals but small droplets referred to as oils. "Oiling out" occurs,

Crystallize at a lower temperature

of necessity, when the temperature of the solution is above the melting point of the crystals. If these droplets solidify and are collected they will be found to be quite impure. Similarly, the melting point of the desired compound may be depressed to a point such that a low-melting eutectic mixture of the solute and the solvent comes out of solution. The simplest remedy for this problem is to lower the temperature at which the solution becomes saturated with the solute by simply adding more solvent. In extreme cases it may be necessary to lower this temperature well below room temperature by cooling the solution with dry ice. If oiling out persists use another solvent.

Crystallization Summary

C

1. **Choosing the solvent.** "Like dissolves like." Some common solvents are water, methanol, ethanol, ligroin, and toluene. When you use a solvent pair, dissolve the solute in the better solvent, and add the poorer solvent to the hot solution until saturation occurs. Some common solvent pairs are ethanol–water, ether–ligroin, and toluene–ligroin.

D

2. **Dissolving the solute.** In an Erlenmeyer flask or reaction tube, add solvent to the crushed or ground solute and heat the mixture to boiling. Add more solvent as necessary to obtain a hot, saturated solution.

E

3. **Decolorizing the solution.** If it is necessary to remove colored impurities, cool the solution to near room temperature and add more solvent to prevent crystallization from occurring. Add decolorizing charcoal in the form of pelletized Norit to the cooled solution, then heat it to boiling for a few minutes, taking care to swirl the solution to prevent bumping. Remove the Norit by filtration, then concentrate the filtrate.

5, H

4. **Filtering suspended solids.** If it is necessary to remove suspended solids, dilute the hot solution slightly to prevent crystallization from occurring during filtration. Filter the hot solution. Add solvent if crystallization begins in the funnel. Concentrate the filtrate to obtain a saturated solution.

8, D

5. **Crystallizing the solute.** Let the hot saturated solution cool to room temperature spontaneously. Do not disturb the solution. Then cool it in ice. If crystallization does not occur, scratch the inside of the container or add seed crystals.

11, 4, F, G

6. **Collecting and washing the crystals.** Collect the crystals using the Pasteur pipette method, the Wilfilter, or by vacuum filtration on a Hirsch funnel or a Büchner funnel. If the latter technique is employed, wet the filter paper with solvent, apply vacuum, break vacuum, add crystals and liquid, apply vacuum until solvent just disappears, break vacuum, add cold wash solvent, apply vacuum, and repeat until crystals are clean and filtrate comes through clear.

7, D

7. **Drying the product.** Press the product on the filter to remove solvent. Then remove it from the filter, squeeze it between sheets of filter paper to remove more solvent, and spread it on a watch glass to dry.

Questions

1. A sample of naphthalene, which should be pure white, was found to have a grayish color after the usual purification procedure. The melting point was correct and the melting point range small. Explain the gray color.

2. How many milliliters of boiling water are required to dissolve 25 g of phthalic acid? If the solution were cooled to 14°C, how many grams of phthalic acid would crystallize out?

3. What is the reason for using activated carbon during a crystallization?

4. If a little activated charcoal does a good job removing impurities in a crystallization, why not use a larger quantity?

5. Under which circumstances is it wise to use a mixture of solvents to carry out a crystallization?

6. Why is gravity filtration and not suction filtration used to remove suspended impurities and charcoal from a hot solution?

7. Why is a fluted filter paper used in gravity filtration?

8. Why are stemless funnels used instead of long-stem funnels to filter hot solutions through fluted filter paper?

9. Why is the final product from the crystallization process isolated by vacuum filtration and not by gravity filtration?

CHAPTER
4

Melting Points, Boiling Points, and Refractive Indices

PRELAB EXERCISE: Predict what the melting points of the three urea-cinnamic acid mixtures will be.

Part 1. Melting Points

The melting point of a pure solid organic compound is one of its characteristic physical properties, along with molecular weight, boiling point, refractive index, and density. A pure solid will melt reproducibly over a narrow range of temperatures, typically less than 1°C. The process of determining this melting "point" is done on a truly micro scale using less than 1 mg of material. The apparatus is simple, consisting of a thermometer, a capillary tube to hold the sample, and a heating bath.

Melting points—a micro technique

Melting points are determined for three reasons: (1) If the compound is a known one, the melting point will help to characterize the sample in hand. (2) If the compound is new, then the melting point is recorded in order to allow future characterization by others. (3) The range of the melting point is indicative of the purity of the compound; an impure compound will melt over a wide range of temperatures. Recrystallization of the compound will purify it and decrease the melting point range. In addition, the entire range will be displaced upward. For example, an impure sample might melt from 120–124°C and after recrystallization melt at 125–125.5°C. A solid is considered pure if the melting point does not rise after recrystallization.

Characterization

An indication of purity

A crystal is an orderly arrangement of molecules in a solid. As heat is added to the solid, the molecules will vibrate and perhaps rotate but still remain a solid. At a characteristic temperature it will suddenly acquire the necessary energy to overcome the forces that attract one molecule to another and will undergo translational motion—in other words, it will become a liquid.

The forces by which one molecule is attracted to another include ionic attraction, van der Waals forces, hydrogen bonds, and dipole–dipole attraction. Most, but by no means all, organic molecules are covalent in nature and melt at temperatures below 300°C. Typical inorganic compounds are ionic and have much higher melting points; e.g., sodium chloride melts at 800°C. Ionic organic

Melting point generalizations

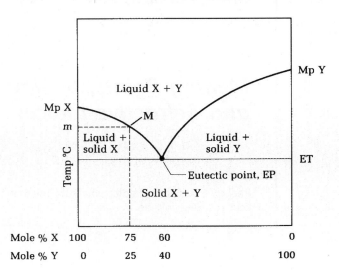

FIG. 4.1 Melting point-composition diagram for mixtures of the solids X and Y.

molecules often decompose before melting, as do compounds having strong hydrogen bonds such as sucrose.

Other factors being equal, larger molecules melt at higher temperatures than smaller ones. Among structural isomers the more symmetrical will have the higher melting point. Among optical isomers the R and S enantiomers will have the same melting points; but the racemate (the mixture of equal parts of R and S) will usually possess a different melting point. Molecules that can form hydrogen bonds will usually possess higher melting points than their counterparts of similar molecular weight.

A phase diagram

The melting point behavior of impure compounds is best understood by consideration of a simple binary mixture of compounds X and Y (Fig. 4.1). This melting point–composition diagram shows the melting point behavior as a function of composition. The melting point of a pure compound is the temperature at which the vapor pressures of the solid and liquid are equal. But in dealing with a mixture the situation is different. Consider the case of a mixture of 75% X and 25% Y. At a temperature below ET (eutectic temperature), the mixture is solid Y and solid X. At ET, the solid begins to melt. The melt is a solution of Y dissolved in liquid X. The vapor pressure of the solution of

Melting point depression

X and Y together is less than that of pure X at the melting point; therefore, the temperature at which X will melt is lower when mixed with Y. This is an application of Raoult's law (*see* Chapter 5). As the temperature is raised, more and more of solid X melts until it is all gone at point **M** (temperature *m*). The melting point range is thus from ET to *m*. In practice it is very difficult to detect point ET when a melting point is determined in a capillary because it represents the point at which an infinitesimal amount of the liquid solution has begun to melt.

The eutectic point

In this hypothetical example the liquid solution becomes saturated with Y at point EP (eutectic point). This is the point at which X and Y and their liquid solutions are in equilibrium. A mixture of X and Y containing 60% X will appear to have a sharp melting point at temperature ET.

The melting point range of a mixture of compounds is generally broad, and the breadth of the range is an indication of purity. The chances of accidentally coming on the eutectic composition are small. Recrystallization will enrich the predominant compound while excluding the impurity and will therefore decrease the melting point range.

It should be apparent that the impurity must be soluble in the compound, so an insoluble impurity such as sand or charcoal will not depress the melting point. The impurity does not need to be a solid. It can be a liquid such as water (if it is soluble) or an organic solvent, such as the one used to recrystallize the compound; hence the necessity for drying the compound before determining the melting point.

Mixed melting points

Advantage is taken of the depression of melting points of mixtures to prove whether or not two compounds having the same melting points are identical. If X and Y are identical, then a mixture of the two will have the same melting point; but if X and Y are not identical, then a small amount of X in Y or of Y in X will reduce the melting point.

Apparatus

The apparatus needed for determining an accurate melting point need not be elaborate; the same results are obtained on the simplest as on the most complex devices.

Thomas–Hoover Uni–Melt

The Thomas–Hoover Uni-Melt apparatus (Fig. 4.2) will accommodate seven capillaries in a small, magnified, lighted beaker of high-boiling silicone oil that is stirred and heated electrically. The heating rate is controlled with a variable transformer that is part of the apparatus. The rising mercury column of the thermometer can be observed with an optional traveling periscope device so the eye need not move away from the capillary. For industrial analytical and control work there is even an apparatus (Mettler) that determines the melting point automatically and displays the result in digital form.

Mel-Temp

The Mel-Temp apparatus (Fig. 4.3) consists of an electrically heated aluminum block that accommodates three capillaries. The sample is illuminated through the lower port and observed with a six-power lens through the upper port. The heating rate can be controlled and, with a special thermometer, the apparatus can be used up to 500°C—far above the useful limit of silicone oil (about 350°C).

In this melting point apparatus it is advisable to use a digital thermometer (Fig. 4.4) rather than the mercury-in-glass thermometer. A digital thermometer has a low heat capacity and fast response time. It is more robust than a glass thermometer and does not of course contain mercury, which is very toxic.

Capillaries may be obtained commercially or may be produced by drawing out 12-mm soft-glass tubing. The tubing is rotated in the hottest part of the Bunsen burner flame until it is very soft and begins to sag. It should not be drawn out during heating, but is removed from the flame and after a moment's hesitation drawn steadily and not too rapidly to arm's length. With some practice it is possible to produce 10 to 15 good tubes in a single drawing. The long

FIG. 4.2 Thomas–Hoover Uni-Melt melting point apparatus.

FIG. 4.3 Mel-Temp melting point apparatus.

Digital thermometer

°C

79

Surface probe

FIG. 4.4 Digital thermometer.

capillary tube can be cut into 100-mm lengths with a glass scorer. Each tube is sealed by rotating the end in the edge of a small flame, as seen in Fig. 4.5.

Filling Melting Point Capillaries

The dry sample is ground to a fine powder on a watch glass or a piece of glassine paper on a hard surface using the flat portion of a spatula. It is formed into a small pile and the melting point capillary forced down into the pile. The sample is shaken into the closed end of the capillary by rapping sharply on a hard surface or by dropping it down a 2-ft length of glass tubing onto a hard surface. The height of the sample should be no more than 2–3 mm.

FIG. 4.5 Sealing a melting point capillary tube.

Sealed Capillaries

Samples that sublime

Some samples sublime (go from the solid directly to the vapor phase without appearing to melt) or undergo rapid air oxidation and decompose at the melting point. These samples should be sealed under vacuum. This can be accomplished by forcing a capillary through a hole previously made in a rubber septum and evacuating the capillary using the water aspirator or a mechanical vacuum pump (Fig. 4.6). Using the flame from a small micro burner, the tube is gently heated about 15 mm above the tightly packed sample. This will cause any material in this region to sublime away. It is then heated more strongly in the same place to collapse the tube, taking care that the tube is straight when it cools. It is also possible to seal the end of a Pasteur pipette, add the sample, pack it down, and seal off a sample under vacuum in the same way.

Handle flame with great care in the organic laboratory.

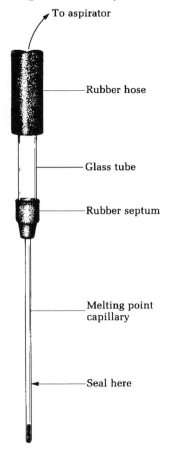

Determining the Melting Point

The accuracy of the melting point depends on the accuracy of the thermometer, so the first exercise in this experiment will be to calibrate the thermometer. Melting points of pure, known compounds will be determined and deviations recorded so that a correction can be applied to future melting points. Be forewarned, however, that thermometers are usually fairly accurate.

The most critical factor in determining an accurate melting point is the rate of heating. At the melting point the temperature rise should not be greater than 1°C per minute. This may seem extraordinarily slow, but it is necessary in order for heat from the bath to be transferred equally to the sample and to the glass and mercury of the thermometer.

From experience you know the rate at which ice melts. Consider doing a melting point experiment on an ice cube. Because water melts at 0°C, you would need to have a melting point bath a few degrees below zero. To observe the true melting point of the ice cube, you would need to raise the temperature extraordinarily slowly. The ice cube would appear to begin to melt at 0°C and, if you waited for temperature equilibrium to be established, it would all be melted at 0.5°C. If you were impatient and raised the temperature too rapidly, the ice might appear to melt over the range 0 to 20°C. Similarly, melting points determined in capillaries will not be accurate if the rate of heating is too fast.

The rate of heating is the most important factor in obtaining accurate melting points. Heat no faster than 1°C per *minute*.

FIG. 4.6 Evacuation of a melting point capillary prior to sealing.

 MICROSCALE

Experiments

1. Calibration of the Thermometer

Determine the melting point of standard substances (Table 4.1) over the temperature range of interest. The difference between the values found and those expected constitutes the correction that must be applied to future temperature readings. If the thermometer has been calibrated previously, then determine one

TABLE 4.1 Melting Point Standards

Compound	Structure	Melting Point (°C)
Naphthalene		80–82
Urea	H_2NCNH_2 with O	132.5–133
Sulfanilamide	NH_2 ... SO_2NH_2	164–165
4-Toluic acid	COOH ... CH_3	180–182
Anthracene		214–217
Caffeine (evacuated capillary)		234–236.5

or more melting points of known substances to familiarize yourself with the technique. If the determinations do not agree within 1°C, then repeat the process. Both mercury-in-glass and digital thermometers will need to be calibrated.

MICROSCALE

$-CH=CH-COOH$

Cinnamic acid

2. Melting Points of Pure Urea and Cinnamic Acid

Using a metal spatula, crush the sample to a fine powder on a hard surface such as a watch glass. Push a melting point capillary into the powder, and force the powder down in the capillary by tapping the capillary or by dropping it through a long glass tube held vertically and resting on a hard surface. The column of solid should be no more than 2–3 mm in height and should be tightly packed.

Except for the Thomas–Hoover and Mel-Temp apparatus, the capillary is held to the thermometer with a rubber band made by cutting a slice off the end of a piece of ³⁄₁₆-in. (5 mm) rubber tubing. This rubber band must be above the level of the oil bath; otherwise, it will break in the hot oil. Insertion of a fresh tube under the rubber band is facilitated by leaving the used tube in place. The sample should be close to and on a level with the center of the thermometer bulb.

Heat rapidly to within 20°C of the melting point.

If the approximate melting temperature is known, the bath can be heated rapidly until the temperature is about 20°C below this point, but the heating during the last 15–20°C should slow down considerably so that *the rate of heating at the melting point is no more than 1°C per minute* while the sample is melting. As the melting point is approached the sample may shrink because of crystal structure changes. However, the melting process begins when the first drops of liquid are seen in the capillary and ends when the last trace of solid disappears. For a pure compound this whole process may occur over a range of only 0.5°C; hence the necessity of having the temperature rise slowly during the determination.

Heat slowly (<1°C/min) near the melting temperature

Two or three melting points at once

If determinations are to be done on two or three samples that differ in melting point by as much as 10°C, two or three capillaries can be secured to the thermometer together and the melting points observed in succession without removal of the thermometer from the bath. As a precaution against interchange of tubes while they are being attached, use some system of identification, such as one, two, and three dots made with a marking pencil.

Determine the melting point (mp) of either urea (mp 132.5–133°C) or cinnamic acid (mp 132.5–133°C). Repeat the determination, and if the two determinations do not check within 1°C, do a third one.

MICROSCALE

3. Melting Points of Urea–Cinnamic Acid Mixtures

IN THIS EXPERIMENT you will see dramatic evidence of the phenomenon of melting point depression that will allow you to make a phase diagram like that in Fig. 4.1.

Make mixtures of urea and cinnamic acid in the approximate proportions 1:4, 1:1, and 4:1 by putting side by side the correct number of equal-sized small piles of the two substances and then mixing them. Grind the mixture thoroughly for at least a minute on a watch glass using a metal spatula. Note the ranges of melting of the three mixtures, and use the temperatures of complete liquefaction to construct a rough diagram of mp versus composition.

MICROSCALE

4. Unknowns

Determine the melting point of one or more of the following unknowns to be selected by the instructor (Table 4.2), and on the basis of the melting point identify the substance. Prepare two capillaries of each unknown. Run a very fast determination on the first sample to ascertain the approximate melting point, and then cool the melting point bath to just below the melting point and make a slow, careful determination using the other capillary.

TABLE 4.2 Melting Point Unknowns

Compound	Melting Point (°C)
Benzophenone	49–51
Maleic anhydride	52–54
4-Nitrotoluene	54–56
Naphthalene	80–82
Acetanilide	113.5–114
Benzoic acid	121.5–122
Urea	132.5–133
Salicylic acid	158.5–159
Sulfanilamide	165–166
Succinic acid	184.5–185
3,5-Dinitrobenzoic acid	205–207
p-Terphenyl	210–211

5. An Investigation: Determination of Molecular Weight Using Melting Point Depression

Before the mass spectrometer came into common usage, the molal freezing point depression of camphor was used to determine molecular weights. Whereas a 1% solid solution of urea in cinnamic acid will cause a relatively small melting point depression, a 1% by weight solid solution in camphor of any organic compound with molecular weight 100 will cause a 4.0°C depression in the melting point of the camphor. Quantitative use of this relationship can be used to determine the molecular weight of an unknown. You can learn more about the details of this technique in very old editions of this book (L.F. Fieser, *Organic Experiments* [Lexington, MA: D.C. Heath, 1979]) or by searching for colligative properties, molal freezing point depression.

Part 2. Boiling Points

The boiling point of a pure organic liquid is one of its characteristic physical properties, just like its density, molecular weight, and refractive index, and the melting point of a solid. The boiling point is used to characterize a new organic liquid, and knowledge of the boiling point helps to compare one organic liquid to another, as in the process of identifying an unknown organic substance.

Comparison of boiling points with melting points is instructive. The process of determining the boiling point is more complex than that for the melting point: It requires more material, and because it is affected less by impurities, it is not as good an indication of purity. Boiling points can be determined on a few microliters of a liquid, but on a small scale it is difficult to determine the boiling point *range*. This requires enough material to distill—about 1 to

2 mL. Like the melting point, the boiling point of a liquid is affected by the forces that attract one molecule to another—ionic attraction, van der Waals forces, dipole–dipole interactions, and hydrogen bonding.

Structure and Boiling Point

In a homologous series of molecules the boiling point increases in a perfectly regular manner. The normal saturated hydrocarbons have boiling points ranging from $-162°C$ for methane to $330°C$ for n-$C_{19}H_{40}$, an increase of about $27°C$ for each CH_2 group. It is convenient to remember that n-heptane with a molecular weight of 100 has a boiling point near $100°C$ ($98.4°C$). A spherical molecule such as 2,2-dimethylpropane has a lower boiling point than n-pentane because it cannot have as many points of attraction to adjacent molecules. For molecules of the same molecular weight, those with dipoles, such as carbonyl groups, will have higher boiling points than those without, and molecules that can form hydrogen bonds will boil even higher. The boiling point of such molecules depends on the number of hydrogen bonds that can be formed, so that an alcohol with one hydroxyl group will boil lower than an alcohol with two if they both have the same molecular weight. A number of other generalizations can be made about boiling point behavior as a function of structure; you will learn about these throughout your study of organic chemistry.

Boiling Point as a Function of Pressure

Boiling points decrease about 0.5° for each 10-mm decrease in atmospheric pressure.

Since the boiling point of a pure liquid is defined as the temperature at which the vapor pressure of the liquid exactly equals the pressure exerted on it, the boiling point will be a function of atmospheric pressure. At an altitude of 14,000 ft the boiling point of water is $81°C$. At pressures near that of the atmosphere at sea level (760 mm), the boiling point of most liquids decreases about $0.5°C$ for each 10-mm decrease in atmospheric pressure. This generalization does not hold for greatly reduced pressures because the boiling point decreases as a nonlinear function of pressure (*see* Fig. 5.1). Under these conditions a nomograph relating observed boiling point, boiling point at 760 mm, and pressure in millimeters should be consulted (*see* Fig. 7.12). This nomograph is not highly accurate; the change in boiling point as a function of pressure also depends on the type of compound (polar, nonpolar, hydrogen bonding, etc.). Consult the *Handbook of Chemistry and Physics* for the correction of boiling points to standard pressure.

The Laboratory Thermometer

CAUTION: Mercury is toxic. Report broken thermometers to your instructor.

Most mercury-in-glass laboratory thermometers have a mark around the stem that is three inches (76 mm) from the bottom of the bulb. This is the immersion line; the thermometer will record accurate temperatures if immersed to this line. Should you break a mercury thermometer, immediately inform your instructor, who will use special apparatus to clean up the mercury. Mercury vapor is very toxic.

Prevention of Superheating—Boiling Sticks and Boiling Stones

A very clean liquid in a very clean vessel will superheat and not boil when subjected to a temperature above its boiling point. This means that a thermometer placed in the liquid will register a temperature higher than the boiling point of the liquid. If boiling does occur under these conditions, it occurs with explosive violence. To avoid this problem, boiling stones are always added to liquids before heating them to boiling—whether to determine a boiling point or to carry out a reaction or distillation. The stones provide the nuclei on which the bubble of vapor indicative of a boiling liquid can form. Some boiling stones, also called boiling chips, are composed of porous unglazed porcelain. This material is filled with air in numerous fine capillaries. Upon heating, this air expands to form the fine bubbles on which even boiling can take place. Once the liquid cools it will fill these capillaries and the boiling chip will become ineffectual, so another must be added each time the liquid is heated to boiling. Sticks of wood—so-called applicator sticks about 1.5 mm in diameter—also promote even boiling and, unlike stones, are removed easily from the solution. None of these work well for vacuum distillation.

Digital thermometer

°C

79

Surface probe

14

Refluxing vapor

Boiling chip   Boiling liquid

FIG. 4.7 Use of a digital thermometer for determining boiling points.

Apparatus and Technique

By Distillation.   When enough material is available, the best method for determining the boiling point of a liquid is to distill it (*see* Chapter 5). Distillation allows the boiling range to be determined and thus gives an indication of purity. Bear in mind, however, that a constant boiling point is not a guarantee of homogeneity and thus purity. Constant-boiling azeotropes such as 95% ethanol abound.

Using a Digital Thermometer and a Reaction Tube.   Boiling points can be measured rapidly and accurately using an electronic digital thermometer as depicted in Fig. 4.7. While digital thermometers are too expensive at present for each student to have, several of these in the laboratory can greatly speed up the determination of boiling points, and are much safer to use because there is no danger from toxic mercury vapor if the thermometer is dropped accidentally.

A surface probe is the active element. Unlike the bulb of mercury at the end of a thermometer, this element has a very low heat capacity and a very fast response time, so boiling points can be determined very quickly in this apparatus. About 0.2–0.3 mL of the liquid and a boiling chip are heated on a sand bath until the liquid refluxes about 3 cm up the tube. The boiling point is the highest temperature recorded by the thermometer and maintained for about 1 min. Application of heat will drive tiny bubbles of air from the boiling chip. Do not mistake these tiny bubbles for true boiling. This can happen if the unknown has a very high boiling point. The probe should not touch the side of the reaction tube but should be placed approximately 5 mm above the liquid.

Thermometer adapter

Refluxing vapor

Boiling chip

Boiling liquid

FIG. 4.8 Small-scale boiling-point apparatus. Be sure the thermometer does not touch the tube.

In a Reaction Tube.

If a digital thermometer is not available, use the apparatus shown in Fig. 4.8. Use of the distilling adapter on the top of the reaction tube allows access to the atmosphere. Place 0.3 mL of the liquid along with a boiling stone in a 10- × 100-mm reaction tube, clamp a thermometer so that the bulb is just above the level of the liquid, and then heat the liquid with a sand bath. It is *very important* that no part of the thermometer touch the reaction tube. Heating is regulated so that the boiling liquid refluxes about 3 cm up the thermometer but does not boil out of the apparatus. If you cannot see the refluxing liquid, carefully run your finger down the side of the reaction tube until you feel heat. This indicates where the liquid is refluxing. Droplets of liquid must drip from the thermometer bulb in order to heat the mercury thoroughly. The boiling point is the highest temperature recorded by the thermometer and maintained over about a 1-min time interval.

Application of heat will drive out tiny air bubbles from the boiling chip. Do not mistake these tiny bubbles for true boiling. This can occur if the unknown has a very high boiling point. It may take several minutes to heat up the mercury in the thermometer bulb. True boiling is indicated by drops dripping from the thermometer and a constant temperature recorded on the thermometer. If the temperature is not constant, then you are probably not observing true boiling.

Using a 3- to 5-mm Tube.

For smaller quantities, the tube is attached to the side of the thermometer (Fig. 4.9) and heated with a liquid bath. The tube, which can be made from tubing 3 to 5 mm in diameter, contains a small inverted capillary. This is made by cutting a 6-mm piece from the sealed end of a melting point capillary, inverting it, and sealing it again to the capillary. A centimeter/millimeter ruler is printed on the inside back cover of this book.

Melting point capillary

Tube, 3 mm dia × 80 mm long

Seal

Sample

Heating bath

FIG. 4.9 Smaller-scale boiling point apparatus.

*Smaller-scale boiling point
apparatus*

When the sample is heated in this device, the air in the inverted capillary will expand and an occasional bubble will escape. At the true boiling point a continuous and rapid stream of bubbles will emerge from the inverted capillary. When this occurs, the heating is stopped and the bath allowed to cool. A time will come when bubbling ceases and the liquid just begins to rise in the inverted capillary. The temperature at which this happens is recorded. The liquid is allowed to partially fill the small capillary, and the heat is applied carefully until the first bubble emerges from the capillary. The temperature is recorded at that point. The two temperatures approximate the boiling point range for the liquid. The explanation: As the liquid was being heated, the air expanded in the inverted capillary and was replaced by vapor of the liquid. The liquid was actually slightly superheated when rapid bubbles emerged from the capillary, but on cooling the point was reached at which the pressure on the inside of the capillary matched the outside (atmospheric) pressure. This is, by definition, the boiling point.

Cleaning Up   Place the boiling point sample in either the halogenated or non-halogenated waste container. Do not pour it down the sink.

Part 3. Refractive Indices

The refractive index n is a physical constant that, like the boiling point, can be used to characterize liquids. It is the ratio of the velocity of light traveling in air to the velocity of light moving in the liquid (Fig. 4.10). It is also equal to the ratio of the sine of the angle of incidence ϕ to the sine of the angle of refraction ϕ':

$$n = \frac{\text{Velocity in air}}{\text{Velocity in liquid}} = \frac{\sin \phi}{\sin \phi'}$$

The angle of refraction is also a function of temperature and the wavelength of light (consider the dispersion of white light by a prism). Because the velocity of light in air (strictly speaking, a vacuum) is always greater than that through a liquid, the refractive index is a number greater than 1; for example, hexane n_D^{20} 1.3751; diiodobenzene, n_D^{20} 1.7179. The superscript 20 indicates that the refractive index was measured at 20°C, and the subscript D refers to the yellow D-line from a sodium vapor lamp, light with a wavelength of 589 nm.

The measurement is made on a refractometer using a few drops of liquid. Compensation is made within the instrument for the fact that white light and not sodium vapor light is used, but a temperature correction must be applied to the observed reading by adding 0.00045 for each degree above 20°C:

$$n_D^{20} = n_D^t + 0.00045(t - 20°\text{C})$$

The refractive index can be determined to 1 part in 10,000, but because the value is quite sensitive to impurities, across the board agreement in the

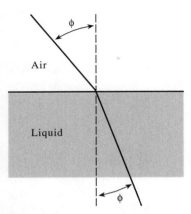

FIG. 4.10   Refraction of light

Thermometer

Place
sample
here

FIG. 4.11 Abbé refractometer. Sample block can be thermostatted.

literature regarding the last figure does not always exist. For this reason, the refractive indices in this book have been rounded to the nearest part per thousand, as have the refractive indices reported in the Aldrich catalog of chemicals. To master the technique of using the refractometer, measure the refractive indices of several known, pure liquids before measuring an unknown.

Specialized hand-held refractometers that read over a narrow range are used to determine the concentration of sugar or alcohol in water.

Procedure

Refractometers come in many designs. In the most common, the Abbé design (Fig. 4.11), two or three drops of the sample are placed on the open prism using a polyethylene Beral pipette (to avoid scratching the prism face). The prism is closed, and the light is turned on and positioned for maximum brightness as seen through the eyepiece. If the refractometer is set to a nearly correct value, then a partially gray image will be seen, as shown in Fig. 4.12(a). Turn the knob so that the line separating the dark and light areas is at the crosshairs, as shown in Fig. 4.12(b). Sometimes the line separating the dark and light areas is fuzzy and colored. Turn the chromatic adjustment until the demarcation line is sharp and colorless. Then read the refractive index. On a newer instrument, press a button to light up the scale in the field of vision. On older models, read the

(a)   (b)   (c)

FIG. 4.12 (a) View into refractometer when index knob is out of adjustment. (b) View into refractometer when properly adjusted. (c) View when chromatic adjustment is incorrect.

refractive index through a separate eyepiece. Read the temperature on the thermometer attached to the refractometer, and make the appropriate temperature correction to the observed index of refraction.

Cleaning Up   When the measurement is completed, open the prism and wipe off the sample with lens paper using ethanol, acetone, or hexane as necessary.

Questions

1. What effect would poor circulation of the melting point bath liquid have on the observed melting point?

2. What is the effect of an insoluble impurity, such as sodium sulfate, on the observed melting point of a compound?

3. Three test tubes, labeled A, B, and C, contain substances with approximately the same melting points. How could you prove the test tubes contain three different chemical compounds?

4. One of the most common causes of inaccurate melting points is too rapid heating of the melting point bath. Under these circumstances, how will the observed melting point compare to the true melting point?

5. Strictly speaking, why is it incorrect to speak of a melting *point*?

6. What effect would the incomplete drying of a sample (for example, the incomplete removal of a recrystallization solvent) have on the melting point?

7. Why should the melting point sample be finely powdered?

8. You suspect that an unknown is acetanilide (mp 113.5–114°C). Give a qualitative estimation of the melting point when the acetanilide is mixed with 10% by weight of naphthalene.

9. You have an unknown with an observed melting point of 90–93°C. Is your unknown compound A with a reported melting point of 95.5–96°C or compound B with a reported melting point of 90.5–91°C? Explain.

10. Why is it important to heat the melting point bath or block slowly and steadily when the temperature gets close to the mp?

11. Why is it important to pack the sample tightly in the melting point capillary?

12. An unknown compound is suspected to be acetanilide (mp 113.5–114°C). What would happen to the mp if this unknown were mixed with (a) an equal quantity of pure acetanilide? (b) an equal quantity of benzoic acid?

13. Which would be expected to have the higher boiling point, *t*-butyl alcohol (2-methyl-2-propanol) or *n*-butyl alcohol (1-butanol)? Explain.

14. When borosilicate glass (Kimax, Pyrex), n^{20} 1.474, is immersed in a solution having the same refractive index, it is almost invisible. Soft glass with n^{20} 1.52 is quite visible. This is an easy way to distinguish between the two types of glass. Calculate the mole percents of toluene and heptane that will have a refractive index of 1.474 assuming a linear relationship between the refractive indices of the two.

Reference

Weissberger, A., and B. W. Rossiter (eds.). *Physical Methods of Chemistry,* Vol. 1, Part V, Wiley-Interscience: New York, 1971.

Surfing the Web

http://ull.chemistry.uakron.edu/organic_lab/melting_point/
The melting points of pure urea and cinnamic acids and mixtures of the two, as well as the melting points of unknowns (Experiments 2, 3, and 4), are carried out on a Thomas–Hoover apparatus and illustrated with 12 extraordinarily clear color photos in this University of Akron site.

CHAPTER

5

Distillation

PRELAB EXERCISE: Predict what a plot of temperature versus volume of distillate will look like for the simple distillation and the fractional distillation of (a) a cyclohexane–toluene mixture and (b) an ethanol–water mixture.

The origins of distillation are lost in antiquity as humans in their thirst for more potent beverages found that dilute solutions of alcohol from fermentation could be separated into alcohol-rich and water-rich portions by heating the solution to boiling and condensing the vapors above the boiling liquid—the process of distillation. Since ethyl alcohol (ethanol) boils at 78°C and water boils at 100°C, one might naively assume that heating a 50:50 mixture of ethanol and water to 78°C would cause the ethanol molecules to leave the solution as a vapor that could be condensed to pure ethanol. Such is not the case. In a mixture of 50:50 ethanol, water boils near 87°C, and the vapor above it is not 100% ethanol.

   Consider a better-behaved mixture: cyclohexane and toluene. The vapor pressures as a function of temperature are plotted in Fig. 5.1. When the vapor

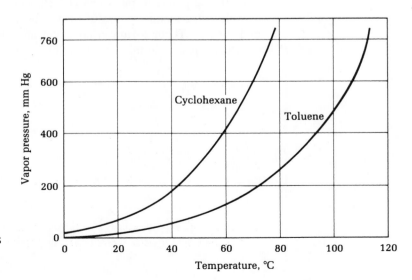

FIG. 5.1 Vapor pressure versus temperature for cyclohexane and toluene.

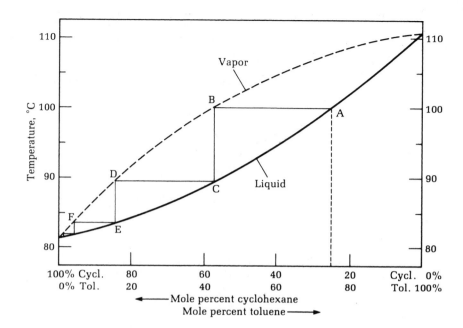

FIG. 5.2 Boiling point–composition curves for cyclohexane–toluene mixture.

pressure of the liquid equals the applied pressure the liquid boils, so this diagram shows that at 760 mm pressure, standard atmospheric pressure, these pure liquids boil at about 78°C and 111°C, respectively. If one of these pure liquids were to be distilled, we would find that the boiling point of the liquid would equal the temperature of the vapor and that the temperature of the vapor would remain constant throughout the distillation.

Figure 5.2 is a boiling point–composition diagram for the cyclohexane–toluene system. If a mixture of 75 mole percent toluene and 25 mole percent cyclohexane is heated, we find (in Fig. 5.2) that it boils at 100°C, or point A. Above a binary mixture of cyclohexane and toluene the vapor pressure has contributions from each component. Raoult's law states that the vapor pressure of the cyclohexane is equal to the product of the vapor pressure of pure cyclohexane and the mole fraction of cyclohexane in the liquid mixture:

$$P_c = P_c^\circ N_c$$

where P_c is the partial pressure of cyclohexane, P_c° is the vapor pressure of pure cyclohexane at the given temperature, and N_c is the mole fraction of cyclohexane in the mixture. Similarly for toluene:

$$P_t = P_t^\circ N_t$$

The total vapor pressure above the solution, P_{Tot}, is given by the sum of the partial pressures due to cyclohexane and toluene:

$$P_{Tot} = P_c + P_t$$

The mole fraction of cyclohexane is equal to the moles of cyclohexane in the mixture divided by the total number of moles (cyclohexane plus toluene) in the mixture.

Dalton's law states that the mole fraction of cyclohexane in the vapor at a given temperature is equal to the partial pressure of the cyclohexane at that temperature divided by the total pressure:

$$X_c = \frac{P_c}{\text{total vapor pressure}}$$

At 100°C cyclohexane has a partial pressure of 433 mm and toluene a partial pressure of 327 mm; the sum of the partial pressures is 760 mm, and so the liquid boils. If some of the liquid in equilibrium with this boiling mixture were condensed and analyzed, it would be found to be 433/760 or 57 mole percent cyclohexane (point B, Fig. 5.2). This is the best separation that can be achieved on a simple distillation of this mixture. As the simple distillation proceeds, the boiling point of the mixture moves toward 111°C along the line from A, and the vapor composition becomes richer in toluene as it moves from B to 110°C. To obtain pure cyclohexane, it would be necessary to condense the liquid at B and redistill it. When this is done it is found that the liquid boils at 90°C (point C) and the vapor equilibrium with this liquid is about 85 mole percent cyclohexane (point D). Therefore, to separate a mixture of cyclohexane and toluene, a series of fractions would be collected and each of these partially redistilled. If this fractional distillation were done enough times the two components could be separated.

This series of redistillations can be done "automatically" in a fractionating column. Perhaps the easiest to understand is the bubble plate column used to distill crude oil fractionally. These columns dominate the skyline of oil refineries, some being 150 ft high and capable of distilling 200,000 barrels of crude oil per day. The crude oil enters the column as a hot vapor (Fig. 5.3). Some of this vapor with high-boiling components condenses on one of the plates. The more volatile substances travel through the bubble cap to the next higher plate where some of the less-volatile components condense. As high-boiling liquid material accumulates on a plate it descends through the overflow pipe to the next lower plate and vapor rises through the bubble cap to the next higher plate. The temperature of the vapor that is rising through a cap is above the boiling point of the liquid on that plate. As bubbling takes place, heat is exchanged, and the less volatile components on that plate vaporize and go on to the next plate. The composition of the liquid on a plate is the same as that of the vapor coming from the plate below. So on each plate a simple distillation takes place. At equilibrium, vapor containing low-boiling material is ascending, and high-boiling liquid is descending through the column.

Fig. 5.2 shows that the condensations and redistillations in a bubble cap column consisting of three plates correspond to moving on the boiling point–composition diagram from point A to point E.

In the laboratory the successive condensations and distillations that occur in the bubble plate column take place in a distilling column. The column is packed with some material on which heat exchange between ascending vapor and descending liquid can take place. A large surface area for this packing is desirable, but the packing cannot be so dense that pressure changes take place

Fractional distillation

Overflow pipe

Plate

Riser
for
vapor

FIG. 5.3 Bubble plate distilling column.

Heat exchange between ascending vapor and descending liquid

within the column causing nonequilibrium conditions. Also, if the column packing has a very large surface area, it will absorb (hold up) much of the material being distilled. A number of different packings for distilling columns have been tried: glass beads, glass helices, carborundum chips, etc. We find one of the best packings is a copper or steel sponge (Chore Boy). It is easy to put into the column; does not come out of the column as beads do; and has a large surface area, good heat transfer characteristics, and low holdup. It can be used in both microscale and macroscale apparatus.

Holdup: unrecoverable distillate that wets the column packing

Column packing

The ability of different column packings to separate two materials of differing boiling points is evaluated by calculating the number of theoretical plates, each theoretical plate corresponding to one distillation and condensation as discussed above. Other things being equal, the number of theoretical plates is proportional to the height of the column, so various packings are evaluated according to the height equivalent to a theoretical plate (HETP); the smaller the HETP, the more plates the column will have and the more efficient it will be. The calculation is made by analyzing the proportion of lower- to higher-boiling material at the top of the column and in the distillation pot.[1]

Height equivalent to a theoretical plate (HETP)

Although not obvious, the most important variable contributing to a good fractional distillation is the rate at which the distillation is carried out. A series of simple distillations take place within a fractionating column, and it is important that complete equilibrium be attained between the ascending vapors and the descending liquid. This process is not instantaneous. It should be an adiabatic process; that is, heat should be transferred from the ascending vapor to the descending liquid with no net loss or gain of heat. In larger, more complex distilling columns, a means is provided for adjusting the ratio between the amount of material that boils up and condenses (refluxes) and is returned to the column (thus allowing equilibrium to take place) and the amount that is removed as distillate. A reflux ratio of 30:1 or 50:1 would not be uncommon for a 40-plate column; distillation would take several hours.

Equilibration is slow.

Good fractional distillation takes a long time.

Carrying out a fractional distillation on the truly microscale (<1 mg) is impossible, and it is even impossible on a small scale (10–400 mg). It can be carried out on a 4-mL scale. As seen in later chapters, various types of chromatography are employed for the separation of micro and semimicro quantities of liquids, whereas distillation is the best method for separating more than a few grams of material.

Azeotropes

Not all liquids form ideal solutions and conform to Raoult's law. Ethanol and water are such liquids. Because of molecular interaction, a mixture of 95.5% (by weight) of ethanol and 4.5% of water boils *below* (78.15°C) the boiling point of pure ethanol (78.3°C). Thus, no matter how efficient the distilling

---

1. See A. Weissberger (ed.), *Technique of Organic Chemistry,* Vol. IV, "Distillation," (New York: Wiley-Interscience), 1951.

The ethanol–water azeotrope

apparatus, 100% ethanol cannot be obtained by distillation of a mixture of, say, 75% water and 25% ethanol. A mixture of liquids of a certain definite composition that distills at a constant temperature without change in composition is called an *azeotrope;* 95% ethanol is such an azeotrope. The boiling point–composition curve for the ethanol–water mixture is seen in Fig. 5.4. To prepare 100% ethanol the water can be removed chemically (reaction with calcium oxide) or by removal of the water as an azeotrope (with still another liquid). An azeotropic mixture of 32.4% ethanol and 67.6% benzene (bp 80.1°C) boils at 68.2°C. A ternary azeotrope (bp 64.9°C) contains 74.1% benzene, 18.5% ethanol, and 7.4% water. Absolute alcohol (100% ethanol) is made by addition of benzene to 95% alcohol and removal of the water in the volatile benzene–water–alcohol azeotrope.

Ethanol and water form a minimum boiling azeotrope. Other substances, such as formic acid (bp 100.7°C) and water (bp 100°C), form maximum boiling azeotropes. For these two compounds the azeotrope boils at 107.3°C.

A constant bp on distillation does not guarantee that the distillate is one pure compound.

A pure liquid has a constant boiling point. A change in boiling point during distillation is an indication of impurity. The converse proposition, however, is not always true, and constancy of a boiling point does not necessarily mean that the liquid consists of only one compound. For instance, two miscible liquids of similar chemical structure that boil at the same temperature individually

FIG. 5.4 Boiling point–composition curves for ethanol–water mixture.

TABLE 5.1   Variation in Boiling Point with Pressure

Pressure (mm)	Water (°C)	Benzene (°C)
780	100.7	81.2
770	100.4	80.8
760	100.0	80.3
750	99.6	79.9
740	99.2	79.5
584*	92.8	71.2

*Instituto de Quimica, Mexico City, altitude 7,700 ft (2,310 m).

will have nearly the same boiling point as a mixture. And, as noted previously, azeotropes have constant boiling points that can be either above or below the boiling points of the individual components.

Distilling a mixture of sugar and water

When a solution of sugar in water is distilled, the boiling point recorded on a thermometer located in the vapor phase is 100°C (at 760 torr) throughout the distillation, whereas the temperature of the boiling sugar solution itself is initially somewhat above 100°C and continues to rise as the concentration of sugar in the remaining solution increases. The vapor pressure of the solution is dependent upon the number of water molecules present in a given volume; hence, with increasing concentration of nonvolatile sugar molecules and decreasing concentration of water, the vapor pressure at a given temperature decreases and a higher temperature is required for boiling. However, sugar molecules do not leave the solution, and the drop clinging to the thermometer is pure water in equilibrium with pure water vapor.

Bp changes with pressure.

When a distillation is carried out in a system open to the air and the boiling point is thus dependent upon existing air pressure, the prevailing barometric pressure should be noted and allowance made for appreciable deviations from the accepted boiling point temperature (Table 5.1). Distillation can also be done at the lower pressures that can be achieved by an oil pump or an aspirator with substantial reduction of boiling point.

Experiments

MICROSCALE

1. Calibration of Thermometer

If you have not previously carried out a calibration, test the 0°C point of your thermometer with a well-stirred mixture of crushed ice and distilled water. To check the 100°C point, put 2 mL of water in a test tube with a boiling chip to prevent bumping and boil the water gently over a hot sand bath with the thermometer in the vapor from the boiling water. Take care to see that the thermometer does not touch the side of the test tube. Then immerse the bulb of the thermometer into the liquid, and see if you can observe superheating.

FIG. 5.5 Small-scale simple distillation apparatus. This apparatus can be adapted for fractional distillation by packing the long neck with a copper sponge. The temperature is regulated by either scraping sand away from or piling sand up around the flask.

Check the atmospheric pressure to determine the true boiling point of the water.

MICROSCALE

Apparatus for simple distillation.

Apparatus

IN THIS EXPERIMENT, the two liquids to be separated are placed in a 5-mL round-bottomed, long-necked flask that is fitted to a distilling head (Fig. 5.5). The flask has a larger surface area exposed to heat than the reaction tube, so the necessary thermal energy can be put into the system to cause the materials to distill. The hot vapor rises and completely envelops the bulb of the thermometer before passing over it and down toward the receiver. The downward-sloping portion of the distilling head functions as an air condenser.

The rate of distillation is determined by the heat input to the apparatus. This is most easily controlled by using a spatula to pile up or scrape away hot sand from around the flask. This works very well. The effect of a column packing on separation efficiency can be evaluated by carrying out a careful distillation of cyclohexane and toluene in this apparatus and then packing the long neck of the flask with a copper sponge and repeating the distillation. Fractional distillation is best carried out using the 10-cm packed column (Fig. 5.6).

FIG. 5.6 Small-scale fractional distillation apparatus. The 10-cm column is packed with 1.5 g of copper sponge (Chore Boy).

Another simple distillation apparatus.

Another design for a simple distillation apparatus is shown in Fig. 5.7. The long air condenser will condense even low-boiling liquids, and the receiver is far from the heat.

 MICROSCALE

2. Instant Microscale Distillation

K   Frequently, a very small quantity of freshly distilled material is needed in an experiment. For example, two compounds that need to be distilled freshly are aniline, which turns black because of the formation of oxidation products, and benzaldehyde, a liquid that easily oxides to solid benzoic acid. The impurities in both these compounds have much higher boiling points than the parent substance, so a very simple distillation suffices to separate them. This is accomplished as follows.

Place a few drops of the impure liquid in a reaction tube along with a boiling chip. Clamp the tube in a hot sand bath and adjust the heat so that the liquid refluxes about halfway up the tube. Expel the air from a Pasteur pipette, thrust it down into the hot vapor, and then pull the hot vapor into the cold upper

FIG. 5.7 Simple distillation apparatus.

Refluxing
vapor

Boiling liquid

Boiling chip

FIG. 5.8 Apparatus for instant
microscale distillation.

portion of the pipette. The vapor will immediately condense and can then be
expelled into another reaction tube held adjacent to the hot one (Fig. 5.8). In
this way enough pure material can be distilled to determine a boiling point, run
a spectrum, make a derivative, or carry out a reaction. Sometimes the first drop
or two will be cloudy, indicating the presence of water. This fraction should be
discarded in order to obtain pure dry material.

Experiments

 MICROSCALE AND MACROSCALE

1. Calibration of Thermometer

If you have not previously carried out a calibration, test the 0°C point of your thermometer with a well-stirred mixture of crushed ice and distilled water. To check the 100°C point, put 2 mL of water in a reaction tube with a boiling chip to prevent bumping and boil the water gently over a hot sand bath with the thermometer in the vapor from the boiling water. Take care to see that the thermometer does not touch the side of the reaction tube. Then immerse the bulb of the thermometer into the liquid and see if you can observe superheating. Check the atmospheric pressure to determine the true boiling point of the water.

MICROSCALE

2. Simple Distillation

IN THIS EXPERIMENT you will set up apparatus like that shown in Fig. 5.5 and distill a mixture of two liquids. The objective is to observe how the boiling point of the mixture changes during the course of its distillation.

17

(A) Simple Distillation of a Cyclohexane–Toluene Mixture.

To a 5-mL long-necked, round-bottomed flask is added 2.0 mL of dry cyclohexane, 2.0 mL of dry toluene, and a boiling chip (Fig. 5.5). This flask is joined by means of a Viton (black) connector to a distilling head fitted with a thermometer using a rubber connector. The thermometer bulb should be completely below the side arm of the Claisen head so that the mercury reaches the same temperature as the vapor that distills. The end of the distilling head dips well down into a vial, which rests on the bottom of a 30-mL beaker filled with ice. The distillation is started by piling up hot sand to heat the flask. As soon as boiling begins, the vapors can be seen to rise up the neck of the flask. Adjust the rate of heating by piling up or scraping away sand from the flask so that it takes *several minutes* for the vapor to rise to the thermometer: **The rate of distillation should be no faster than two drops per minute.**

Record the temperature versus the number of drops during the entire distillation process. If the rate of distillation is as slow as it should be, there will be sufficient time between drops to read and record the temperature. Continue the distillation until only about 0.4 mL remains in the distilling flask. Never distill to dryness. On a larger scale explosive peroxides can sometimes accumulate. At the end of the distillation, measure as accurately as possible, perhaps using a syringe, the volume of the distillate and, after it cools, the volume left in the pot; the difference is the holdup of the column if none has been lost by evaporation. Note the barometric pressure, make any thermometer corrections necessary, and make a plot of milliliters (drop number) versus temperature for the distillation.

Viton is resistant to hot aromatic vapors.

The thermometer bulb must be completely below the side arm.

Cyclohexane
bp 81°C
MW 84.16
n_D^{20} 1.4260

Toluene
bp 111°C
MW 92.14
n_D^{20} 1.4960

There are 21 ± 3 drops per milliliter.

Cleaning Up   The pot residue should be placed in the organic solvents container. The distillate can be placed there, or it can be recycled.

(B) Simple Distillation of an Ethanol–Water Mixture.

In a 5-mL round-bottomed, long-necked flask place 4 mL of a 10% to 20% ethanol–water mixture. It could come from the fermentation of glucose (*see* Chapter 59). Assemble the apparatus as described above, and carry out the distillation until you believe a representative sample of ethanol has collected in the receiver. In the hood place three drops of this sample on a watch glass, and try to ignite it with the blue cone of a microburner flame. Does it burn? Is any unburned residue observed? There was a time when alcohol–water mixtures were mixed with gunpowder and ignited to give proof that the alcohol had not been diluted. One hundred proof alcohol is 50% ethanol by volume.

Cleaning Up   The distillate and pot residue can be flushed down the drain.

MICROSCALE

3. Fractional Distillation

Apparatus

20
18

Assemble the apparatus shown in Fig. 5.6. The 10-cm column is packed with 1.5 g of copper sponge and connected to the 5-mL short-necked flask using the black (Viton) connector. The column should be vertical, and care should be taken to ensure that the bulb of the thermometer does not touch the side of the distilling head. The column, but not the distilling head, will be insulated with glass wool or cotton at the appropriate time to ensure that the process is adiabatic. Alternatively, the column can be insulated with a cut-off 15-mL polyethylene-centrifuge tube.

Adjust the heat input to the flask by piling up or scraping away sand around the flask.

IN THIS EXPERIMENT, just as in the last one, you will distill a mixture of two liquids and again record the boiling points as a function of volume of distillate (drops). The necessity for a very slow rate of distillation cannot be overemphasized.

(A) Fractional Distillation of a Cyclohexane–Toluene Mixture.

Never distill in an airtight system.

To the short-necked flask is added 2.0 mL of cyclohexane, 2.0 mL of toluene, and a boiling chip. The distilling column is packed with 1.5 g of copper sponge (Fig. 5.6). The mixture is brought to a boil over a hot sand bath. Observe the ring of condensate that should rise slowly through the column; if you cannot at first see this ring, locate it by touching the column with the fingers. Reduce the heat by scraping sand away from the flask, and wrap the column, but not the distilling head, with glass wool or cotton if it is not already insulated.

Insulate the distilling column but not the head.

The distilling head and the thermometer function as a small reflux condenser. Again, apply the heat, and as soon as the vapor reaches the thermometer bulb, reduce the heat by scraping away sand. **Distill the mixture at a rate no faster than two drops per minute,** and record the temperature as a function of the number of drops. If the heat input has been *very* carefully adjusted, the distillation will cease and the temperature reading will drop after the cyclohexane has distilled. Increase the heat input by piling up the sand around the flask in order to cause the toluene to distill. Stop the distillation when only about

FIG. 5.9   Simple and fractional distillation curves for cyclohexane and toluene.

21 ± 3 drops = 1 mL

0.4 mL remains in the flask and measure the volume of distillate and the pot residue as before. Make a plot of boiling point versus milliliters of distillate (drops) and compare it to the simple distillation carried out in the same apparatus. Compare your results with those of Fig. 5.9.

Cleaning Up   The pot residue should be placed in the organic solvents container. The distillate can be placed there or recycled.

(B) Fractional Distillation of an Ethanol–Water Mixture.

Distill 4 mL of the same ethanol–water mixture used in the simple distillation experiment following the procedure used for cyclohexane–toluene with either the short or the long distilling column. Remove what you regard to be the ethanol fraction and repeat the ignition test. Is any difference noted?

Cleaning Up   The pot residue and distillate can be flushed down the drain.

(C) Fractional Distillation of an Unknown Mixture.

Distill 4 mL of a mixture of two of the compounds from Table 5.2 (p. 95). The two liquids will have boiling points at least 20°C apart. The composition of the mixture will be 20:80, 30:70, 40:60, 50:50, 60:40, 70:30, or 80:20 percents of the two components. Identify the two compounds, and determine the percent composition of each.

Once the mixture has been distilled and the volumes of the lower- and higher-boiling components determined, the mixture might be redistilled and separated into three fractions: the lower-boiling one, a small middle fraction, and the higher-boiling one. The composition and purity of the lower- and higher-boiling fractions can be determined by measuring the refractive indices of each.

Cleaning Up   Place all fractions and the pot residue in the organic solvents waste container.

MACROSCALE

CAUTION: Cyclohexane and toluene are flammable; make sure distilling apparatus is tight.

CH₃

Cyclohexane
MW 84.16
bp 81.4°C
den 0.78
n_D^{20} 1.4260

Toluene
MW 92.14
bp 111°C
den 0.87
n_D^{20} 1.4960

Throughout this text information regarding the physical properties of substances has been placed in the margins. MW is molecular weight, bp is boiling point, mp is melting point, den is density in g/mL, and n_D^{20} is the refractive index.

4. Simple Distillation

Apparatus

In any distillation, the flask should be no more than two-thirds full at the start. Great care should be taken not to distill to dryness because, in some cases, high-boiling explosive peroxides can become concentrated.

Assemble the apparatus for simple distillations as shown in Fig. 5.10, starting with the support ring followed by the electric flask heater (*see* Fig. 1.16n) and then the flask. One or two boiling stones are put in the flask to promote even boiling. Each ground joint is greased by putting three or four stripes of grease lengthwise around the male joint and pressing the joint firmly into the other without twisting. The air is thus eliminated, and the joint will appear almost transparent. (Do not use excess grease because it will contaminate the product.) Water enters the condenser at the tublature nearest the receiver. Because of the large heat capacity of water, only a very small stream (3 mm

FIG. 5.10 Apparatus for simple distillation.

diameter) is needed; too much water pressure will cause the tubing to pop off. A heavy rubber band, or better, a Keck clamp, can be used to hold the condenser to the distillation head. Note that the bulb of the thermometer is below the opening into the side arm of the distillation head.

(A) Simple Distillation of a Cyclohexane–Toluene Mixture.

Do not add a boiling chip to a hot liquid. It may boil over.

Place a mixture of 30 mL cyclohexane and 30 mL toluene and a boiling chip in a dry 100-mL round-bottomed flask, and assemble the apparatus for simple distillation. After assuring that all connections are tight, heat the flask strongly until boiling begins. Then adjust the heat until the distillate drops at a regular rate of about one drop per second. Record both the temperature and the volume of distillate at regular intervals. After 50 mL of distillate is collected, discontinue the distillation. Record the barometric pressure, make any thermometer correction necessary, and plot boiling point versus volume of distillate. Save the distillate for fractional distillation.

Dispose of cyclohexane and toluene in the container provided. Do not pour them down the drain.

Cleaning Up   The pot residue should be placed in the organic solvents container. The distillate also can be placed there or it can be recycled.

(B) Simple Distillation of an Ethanol–Water Mixture.

A 10% to 12% solution of ethanol in water is produced by fermentation. See Chapter 59.

In a 500-mL round-bottomed flask place 200 mL of a 20% aqueous solution of ethanol. Follow the procedure (above) for the distillation of a cyclohexane–toluene mixture. Discontinue the distillation after 50 mL of distillate has been collected. Working in the hood place three drops of distillate on a Pyrex watch glass, and try to ignite it with the blue cone of a microburner flame. Does it burn? Is any unburned residue observed?

Cleaning Up   The pot residue and distillate can be flushed down the drain.

 MACROSCALE

5. Fractional Distillation

Apparatus

Assemble the apparatus shown in Figs. 5.11 and 5.12. The fractionating column is packed with one-fourth to one-third of a metal sponge. The column should be perfectly vertical and be insulated with glass wool covered with shiny-side in aluminum foil. However, in order to observe what is taking place within the column, insulation is omitted for this experiment.

(A) Fractional Distillation of a Cyclohexane–Toluene Mixture.

After the flask from the simple distillation experiment has cooled, pour the 50 mL of distillate back into the distilling flask, add one or two new boiling chips, and assemble the apparatus for fractional distillation. The stillhead delivers into a short condenser fitted with a bent adapter leading into a 10-mL graduated cylinder. Gradually turn up the heat to the electric flask heater until the mixture of cyclohexane and toluene just begins to boil. As soon as boiling starts,

Keck clamp

Rubber tubing

Keck clamp

Fractionating column

Stainless steel sponge packing

Water out

Water in

FIG. 5.11 Apparatus for fractional distillation. The position of the thermometer bulb is critical.

FIG. 5.12 Fractionating column and packing. Use one-third of sponge (Chore Boy).

turn down the power. Heat slowly at first. A ring of condensate will rise slowly through the column; if you cannot at first see this ring, locate it by cautiously touching the column with the fingers. The rise should be very gradual so that the column can acquire a uniform temperature gradient. Do not apply more heat until you are sure that the ring of condensate has stopped rising; then increase the heat gradually. In a properly conducted operation, the vapor-condensate mixture reaches the top of the column only after several minutes. Once distillation has commenced, it should continue steadily without any drop in temperature at a rate no greater than 1 mL in 1.5–2 min. Observe the flow, and keep it steady by slight increases in heat as required. Protect the column from drafts by wrapping it with aluminum foil, glass wool, or even a towel. This insulation will help prevent flooding of the column, as will slow and steady distillation.

Record the temperature as each milliliter of distillate collects, and take more frequent readings when the temperature starts to rise abruptly. Each time the graduated cylinder fills, quickly empty it into a series of labeled 25-mL Erlenmeyer flasks. Stop the distillation when a second constant temperature is reached. Plot a distillation curve, and record what you observed inside the column in the course of the fractionation. Combine the fractions that you think are pure, and turn in the product in a bottle labeled with your name, desk number, the name of the product, the bp range, and the weight.

Cleaning Up   The pot residue should be placed in the organic solvents container. The cyclohexane and toluene fractions can be placed there also, or they can be recycled.

(B) Fractional Distillation of Ethanol–Water Mixture.   Place the 50 mL of distillate from the simple distillation experiment in a 100-mL round-bottomed flask, add one or two boiling chips, and assemble the apparatus for fractional distillation. Follow the procedure (above) for the fractional distillation of a cyclohexane–toluene mixture. Repeat the ignition test. Is any difference noted? Alternatively distill 60 mL of the 10–20% ethanol–water mixture that results from the fermentation of sucrose (*see* Chapter 65).

Cleaning Up   The pot residue and distillate can be flushed down the drain.

 MICROSCALE AND MACROSCALE

6. Unknowns

You will be supplied with an unknown, prepared by the instructor, that is a mixture of two solvents from those listed in Table 5.2, only two of which form azeotropes. The solvents in the mixture will be mutually soluble and differ in boiling point by more than 20°C. Fractionate the unknown, and identify the components from the boiling points. Prepare a distillation curve. You may be

TABLE 5.2   Some Properties of Common Solvents

Solvent	Boiling Point (°C)
Acetone	56.5
Methanol	64.7
Hexane	68.8
1-Butanol	117.2
2-Methyl-2-propanol	82.2
Water	100.0
Toluene*	110.6

*Methanol and toluene form an azeotrope, bp 63.8°C (69% methanol).

directed to analyze your distillate by gas chromatography (*see* Chapter 11) or refractive index (*see* Chapter 4).

Cleaning Up   Organic material goes in the organic solvents container. Water and aqueous solutions can be flushed down the drain.

Questions

1. In the simple distillation experiment (2), can you account for the boiling point of your product in terms of the known boiling points of the pure components of your mixture? If so, how? If not, why not?

2. From the plot of boiling point versus volume of distillate in the simple distillation experiment, what can you conclude about the purity of your product?

3. From the boiling point versus volume of distillate plot in the fractional distillation of the cyclohexane–toluene mixture (3), what conclusion can you draw about the homogeneity of the distillate?

4. From the boiling point versus volume of distillate in the fractional distillation of the ethanol–water mixture (3), what conclusion can you draw about the homogeneity of the distillate? Does it have a constant boiling point? Is it a pure substance because it has a constant boiling point?

5. What is the effect on the boiling point of a solution (e.g., water) produced by a soluble nonvolatile substance (e.g., sodium chloride)? What is the effect of an insoluble substance such as sand or charcoal? What is the temperature of the vapor above these two boiling solutions?

6. In the distillation of a pure substance (e.g., water), why doesn't all the water vaporize at once when the boiling point is reached?

7. In fractional distillation, liquid can be seen running from the bottom of the distillation column back into the distilling flask. What effect does this returning condensate have on the fractional distillation?

8. Why is it extremely dangerous to attempt to carry out a distillation in a completely closed apparatus (one with no vent to the atmosphere)?

9. Why is better separation of two liquids achieved by slow rather than fast distillation?

10. Explain why a packed fractionating column is more efficient than an unpacked one.

11. In the distillation of the cyclohexane–toluene mixture, the first few drops of distillate may be cloudy. Explain.

12. What effect does the reduction of atmospheric pressure have on the boiling point? Can cyclohexane and toluene be separated if the external pressure is 350 mm Hg instead of 760 mm Hg?

13. When water-cooled condensers are used for distillation or for refluxing a liquid, the water enters the condenser at the lowest point and leaves at the highest. Why?

Surfing the Web

http://www.elmhurst.edu/~chm/onlcourse/chm110/outlines/distill.html
A simple one-page site from Elmhurst College illustrating the fractional distillation of crude oil.

CHAPTER

6

Steam Distillation

PRELAB EXERCISE: If a mixture of toluene and water is distilled at 97°C, what weight of water would be necessary to carry over 1 g of toluene?

Each liquid exerts its own vapor pressure.

The boiling point of immiscible liquids is below *the boiling point of either pure liquid.*

When a mixture of cyclohexane and toluene is distilled (*see* Chapter 5) the boiling point of these two miscible liquids is *between* the boiling points of each of the pure components. By contrast, if a mixture of benzene and water (immiscible liquids) is distilled, the boiling point of the mixture will be *below* the boiling point of each pure component. Since the two liquids are essentially insoluble in each other, the benzene molecules in a droplet of benzene are not diluted by water molecules from nearby water droplets; hence the vapor pressure exerted by the benzene is the same as that of benzene alone at the existing temperature. The same is true of the water present. Because they are immiscible, the two liquids exert pressures against the common external pressure independently, and when the sum of the two partial pressures equals the external pressure, boiling occurs. Benzene has a vapor pressure of 760 torr at 80.1°C and, if it is mixed with water, the combined vapor pressure must equal 760 torr at some temperature below 80.1°C. This temperature, the boiling point of the mixture, can be calculated from known values of the vapor pressures of the separate liquids at that temperature. Vapor pressures found for water and benzene in the range 50–80°C are plotted in Fig. 6.1. The dotted line cuts the two curves at points where the sum of the vapor pressures is 760 torr; hence this temperature is the boiling point of the mixture (69.3°C).

Practical use can sometimes be made of the fact that many water-insoluble liquids and solids behave as benzene does when mixed with water, volatilizing at temperatures below their boiling points. Thus, naphthalene, a solid, boils at 218°C but distills with water at a temperature below 100°C. Because naphthalene is not very volatile, considerable water is required to entrain it, and the conventional way of conducting the distillation is to pass steam into a boiling flask containing naphthalene and water. This process is called *steam distillation.* With more volatile compounds, or with a small amount of material, the substance can be heated with water in a simple distillation flask and the steam generated in situ.

Some high-boiling substances decompose before the boiling point is reached and, if impure, cannot be purified by ordinary distillation. However,

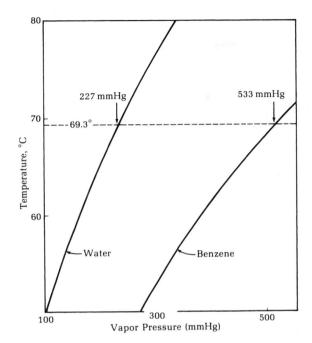

FIG. 6.1 Vapor pressure versus temperature curves for water and benzene.

Used for isolation of perfume and flavor oils.

these can be freed from contaminating substances by steam distillation at a lower temperature, at which they are stable. Steam distillation also offers the advantage of selectivity because some water-insoluble substances are volatile with steam and others are not, and some volatilize so slowly that sharp separation is possible. This technique is useful in processing natural oils and resins, which can be separated into steam-volatile and nonsteam-volatile fractions. It is useful for recovery of a nonsteam-volatile solid from its solution in a high-boiling solvent such as nitrobenzene, bp 210°C; all traces of the solvent can be eliminated and the temperature can be kept low.

The boiling point remains constant during a steam distillation so long as adequate amounts of both water and the organic component are present to saturate the vapor space. Determination of the boiling point and correction for any deviation from normal atmospheric pressure permits calculation of the amount of water required for distillation of a given amount of organic substance.

Dalton's law

According to Dalton's law, the molecular proportion of the two components in the distillate is equal to the ratio of their vapor pressures (p) in the boiling mixture; the more volatile component contributes the greater number of molecules to the vapor phase. Thus,

$$\frac{\text{Moles of water}}{\text{Moles of substance}} = \frac{p_{\text{water}}}{p_{\text{substance}}}$$

The vapor pressure of water (p_{water}) at the boiling temperature in question can be found by interpolation of the data of Table 6.1, and that of the organic

TABLE 6.1 Vapor Pressure of Water in Millimeters of Mercury

t (°C)	p	t (°C)	p	t (°C)	p	t (°C)	p
60	149.3	70	233.7	80	355.1	90	525.8
61	156.4	71	243.9	81	369.7	91	546.0
62	163.8	72	254.6	82	384.9	92	567.0
63	171.4	73	265.7	83	400.6	93	588.6
64	179.3	74	277.2	84	416.8	94	610.9
65	187.5	75	289.1	85	433.6	95	633.9
66	196.1	76	301.4	86	450.9	96	657.6
67	205.0	77	314.1	87	468.7	97	682.1
68	214.2	78	327.3	88	487.1	98	707.3
69	223.7	79	341.0	89	506.1	99	733.2

substance is, of course, equal to $760 - p_{water}$. Hence, the weight of water required per gram of substance is given by the expression

$$\frac{\text{Wt of water per}}{\text{g of substance}} = \frac{18 \times p_{water}}{\text{MW of substance} \times (760 - p_{water})}$$

From the data given in Fig. 6.1 for benzene–water, the fact that the mixture boils at 69.3°C, and the molecular weight of 78.11 for benzene, the water required for steam distillation of 1 g of benzene is only $227 \times \frac{18}{533} \times \frac{1}{78} = 0.10$ g. Nitrobenzene (bp 210°C, MW 123.11) steam distills at 99°C and requires 4.0 g of water per gram. The low molecular weight of water makes water a favorable liquid for two-phase distillation of organic compounds.

Steam distillation is employed in a number of experiments in this text. On a small scale steam is generated in the flask that contains the substance to be steam distilled by simply boiling a mixture of water and the immiscible substance.

Ice

Hot sand bath

Boiling chip

FIG. 6.2 Small-scale steam distillation apparatus. Add water via syringe at A.

Terpenes

Apparatus

The apparatus (Fig. 6.2) consists of a 5-mL short-necked boiling flask, addition port, and distilling head leading to an ice-cooled receiver. As the steam distillation proceeds, it may be necessary to add more water to the flask. This is done via syringe through the septum on the addition port (A).

Isolation of Citral

Citral is an example of a very large group of *natural products* called *terpenes*. They are responsible for the characteristic odors of plants such as eucalyptus, pine, mint, peppermint, and lemon. The odors of camphor, menthol, lavender, rose, and hundreds of other fragrances are due to terpenes, which have 10 carbon atoms with double bonds, and aldehyde, ketone, or alcohol functional groups (Fig. 6.3).

FIG. 6.3 Structures of some terpenes.

Geranial

Isopentenyl pyrophosphate

Isoprene
(2-Methy 1-1,3-butadiene)

Neral

Limonene
(lemons)

Myrcene
(bayberry)

α-Pinene
(turpentine)

Menthol
(mint)

Carvone
(caraway seeds)

Camphor

1,8-Cineole
(eucalyptus)

Pulegone
(pennyroyal oil)

Anethole
(anlse seed)

The isoprene rule

In nature these terpenes all arise from a common precursor: isopentenyl pyrophosphate. At one time these were thought to come from the simple diene, isoprene (2-methyl-1,3-butadiene), because the skeletons of terpenes can be dissected into isoprene units, having 5 carbon atoms arranged as in 2-methylbutane. These isoprene units are almost always arranged in a "head-to-tail" fashion.

In the present experiment citral, a mixture of geranial and neral, is isolated by steam distillation of lemongrass oil, which is used to make lemongrass tea, a popular drink in Mexico. The distillate contains 90% geranial and 10% neral, the isomer about the 2,3-bond. Citral is used in a commercial synthesis of vitamin A.

Lemongrass oil contains a number of substances; simple or fractional distillation would not be a practical method for obtaining pure citral. And because it boils at 229°C, it has a tendency to polymerize, oxidize, and decompose during distillation. For example, heating with potassium bisulfate, an acidic compound, converts citral to 1-methyl-4-isopropylbenzene (p-cymene).

Steam distillation: the isolation of heat-sensitive compounds

Steam distillation is thus a very gentle method for isolating citral. The distillation takes place below the boiling point of water. The distillate consists of a mixture of citral (and some neral) and water. It is isolated by shaking the mixture with *t*-butyl methyl ether. The citral dissolves in the *t*-butyl methyl ether, which is immiscible with water, and the two layers are separated. The *t*-butyl methyl ether is dried (it dissolves some water) and evaporated to leave citral.

Geranial and neral are geometric isomers.

Store the citral in the smallest possible container in the dark for later characterization. The homogeneity of the substance can be investigated using thin-layer chromatography (*see* Chapter 9) or gas chromatography (*see* Chapter 11). An infrared spectrum (*see* Chapter 12) would confirm the presence of the aldehyde; an ultraviolet spectrum (*see* Chapter 14) would indicate it is a conjugated aldehyde; and a nuclear magnetic resonance (NMR) spectrum (*see* Chapter 13) would clearly show the aldehyde proton, the three methyl groups, and the two olefinic protons. Chemically the molecule can be characterized by reaction with bromine and also permanganate, which shows it contains double bonds; and by the Tollens test, which confirms the presence of an aldehyde (*see* Chapter 36). Finally, the molecule can be reacted with another substance to form a crystalline derivative for further identification (*see* Chapter 70). You will probably not be required to carry out all of these analyses; however, these are the major tools available to the organic chemist for ascertaining purity and determining the structure of an organic molecule.

Experiments

MICROSCALE

Steam Distillation Apparatus

L   Into a 5-mL short-necked, round-bottomed flask place a boiling chip, 0.5 mL of lemongrass oil[1] (*not* lemon oil), and 3 mL of water. Assemble the apparatus as

---

1. Obtained from Pfaltz and Bauer, 172 E. Aurora St., Waterbury, CT 06708.

*Wrap up the vertical part of
the apparatus in cotton or
glass wool to speed the
distillation.*

depicted in Fig. 6.2 and distill as rapidly as possible, taking care that all the
distillate condenses. Using the syringe, inject water dropwise through the septum to keep the volume in the flask constant. Distill into an ice-cooled vial, as
shown, or, better, into the 15-mL centrifuge tube until no more oily drops can
be detected, about 10 to 12 mL.

▯ MICROSCALE

12, V

1. Extraction of Citral

IN THIS EXPERIMENT you will extract the pleasant-smelling liquid citral from
water using ether as the solvent. The ether solution is dried and the ether evaporated to leave pure citral. Extraction is a common isolation technique (*see* Chapter 8 for information on the theory and practice of extraction).

Add 2.5 mL of *tert*-butyl methyl ether to the cold distillate. Shake, let the
layers separate, and then draw off the aqueous layer with a Pasteur pipette and
transfer it to another centrifuge tube. Continue this extraction process by again
adding 1.5 mL of ether to the aqueous layer, shaking, and separating to extract
the citral from the steam distillate.

See the sidebar in Chapter 8 for the many advantages of *t*-butyl methyl
ether as an extraction solvent.

*In Sweden they say, "Add
anhydrous drying agent until it
begins to snow."*

Place the ether in a reaction tube, and then add about 2 mL of saturated
sodium chloride solution to the ether. Stopper the tube, flick the tube or shake
it, and then remove and discard the aqueous layer. Add anhydrous calcium
chloride pellets to the ether until these no longer clump together, stopper the
tube, and shake it over a period of 5 to 10 minutes. This removes water adhering to the reaction tube and dissolved in the ether. Force a Pasteur pipette to
the bottom of the reaction tube, expel the air from the pipette, draw up the
ether, and expel it into another tared reaction tube. Add fresh ether, which will
serve to wash off the drying agent, and add that ether to the tared reaction tube.
Add a boiling stick or boiling chip to the ether in the reaction tube, place it in
a beaker of hot water, and evaporate the ether by boiling and drawing the ether
vapors into the water aspirator or, better, by blowing a gentle stream of air or
nitrogen into the tube (in the hood). The last traces of ether may be removed
by connecting the reaction tube directly to the water aspirator. The residue
should be a clear, fragrant oil. If it is cloudy, it is wet. Determine the weight
of the citral and calculate the percentage of citral recovered from the lemongrass oil, assuming that the density of the lemongrass oil is the same as that
of citral (0.89). Transfer the product to the smallest possible airtight container
and store it in the dark for later analysis to confirm the presence of double
bonds and the aldehyde group (*see* Chapters 18 and 36). Analyze the infrared
spectrum in detail.

See page 137 *for the removal
of water from ether solutions.*

Cleaning Up   The aqueous layer can be flushed down the drain. Any ether
goes into the organic solvents container. Allow ether to evaporate from the calcium chloride in the hood and then place it in the nonhazardous solid waste
container.

MACROSCALE

Anthracene
mp 216°C

Toluene
bp 110.8°C
den 0.866

2. Recovery of a Dissolved Substance

Steam Distillation Apparatus

In the assembly shown in Fig. 6.4 steam is passed into a 250-mL, round-bottomed flask through a section of 6-mm glass tubing fitted into a stillhead with a piece of 5-mm rubber tubing connected to a trap, which in turn is connected to the steam line. The trap serves two purposes: it allows water, which is in the steam line, to be removed before it reaches the round-bottomed flask; and adjustment of the clamp on the hose at the bottom of the trap allows precise control of the steam flow. As shown, the stopper in the trap should be wired on as a precaution. A bent adapter attached to a *long* condenser delivers the condensate into a 250-mL Erlenmeyer flask.

Measure 50 mL of a 0.2% solution of anthracene in toluene into the 250-mL round-bottomed flask and add 100 mL of water. For an initial distillation to determine the boiling point and composition of the toluene–water azeotrope, fit the stillhead with a thermometer instead of the steam-inlet tube (*see* Fig. 5.5). Heat the mixture with a hot plate and sand bath or electric flask heater, distill about 50 mL of the azeotrope, and record a value for the boiling point. After removing the heat, pour the distillate into a graduated cylinder and measure the volumes of toluene and water. Calculate the weight of water per gram of toluene and compare the result to the theoretical value calculated from the vapor pressure of water at the observed boiling point (Table 6.1).

FIG. 6.4 Steam distillation apparatus.

CAUTION: *Live steam causes*
severe burns. If apparatus leaks
steam, turn off steam valve
immediately.

Replace the thermometer with the steam-inlet tube. To start the steam distillation, heat the flask containing the mixture with a Thermowell to prevent water from condensing in the flask to the point where water and product splash over into the receiver. Then turn on the steam valve, being sure the screw clamp on the bottom of the trap is open. Slowly close the clamp, and allow steam to pass into the flask. Try to adjust the rate of steam addition and the rate of heating so that the water level in the flask remains constant. Unlike ordinary distillations, steam distillations are usually run as fast as possible, with proper care to avoid having material splash into the receiver and to avoid having uncondensed steam escape.

Continue distillation by passing in steam until the distillate is clear and then until fluorescence appearing in the stillhead indicates that a trace of anthracene is beginning to distill. Stop the steam distillation by first opening the clamp at the bottom of the trap and then turning off the steam valve. Grasp the round-bottomed flask with a towel when disconnecting it and, using the clamp to support it, cool it under the tap. The bulk of the anthracene can be dislodged from the flask walls and collected on a small suction filter. To recover any remaining anthracene, add a small amount of acetone to the flask, warm the flask on the steam bath to dissolve the material, add water to precipitate it, and then collect the precipitate on the same suction filter. About 80% of the hydrocarbon in the original toluene solution should be recoverable. When dry, crystallize the material from about 1 mL of toluene and observe that the crystals are more intensely fluorescent than the solution or the amorphous solid. The characteristic fluorescence is quenched by mere traces of impurities.

Cleaning Up Place the toluene and the anthracene in the organic solvents container. The aqueous layer can be flushed down the drain.

 MACROSCALE

3. Isolation of Citral

Citral, a fragrant terpene aldehyde made up of two isoprene units, is the main component of the steam-volatile fraction of lemongrass oil and (as mentioned above) is used in a commercial synthesis of vitamin A.

Using a graduated cylinder, measure out 10 mL of lemongrass oil (*not* lemon oil) into the 250-mL boiling flask. Rinse the remaining contents of the graduated cylinder into the flask with a small amount of *t*-butyl methyl ether. Add 100 mL of water, make connections as in Fig. 6.4, heat the flask with a low flame, and pass in the steam. Distill as rapidly as the cooling facilities allow and continue until droplets of oil no longer appear at the tip of the condenser (about 250 mL of distillate).

Pour 50 mL of *t*-butyl methyl ether into a 125-mL separatory funnel, cool the distillate if necessary, and pour a part of it into the funnel. Shake, let the layers separate, discard the lower layer, add another portion of distillate, and repeat. When the last portion of distillate has been added, rinse the flask with a small amount of *t*-butyl methyl ether to recover adhering citral. Use the techniques described in Chapter 8 for drying, filtering, and evaporating the *t*-butyl

Citral (mixture of geranial
and neral)
MW 152.24
bp 229°C, den 0.888
n_D^{20} 1.4880

methyl ether. Take the tare of a 1-g tincture bottle, transfer the citral to it with a Pasteur pipette, and determine the weight and the yield from the lemongrass oil. Label the bottle and store (in the dark) for later testing for the presence of the double bonds and the aldehyde group (*see* Chapters 18 and 36).

Cleaning Up　The aqueous layer can be flushed down the drain. Any *t*-butyl methyl ether goes in the organic solvents container. Allow *t*-butyl methyl ether to evaporate from the calcium chloride pellets in the hood, then place it in the nonhazardous solid waste container.

🝛 MACROSCALE

Eugenol

Acetyleugenol

4. Isolation of Eugenol from Cloves

In the fifteenth century Theophrastus Bombastus von Hohenheim, otherwise known as Paracelsus, urged all chemists to make extractives for medicinal purposes rather than try to transmute base metals into gold. He believed every extractive possessed a quintessence that was the most effective part in effecting cures. There was then an upsurge in the isolation of essential oils from plant materials, some of which are still used for medicinal purposes. Among these are camphor, quinine, oil of cloves, cedarwood, turpentine, cinnamon, gum benzoin, and myrrh. Oil of cloves, which consists almost entirely of eugenol and its acetate, is a food flavoring agent as well as a dental anesthetic. The Food and Drug Administration has declared clove oil to be the most effective nonprescription remedy for toothache.

The biggest market for essential oils is for perfumes and, as might be expected, prices for these oils reflect their rarity. Recently, worldwide production of orange oil was 1500 tons and sold for $0.75 per lb, whereas 400 tons of clove oil sold for $14.00 per lb, and 10 tons of jasmine oil sold for $2000 per lb. These three oils represent the most common extractive processes. Orange oil is obtained by expression (squeezing) of the peel in presses; clove oil is obtained by steam distillation, as performed in this experiment; and jasmine oil is obtained by extraction of the flower petals using ethanol.

Cloves are the flower buds from a tropical tree that can grow to 50 feet in height. The buds are handpicked in the Moluccas (the Spice Islands) of Indonesia, the East Indies, and the islands of the Indian Ocean, where a single tree can yield up to 75 lb of the sun-dried buds we know as cloves.

Cloves contain between 14 and 20% by weight of essential oil, of which only about 50% can be isolated. The principal constituent of clove oil is eugenol and its acetyl derivative. Eugenol boils at 255°C, but, being insoluble in water, it will form an azeotrope with water and steam distill at a temperature slightly below the boiling point of water. Being a phenol, eugenol will dissolve in aqueous alkali to form the phenolate anion, which forms the basis for its separation from its acetyl derivative. The relative amounts of eugenol and acetyleugenol and the effectiveness of the alkali extraction in separating them can be analyzed by thin-layer chromatography.

Procedure

IN THIS EXPERIMENT a mixture of the essential oils—eugenol and acetyleugenol—are steam distilled from cloves. These compounds are isolated from the aqueous distillate by extraction into dichloromethane. The dichloromethane solution is shaken with aqueous sodium hydroxide, which reacts with the acidic eugenol. The dichloromethane layer is dried and evaporated to give acetyleugenol. The basic layer is acidified and the eugenol extracted into dichloromethane, which is in turn dried and evaporated to give pure eugenol.

Place 25 g of whole cloves in a 250-mL round-bottomed flask, add 100 mL of water, and set up an apparatus for steam distillation (Fig. 6.4) or simple distillation (*see* Fig. 5.10). In the latter procedure steam is generated in situ. Heat the flask strongly until boiling begins, then reduce the heat just enough to prevent foam from being carried over into the receiver. Instead of using a graduated cylinder as a receiver, use an Erlenmeyer flask and transfer the distillate periodically to the graduated cylinder; then, if any material does foam over, the entire distillate will not become contaminated. Collect 60 mL of distillate, remove the flame, and add 60 mL of water to the flask. Resume the distillation, and collect an additional 60 mL of distillate.

The eugenol is sparingly soluble in water and is extracted easily from the distillate with dichloromethane. Place the 120 mL of distillate in a 250-mL separatory funnel and extract with three 15-mL portions of dichloromethane. In this extraction very gentle shaking will fail to remove all of the product, and long and vigorous shaking will produce an emulsion of the organic layer and water. The separatory funnel will appear to have three layers in it. It is better to err on the side of vigorous shaking and draw off the clear lower layer to the emulsion line for the first two extractions. For the third extraction, shake the mixture less vigorously and allow a longer period of time for the two layers to separate.

Combine the dichloromethane extracts (the aqueous layer can be discarded), and add just enough anhydrous calcium chloride pellets so that the drying agent no longer clumps together but appears to be a dry powder as it settles in the solution. This may require as little as 2 g of drying agent. Swirl the flask for a minute or two to complete the drying process and then decant the solvents into an Erlenmeyer flask. It is quite easy to decant the dichloromethane from the drying agent, so it is not necessary to set up a filtration apparatus to accomplish this separation.

Measure the volume of the dichloromethane in a dry graduated cylinder, place exactly one-fifth of the solution in a tared Erlenmeyer flask, add a wood boiling stick (easier to remove than a boiling chip), and evaporate the solution on a steam bath in a hood. The residue of crude clove oil will be used in the thin-layer chromatography analysis. From its weight, the total yield of crude clove oil can be calculated.

See Chapter 8 for the theory of acid/base extractions.

To separate eugenol from acetyleugenol, extract the remaining four-fifths of the dichloromethane solution (about 30 mL) with 5% aqueous sodium hydroxide solution. Carry out this extraction three times, using 10-mL portions of sodium hydroxide each time. Dry the dichloromethane layer over anhydrous calcium chloride pellets, decant the solution into a tared Erlenmeyer flask, and evaporate the solvent. The residue should consist of acetyleugenol and other steam-volatile neutral compounds from cloves.

Acidify the combined aqueous extracts to pH 1 with concentrated hydrochloric acid (use Congo red or litmus paper), and then extract the liberated eugenol with three 8-mL portions of dichloromethane. Dry the combined extracts, decant into a tared Erlenmeyer flask, and evaporate the solution on a steam bath. Calculate the weight percent yields of eugenol and acetyleugenol on the basis of the weight of cloves used.

Analyze your products using infrared spectroscopy and thin-layer chromatography. Obtain an infrared spectrum of either eugenol or acetyleugenol using the thin-film method. Compare your spectrum to the spectrum of a fellow student who has examined the other compound.

Use plastic sheets precoated with silica gel for thin-layer chromatography. One piece the size of a microscope slide should suffice. Spot crude clove oil, eugenol, and acetyleugenol (1% solutions) side by side about 5 mm from one end of the slide. The spots should be very small. Immerse the end of the slide in a dichloromethane–hexane mixture (1:2 or 2:1) about 3-mm deep in a covered beaker. After running the chromatogram observe the spots under an ultraviolet lamp or by developing them in an iodine chamber.

Cleaning Up   Combine all aqueous layers, neutralize with sodium carbonate, dilute with water, and flush down the drain. Any solutions containing dichloromethane should be placed in the halogenated organic solvents container. Allow the solvent to evaporate from the calcium chloride pellets in the hood and then place the drying agent in the nonhazardous solid waste container.

Questions

1. Assign the peaks in the ^{1}H NMR spectrum of eugenol to specific protons in the molecule (Fig. 6.5). The OH peak is at 5.1 ppm.

2. A mixture of ethyl iodide (C_2H_5I, bp 72.3°C) and water boils at 63.7°C. What weight of ethyl iodide would be carried over by 1 g of steam during steam distillation?

3. Iodobenzene (C_6H_5I, bp 188°C) steam distills at a temperature of 98.2°C. How many molecules of water are required to carry over 1 molecule of iodobenzene? How many grams per gram of iodobenzene?

4. The condensate from a steam distillation contains 8 g of an unknown compound and 18 g of water. The mixture steam distilled at 98°C. What is the molecular weight of the unknown?

5. Bearing in mind that a sealed container filled with steam will develop a vacuum if the container is cooled, explain what would occur if a steam

FIG. 6.5 [^1]H NMR spectrum of eugenol (250 MHz).

distillation was stopped by turning off the steam valve before opening the screw clamp on the adapter trap.

6. A mixture of toluene (bp 110.8°C) and water is steam distilled. Visual inspection of the distillate reveals that there is a greater volume of toluene than water present, yet water (bp 100°C) has the higher vapor pressure. Explain this observation.

Surfing the Web

http//www.deancoleman.com/whatareoils.htm
This website explains all about essential oils—how they are isolated, their sources, uses, and characteristics.

http//www.essential-oil.org/shop/oilsa.htm
This website lists the prices of 450 essential oils, most of which are isolated via steam distillation.

CHAPTER

7

Vacuum Distillation and Sublimation

PRELAB EXERCISE: Compare the operation of a barometer, used to measure atmospheric pressure, and a mercury manometer, used to measure the pressure in an evacuated system.

Part 1. Vacuum Distillation

Many substances cannot be distilled satisfactorily in the ordinary way, either because they boil at such high temperatures that decomposition occurs or because they are sensitive to oxidation. In such cases purification can be accomplished by distillation at diminished pressure. A few of the many pieces of apparatus for vacuum distillation are described on the following pages. Although round-bottomed Pyrex ware and thick-walled suction flasks are not liable to collapse, safety glasses should be worn at all times when carrying out this type of distillation.

Vacuum Distillation Assemblies

Carry out vacuum distillation behind a safety shield. Check apparatus for scratches and cracks.

A typical macroscale vacuum distillation apparatus is illustrated in Fig. 7.1. It is constructed of a round-bottomed flask (often called the "pot") containing the material to be distilled, a Claisen distilling head fitted with a hair-fine capillary mounted through a rubber tubing sleeve, and a thermometer with the bulb extending below the side arm opening. The condenser fits into a vacuum adapter that is connected to the receiver and, via heavy-walled rubber tubing, to a mercury manometer and thence to the trap and water aspirator.

Prevention of bumping

Liquids usually bump vigorously when boiled at reduced pressure and most boiling stones lose their activity in an evacuated system; it is therefore essential to make a special provision for controlling the bumping. This is done by allowing a fine stream of air bubbles to be drawn into the boiling liquid through a glass tube drawn to a hair-fine capillary. The capillary should be so fine that even under vacuum only a few bubbles of air are drawn in each second; smooth boiling will be promoted, and the pressure will remain low. The capillary should extend to the very bottom of the flask, and should be slender and flexible so that it will whip back and forth in the boiling liquid. Another method used to prevent bumping when small quantities of material are being distilled, is to introduce

110

Thermometer bulb
below side arm
of Claisen
distilling head

Keck clamp

Water out

Capillary

Claisen
distilling head

Pot

Condenser

Keck
clamp

Vacuum
adapter

To trap
and aspirator

Water in

Keck
clamp

Receiver

Manometer

FIG. 7.1 Vacuum distillation
apparatus.

Making a hair-fine capillary

*Handle flames in the organic
laboratory with great care.*

sufficient glass wool into the flask to fill a part of the space above the liquid.
Rapid magnetic stirring will also prevent bumping.

The capillary is made in three operations. First, a 6-in. length of 6-mm
glass tubing is rotated and heated in a small area over a *very hot* flame to collapse the glass and thicken the side walls as seen in Fig. 7.2(a). The tube is
removed from the flame, allowed to cool slightly, and then drawn into a thick-
walled, coarse diameter capillary [Fig. 7.2(b)]. This coarse capillary is heated
at point X over the wing top of a Bunsen burner turned 90°. When the glass is
very soft, but not soft enough to collapse the tube entirely, the tubing is lifted
from the flame and without hesitation drawn smoothly and rapidly into a
hair-fine capillary by stretching the hands as far as they will reach (about 2 m)
[Fig. 7.2(c)]. The two capillaries so produced can be snapped off to the desired
length. To ascertain that there is indeed a hole in the capillary, place the end
beneath a low-viscosity liquid such as acetone or *t*-butyl methyl ether, and blow
in the large end. A stream of very small bubbles should be seen. If the stream of
bubbles is not extremely fine, make a new capillary. The flow of air through the
capillary *cannot* be controlled by attaching a rubber tube and clamp to the top of
the capillary tube. Should the right-hand capillary of Fig. 7.2(c) break when in
use, it can be fused to a scrap of glass (for use as a handle) and heated again at
point Y [Fig. 7.2(c)]. In this way the capillary can be redrawn many times.

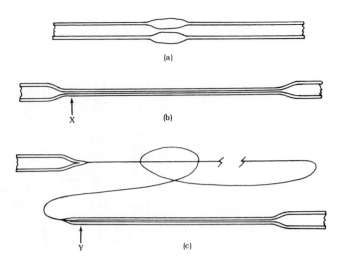

FIG. 7.2 Capillary for vacuum distillation.

Heating baths

The pot is heated via a heating bath rather than a Thermowell to promote even boiling and make possible accurate determination of the boiling point. The bath is filled with a suitable heat transfer liquid (water, cottonseed oil, silicone oil, or molten metal) and heated to a temperature of about 20°C higher than that at which the substance in the flask distills. The bath temperature is kept constant throughout the distillation. The surface of the liquid in the flask should be below that of the heating medium because this condition lessens the tendency to bump. Heating of the flask is begun only after the system has been evacuated to the desired pressure; otherwise the liquid might boil too suddenly on reduction of the pressure.

Changing fractions

To change fractions the following must be done in sequence: Remove the source of heat, release the vacuum, change the receiver, restore the vacuum to the former pressure, resume heating.

Mercury manometer

The pressure of the system is measured with a closed-end mercury manometer. The manometer (Fig. 7.3) is connected to the system by turning the stopcock until the V-groove in the stopcock is aligned with the side arm. To avoid contamination of the manometer, it should be connected to the system only when a reading is being made. The pressure (in mm Hg) is given by the height (in mm) of the central mercury column above the reservoir of mercury and represents the difference in pressure between the nearly perfect vacuum in the center tube (closed at the top, open at the bottom) and the large volume of the manometer, which is at the pressure of the system.

Another common type of closed-end mercury manometer is shown in Fig. 7.4. At atmospheric pressure, the manometer is completely full of mercury, as shown in Fig. 7.4(a). When the open end is connected to a vacuum, the pressure is measured as the distance in millimeters between the mercury in the right and left legs. Note that the pressure in the left leg is essentially zero (mercury has a low vapor pressure). If the applied vacuum were perfect (0 mm Hg), then the two columns would have the same height.

FIG. 7.3   Closed-end mercury manometer.

FIG. 7.4   Another type of closed-end mercury manometer.

A better vacuum distillation apparatus is shown in Fig. 7.5. The distillation neck of the Claisen adapter is longer than other adapters and has a series of indentations made from four directions, so that the points nearly meet in the center. These indentations increase the surface area over which rising vapor can come to equilibrium with descending liquid, and it then serves as a fractionating column (a Vigreux column). A column packed with a metal sponge has a high tendency to become filled with liquid (flood) at reduced pressure. The apparatus illustrated in Fig. 7.5 also has a fraction collector, which allows the removal of a fraction without disturbing the vacuum in the system. While the receiver is being changed, the distillate collects in the small reservoir A. The clean receiver is evacuated by another aspirator at tube B before being connected again to the system.

If only a few milliliters of a liquid are to be distilled, the apparatus shown in Fig. 7.6 has the advantage of low hold-up—that is, not much liquid is lost

FIG. 7.5   Vacuum distillation apparatus with Vigreux column and fraction collector.

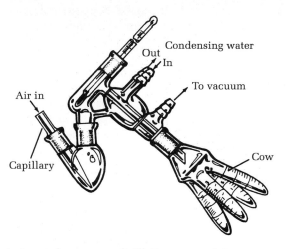

FIG. 7.6   Semimicroscale vacuum distillation apparatus.

FIG. 7.7 Vacuum distillation head.

wetting the surface area of the apparatus. The fraction collector illustrated is known as a "cow." Rotation of the cow about the standard taper joint will allow four fractions to be collected without interrupting the vacuum.

A distillation head of the type shown in Fig. 7.7 allows fractions to be removed without disturbing the vacuum, and it also allows control of the reflux ratio (*see* Chapter 5) by manipulation of the condenser and stopcock A. These can be adjusted to remove all the material that condenses or only a small fraction, with the bulk of the liquid being returned to the distilling column to establish equilibrium between descending liquid and ascending vapor. In this way liquids with small boiling-point differences can be separated.

Microscale Vacuum Distillation Assemblies

On a truly micro scale (<10 mg), simple distillation is not practical because of mechanical losses. On a small scale (10–500 mg), distillation is still not a good method for isolating material, again because of mechanical losses, but bulb-to-bulb distillations can serve to rid a sample of all low-boiling material and nonvolatile impurities. In research, preparative-scale gas chromatography (*see* Chapters 10 and 11) and high-performance liquid chromatography (HPLC) have supplanted vacuum distillation of very small quantities of material.

Fractional distillation of small quantities of liquids is even more difficult. The necessity for maintaining an equilibrium between ascending vapors and descending liquid means there will inevitably be large mechanical losses. The best apparatus for the fractional distillation of about 0.5 to 20 mL under reduced pressure is the so-called micro spinning band column, which has a holdup of about 0.1 mL. Again, preparative-scale gas chromatography and HPLC are the best means for separating mixtures of liquids.

Microscale Apparatus

It is possible to assemble several pieces of apparatus that can be used for simple vacuum distillation using components from the microscale kit. One such assembly is shown in Fig. 7.8. The material to be distilled is placed in the 5-mL short-necked flask packed loosely with glass wool, which will help prevent bumping. The thermometer bulb extends entirely below the side arm, and the distillate is collected in a reaction tube, which can be cooled in a beaker of ice. The vacuum source is connected to a syringe needle, or the rubber tubing from the aspirator, if of the proper diameter, can be connected directly to the adapter, dispensing with the septum and needle.

The Water Aspirator in Vacuum Distillation

A water aspirator in good order produces a vacuum nearly corresponding to the vapor pressure of the water flowing through it. Polypropylene aspirators afford good service and are not subject to corrosion, as are the brass ones. If a manometer is not available and the assembly is free of leaks and the trap and

To aspirator

Glass wool

FIG. 7.8 Microscale apparatus for simple vacuum distillation.

lines clean and dry, an approximate estimate of the pressure can be made by measuring the water temperature and reading the pressure from Table 7.1.

The Rotary Oil Pump

To obtain pressures below 10 mm Hg, a mechanical vacuum pump of the type illustrated in Fig. 7.9(a) is used. A pump of this type in good condition can obtain pressures as low as 0.1 mm Hg. These low pressures are measured with a tilting-type McLeod gauge [Fig. 7.9(b)]. When a reading is being made, the gauge is tilted to the vertical position shown and the pressure is read as the difference between the heights of the two columns of mercury. Between readings the gauge is rotated clockwise 90°.

Dewar should be wrapped with tape or otherwise protected from implosion.

Never use a mechanical vacuum pump before placing a mixture of dry ice and isopropyl alcohol in a Dewar flask [Fig. 7.9(c)] around the trap, and never pump corrosive vapors (e.g., HCl gas) into the pump. Should this happen, change the pump oil immediately. With care, it will give many years of good

TABLE 7.1 Vapor Pressure of Water at Different Temperatures

t (°C)	p (mm Hg)	t (°C)	p (mm Hg)	t (°C)	p (mm Hg)	t (°C)	p (mm Hg)
0	4.58	20	17.41	24	22.18	28	28.10
5	6.53	21	18.50	25	23.54	29	29.78
10	9.18	22	19.66	26	24.99	30	31.55
15	12.73	23	20.88	27	26.50	35	41.85

FIG. 7.9 (a) Rotary oil pump, (b) tilting McLeod gauge, (c) vacuum system.

service. The dry ice trap condenses organic vapors and water vapor, both of which would otherwise contaminate the vacuum pump oil and exert enough vapor pressure to destroy a good vacuum.

For an exceedingly high vacuum (5×10^{-8} mm Hg) a high-speed, three-stage mercury diffusion pump is used (Fig. 7.10).

Relationship Between Boiling Point and Pressure

It is not possible to calculate the boiling point of a substance at some reduced pressure from a knowledge of the boiling temperature at 760 mm Hg because the relationship between boiling point and pressure varies from compound to

FIG. 7.10 High-speed, three-stage mercury diffusion pump capable of producing a vacuum of 5×10^{-8} mm Hg. Mercury is boiled in the flask; the vapor rises in the center tube, is deflected downward in the inverted cups, and entrain gas molecules, which diffuse in from the space to be evacuated, A. The mercury condenses to a liquid and is returned to the flask; the gas molecules are removed at B by an ordinary rotary vacuum pump.

compound and is somewhat unpredictable. It is true, however, that boiling point curves for organic substances have much the same general disposition, as illustrated by the two lower curves in Fig. 7.11. These are similar and do not differ greatly from the curve for water. For substances boiling in the region of 150–250°C at 760 mm Hg, the boiling point at 20 mm Hg is 100–120°C lower

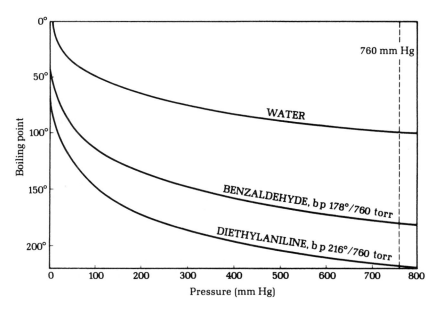

FIG. 7.11   Boiling point curves.

TABLE 7.2   Distillation of a (Hypothetical) Substance at Various Pressures

Method		Pressure (mm Hg)	bp (°C)
Ordinary distillation		760	250
Aspirator { summer		25	144
{ winter		15	134
	poor condition	10	124
Rotary oil pump { good condition		3	99
	excellent condition	1	89
Mercury vapor pump (high vacuum distillation)		0.01	30

than at 760 mm Hg. Benzaldehyde, which is very sensitive to air oxidation at the normal boiling point of 178°C, distills at 76°C at 20 mm Hg, and the concentration of oxygen in the rarefied atmosphere is just $\frac{20}{760}$, or 3% of that in an ordinary distillation.

The curves all show a sharp upward inclination in the region of very low pressure. The lowering of the boiling point attending a reduction in pressure is far more pronounced at low than at high pressures. A drop in the atmospheric pressure of 10 mm Hg lowers the normal boiling point of an ordinary liquid by less than a degree, but a reduction of pressure from 20 to 10 mm Hg causes a drop of about 15°C in the boiling point. The effect at pressures below 1 mm is still more striking, and with development of practical forms of the highly efficient oil vapor or mercury vapor diffusion pump, distillation at a pressure of a few thousandths or ten thousandths of a millimeter has become a standard operation in many research laboratories. High-vacuum distillation—that is, at a pressure below 1 mm Hg—affords a useful means of purifying extremely sensitive or very slightly volatile substances. Table 7.2 indicates the order of magnitude of the reduction in boiling point attainable by operating in different ways and illustrates the importance of keeping vacuum pumps in good repair.

The boiling point of a substance at varying pressures can be estimated from a pressure–temperature nomograph such as the one shown in Fig. 7.12. If the boiling point of a nonpolar substance at 760 mm Hg is known, for example, 145°C (column B), and the new pressure measured, for example, 28 mm Hg (column C), then a straight line connecting these values on columns B and C when extended intersects column A to give the observed boiling point of 50°C. Conversely, a substance observed to boil at 50°C (column A) at 1.0 mm Hg (column C) will boil at approximately 212°C at atmospheric pressure (column B). If the material being distilled is polar, such as a carboxylic acid, column D is used. Thus a substance that boils at 145°C at atmospheric pressure (column B) will boil at 28 mm Hg (column C) if it is nonpolar and at a pressure of 10 mm Hg (column D) if it is polar. The boiling point will be 50°C (column A).

Vacuum distillation is not confined to the purification of substances that are liquid at ordinary temperatures but can often be used to advantage for solid substances. This operation is conducted for a different purpose and by a different technique. A solid is seldom distilled to cause a separation of constituents

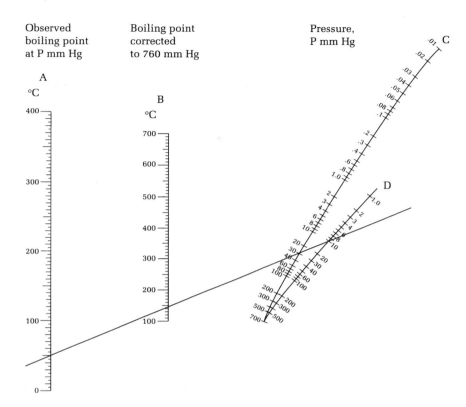

Observed
boiling point
at P mm Hg

Boiling point
corrected
to 760 mm Hg

Pressure,
P mm Hg

FIG. 7.12 Pressure–temperature nomograph.

of differing degrees of volatility but rather to purify the solid. It is often possible in one vacuum distillation to remove foreign coloring matter and tar without any appreciable loss of product, whereas several wasteful crystallizations might be required to attain the same purity. It is often good practice to distill a crude product and then to crystallize it. Time is saved in the latter operation because the hot solution usually requires neither filtration nor clarification. The solid must be dry and a test should be made to determine if it will distill without decomposition at the pressure of the pump available. That a compound lacks the required stability at high temperatures is sometimes indicated by the structure, but a high melting point should not be taken as an indication that distillation will fail. Substances melting as high as 300°C have been distilled with success at the pressure of an ordinary rotary vacuum pump.

Molecular Distillation

At 1×10^{-3} mm Hg the mean free path of nitrogen molecules is 56 mm at 25°C. This means that an average N_2 molecule can travel 56 mm before bumping into another N_2 molecule. In specially designed apparatus it is possible to distill almost any volatile molecule by operating at a very low pressure and

FIG. 7.13 Molecular distillation apparatus.

having the condensing surface close to the material being distilled. The thermally energized molecule escapes from the liquid, moves about 10 mm without encountering any other molecules, and condenses on a cold surface. A simple apparatus for molecular distillation is illustrated in Fig. 7.13. The bottom of the apparatus is placed on a hot surface, and the distillate moves a very short distance before condensing. If it is not too viscous it will drip from the point on the glass condensing surface and run down to the receiver.

The efficiency of molecular distillation apparatus is less than one theoretical plate (*see* Chapter 5). It is used to remove very volatile substances such as solvents and to separate volatile, high-boiling substances at low temperatures from nonvolatile impurities.

In more sophisticated apparatus of quite different design, the liquid to be distilled falls down a heated surface, which is again close to the condenser. This moving film prevents a buildup of nonvolatile material on the surface of the material to be distilled, which would cause the distillation to cease. Vitamin A is distilled commercially in this manner.

Part 2. Sublimation

22   Sublimation is the process whereby a solid evaporates from a warm surface and condenses on a cold surface, again as a solid (Fig. 7.14 and Fig. 7.15). This technique is particularly useful for the small-scale purification of solids because there is so little loss of material in transfer. If the substance possesses the correct properties, sublimation is preferred over crystallization when the amount of material to be purified weighs less than 100 mg.

As demonstrated in the experiment on page 123, sublimation can occur readily at atmospheric pressure. For substances with lower vapor pressures vacuum sublimation is used. At very low pressure the sublimation becomes very similar to molecular distillation, where the molecule leaves the warm solid and passes unobstructed to a cold condensing surface and condenses in the form of a solid.

15-mL **Centrifuge**
tube, to be filled
with ice

Adapter (Pluro stopper)

Pipette
bulb

25-mL Filter flask

Material to
be sublimed

Sublimate

Heat source

FIG. 7.14   Small-scale vacuum
sublimation apparatus.

Vacuum

Sublimate
Water in

Rubber O-ring

Material to
be sublimed

Heat here

Vacuum

Rubber O-ring

Ice

Sublimate goes to here
Material to be sublimed
Heat this surface

(a)   (b)

FIG. 7.15   (a) Mallory sublimator; (b) large vacuum sublimator.

Since sublimation occurs from the surface of the warm solid, impurities can accumulate and slow down or even stop the sublimation, in which case it is necessary to open the apparatus, grind the impure solid to a fine powder, and restart the sublimation.

Sublimation is much easier to carry out on a small scale than on a large one. It would be unusual for a research chemist to sublime more than about 10 g of material because the sublimate tends to fall back to the bottom of the apparatus. In an apparatus such as that illustrated in Fig. 7.15(a), the solid to be sublimed is placed in the lower flask and connected via a lubricant-free rubber O-ring to the condenser, which in turn is connected to a vacuum pump. The lower flask is immersed in an oil bath at the appropriate temperature and the product sublimed and condensed onto the cool walls of the condenser. The parts of the apparatus are gently separated and the condenser inverted; the vacuum connection serves as a convenient funnel for product removal. For large-scale work the sublimator of Fig. 7.15(b) is used. The inner well is filled with a coolant (ice or dry ice). The sublimate clings to this cool surface, from which it can be removed by scraping and dissolving in an appropriate solvent.

Lyophilization

Lyophilization, also called freeze-drying, is the process of subliming a solvent, usually water, with the object of recovering the solid that remains after the solvent is removed. This technique is extensively used to recover heat- and oxygen-sensitive substances of natural origin, such as proteins, vitamins, nucleic acids, and other biochemicals from dilute aqueous solution. The aqueous solution of the substance to be lyophilized is usually frozen to prevent bumping and then subjected to a vacuum of about 1×10^{-3} mm Hg. The water sublimes and condenses as ice on the surface of a large and very cold condenser. The sample remains frozen during this entire process, without any external cooling being supplied, because of the very high heat of vaporization of water; thus the temperature of the sample never exceeds 0°C. Freeze-drying on a large scale is employed to make "instant" coffee, tea, soup, rice, and all sorts of dehydrated foods.

The Kugelrohr

The Kugelrohr (German, meaning "bulb-tube") is a widely used piece of research apparatus that consists of a series of bulbs that can be rotated and heated under vacuum. Bulb-to-bulb distillation frees the desired compound of very low-boiling and very high-boiling or nonvolatile impurities. The crude mixture is placed in bulb A (Fig. 7.16) in the heated glass chamber. At C is a shutter mechanism that holds in the heat but allows the bulbs to be moved out one by one as distillation proceeds. The lowest boiling material collects in bulb D; then bulb C is moved out of the heated chamber, the temperature increased, and the next fraction collected in bulb C. Finally this process is repeated for bulb B. The bulbs rotate under vacuum using a mechanism such as the one used on rotary evaporators. The same apparatus is used for bulb-to-bulb fractional sublimation.

FIG. 7.16   Kugelrohr bulb-to-bulb distillation apparatus.

Experiment

Sublimation of an Unknown Substance

Apparatus and Technique

The apparatus consists of a 15-mL centrifuge tube thrust through an adapter (use a drop of glycerol to lubricate the adapter) fitted in a 25-mL filter flask. Once the adapter is properly positioned on the centrifuge tube it should remain there permanently. This tube is used only for sublimation.

The sample is either ground to a fine powder and uniformly distributed on the bottom of the flask or is introduced into the flask as a solution and the solvent evaporated to deposit the substance on the bottom of the filter flask. If the compound sublimes easily, care must be exercised using the latter technique to ensure that the sample does not evaporate as the last of the solvent is being removed.

The 15-mL centrifuge tube and adapter are placed in the flask so that the tip of the centrifuge tube is about 3 to 8 mm above the bottom of the flask (Fig. 7.14). The flask is clamped with a three-prong clamp. Many substances sublime at atmospheric pressure, including the sublimation unknowns listed in Table 7.3. For vacuum sublimation, the side arm of the flask leads to an aspirator or vacuum pump for reduced pressure sublimation. The centrifuge tube is filled with ice and water. The ice is not added before closing the apparatus, so atmospheric moisture will not condense on the tube.

Sublimation: Add sample to flask, close flask openings, add ice, sublime sample, remove ice, add room-temperature water, open apparatus, and scrape off product.

The filter flask is warmed cautiously on a hot sand bath until the product just begins to sublime. The heat is maintained at that temperature until sublimation is complete. Because some product will collect on the cool upper parts of the flask, it should be fitted with a loose cone of aluminum foil to direct heat

TABLE 7.3 Sublimation Unknowns

Substance	mp (°C)	Substance	mp (°C)
1,4-Dichlorobenzene	55	Benzoic acid	122
Naphthalene	82	Salicylic acid	159
1-Naphthol	96	Camphor	177
Acetanilide	114	Caffeine	235

there and cause the material to collect on the surface of the centrifuge tube. Alternatively, tilt the flask and rotate it in the hot sand, or remove the flask from the sand bath and then use a heat gun to warm the flask.

Once sublimation is judged complete, the ice water is removed from the centrifuge tube with a pipette and replaced with water at room temperature. This will prevent moisture from condensing on the product once the vacuum is turned off and the tube removed from the flask. The product is scraped from the centrifuge tube with a metal spatula onto a piece of glazed paper. It is much easier to scrape the product from a centrifuge tube than from a round-bottomed test tube. The last traces can be removed by washing off the tube with a few drops of an appropriate solvent, if that is deemed necessary.

Procedure

A very simple sublimation apparatus: an inverted stemless funnel on a watch glass

Roll the filter flask in the sand bath or heat it with a heat gun to drive material from the upper walls of the flask.

Into the bottom of a 25-mL filter flask, place 50 mg of an impure unknown taken from the list in Table 7.3. These substances can be sublimed at atmospheric pressure, although some will sublime more rapidly at reduced pressure. Close the flask with a rubber pipette bulb, and then place ice water in the centrifuge tube. Cautiously warm the flask until sublimation starts, and then maintain that temperature throughout the sublimation. Fit the flask with a loose cone of aluminum foil to direct heat up the sides of the flask, causing the product to collect on the tube. Once sublimation is complete, remove the ice water from the centrifuge tube and replace it with water at room temperature. Collect the product, determine its weight and the percent recovery, and from the melting point identify the unknown. Hand in the product in a neatly labeled vial.

Cleaning Up Wash material from the apparatus with a minimum quantity of acetone, which, except for the chloro compound, can be placed in the organic solvents container. The 1,4-dichlorobenzene solution must be placed in the halogenated organic waste container.

For Further Investigation

Room deodorants, for example the Renuzit Long Last adjustable air freshener, appear to sublime. Place about 150 mg, carefully weighed, of the green solid in the filter flask and sublime it with very little heat applied to the flask. Identify the substance that sublimes. Weigh the residue. As an advanced experiment run the IR spectrum (*see* Chapter 12) of the residue (*not* of the substance that sublimes). Comment on the economics of air fresheners.

Questions

1. Has sublimation aided in the purification of the unknown? Justify your answer.

2. From your experience and a knowledge of the process of sublimation, cite some examples of substances that sublime.

3. How might freeze-dried foods be prepared?

4. Describe the mercury level in a manometer like that shown in Fig. 7.4(a) if the left arm is 100 cm tall. [Answer: The difference in height between the column of mercury on the left and the one on the right would be 760 mm, atmospheric pressure.]

CHAPTER

8

Extraction of Acids and Bases and the Isolation of Caffeine from Coffee, Tea, and Cola Syrup

Extraction is one of humankind's oldest chemical operations. The preparation of a cup of coffee or tea involves the extraction of flavor and odor components from dried vegetable matter with hot water. Aqueous extracts of bay leaves, stick cinnamon, peppercorns, and cloves are used as food flavorings, along with alcoholic extracts of vanilla and almond. For the past century and a half, organic chemists have extracted, isolated, purified, and characterized the myriad compounds produced by plants that for centuries have been used as drugs and perfumes—substances such as quinine from cinchona bark, morphine from the opium poppy, cocaine from coca leaves, and menthol from peppermint oil. In research a Soxhlet extractor is often used (Fig. 8.1). The organic chemist commonly employs, in addition to solid/liquid extraction, two other types of extraction: liquid/liquid extraction and acid/base extraction.

Part 1. Liquid/Liquid Extraction

After a chemical reaction has been carried out, the organic product is often separated from inorganic substances by liquid/liquid extraction. For example, in the synthesis of 1-bromobutane (*see* Chapter 16)

$$2\ CH_3CH_2CH_2CH_2OH + 2\ NaBr + H_2SO_4 \rightarrow$$
$$2\ CH_3CH_2CH_2CH_2Br + 2\ H_2O + Na_2SO_4$$

1-butanol, also a liquid, is heated with an aqueous solution of sodium bromide and sulfuric acid to produce the product and sodium sulfate. The 1-bromobutane is isolated from the reaction mixture by extraction with *t*-butyl methyl ether, a solvent in which 1-bromobutane is soluble and in which water and sodium sulfate are insoluble. The extraction is accomplished by simply adding *t*-butyl

Paper thimble

FIG. 8.1 Soxhlet extractor; for extraction of solids, for example, dried leaves or seeds. This solid is put in a filter paper thimble. Solvent vapor rises in the tube on the right, and condensate drops onto the solid in the thimble, leaches out soluble material and, after initiating an automatic siphon, carries it to the flask where nonvolatile extracted material accumulates. Substances of very slight solubility can be extracted by prolonged operation.

methyl ether to the aqueous mixture and shaking it. The *t*-butyl methyl ether is less dense than water and floats on top; it is removed and evaporated to leave the bromo compound free of inorganic substances.

Properties of Extraction Solvents

The solvent used for extraction should possess many properties of a satisfactory recrystallization solvent. It should readily dissolve the substance to be extracted; it should have a low boiling point so that it can be removed readily; it should not react with the solute or the other solvent; it should not be flammable or toxic; and it should be relatively inexpensive. In addition, it should not be miscible with water (the usual second phase). No solvent meets all the criteria, but several do come close. Diethyl ether, usually referred to simply as ether, is probably the most common solvent used for extraction, but it is highly flammable.

$$CH_3CH_2 - O - CH_2CH_3$$

Diethyl ether
"Ether"
MW 74.12, den. 0.708
bp 34.6°C, n_D^{20} 1.3530

In the past, diethyl ether has been the most common solvent for extraction in the laboratory. It has high solvent power for hydrocarbons and for oxygen-containing compounds. It is highly volatile (bp 34.6°C) and is therefore easily removed from an extract. However, diethyl ether has two big disadvantages: it is highly flammable and so poses a great fire threat, and it easily forms peroxides. The reaction of diethyl ether with air is catalyzed by light. The resulting peroxides are higher boiling than the ether and are left as a residue when the ether evaporates. If the residue is heated, it will explode because ether peroxides are treacherous high explosives. In recent years, a new solvent has come on the scene.

tert-Butyl Methyl Ether, the Extraction Solvent of Choice.

$$\begin{array}{c} CH_3 \\ | \\ H_3C - C - O - CH_3 \\ | \\ CH_3 \end{array}$$

tert-Butyl methyl ether
MW 88.14, den. 0.741
bp 55.2°C, n_D^{20} 1.369

tert-Butyl methyl ether, called methyl *tert*-butyl ether (MTBE) in industry, has many advantages over diethyl ether as an extraction solvent. Most important, it does not easily form peroxides, so it can be stored for much longer periods than diethyl ether. And, in the United States, it is less than two-thirds the price of diethyl ether. It is slightly less volatile (bp 55°C), so it does not pose the same fire threat as diethyl ether, although one must be as careful in handling this solvent as in handling any other highly volatile, flammable substance. The explosion limits for *tert*-butyl methyl ether mixed with air are much narrower than for diethyl ether, the toxicity is less (it is not a carcinogen), the solvent power is the same, and the ignition temperature is higher (224 versus 180°C).

The weight percent solubility of diethyl ether dissolved in water is 7.2%, whereas that of the butyl ether is 4.8%. The solubility of water in diethyl ether is 1.2%, while in the butyl ether it is 1.5%. Unlike diethyl ether, *t*-butyl methyl ether forms an azeotrope with water (4% water) that boils at 52.6°C. This means that evaporation of any *t*-butyl methyl ether solution that is saturated with water should leave no water residue, unlike diethyl ether.

The low price and ready availability of *tert*-butyl methyl ether came about because it replaced tetraethyl lead as the antiknock additive for high-octane gasoline and as a fuel oxygenate, which helps reduce air pollution, but its water solubility has allowed it to contaminate drinking water supplies in states where leaking fuel tanks are not well regulated. Consequently, in some areas it is being replaced with much more expensive ethanol. In this text, *tert*-butyl methyl ether is *strongly* suggested wherever diethyl ether formerly would have been used in an extraction. It will not, however, work as the only solvent in the Grignard reaction, probably because of steric hindrance. So whenever the word "ether" appears in this text as an extraction solvent, it is suggested that *tert*-butyl methyl ether be used and not diethyl ether.

Partition Coefficient

The extraction of a compound such as 1-butanol, which is slightly soluble in water as well as very soluble in ether, is an equilibrium process governed by the solubilities of the alcohol in the two solvents. The ratio of the solubilities is known as the *distribution coefficient,* also called the *partition coefficient, k,* and is an equilibrium constant with a certain value for a given substance, pair of solvents, and temperature.

To a good approximation the *concentration* of the solute in each solvent can be correlated with the *solubility* of the solute in the pure solvent, a figure that can be found readily in tables of solubility in reference books. For substance C

$$k = \frac{\text{Concentration of C in } t\text{-butyl methyl ether}}{\text{Concentration of C in water}}$$

$$> \frac{\text{Solubility of C in } t\text{-butyl methyl ether (g/100 mL)}}{\text{Solubility of C in water (g/100 mL)}}$$

Consider a compound, A, that dissolves in *t*-butyl methyl ether to the extent of 12 g/100 mL and dissolves in water to the extent of 6 g/100 mL.

$$k = \frac{12 \text{ g/100 mL } t\text{-butyl methyl ether}}{6 \text{ g/100 mL water}} = 2$$

If a solution of 6 g of A in 100 mL of water is shaken with 100 mL of *t*-butyl methyl ether, then

$$k = \frac{(x \text{ grams of A/100 mL } t\text{-butyl methyl ether})}{(6 - x \text{ grams of A/100 mL water})} = 2$$

from which

$$x = 4.0 \text{ g of A in the ether layer}$$

$$6 - x = 2.0 \text{ g left in the water layer}$$

It is, however, more efficient to extract the 100 mL of aqueous solution twice with 50-mL portions of *t*-butyl methyl ether rather than once with a 100-mL portion.

$$k = \frac{(x \text{ g of A/50 mL})}{(6 - x \text{ g of A/100 mL})} = 2$$

from which

$$x = 3.0 \text{ g in the } t\text{-butyl methyl ether layer}$$

$$6 - x = 3.0 \text{ g in the water layer}$$

If this 3.0 g/100 mL of water is extracted once more with 50 mL of *t*-butyl methyl ether, we can calculate that 1.5 g will be in the ether layer, leaving 1.5 g in the water layer. So two extractions with 50-mL portions of ether will extract 3.0 g + 1.5 g = 4.5 g of A, whereas one extraction with a 100-mL portion of *t*-butyl methyl ether removes only 4.0 g of A. Three extractions with $33\frac{1}{3}$-mL portions of *t*-butyl methyl ether would extract 4.7 g. Obviously there is a point at which the increased amount of A extracted does not repay the effort of multiple extractions, but keep in mind that several small-scale extractions are more effective than one large-scale extraction.

MICROSCALE

13, W

FIG. 8.2 Mixing the contents of a reaction tube by flicking it. Grasp the tube firmly at the very top and flick it vigorously at the bottom. The contents will mix without coming out of the tube.

Always draw out the lower layer and place it in another container.

Technique of Liquid/Liquid Extraction

Place 1 to 2 mL of an aqueous solution of the compound to be extracted in a reaction tube. Add about 1 mL of dichloromethane. Note, as you add the dichloromethane, whether it is the top or bottom layer.

Mixing the Layers.   An effective way to do this is to flick the tube with a finger. Grasp the tube firmly at the very top between thumb and forefinger, and flick it vigorously at the bottom (Fig. 8.2). You will find that this violent motion mixes the contents well, but nothing comes out the top. Another good mixing technique is to pull the contents of the reaction tube into a Pasteur pipette and then expel the mixture back into the tube with force. Doing this several times will effect good mixing of the two layers. A stopper can be placed in the top of the tube and the contents mixed by shaking the tube, but the problem with this technique is that the high vapor pressure of the solvent will often force liquid out around the cork or stopper.

Separating the Layers.   After thoroughly mixing the two layers, allow them to separate. Tap the tube if droplets of one layer are in the other layer or on the side of the tube. After the layers separate completely, draw up the lower dichloromethane layer into a Pasteur pipette. Leave behind any middle emulsion layer. The easiest way to do this is to attach the pipette to a pipette pump (Fig. 8.3). This allows very precise control of the liquid being removed. It takes more skill and practice to remove the lower layer cleanly with a 2-mL rubber bulb attached to the pipette because the high vapor pressure of the solvent tends to make it dribble out. To avoid losing any of the solution, it is best to grasp a clean, dry, empty tube in the same hand as the full tube to receive the organic layer (Fig. 8.4).

From the discussion of the distribution coefficient in the preceding section you know that several small extractions are better than one large one, so repeat the extraction process with two further 1-mL portions of dichloromethane. An

2-mL Pipette
pump

1-mL Pipette
graduated to
± 0.01 mL

Reaction tube

FIG. 8.3   Removal of a solvent
from a reaction tube using a
pipette and pipette pump.

FIG. 8.4   Grasp both reaction
tubes in one hand when
transferring material from one
tube to another using a Pasteur
pipette.

Polyethylene
cap

Glass
column

Micro
Büchner
funnel

FIG. 8.5   Microscale separatory
funnel. Remove the polyethylene
frit from the micro Büchner
funnel before using.

experienced chemist might summarize all the preceding with the notebook entry,
"Aqueous layer extracted 3 × 1-mL portions CH_2Cl_2," and in a formal report
would write, "The aqueous layer was extracted three times with 1-mL portions
of dichloromethane." If any water droplets have been transferred inadvertently,
the easiest way to eliminate them is to again transfer the organic layer to a clean,
dry reaction tube.

 Larger Microscale Technique

A separatory funnel, regardless of size, should be filled to only about two-thirds
of its capacity so the layers can be mixed by shaking. The microscale separatory funnel (Fig. 8.5) has a capacity of 8.5 mL when full, so it is useful for an
extraction with a total volume of about 6 mL.

Poke out the polyethylene frit from the bottom part of the separatory funnel using a wood boiling stick. Store it for later replacement. Close the valve, add up to 5 mL of the solution to be extracted to the separatory funnel, then add the extraction solvent so that the total volume does not exceed 6 mL.

Cap the separatory funnel, and mix the contents by inverting the funnel several times. If the two layers separate fairly easily, then the contents can be shaken more thoroughly. If the layers do not separate easily, be careful not to shake the funnel too vigorously because intractable emulsions could form.

Remove the stopper from the funnel, clamp it, and then, grasping the valve with two hands, empty the bottom layer into an Erlenmeyer flask or other container. If the top layer is desired, pour it out through the top of the separatory funnel at this time—don't drain it through the valve, which may have a drop of the lower layer remaining in it.

Drying the Solvent.   Dichloromethane dissolves a very small quantity of water, and microscopic droplets of water are suspended in the organic layer, often making it cloudy. To remove the water, a drying agent, anhydrous calcium chloride pellets, is added to the dichloromethane solution.

How Much Drying Agent Should Be Used?   When a small quantity of the drying agent is added, the crystals or pellets become sticky with water, clump together, and fall rapidly as a lump to the bottom of the reaction tube. There will come a point when a new small quantity of drying agent no longer clumps together, but the individual particles settle slowly throughout the solution. As they say in Scandinavia, "Add drying agent until it begins to snow." The drying process takes about 10 to 15 min, during which time the tube contents should be mixed occasionally by flicking the tube. The solution should no longer be cloudy, but clear (although it may be colored).

Once drying is judged complete, the solvent is removed by forcing a Pasteur pipette to the bottom of the reaction tube and pulling the solvent in. Air is expelled from the pipette as it is being pushed through the crystals or pellets so that no drying agent will enter the pipette. It is very important to wash the drying agent left in the reaction tube with several small quantities of pure solvent to transfer all the extract.

To water aspirator or to nitrogen or air supply

— Pasteur pipette

FIG. 8.6 Aspirator tube being used to remove solvent vapors.

Removing the Solvent.   If the quantity of extract is relatively small, say three mL or less, then the easiest way to remove the solvent is to blow a stream of air (or nitrogen) onto the surface of the solution from a Pasteur pipette (Fig. 8.6). Be sure that the stream of air is very gentle before inserting it into the reaction tube. The heat of vaporization of the solvent will cause the tube to become rather cold during the evaporation and, of course, slow down the process. The easiest way to add heat is to hold the tube in your hand.

Another way to remove the solvent is to attach the Pasteur pipette to an aspirator and pull air over the surface of the liquid. This is not quite as fast as blowing air onto the surface of the liquid and runs the danger of sucking up the liquid into the aspirator.

If the volume of liquid is more than about three mL, then put it into the 25-mL filter flask, put the plastic Hirsch funnel in place, and attach the flask to the aspirator. By placing your thumb in the Hirsch funnel, the vacuum can be controlled, and heat can be applied by holding the flask in the other hand while swirling the contents (Fig. 8.7).

The reaction tube or filter flask in which the solvent is evaporated should be tared (weighed empty), and this weight recorded in your notebook. In this way, the weight of material extracted can be determined by again weighing the container.

6

Record the tare of the final container.

Experiment

To aspirator

FIG. 8.7 Apparatus for removal of a solvent under vacuum.

⎕ MICROSCALE

Partition Coefficient of Benzoic Acid

IN THIS EXPERIMENT you will shake a solution of benzoic acid in water with the immiscible solvent, dichloromethane. The benzoic acid will distribute (partition) itself between the two layers. By removing the organic layer, drying, and evaporating it, the weight of benzoic acid in the dichloromethane can be determined and thus the ratio in the two layers. This ratio is a constant known as the partition coefficient.

In a reaction tube, place about 100 mg of benzoic acid (weighed to the nearest milligram), and add to this exactly equal volumes of water followed by dichloromethane (about 1.6 mL each). While making this addition, note which layer is the organic layer and which the aqueous. Put a septum on the tube, and shake the contents vigorously for at least 2 min. Allow the tube to stand undisturbed until the layers separate and then carefully draw off, using a Pasteur pipette, *all* the aqueous layer without removing any of the organic layer. It may be of help to draw out the tip of the pipette to a fine point in a flame and, using this, to tilt the reaction tube on its side to make this separation as clean as possible.

Add anhydrous calcium chloride pellets to the dichloromethane in very small quantities until it no longer clumps together. Mix the contents of the tube by flicking it, and allow it to stand for about 5 min to complete the drying process. Using a dry Pasteur pipette, transfer the dichloromethane to a tared dry reaction tube or 10-mL Erlenmeyer flask containing a boiling chip. Complete the transfer by washing the drying agent with two more portions of solvent that are added to the original solution, and then evaporate the solvent. This can be done by boiling off the solvent while removing solvent vapors with an aspirator tube or by blowing a stream of air or nitrogen into the container while warming it in the hand (Fig. 8.6). This operation should be performed in a hood.

From the weight of the benzoic acid in the dichloromethane layer, the weight in the water layer can be obtained by difference. The ratio of the weight in dichloromethane to the weight in water is the distribution coefficient because the volumes of the two solvents were equal. Report the value of the distribution coefficient in your notebook.

Cleaning Up The aqueous layer can be flushed down the drain. Dichloromethane goes into the halogenated organic solvents container and, after allowing the solvent to evaporate from the sodium sulfate in the hood, place it in the nonhazardous solid waste container.

Part 2. Acid/Base Extraction

The third type of extraction, acid/base extraction, involves carrying out simple acid/base reactions in order to separate strong organic acids, weak organic acids, neutral organic compounds, and basic organic substances. The chemistry involved is given in the equations that follow, using benzoic acid, phenol, naphthalene, and aniline as examples of the four types of compounds. Chapter 44 is also an acid/base extraction experiment; the components of analgesic tablets are separated.

Here is the strategy: The four organic compounds are dissolved in *t*-butyl methyl ether. The ether solution is shaken with a saturated aqueous solution of sodium bicarbonate, a weak base. This will react only with the strong acid, benzoic acid (**1**) to form the ionic salt, sodium benzoate (**5**), which dissolves in the aqueous layer and is removed. The ether solution now contains just phenol (**2**), naphthalene (**4**), and aniline (**3**). A 3 *M* aqueous solution of sodium hydroxide is added and the mixture shaken. The hydroxide, a strong base, will react only with the phenol (**2**) a weak acid, to form sodium phenoxide (**6**), an ionic compound that dissolves in the aqueous layer and is removed. The ether now contains only naphthalene (**4**) and aniline (**3**). Shaking it with dilute hydrochloric acid removes the aniline, a base, as the ionic anilinium chloride (**7**). The aqueous layer is removed. Evaporation of the *t*-butyl methyl ether now leaves naphthalene (**4**), the neutral compound. The other three compounds are recovered by adding acid to the sodium benzoate (**5**) and sodium phenoxide (**6**) and base to the anilinium chloride (**7**) to regenerate the covalent compounds benzoic acid (**1**), phenol (**2**), and aniline (**3**). These operations are conveniently represented in a flow sheet (Fig. 8.8).

The ability to separate strong from weak acids depends on the acidity constants of the acids and the basicity constants of the bases as follows. In the first equation consider the ionization of benzoic acid, which has an equilibrium constant, K_a, of 6.8×10^{25}. The conversion of benzoic acid to the benzoate anion in Eq. 4 is governed by the equilibrium constant, K (Eq. 5), obtained by combining the third and fourth equations.

The pK$_a$ of carbonic acid, H$_2$CO$_3$, is 6.35.

$$C_6H_5COOH + H_2O \rightleftharpoons C_6H_5COO^- + H_3O^+ \tag{1}$$

$$K_a = \frac{[C_6H_5COO^-][H_3O^+]}{[C_6H_5COOH]} = 6.8 \times 10^{-5}, pK_a = 4.17 \tag{2}$$

$$K_w = [H_3O^+][OH^-] = 10^{-14} \tag{3}$$

$$C_6H_5COOH + OH^- \rightleftharpoons C_6H_5COO^- + H_2O \tag{4}$$

$$K = \frac{[C_6H_5COO^-]}{[C_6H_5COOH][OH^-]} = \frac{K_a}{K_w} = \frac{6.8 \times 10^{-5}}{10^{-14}} = 3.2 \times 10^8 \tag{5}$$

If 99% of the benzoic acid is converted to $C_6H_5COO^-$

$$\frac{[C_6H_5COO^-]}{[C_6H_5COOH]} = \frac{99}{1} \tag{6}$$

then from Eq. 5 the hydroxide ion concentration would need to be $6.8 \times 10^{-7} M$. Because saturated $NaHCO_3$ has $[OH^-] = 3 \times 10^{-4} M$, the hydroxide ion concentration is high enough to convert benzoic acid completely to sodium benzoate.

$$+ \; Na^+HCO_3^- \longrightarrow \qquad + \; H_2O \; + \; CO_2$$

1
Benzoic acid
$pK_a = 4.17$
Covalent, sol. in org. solvents

5
Sodium benzoate
Ionic, sol. in water

$$+ \; H^+Cl^- \longrightarrow \qquad + \; Na^+Cl^-$$

5

1

$$+ \; Na^+OH^- \longrightarrow \qquad + \; H_2O$$

2
Phenol
$pK_a = 10$
Covalent, sol. in org. solvents

6
Sodium phenoxide
Ionic, sol. in water

$$+ \; H^+Cl^- \longrightarrow \qquad + \; Na^+Cl^-$$

6

2

$$+ \; H^+Cl^- \longrightarrow$$

3
Aniline
$pK_b = 9.30$
Covalent, sol. in org. solvents

7
Anilinium chloride
Ionic, sol. in water

$$+ \; Na^+OH^- \longrightarrow \qquad + \; H_2O \; + \; Na^+Cl^-$$

7

3

In reaction tube A,
1) Dissolve all four compounds in *t*-butyl methyl ether.
2) Mix with HCO_3^-, remove lower aqueous layer, and place it in tube B.

Aqueous layer — Tube B
Ether layer — Tube A

1) Add OH^-, mix, remove lower aqueous layer, and place it in tube C.

Aqueous layer — Tube C
Ether layer — Tube A

1) Add HCl, mix, remove lower aqueous layer, and place it in tube D.

Aqueous layer — Tube D
Ether layer — Tube A

1) Dry solution over anhydrous calcium chloride pellets, remove solvent, and evaporate it to dryness in a clean, dry, tared reaction tube.

5 Add HCl

6 Add HCl

7 Add NaOH

1
Benzoic acid
Forms a white, crystalline precipitate that can be removed by filtration

2
Phenol

3
Aniline

4
Naphthalene

Phenol and aniline each form oily layers on the top of the aqueous layer. Extract each with t-butyl methyl ether: Add ether to the tube, mix, separate layers, dry the ether layer over anhydrous calcium chloride pellets, remove solution from drying agent, and evaporate the solvent.

FIG. 8.8 Flow sheet for the separation of a strong acid, a weak acid, a neutral compound, and a base: benzoic acid, phenol, naphthalene, and aniline.

For phenol with a K_a of 10^{-10}, the minimum hydroxide ion concentration that will produce the phenoxide anion in 99% conversion is 10^{-2} M. The concentration of hydroxide in 10% sodium hydroxide solution is 10^{-1} M, and so phenol in strong base is entirely converted to the water-soluble salt.

Liquid/liquid extraction and acid/base extraction are employed in the majority of organic reactions because it is unusual to have the product crystallize from the reaction mixture or to be able to distill the reaction product directly from the reaction mixture. In the research literature, one will often see the statement "the reaction mixture was worked up in the usual way," which implies an extraction process of the type described here. Good laboratory practice dictates, however, that the details of the process be written out.

Practical Considerations

Emulsions

Imagine trying to extract a soap solution (e.g., a nonfoaming dishwasher detergent) into an organic solvent. After a few shakes with an organic solvent, you would have an absolutely intractable emulsion. An emulsion is a suspension of one liquid as droplets in another. Detergents stabilize emulsions, and so any time a detergentlike molecule happens to be in the material being extracted there is the danger that emulsions will form. Substances of this type are commonly found in nature, so one must be particularly wary of emulsion formation when creating organic extracts of aqueous plant material, such as caffeine from tea. Emulsions, once formed, can be quite stable. You would be quite surprised to open your refrigerator one morning and see a layer of clarified butter floating on the top of a perfectly clear aqueous solution that had once been milk, but that is the classic example of an emulsion.

Shake gently to avoid emulsions.

Prevention is the best cure for emulsions. This means shaking the solution to be extracted *very gently* until you see that the two layers will separate readily. If a bit of emulsion forms it may break simply on standing for a sufficient length of time. Making the aqueous layer highly ionic will help. Add as much sodium chloride as will dissolve, and shake the mixture gently. Vacuum filtration sometimes works and, when the organic layer is the lower layer, filtration through silicone-impregnated filter paper is an aid. Centrifugation works very well for breaking emulsions. This is easy on a small scale, but often the equipment is not available for large-scale centrifugation of organic liquids.

Pressure Buildup

The heat of the hand or heat from acid/base reactions will cause pressure buildup in an extraction mixture that contains a very volatile solvent such as dichloromethane. The extraction container—be it a test tube or a separatory funnel—must be opened carefully to vent this pressure.

Sodium bicarbonate solution is often used to neutralize acids when carrying out acid/base extractions. The result is the formation of carbon dioxide, which can cause foaming and high pressure buildup. Whenever bicarbonate is used, add it very gradually with thorough mixing and frequent venting of the extraction device. If a large amount of acid is to be neutralized with bicarbonate, the process should be carried out in a beaker.

Removal of Water from Extraction Solvents

Saturated aqueous sodium chloride solution removes water from ether.

The organic solvents used for extraction dissolve not only the compound being extracted but also water. Evaporation of the solvent then leaves the desired compound contaminated with water. At room temperature water dissolves 4.8% of *t*-butyl methyl ether by weight, and the ether dissolves 1.5% of water. But ether is virtually insoluble in water saturated with sodium chloride (36.7 g/100 mL). If ether that contains dissolved water is shaken with a saturated aqueous solution of sodium chloride, water will be transferred from the *t*-butyl methyl ether to the aqueous layer. So, strange as it may seem, ethereal extracts are routinely dried by shaking them with an aqueous saturated sodium chloride solution.

Solvents such as dichloromethane do not dissolve nearly as much water and are therefore dried over a chemical drying agent. Many choices of chemical drying agents are available for this purpose, and the choice of which one to use is governed by four factors: the possibility of reaction with the substance being extracted, the speed with which it removes water from the solvent, the efficiency of the process, and the ease of recovery from the drying agent.

Some very good but specialized and reactive drying agents are potassium hydroxide, anhydrous potassium carbonate, sodium metal, calcium hydride, lithium aluminum hydride, and phosphorus pentoxide. Substances that are essentially neutral and unreactive and are widely used as drying agents include anhydrous calcium sulfate (Drierite), magnesium sulfate, molecular sieves, calcium chloride, and sodium sulfate.

Drierite, $CaSO_4$

Drierite, a specially prepared form of calcium sulfate, is a fast and effective drying agent. However, it is difficult to ascertain whether enough has been used. An indicating type of Drierite is impregnated with cobalt chloride, which turns from blue to red when it is saturated with water. This works well when gases are being dried, but should not be used for liquid extractions because the cobalt chloride dissolves in many protic solvents.

Magnesium sulfate, $MgSO_4$

Magnesium sulfate is also a fast and fairly effective drying agent, but it is so finely powdered that it always requires careful filtration for removal.

Molecular sieves, zeolites

Molecular sieves are sodium alumino-silicates (zeolites) that have well-defined pore sizes. The 4A size adsorbs water to the exclusion of almost all organic substances and is a fast and effective drying agent but, like Drierite, it is impossible to ascertain by appearance whether enough has been used. Molecular sieves in the form of 1/16-in. pellets are often used to dry solvents by simply adding them to the container.

Calcium chloride ($CaCl_2$) pellets, the drying agent of choice for small-scale experiments

Calcium Chloride Pellets, the Drying Agent of Choice   *Calcium chloride,* recently available in the form of pellets[1] (4 to 80 mesh), is a very fast

---

1. Fisher, Cat. No. 614-3.

Add anhydrous drying agent until it begins to snow.

and effective drying agent. It has the advantage that it clumps together when excess water is present so that it is possible to know how much to add by observing its behavior. Unlike the older granular form, the pellets do not disintegrate to give a fine powder. These pellets are admirably suited to microscale experiments where the solvent is removed from the drying agent with a Pasteur pipette. It is much faster and far more effective than anhydrous sodium sulfate; after much experimentation, we have decided that this is the agent of choice for microscale experiments in particular. These pellets are used for most of the drying operations in this text. But calcium chloride reacts with some alcohols, phenols, amides, and some carbonyl-containing compounds. Advantage is sometimes taken of this property to remove not only water from a solvent but also, for example, a contaminating alcohol (*see* Chapter 16—the synthesis of 1-bromobutane from 1-butanol). Since *t*-butyl methyl ether forms an azeotrope with water its solutions should, theoretically, not need to be dried; evaporation carries away the water. Drying these ether solutions with calcium chloride pellets removes water droplets that get carried into the ether solution.

Sodium sulfate, Na$_2$SO$_4$

   Sodium sulfate is a very poor drying agent. It has a very high capacity for water but is slow and not very efficient in the removal of water. It, like calcium chloride pellets, clumps together when wet, and solutions are easily removed from it using a Pasteur pipette. It has been used extensively in the past and should still be used for compounds that react with calcium chloride.

MICROSCALE

Benzoic acid
mp 122°C, pK_a 4.17

1,4-Dimethoxybenzene
(Hydroquinone dimethyl ether)
mp 57°C

1. Separation of a Carboxylic Acid, a Phenol, and a Neutral Substance

A mixture of equal parts of a carboxylic acid, a phenol, and a neutral substance is to be separated by extraction from an ether solvent. Note carefully the procedure for this extraction. In the next experiment you are to work out your own extraction procedure. Your unknown will consist of either benzoic acid or 2-chlorobenzoic acid (the carboxylic acid), 4-*tert*-butyl phenol or 4-bromophenol and biphenyl or 1,4-dimethoxybenzene (the neutral substance). The object of this experiment is to identify the three substances in the mixture and to determine the percent recovery of each from the mixture.

Procedure

IN THIS EXPERIMENT three organic solids are separated by reaction with base followed by extraction. Bicarbonate converts carboxylic acids (but not phenols) to ions. Hydroxide ion converts phenols (as well as carboxylic acids) to ions. Ionic substances are soluble in water. Addition of hydrochloric acid to the aqueous ionic solutions regenerates nonionic substances. At each step you should ask yourself, "Have I converted a nonionic substance to an ionic one?" (or vice versa). The ionic substances will be in the aqueous layer, the nonionic ones in the organic layer.

12, V   Dissolve about 0.18 g of the mixture (record the exact weight) in 2 mL of *tert*-butyl methyl ether or diethyl ether in a reaction tube. Then add 1 mL of a saturated aqueous solution of sodium bicarbonate to the tube. Use the graduations on the side of the tube to measure the amounts because they do not need to be exact. Mix the contents of the tube thoroughly by pulling the two layers into a Pasteur pipette and expelling them forcefully into the reaction tube. Do this for about 3 min. Allow the layers to separate completely and then draw off the lower layer into another reaction tube (tube 2). Add another 0.15 mL of sodium bicarbonate solution to the tube, mix the contents as before, and add the lower layer to tube 2. Exactly which chemical species is in tube 2? Add 0.2 mL of ether to tube 2, mix it thoroughly, remove the ether layer, and discard it. This is called *backwashing* and serves to remove any organic material that might contaminate the contents of tube 2.

OH

Br

4-Bromophenol
mp 66°C, pK_a 10.2

Add 1.0 mL of 3 *M* aqueous sodium hydroxide to tube 1, shake the mixture thoroughly, allow the layers to separate, draw off the lower layer using a clean Pasteur pipette, and place it in tube 3. Extract tube 1 with two 0.15-mL portions of water, and add these to tube 3. Backwash the contents of tube 3 with 0.15 mL of ether, and discard the ether wash just as was done for tube 2. Exactly which chemical species is in tube 3?

To tube 1 add saturated sodium chloride solution, mix, remove the aqueous layer, and then add to the ether anhydrous calcium chloride pellets until the drying agent no longer clumps together. Wash it off with ether after the drying process is finished. Allow 5 to 10 min for drying of the ether solution.

Using the concentration information given in the inside back cover of this book, calculate exactly how much concentrated hydrochloric acid is needed to neutralize the contents of tube 2. Then, by dropwise addition of concentrated hydrochloric acid, carry out this neutralization while testing the solution with litmus paper. An excess of hydrochloric acid does no harm. This reaction must be carried out with *extreme care* because much carbon dioxide is released in the neutralization. Add a boiling stick to the tube and very cautiously heat the tube to bring most of the solid carboxylic acid into solution. Allow the tube to cool slowly to room temperature and then cool it in ice. Remove the solvent with a Pasteur pipette and recrystallize the residue from boiling water. Again, allow the tube to cool slowly to room temperature, and then cool it in ice. At the appropriate time stir the crystals and collect them on the Hirsch funnel using the procedures detailed in Chapter 3. The crystals can be transferred and washed on the funnel using a small quantity of ice water. The solubility of benzoic acid in water is 1.9 g/L at 0°C and 68 g/L at 95°C. The solubility of chlorobenzoic acid is similar. Turn the crystals out onto a tared piece of paper, allow them to dry thoroughly, and determine the percent recovery of the acid. Assess the purity of the product by melting point.

In exactly the same way, neutralize the contents of tube 3 with concentrated hydrochloric acid. This time, of course, there will be no carbon dioxide evolution. Again, heat the tube to bring most of the material into solution, allow it to cool slowly, remove the solvent, and recrystallize the phenol from boiling water. At the appropriate time, after the product has cooled slowly to room

Add HCl with care. CO$_2$ is released.

Biphenyl
mp 71°C

G

F

OH

H$_3$C—C—CH$_3$
|
CH$_3$

4-*tert*- Butylphenol
mp 101°C, pK_a 10.17

temperature and then in ice, it is also collected on the Hirsch funnel, washed with a very small quantity of ice water, and allowed to dry. The percent recovery and melting point are determined.

The neutral compound is recovered using the Pasteur pipette to remove the ether from the drying agent and to transfer it to a tared reaction tube. The drying agent is washed two or three times with additional ether to ensure complete transfer of the product.

Best way to remove the solvent: under a gentle stream of air or nitrogen.

Evaporate the solvent by placing the tube in a warm water bath and directing a stream of nitrogen or air onto the surface of the ether in the hood (Fig. 8.6). An aspirator tube also can be used for this purpose. Determine the weight of the crude product, and then recrystallize it from methanol–water if it is the low-melting compound. Reread Chapter 3 for detailed instructions on carrying out this process of crystallization from a mixed solvent. The product is dissolved in about 0.5 to 1 mL of methanol and water is added until the solution gets cloudy, indicating the solution is saturated. This process is best carried out while heating the tube in a hot water bath at 50°C. Allow the tube to cool slowly to room temperature and then cool it thoroughly in ice. If you have the high-melting compound, recrystallize it from ethanol (8 mL/g).

The products are best isolated by collection on the Hirsch funnel using an ice-cold alcohol–water mixture to transfer and wash the compounds. Determine the percent recovery and the melting point. Turn in the products in neatly labeled 1 ½-in. × 1 ½-in. (4 cm × 4 cm) ziplock plastic bags attached to the laboratory report. If the yield on crystallization is low, concentrate the filtrate (the mother liquor) and obtain a second crop of crystals.

2-Chlorobenzoic acid
mp 141°C, pK_a 2.92

☐ MICROSCALE

2. Separation of a Neutral and Basic Substance

In this experiment remember that hydrochloric acid will convert a nonionic amine to an ionic substance and that base will regenerate the nonionic substance from the ionic form. The nonionic and neutral substances are ether-soluble and the ionic substances will be found in the aqueous layer.

Ether vapors are heavier than air and can travel along bench tops, run down drain troughs, and collect in sinks. Be extremely careful to avoid flames when working with volatile ethers.

A mixture of equal parts of a neutral substance, naphthalene or 1,4-dichlorobenzene, and a basic substance, 4-chloroaniline or ethyl 4-aminobenzoate, is to be separated by extraction from an ether solution. Naphthalene and 1,4-dichlorobenzene are completely insoluble in water. The bases will dissolve in hydrochloric acid, while the neutral compounds will remain in ether solution. The bases are insoluble in cold water but will dissolve to some extent in hot water and are soluble in ethanol. Naphthalene and 1,4-dichlorobenzene can be purified as described in Chapter 3. They also sublime very easily. Keep the samples covered.

Plan a step-by-step procedure for separating 200 mg of the mixture into its components, and have the plan checked by the instructor before proceeding. A flow sheet is a convenient way to present the plan. Select the correct solvent or mixture of solvents for the recrystallization of the bases on the basis of solubility tests. Determine the weights and melting points of the isolated and purified products, and calculate the percent recovery of each. Turn in the

Naphthalene
mp 82°C

1,4-Dichlorobenzene
mp 56°C

4-Chloroaniline
mp 68–71°C, pK_b 4.15

Ethyl 4-aminobenzoate
mp 90°C, pK_b 4.92

products in neatly labeled vials or 1 ½-in. × 1 ½-in. ziplock plastic bags attached to the report.

Cleaning Up Combine all aqueous filtrates and solutions, neutralize them, and flush the resulting solution down the drain. Used ether should be placed in the organic solvents container, and the drying agent, once the solvent has evaporated from it, can be placed in the nonhazardous solid waste container. Any 4-chloroaniline or 1,4-dichlorobenzene should be placed in the halogenated waste container.

 MACROSCALE

Apparatus and Operations

In macroscale experiments, a frequently used method of working up a reaction mixture is to dilute the mixture with water and extract with ether in a separatory funnel (Fig. 8.9). When the stoppered funnel is shaken to distribute the components between the immiscible solvents *t*-butyl methyl ether and water, pressure always develops through volatilization of ether from the heat of the hands, and the liberation of a gas (CO_2) can increase the pressure. Consequently, the funnel is grasped so that the stopper is held in place by one hand and the stopcock by the other, as illustrated. After a brief shake or two, the funnel is held in the inverted position shown and the stopcock opened cautiously (with the funnel stem pointed away from nearby persons) to release pressure. The mixture can then be shaken more vigorously and pressure released as necessary. When equilibration is judged to be complete, the slight, constant terminal

Foaming occurs when bicarbonate is added to acid; use care.

2-Chlorobenzoic acid
mp 141°C, pK_a 2.92

1,4-Dichlorobenzene
mp 56°C

 Biphenyl
mp 71°C

4-*t*-Butylphenol
mp 101°C

FIG. 8.9 Correct positions for holding a separatory funnel when shaking. Point outlet away from yourself and your neighbors.

FIG. 8.10 Separatory funnel with Teflon stopcock.

pressure due to ether is released, the stopper is rinsed with a few drops of ether delivered by a Pasteur pipette, and the layers allowed to separate. The organic reaction product is distributed wholly or largely into the upper ether layer, whereas inorganic salts, acids, and bases pass into the water layer, which can be drawn off and discarded. If the reaction was conducted in alcohol or some other water-soluble solvent, the bulk of the solvent is removed in the water layer and the remainder can be eliminated in two or three washings with 1–2 volumes of water conducted with the techniques used in the first equilibration. The separatory funnel should be supported in a ring stand as shown in Fig. 8.10.

If acetic acid was used as the reaction solvent it would also be distributed largely into the aqueous phase, but if the reaction product is a neutral substance the residual acetic acid in the ether can be removed by one washing with excess 5% sodium bicarbonate solution. If the reaction product is a higher molecular weight acid, for example benzoic acid (C_6H_5COOH), it will stay in the ether layer, while acetic acid is being removed by repeated washing

OCH₃

OCH₃

1,4-Dimethoxybenzene
(Hydroquinone dimethyl ether)
mp 57°C

with water; the benzoic acid can then be separated from neutral byproducts by extraction with sodium bicarbonate or sodium hydroxide solution and acidification of the extract. Acids of high molecular weight are extracted only slowly by sodium bicarbonate, so sodium carbonate is used in its place; however, carbonate is more prone than bicarbonate to produce emulsions. Sometimes an emulsion in the lower layer can be settled by twirling the separatory funnel by its stem. An emulsion in the upper layer can be broken by grasping the funnel by the neck and swirling it. Because the tendency to emulsify increases with removal of electrolytes and solvents, a little sodium chloride or hydrochloric acid solution is added with each portion of wash water. If the layers are largely clear but an emulsion persists at the interface, the clear part of the water layer can be drawn off and the emulsion run into a second funnel and shaken with fresh ether.

Before adding a liquid to the separatory funnel, check the stopcock. If it is glass, see that it is properly greased, bearing in mind that too much grease will clog the hole in the stopcock and also contaminate the extract. If the stopcock is Teflon, see that it is adjusted to a tight fit in the bore. Store the separatory funnel with the Teflon stopcock loosened to prevent sticking. Because Teflon has a much larger temperature coefficient of expansion than glass, a stuck stopcock can be loosened by cooling the stopcock in ice or dry ice. Do not store liquids in the separatory funnel; they often leak or cause the stopper or stopcock to freeze. To have sufficient room for mixing the layers, fill the separatory funnel no more than three-fourths full. Withdraw the lower layer from the separatory funnel through the stopcock, and pour the upper layer out through the neck.

All too often the inexperienced chemist discards the wrong layer when using a separatory funnel. Through incomplete neutralization, a desired component may still remain in the aqueous layer or the densities of the layers may change. Cautious workers save all layers until the desired product has been isolated. The organic layer is not always the top layer. If in doubt, test the layers by adding a few drops of each to water in a test tube.

MACROSCALE

$pH = -log\ [H^+]$

$pK_a = acidity\ constant$

$pK_b = basicity\ constant$

3. Separation of Acidic and Neutral Substances

A mixture of equal proportions of benzoic acid, 4-*t*-butylphenol, and 1,4-dimethoxybenzene is to be separated by extraction from *t*-butyl methyl ether. Note the detailed directions for extraction carefully. Prepare a flow sheet (Fig. 8.8) for this sequence of operations. In the next experiment you will work out your own extraction procedure.

Procedure

Dissolve 3 g of the mixture in 30 mL of *t*-butyl methyl ether, and transfer the mixture to a 125-mL separatory funnel (Fig. 8.10) using a little *t*-butyl methyl ether to complete the transfer. Add 10 mL of water, and note which layer is organic and which is aqueous. Add 10 mL of a 3 *M* aqueous solution of

O $\diagdown$ C $\diagup$ OH

Benzoic acid
mp 123°C, pK_a 4.17

OH

H$_3$C — C — CH$_3$

CH$_3$

4-*t*-Butylphenol
mp 101°C

OCH$_3$

OCH$_3$

**1,4-Dimethoxybenzene
(Hydroquinone dimethyl ether)**
mp 57°C   **I**

*Extinguish all flames when
working with* t-*butyl methyl*   **F**
*ether! The best method for
removing the ether is by simple
distillation. Dispose of waste
ether in container provided.*

sodium bicarbonate to the funnel. Swirl or stir the mixture to allow carbon dioxide to escape. Stopper the funnel, and cautiously mix the contents. Vent the liberated carbon dioxide and then shake the mixture thoroughly with frequent venting of the funnel. Repeat the process with another 10 mL of bicarbonate solution. Allow the layers to separate completely, then draw off the lower layer into a 50-mL Erlenmeyer flask (labeled Flask 1). What does this layer contain?

Add 10 mL of 1.5 *M* aqueous sodium hydroxide to the separatory funnel, shake the mixture thoroughly, allow the layers to separate, and draw off the lower layer into a 50-mL Erlenmeyer flask (labeled Flask 2). Repeat the process with another 10 mL of base. Then add an additional 5 mL of water to the separatory funnel, shake the mixture as before, and add this to Flask 2. What does Flask 2 contain?

Add 15 mL of a saturated aqueous solution of sodium chloride to the separatory funnel, shake the mixture thoroughly, allow the layers to separate, and draw off the lower layer, which can be discarded. What is the purpose of adding saturated sodium chloride solution? Carefully pour the ether layer into a 50-mL Erlenmeyer flask (labeled Flask 3) from the top of the separatory funnel, taking great care not to allow any water droplets to be transferred. Add about 4 g of anhydrous calcium chloride pellets to the ether extract, and set it aside.

Acidify the contents of Flask 2 by dropwise addition of concentrated hydrochloric acid while testing with litmus paper. Cool the flask in an ice bath.

Cautiously add concentrated hydrochloric acid dropwise to Flask 1 until the contents are acidic to litmus and then cool the flask in ice.

Decant (pour off) the ether from Flask 3 into a tared flask, taking care to leave all of the drying agent behind. Wash the drying agent with additional ether to ensure complete transfer of the product. If decantation is difficult then remove the drying agent by gravity filtration (*see* Fig. 3.2). Put a boiling stick in the flask, and evaporate the ether in the hood. An aspirator tube can be used for this purpose (Fig. 8.11). Determine the weight of the crude *p*-dimethoxybenzene, and then recrystallize it from methanol. See Chapter 3 for detailed instructions on how to carry out crystallization.

Isolate the *t*-butylphenol from Flask 2 employing vacuum filtration on a Hirsch funnel (*see* Fig. 3.2), and wash it on the filter with a small quantity of ice water. Determine the weight of the crude product and then recrystallize it from ethanol. Similarly isolate, weigh, and recrystallize from boiling water the benzoic acid in Flask 1. The solubility of benzoic acid in water is 1.9 g/L at 0°C and 68 g/L at 95°C.

Dry the purified products, determine their melting points and weights, and calculate the percent recovery of each substance, bearing in mind that the original mixture contained 1 g of each compound. Hand in the three products in neatly labeled vials.

Cleaning Up   Combine all aqueous layers, washes, and filtrates. Dilute with water, neutralize using either sodium carbonate or dilute hydrochloric acid. Methanol filtrate and any ether go in the organic solvents container. Allow ether

FIG. 8.11   Aspirator tube in use.

to evaporate from the calcium chloride in the hood. It can be placed in the non-hazardous solid waste container.

4. Separation of a Neutral and Basic Substance

Naphthalene
mp 82°C

A mixture of equal parts of a neutral substance, naphthalene, and a basic substance, 4-chloroaniline, are to be separated by extraction from *t*-butyl methyl ether solution. The base will dissolve in hydrochloric acid whereas the neutral naphthalene will remain in the *t*-butyl methyl ether solution. 4-Chloroaniline is insoluble in cold water but will dissolve to some extent in hot water and is soluble in ethanol. Naphthalene can be purified as described in Chapter 3.

Plan a procedure for separating 2.0 g of the mixture into its components and have the plan checked by the instructor before proceeding. A flow sheet is a convenient way to present the plan. Using solubility tests, select the correct solvent or mixture of solvents to crystallize 4-chloroaniline. Determine the weights and melting points of the isolated and purified products and calculate the percent recovery of each. Turn in the products in neatly labeled vials.

Handle aromatic amines with care. Most are toxic and some are carcinogenic. Avoid breathing the dust and vapor from the solid and keep the compounds off the skin, best done by wearing gloves.

Cleaning Up   Combine all aqueous filtrates and solutions, neutralize them, and flush the resulting solution down the drain with a large excess of water. Used *t*-butyl methyl ether should be placed in the organic solvents container, and the calcium chloride, once the solvent has evaporated from it, can be placed in the nonhazardous solid waste container. Any 4-chloroaniline should be placed in the chlorinated organic compounds container.

5. Extraction of Caffeine from Tea

Tea and coffee have been popular beverages for centuries, primarily because they contain the stimulant caffeine. It stimulates respiration, the heart, and the central nervous system, and is a diuretic (promotes urination). It can cause nervousness and insomnia and, like many drugs, can be addictive, making it difficult to reduce the daily dose. A regular coffee drinker who consumes just four

NH₂

4-Chloroaniline
mp 68–71°C, pK_b 10.0

cups per day can experience headache, insomnia, and even nausea upon withdrawal from the drug. On the other hand, it helps people to pay attention and can sharpen moderately complex mental skills as well as prolong the ability to exercise.

Caffeine may be the most widely abused drug in the United States. During the course of a day an average person may unwittingly consume up to a gram of this substance. The caffeine content of some common foods and drugs is given in Table 8.1.

Caffeine belongs to a large class of compounds known as alkaloids. These are of plant origin, contain basic nitrogen, often have a bitter taste and complex structure, and usually have physiological activity. Their names usually end in "ine"; many are quite familiar by name if not chemical structure—nicotine, cocaine, morphine, strychnine.

Tea leaves contain tannins, which are acidic, as well as a number of colored compounds and a small amount of undecomposed chlorophyll (soluble in dichloromethane). To ensure that the acidic substances remain water soluble and that the caffeine will be present as the free base, sodium carbonate is added to the extraction medium.

The solubility of caffeine in water is 2.2 mg/mL at 25°C, 180 mg/mL at 80°C, and 670 mg/mL at 100°C. It is quite soluble in dichloromethane, the solvent used in this experiment to extract the caffeine from water.

Caffeine can be extracted from tea bags easily. The procedure one would use to make a cup of tea—simply "steeping" the tea with very hot water for about 7 min—extracts most of the caffeine. There is no advantage to boiling the tea leaves with water for 20 min. Since caffeine is a white, slightly bitter, odorless, crystalline solid, it is obvious that water extracts more than just caffeine. When the brown aqueous solution is subsequently extracted with dichloromethane, primarily caffeine dissolves in the organic solvent. Evaporation

TABLE 8.1 Caffeine Content of Common Foods and Drugs

Espresso	120 mg per 2 oz
Coffee, regular, brewed	103 mg per cup
Instant coffee	57 mg per cup
Coffee, decaffeinated	2 to 4 mg per cup
Tea	30 to 75 mg per cup
Cocoa	5 to 40 mg per cup
Milk chocolate	6 mg per oz
Baking chocolate	35 mg per oz
Coca-Cola, Classic	46 mg per 12 oz
Jolt Cola	72 mg per 12 oz
Anacin, Bromo-Seltzer, Midol	32 mg per pill
Excedrin, extra strength	65 mg per pill
Dexatrim, Dietac, Vivarin	200 mg per pill
Dristan	16 mg per pill
No-Doz	100 mg per pill

of the solvent leaves crude caffeine, which on sublimation yields a relatively pure product. When the concentrated tea solution is extracted with dichloromethane, emulsions can form very easily. There are substances in tea that cause small droplets of the organic layer to remain suspended in the aqueous layer. This emulsion formation results from vigorous shaking. To avoid this problem, it might seem that one could boil the tea leaves with dichloromethane first and then extract the caffeine from the dichloromethane solution with water. In fact this does not work. Boiling 25 g of tea leaves with 50 mL of dichloromethane gives only 0.05 g of residue after evaporation of the solvent. Subsequent extractions give less material. Hot water causes the tea leaves to swell and is obviously a far more efficient extraction solvent. An attempt to sublime caffeine directly from tea leaves was also unsuccessful.

Microscale Procedure

M In a 30-mL beaker place 15 mL of water, 2 g of sodium carbonate, and a wooden boiling stick. Bring the water to a boil on the sand bath, remove the boiling stick, and brew a very concentrated tea solution by immersing a tea bag (2.4 g tea) in the very hot water for 5 min. After the tea bag cools enough to handle, and being careful not to break the bag, squeeze as much water from the bag as possible. Again bring the water to a boil and add a new tea bag to the hot solution. After 5 min, remove the tea bag, and squeeze out as much water as possible. This can be done easily on the Hirsch funnel. Rinse the bag with a few mL of very hot water, but be sure the total volume of aqueous extract does not exceed 12 mL. Pour the extract into a 15-mL centrifuge tube, and cool the solution in ice to below 40°C (the boiling point of dichloromethane).

CAUTION: Do not breathe the vapors of dichloromethane and, if possible, work with this solvent in the hood.

Using three 2-mL portions of dichloromethane, extract the caffeine from the tea. Cork the tube and use a gentle rocking motion to carry out the extraction. Vigorous shaking will produce an intractable emulsion, whereas extremely gentle mixing will fail to extract the caffeine. If you have ready access to a centrifuge, the shaking can be very vigorous because any emulsions formed can be broken fairly well by centrifugation for about 90 sec. After each extraction, remove the lower organic layer into a reaction tube, leaving any emulsion layer behind. Dry the combined extracts over anhydrous calcium chloride pellets for 5 or 10 min in an Erlenmeyer flask. Add the drying agent in portions with shaking until it no longer clumps together. Transfer the dry solution to a tared 25-mL filter flask, wash the drying agent twice with 2-mL portions of dichloromethane, and evaporate it to dryness (Fig. 8.7). The residue will be crude caffeine (determine its weight) that is to be purified by sublimation.

Balance the centrifuge tubes.

Fit the filter flask with a Pluro stopper or no. 2 neoprene adapter through which is thrust a 15-mL centrifuge tube. Put a pipette bulb on the side arm. Clamp the flask with a large three-prong clamp, fill the centrifuge tube with ice and water, and heat the flask on a hot sand bath (Fig. 8.12). Caffeine is reported to sublime at about 170°C. Tilt the filter flask and rotate it in the hot sand bath to drive more caffeine onto the centrifuge tube. Use a heat gun to heat the upper walls of the filter flask. When sublimation ceases, remove the ice water from

Labels on the figure:

- 15-mL Centrifuge tube, to be filled with ice
- Adapter (Pluro stopper)
- Pipette bulb
- 25-mL Filter flask
- Material to be sublimed
- Sublimate
- Heat source

FIG. 8.12 Sublimation apparatus.

the centrifuge tube, and allow the flask to cool somewhat before removing the centrifuge tube. Scrape the caffeine onto a tared weighing paper, weigh, and using the plastic funnel, transfer it to a small vial or a plastic bag. At the discretion of the instructor, determine the melting point using a sealed capillary. The melting point of caffeine is 238°C. Using the centrifugation technique to separate the extracts, about 30 mg of crude caffeine can be obtained. This will give you 10 to 15 mg of sublimed material, depending on the caffeine content of the particular tea being used. The isolated caffeine can be used to prepare caffeine salicylate (Experiment 7).

Cleaning Up Discard the tea bags in the nonhazardous solid waste container. Allow the solvent to evaporate from the drying agent, and discard in the same container. Place any unused and unrecovered dichloromethane in the chlorinated organic compounds container. The apparatus can be cleaned with soap and hot water. Caffeine can be flushed down the drain, since it is biodegradable.

Macroscale Procedure

To an Erlenmeyer flask containing 25 g of tea leaves (or 10 tea bags) and 20 g of sodium carbonate, add 225 mL of vigorously boiling water. Allow the mixture to stand for 7 min and then decant into another Erlenmeyer flask. To the hot tea leaves add another 50 mL of hot water and then immediately decant and combine with the first extract. Very little, if any, additional caffeine is extracted by boiling the tea leaves for 20 min. Decantation works nearly as well as vacuum filtration and is much faster.

CAUTION: Carry out this work with dichloromethane in the hood.

Rock the separatory funnel very gently to avoid emulsions.

Cool the aqueous solution to near room temperature, and extract it twice with 30-mL portions of dichloromethane. Take great care not to shake the separatory funnel so vigorously as to cause emulsion formation, bearing in mind that if it is not shaken vigorously enough the caffeine will not be extracted into the organic layer. Use a gentle rocking motion of the separatory funnel. Drain off the dichloromethane layer on the first extraction; include the emulsion layer on the second extraction. Dry the combined dichloromethane solutions and any emulsion layer with anhydrous calcium chloride pellets. Add sufficient drying agent until it no longer clumps together on the bottom of the flask. Carefully decant or filter the dichloromethane solution into a tared Erlenmeyer or distilling flask. Silicone-impregnated filter paper passes dichloromethane and retains water. Wash the drying agent with a further portion of solvent and evaporate or distill the solvent. A wooden stick is better than a boiling chip to promote smooth boiling because it is easily removed once the solvent is gone. The residue of greenish-white crystalline caffeine should weigh about 0.25 g.

Dispose of used dichloromethane in the container provided.

 D Crystallization of Caffeine. To recrystallize the caffeine, dissolve it in 5 mL of hot acetone, transfer it with a Pasteur pipette to a small Erlenmeyer flask and, while it is hot, add ligroin to the solution until a faint cloudiness appears. Set the flask aside and allow it to cool slowly to room temperature. This mixed-solvent method of recrystallization depends on the fact that caffeine is far more soluble in acetone than ligroin, so a combination of the two solvents can be found where the solution is saturated in caffeine (the cloud point). Cool the solution containing the crystals and remove them by vacuum filtration, employing the Hirsch funnel or a very small Büchner funnel. Use a few drops of ligroin to transfer the crystals and wash the crystals. If you wish to obtain a second crop of crystals, collect the filtrate in a test tube, concentrate it to the cloud point using the aspirator tube (*see* Fig. 3.21), and repeat the crystallization process.

Cleaning Up The filtrate can be diluted with water and washed down the drain. Any dichloromethane collected goes into the halogenated organic waste container. After the solvent is allowed to evaporate from the drying agent in the hood, it can be placed in the nonhazardous solid waste container; otherwise it goes in the hazardous waste container. The tea leaves go in the nonhazardous solid waste container.

 MICROSCALE AND MACROSCALE

6. Extraction of Caffeine from Cola Syrup

Coca-Cola was originally flavored with extracts from the leaves of the coca plant and the kola nut. Coca is grown in northern South America; the Indians of Peru and Bolivia have for centuries chewed the leaves to relieve the pangs of hunger and sensitivity to high mountain cold. The cocaine from the leaves causes local anesthesia of the stomach. It has limited use as a local anesthetic for surgery on the eye, nose, and throat. Unfortunately, it is now a widely abused illicit drug. Kola nuts contain about 3% caffeine as well as a number of other

Caffeine
mp 238°C

Cocaine

CAUTION: Do not breathe the vapor of dichloromethane. Work with this solvent in the hood.

alkaloids. The kola tree is in the same family as the cacao tree from which cocoa and chocolate are obtained. Modern cola drinks do not contain cocaine; however, Coca-Cola contains 43 mg of caffeine per 12-oz serving. The acidic taste of many soft drinks comes from citric, tartaric, phosphoric, and benzoic acids.

Automatic soft drink dispensing machines mix a syrup with carbonated water. In the following experiment caffeine is extracted from concentrated cola syrup.

Microscale Procedure

Add 1 mL of concentrated ammonium hydroxide to a mixture of 5 mL commercial cola syrup and 5 mL of water in a 15-mL centrifuge tube. Add 1 mL dichloromethane and tip the tube gently back and forth for 5 min. Do not shake the mixture as in a normal extraction because an emulsion will form and the layers will not separate. After the layers have separated as much as possible, remove the clear lower layer, leaving the emulsion behind. Using 1.5 mL dichloromethane, repeat the extraction in the same way twice more. At the final separation, include the emulsion layer with the dichloromethane. If a centrifuge is available, the mixture can be shaken vigorously and the emulsion broken by centrifugation for 90 sec. Combine the extracts in a reaction tube and dry the solution with anhydrous calcium chloride pellets. Add the drying agent with shaking until it no longer clumps together. After 5 to 10 min, remove the solution with a Pasteur pipette and place it in a tared filter flask. Wash off the drying agent with more dichloromethane and evaporate the mixture to dryness. Determine the crude weight of caffeine, then sublime it as described in the preceding experiment.

Macroscale Procedure

Add 10 mL of concentrated ammonium hydroxide to a mixture of 50 mL of commercial cola syrup and 50 mL of water. Place the mixture in a separatory funnel, add 50 mL of dichloromethane, and swirl the mixture and tip the funnel back and forth for at least 5 min. Do not shake the solutions together as in a normal extraction because an emulsion will form and the layers will not separate. An emulsion is made up of droplets of one phase suspended in the other (milk is an emulsion). Separate the layers. Repeat the extraction with a second 50-mL portion of dichloromethane. From your knowledge of the density of dichloromethane and water you should be able to predict which is the top layer and which is the bottom layer. If in doubt, add a few drops of each layer to water. The aqueous layer will be soluble; the organic layer will not. Combine the dichloromethane extracts and any emulsion that has formed in a 125-mL Erlenmeyer flask, then add anhydrous calcium chloride pellets to remove water from the solution. Add the drying agent until it no longer clumps together at the bottom of the flask but swirls freely in solution. Swirl the flask with the drying agent from time to time over a 10-min period. Carefully decant (pour off) the dichloromethane or remove it by filtration through a fluted filter paper, add

Chlorinated solvents are toxic, insoluble in water, expensive, and should never be poured down the drain.

about 5 mL more solvent to the drying agent to wash it, and decant this also. Combine the dried dichloromethane solutions in a tared flask and remove the dichloromethane by distillation or evaporation on the steam bath. Remember to add a wooden boiling stick to the solution to promote even boiling. Determine the weight of the crude product.

Crystallization of Caffeine

To recrystallize the caffeine dissolve it in 5 mL of hot acetone, transfer it with a Pasteur pipette to a small Erlenmeyer flask and, while it is hot, add ligroin to the solution until a faint cloudiness appears. Set the flask aside and allow it to cool slowly to room temperature. This mixed-solvent method of recrystallization depends on the fact that caffeine is far more soluble in acetone than ligroin, so a combination of the two solvents can be found where the solution is saturated in caffeine (the cloud point). Cool the solution containing the crystals and remove them by vacuum filtration, employing the Hirsch funnel or a very small Büchner funnel. Use a few drops of ligroin to transfer the crystals and wash the crystals. If you wish to obtain a second crop of crystals, collect the filtrate in a test tube, concentrate it to the cloud point using the aspirator tube (*see* Fig. 3.9), and repeat the crystallization process.

Cleaning Up   Combine all aqueous filtrates and solutions, neutralize them, and flush the resulting solution down the drain. Used dichloromethane should be placed in the halogenated waste container, and the drying agent, once the solvent has evaporated from it, can be placed in the nonhazardous solid waste container. The ligroin–acetone filtrates should be placed in the organic solvents container.

Sublimation of Caffeine

Sublimation is a fast and easy way to purify caffeine. Using the apparatus depicted in Fig. 8.12, sublime the crude caffeine at atmospheric pressure following the procedure in Part 2 of Chapter 7.

MICROSCALE

7. Isolation of Caffeine from Instant Coffee

Instant coffee, according to manufacturers, contains between 55 and 62 mg of caffeine per 6-oz cup, and a cup is presumably made from a teaspoon of the powder, which weighs 1.3 g; so 2 g of the powder should contain 85 to 95 mg of caffeine. Unlike tea, however, coffee contains other compounds that are soluble in dichloromethane, so obtaining pure caffeine from coffee is not easy. The object of this experiment is to extract instant coffee with dichloromethane (the easy part) and then to try to devise a procedure for obtaining pure caffeine from the extract.

From the thin-layer chromatography you may deduce that certain impurities have a high R_f value in hydrocarbons (in which caffeine is insoluble). Consult reference books (see especially the *Merck Index*) to determine the solubility (and lack of solubility) of caffeine in various solvents. You might try trituration (grinding the crude solid with a solvent) to dissolve impurities preferentially. Column chromatography is another possible means of purifying the product. Or you might convert all of it to the salicylate and then regenerate the caffeine from the salicylate. Experiment! Or you can simply follow the following procedure.

Procedure

IN THIS EXPERIMENT a very concentrated aqueous solution of coffee is prepared and shaken vigorously with an organic solvent to make an intractable emulsion that can be broken (separated into two layers) by centrifugation. Caffeine is isolated by crystallization.

    In a 10-mL Erlenmeyer flask, place 2 g of sodium carbonate and 2 g of instant coffee powder. Add to this 9 mL of boiling water, stir the mixture well, bring it to a boil again with stirring, cool it to room temperature, and then pour it into a 15-mL plastic centrifuge tube fitted with a screw cap. Add 2 mL of dichloromethane, cap the tube, shake it vigorously for 60 sec; then centrifuge it at high speed for 90 sec. Remove the clear yellow dichloromethane layer and place it in a 10-mL Erlenmeyer flask. Repeat this process twice more. To the combined extracts add anhydrous calcium chloride pellets until they no longer clump together, allow the solution to dry for a few minutes, then transfer it to a tared 25-mL filter flask and wash the drying agent with more solvent. Remove the solvent as was done in the tea extraction experiment and determine the weight of the crude caffeine. You should obtain about 60 mg of crude product. Sublimation of this orange powder gives an impure orange sublimate that smells strongly of coffee, so sublimation is not a good way to purify this material.

Caffeine has no odor.

    Dissolve a very small quantity of the product in a drop of dichloromethane and analyze the crude material by thin-layer chromatography. Dissolve the remainder of the material in 1 mL of boiling 95% ethanol, then dilute the mixture with 1 mL of *tert*-butyl methyl ether, heat to boiling, and allow to cool slowly to room temperature. Long, needlelike crystals should form in the orange

D   solution. Alternatively, crystallize the product from a 1:1 mixture of ligroin [hexane(s)] and 2-propanol, using about 2 mL. Cool the mixture in ice for at least 10 min, and then collect the product on the Hirsch funnel. Complete the transfer with the filtrate and then wash the crystals twice with cold 50/50 ethanol/*tert*-butyl methyl ether. The yield of white fluffy needles of caffeine should be more than 30 mg.

Cleaning Up   Allow the solvent to evaporate from the drying agent and discard it in the nonhazardous waste container. Place any unused and unrecovered dichloromethane in the chlorinated organic solvents container.

MICROSCALE AND MACROSCALE

8. Caffeine Salicylate

Preparation of a derivative of caffeine.

One way to confirm the identity of an organic compound is to prepare a derivative of it. Caffeine melts and sublimes at 238°C. It is an organic base and can therefore accept a proton from an acid to form a salt. The salt formed when caffeine combines with hydrochloric acid, like many amine salts, does not have a sharp melting point; it merely decomposes when heated. But the salt formed from salicylic acid, even though ionic, has a sharp melting point and can thus be used to help characterize caffeine. See Fig. 8.13 for the ^{1}H NMR spectrum of caffeine.

Caffeine   **Salicylic acid**   **Caffeine salicylate**

Procedure

CAUTION: Petroleum ether is very flammable. Extinguish all flames.

The quantities given can be multiplied by 5 or 10 if necessary. To 10 mg of sublimed caffeine in a tared reaction tube add 7.5 mg of salicylic acid and 0.5 mL of dichloromethane. Heat the mixture to boiling and add petroleum

FIG. 8.13 ^{1}H NMR spectrum of caffeine (250 MHz).

Crystallization from mixed solvents

ether (a poor solvent for the product) dropwise until the mixture just turns cloudy, indicating the solution is saturated. If too much petroleum ether is added, then clarify it by adding a very small quantity of dichloromethane. Insulate the tube in order to allow it to cool slowly to room temperature, then cool it in ice. The needlelike crystals are isolated by removing the solvent with a Pasteur pipette while the reaction tube is in the ice bath. Evaporate the last traces of solvent under vacuum (Fig. 8.14) and determine the weight of the derivative and its melting point. Caffeine salicylate is reported to melt at 137°C.

G

7

Cleaning Up   Place the filtrate in the halogenated organic solvents container.

To aspirator

Glass tube

Thermometer adapter

Reaction tube

Beaker of warm water

Crystals to be dried

FIG. 8.14 Drying of crystals under vacuum in beaker of warm water.

Questions

1. Suppose a reaction mixture, when diluted with water, afforded 300 mL of an aqueous solution of 30 g of the reaction product malononitrile, $CH_2(CN)_2$, which is to be isolated by extraction with ether. The solubility of malononitrile in ether at room temperature is 20.0 g per 100 mL, and in water is 13.3 g per 100 mL. What weight of malononitrile would be recovered by extraction with (a) three 100-mL portions of ether; (b) one 300-mL portion of ether? *Suggestion:* For each extraction let x equal the weight extracted into the ether layer. In case (a) the concentration in the ether layer is $x/100$, and in the water layer is $(30 - x)/300$; the ratio of these quantities is equal to $k = 20/13.3$.

2. Why is it necessary to remove the stopper from a separatory funnel when liquid is being drained from it through the stopcock?

3. The pK_a of *p*-nitrophenol is 7.15. Would you expect this to dissolve in sodium bicarbonate solution? The pK_a of 2,5-dinitrophenol is 5.15. Will it dissolve in bicarbonate solution?

4. The distribution coefficient, k = (conc. in ligroin/conc. in water), between ligroin and water for solute A is 7.5. What weight of A would be removed from a solution of 10 g of A in 100 mL of water by a single extraction with 100 mL of ligroin? What weight of A would be removed by four successive extractions with 25-mL portions of ligroin? How much ligroin would be required to remove 98.5% of A in a single extraction?

5. In Experiment 1, how many moles of benzoic acid are present? How many moles of sodium bicarbonate are contained in 1 mL of a 10% aqueous solution? (A 10% solution has 1 g of solute in 9 mL of solvent.) Is the amount of sodium bicarbonate sufficient to react with all of the benzoic acid?

6. To isolate the benzoic acid from the bicarbonate solution, it is acidified with concentrated hydrochloric acid in Experiment 1. What volume of acid is needed to neutralize the bicarbonate? The concentration of hydrochloric acid is expressed in various ways on the inside back cover of this laboratory manual.

7. How many moles of 2-naphthol are in the mixture to be separated in Experiment 1? How many moles of sodium hydroxide are contained in 1 mL of 5% sodium hydroxide solution? (Assume the density of the solution is 1.0.) What volume of concentrated hydrochloric acid is needed to neutralize this amount of sodium hydroxide solution?

8. Draw a flow sheet to show how you would separate the components of a mixture containing an acid substance, toluic acid, a basic substance, *p*-bromo-aniline, and a neutral substance, anthracene.

Surfing the Web

http://ull.chemistry.uakron.edu/organic_lab/distribution/
This University of Akron site with some 15 graphics shows the macroscale determination of the distribution coefficient (partition coefficient) of crotonic acid and benzoic acid in the water/dichloromethane system. The concentration of acid in the aqueous phase is determined by titration.

http://ull.chemistry.uakron.edu/organic_lab/cola/index.html
The extraction of caffeine from 10 mL of cola syrup (Experiment 4) is very clearly demonstrated in 14 color photos. Preparation of caffeine salicylate (Experiment 5) is demonstrated with 8 close-up color photos.

CHAPTER

9

Thin-Layer Chromatography: Analysis of Analgesics and Isolation of Lycopene from Tomato Paste

PRELAB EXERCISE: Compare thin-layer chromatography with column chromatography with regard to: (1) quantity of material that can be separated; (2) the time needed for the analysis; (3) the solvent systems; and (4) the ability to separate compounds.

Thin-layer chromatography (TLC) is a sensitive, fast, simple, and inexpensive analytical technique that you will be using repeatedly while carrying out organic experiments. It is a micro technique; as little as 10^{-9} g of material can be detected, although the usual sample size is from 1 to 100×10^{-6} g.

TLC requires micrograms of material.

TLC involves spotting the sample to be analyzed near one end of a sheet of glass or plastic that is coated with a thin layer of an adsorbent. The sheet, which can be the size of a microscope slide, is placed on end in a covered jar containing a shallow layer of solvent. As the solvent rises by capillary action up through the adsorbent, differential partitioning occurs between the components of the mixture dissolved in the solvent and the stationary adsorbent phase. The more strongly a given component of the mixture is adsorbed onto the stationary phase, the less time it will spend in the mobile phase, and the more slowly it will migrate up the TLC plate.

Uses of Thin-Layer Chromatography

1. **To determine the number of components in a mixture.** TLC affords a quick and easy method for analyzing such things as a crude reaction mixture, an extract from some plant substance, or a painkiller. Knowing the number and relative amounts of the components aids in planning further analytical and separation steps.
2. **To determine the identity of two substances.** If two substances spotted on the same TLC plate give spots in identical locations, they *may* be identical. If the spot positions are not the same, the substances cannot be the same. It is possible for two closely related compounds that are not identical to have the same positions on a TLC plate.

3. **To monitor the progress of a reaction.** By sampling a reaction from time to time it is possible to watch the reactants disappear and the products appear using TLC. Thus, the optimum time to halt the reaction can be determined, and the effect of changing such variables as temperature, concentrations, and solvents can be followed without having to isolate the product.

4. **To determine the effectiveness of a purification.** The effectiveness of distillation, crystallization, extraction, and other separation and purification methods can be monitored using TLC, with the caveat that a single spot does not guarantee a single substance.

5. **To determine the appropriate conditions for a column chromatographic separation.** Thin-layer chromatography is generally unsatisfactory for purifying and isolating macroscopic quantities of material; however, the adsorbents most commonly used for TLC—silica gel and alumina—are used for column chromatography, discussed in the next chapter. Column chromatography is used to separate and purify up to a gram of a solid mixture. The correct adsorbent and solvent used to carry out the chromatography can be determined rapidly by TLC.

6. **To monitor column chromatography.** As column chromatography is carried out, the solvent is collected in a number of small flasks. Unless the desired compound is colored, the various fractions must be analyzed in some way to determine which ones have the desired components of the mixture. TLC is a fast and effective method for doing this.

Adsorbents and Solvents

The two most common coatings for thin-layer chromatography plates are alumina (Al_2O_3) and silica gel (SiO_2).These are the same adsorbents most commonly used in column chromatography (*see* Chapter 10) for the purification of macroscopic quantities of material. Of the two, alumina, when anhydrous, is the more active, that is, it will adsorb substances more strongly. It is thus the adsorbent of choice when the separation involves relatively nonpolar substrates such as hydrocarbons, alkyl halides, ethers, aldehydes, and ketones. To separate the more polar substrates such as alcohols, carboxylic acids, and amines, the less active adsorbent, silica gel, is used. In an extreme situation very polar substances on alumina do not migrate very far from the starting point (give low R_f values), and nonpolar compounds travel with the solvent front (give high R_f values) if chromatographed on silica gel. These extremes of behavior are markedly affected, however, by the solvents used to carry out the chromatography. A polar solvent will carry along with it polar substrates, and nonpolar solvents will do the same with nonpolar compounds—another example of the generalization "like dissolves like."

R_f is the ratio of the distance the spot travels from the origin to the distance the solvent travels.

Avoid the use of benzene, carbon tetrachloride, and chloroform. Benzene is a carcinogen; the others are suspected carcinogens.

Table 9.1 lists common solvents used in chromatography, both thin-layer and column. Only the environmentally safe solvents are listed; the polarities of such solvents as benzene, carbon tetrachloride, or chloroform can be matched by other less toxic solvents. In general these solvents are characterized by

TABLE 9.1 Chromatography Solvents

Solvent	bp (°C)
Petroleum ether (pentanes)	35–36
Ligroin (hexanes)	60–80
Dichloromethane	40
t-Butyl methyl ether	55
Ethyl acetate	77
Acetone	56
2-Propanol	82
Ethanol	78
Methanol	65
Water	100
Acetic acid	118

TABLE 9.2 Order of Solute Migration on Chromatography

Solute	Solute
Fastest	*Slowest*
Alkanes	Ketones
Alkyl halides	Aldehydes
Alkenes	Amines
Dienes	Alcohols
Aromatic hydrocarbons	Phenols
Aromatic halides	Carboxylic acids
Ethers	Sulfonic acids
Esters	

having low boiling points and low viscosities that allow them to migrate rapidly. They are listed in order of increasing polarity. A solvent more polar than methanol is seldom needed. Often just two solvents are used in varying proportions; the polarity of the mixture is a weighted average of the two. Ligroin–ether mixtures are often employed in this way.

The order in which solutes migrate on thin-layer chromatography is the same as the order of solvent polarity. The largest R_f values are shown by the least polar solutes. In Table 9.2 the solutes are arranged in order of increasing polarity.

Apparatus and Procedure

A very dilute solution (1%) of the test substance is employed for TLC.

A 1% solution of the substance to be examined is spotted onto the plate about 1 cm from the bottom end, then the plate is inserted into a beaker or a 4-oz wide-mouth bottle containing 4 mL of an organic solvent. The bottle is lined with filter paper wet with solvent to saturate the atmosphere within the container. The top is put in place and the time noted. The solvent travels rapidly up in the thin layer by capillary action, and if the substance is a pure colored compound, one soon sees a spot traveling either along with the solvent front or, more usually, at some distance behind the solvent front. One can remove the slide, quickly mark the front before the solvent evaporates, and calculate the R_f value. The R_f value is the ratio of the distance the spot travels from the point of origin to the distance the solvent travels (Fig. 9.1). The best separations are achieved when the R_f value falls between 0.3 and 0.7.

Visualization of the Chromatogram

Colored compounds

And colorless ones

If the substances being chromatographed are colored, then it is possible to detect the compounds visually. Colorless substances can be detected when the solvent is allowed to evaporate and the plate allowed to stand in a stoppered 4-oz bottle containing a few crystals of iodine. Iodine vapor is adsorbed by the organic compound to form a brown spot. A spot should be outlined at once with a pencil

FIG. 9.1 Thin-layer chromatography plate.

because it will soon disappear as the iodine sublimes away; brief return to the iodine chamber will regenerate the spot. The order of elution and the elution power for solvents are the same as for column chromatography.

The use of commercial TLC sheets such as Whatman flexible plates for TLC, cat. no. 4410 222 (Fisher cat. no. 05-713-162), is strongly recommended. These poly(ethylene terephthalate) (Mylar) sheets are coated with silica gel using polyacrylic acid as a binder. A fluorescent indicator has been added to the silica gel so that when the sheet is observed under 254-nm UV (ultraviolet) light, spots that either quench or enhance fluorescence can be seen. Iodine can also be used to visualize spots. The coating on these sheets is only 100 μm thick, so very small spots must be applied. Unlike student-prepared plates, these coated sheets (cut with scissors to 1" $\times$ 3") give very consistent results. A light pencil mark 1 cm from the end will guide spotting. A supply of these precut sheets makes it a simple matter to examine most of the reactions in this book for completeness of reaction, purity of product, and side reactions.

Many specialized spray reagents have been developed that give specific colors for certain types of compounds. There is a large amount of literature on the solvents and adsorbents for use in the separation of a wide variety of substances.[1]

TLC tests for
1. Completeness of reaction
2. Purity of product
3. Side reactions

Spotting Test Solutions

It is extremely important that the spots be as small as possible and that they be applied using a 1% (not 2% or more) solution of the compounds being separated. This is done with micropipettes made by drawing open-end mp

---

1. Egon Stahl, *Thin-Layer Chromatography* (New York: Springer Verlag), 1969.

FIG. 9.2 (a) Micropipette. (b) Making a micropipette, which is pulled from a melting point capillary that is open on each end. Heat it at the base of the flame as shown.

capillaries in a burner flame (Fig. 9.2). The bore of these capillaries should be so small that once a liquid is drawn in to them it will not flow out to form a drop. To spot a test solution, let a 2–3 cm column of solution flow into the pipette by capillary action, hold this vertically over a coated plate, aim it at a point on the right side of the plate and about 1 cm from the bottom, and lower the pipette until the tip just touches the adsorbent. Only then will liquid flow onto the plate; withdraw the capillary when the spot is about 1 mm in diameter. Make a second 1-mm spot on the left side of the plate, let it dry, and make two more applications of the same size (1 mm) at the same place. Determine whether the large or the small spot gives the better results. The center of the letter *o* on this page is more than 1 mm in diameter. The distance between the sides of the letter *n* is 1 mm.

Experiments

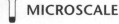 **MICROSCALE**

1. Analgesics

Analgesics are substances that relieve pain. The most common of these is aspirin, a component of more than 100 nonprescription drugs. In Chapter 41, the history and background of this most popular drug is discussed. In the present experiment, analgesic tablets will be analyzed by thin-layer chromatography to determine which analgesics they contain and whether they contain caffeine, which is often added to counteract the sedative effects of the analgesic.

In addition to aspirin and caffeine, the most common components of analgesics are at present acetaminophen and ibuprofen (Motrin). In addition to one

Aspirin
Acetylsalicylic acid

Acetaminophen
4-Acetamidophenol

Ibuprofen
2-(4-Isobutylphenyl)propionic acid

Caffeine

or more of these substances, each tablet contains a binder, often starch, micro-crystalline cellulose, or silica gel. And to counteract the acidic properties of aspirin, an inorganic buffering agent is added to some analgesics. Inspection of labels will reveal that most cold remedies and decongestants contain both aspirin and caffeine in addition to the primary ingredient.

Because of the insoluble binder, not all the unknown will dissolve.

To identify an unknown by TLC, the usual strategy is to run chromatograms of known substances (the standards) and the unknown at the same time. If the unknown has one or more spots that correspond to spots with the same R_f values as the standards, then those substances are probably present.

Proprietary drugs that contain one or more of the common analgesics and sometimes caffeine are sold under the names of Bayer Aspirin, Anacin, Datril, Advil, Excedrin, Extra Strength Excedrin, Tylenol, and Vanquish. Note that ibuprofen has a chiral carbon atom. One enantiomer is more effective than the other.

Procedure

Following the procedure outlined earlier, draw a light pencil line about 1 cm from the end of a chromatographic plate. On this line spot aspirin, acetaminophen, ibuprofen, and caffeine, which are available as reference standards. Use a

FIG. 9.3   A method for developing TLC plates.

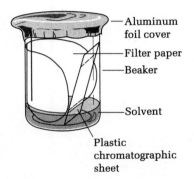

FIG. 9.4   An alternative method for developing TLC plates.

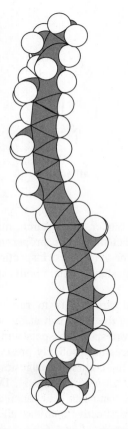

FIG. 9.5   An energy-minimized, space-filling model of lycopene. The molecule is flat, but steric hindrance of the methyl groups causes the molecule to bend into the S shape.

separate capillary for each standard, or rinse the capillary carefully. Make each spot as small as possible, preferably less than 0.5 mm in diameter. Examine the plate under the ultraviolet (UV) light to see that enough of each compound has been applied; if not, add more. On a separate plate run the unknown and one or more of the standards.

The unknown sample is prepared by crushing a part of a tablet, adding this powder to a test tube or small vial along with an appropriate amount of ethanol, and then mixing the suspension. Not all of the crushed tablet will dissolve, but enough will go into solution to spot the plate. The binder—starch or silica—will not dissolve. Try to prepare a 1% solution of the unknown.

Use as the solvent for the chromatogram a mixture of 95% ethyl acetate and 5% acetic acid (Fig. 9.3 or 9.4). After the solvent has risen to near the top of the plate, mark the solvent front with a pencil, remove the plate from the developing chamber, and allow the solvent to dry. Examine the plate under UV light to see the components as dark spots against a bright green-blue background. Outline the spots with a pencil. The spots can also be visualized by putting the plate in an iodine chamber made by placing a few crystals of iodine in the bottom of a capped 4-oz jar. Calculate the R_f values for the spots, and identify the components in the unknown.

Cleaning Up   Solvents should be placed in the organic solvents container, and dry, used chromatographic plates can be discarded in the nonhazardous solid waste container.

2. Plant Pigments

The botanist Michael Tswett discovered the technique of chromatography and applied it, as the name implies, to colored plant pigments. The leaves of plants contain, in addition to chlorophyll-a and -b, other pigments that are revealed in the fall when the leaves die and the chlorophyll rapidly decomposes. Among the most abundant of the other pigments are the carotenoids, which include the carotenes and their oxygenated homologs, the xanthophylls. The bright orange β-carotene is the most important of these because it is transformed in the liver to vitamin A, which is required for night vision.

Cows eat fresh, green grass that contains carotene, but they do not metabolize the carotene entirely, so it ends up in their milk. Butter made from this milk is therefore yellow. In the winter the silage cows eat does not contain carotene because it readily undergoes air oxidation, and the butter made at that time is white. For some time an azo dye called Butter Yellow was added to winter butter to give it the accustomed color, but the dye was found to be a carcinogen. Now winter butter is colored with synthetic carotene, as is all margarine.

Lycopene (Fig. 9.5), the red pigment of the tomato, is a C_{40}-carotenoid made up of eight isoprene units. β-Carotene, the yellow pigment of the carrot, is an isomer of lycopene in which the double bonds at C_1—C_2 and C'_1—C'_2 are replaced by bonds extending from C_1 to C_6 and from C'_1 to C'_6 to form rings. The chromophore in each case is a system of 11 all-*trans* conjugated double bonds; the closing of the two rings renders β-carotene less highly pigmented than lycopene.

Fresh tomato fruit is about 96% water, and R. Willstätter and H. R. Escher isolated from this source 20 mg of lycopene per kilogram of fruit. They then found a more convenient source in commercial tomato paste, from which seeds and skin have been eliminated and the water content reduced by evaporation in vacuum to a content of 26% solids. From this they isolated 150 mg of lycopene per kilogram of paste. The expected yield in the present experiment is 0.075 mg.

A jar of strained carrots sold as baby food serves as a convenient source of β-carotene. The German investigators isolated 1 g of β-carotene per kilogram of "dried" shredded carrots of unstated water content.

The following procedure calls for dehydration of tomato or carrot paste with ethanol and extraction with dichloromethane, an efficient solvent for lipids.

Lycopene and β-carotene from tomato paste and strained carrots

As an interesting variation, try extraction of lycopene from commercial catsup.

Experimental Considerations

Carotenoids are very sensitive to light-catalyzed air oxidation. Perform this experiment as rapidly as possible; keep solutions as cool and dark as possible. This extraction produces a mixture of products that can be analyzed by both TLC and column chromatography (*see* Chapter 10). If enough material for TLC only is desired, use one-tenth the quantities of starting material and solvents employed in the following procedure. This extraction can also be carried out with hexane if the ventilation is not adequate to use dichloromethane. Hexane is more prone to form emulsions than the chlorinated solvent.

CAUTION: *Do not breathe the vapors of dichloromethane. Carry out the extraction in the hood. Dichloromethane is a suspected carcinogen.*

 MICROSCALE AND MACROSCALE

Procedure

IN THIS EXPERIMENT some tomato or carrot paste is treated with acetone, which will remove water and lipids but not the highly colored carotenoid hydrocarbons.

Chlorophyll-a

β-Carotene (C₄₀H₅₆)
mp 183°C, λ_{max}^{hexane} 451 nm

3′-Dehydrolutein (a xanthophyll)

Butter Yellow
(carcinogenic)

Lycopene (C₄₀H₅₆)
MW 536.85
mp 173°C, λ_{max}^{hexane} 475 nm

The carotenoids are extracted by dichloromethane and analyzed by thin-layer chromatography.

A 5-g sample of fresh tomato or carrot paste (baby food) is transferred to the bottom of a 25 × 150 mm test tube followed by 10 mL of acetone. The mixture is stirred and shaken before being filtered on the Hirsch funnel. Scrape as much of the material from the tube as possible, and press it dry on the funnel. Let the tube drain thoroughly. Place the filtrate in a 125-mL Erlenmeyer flask.

Return the solid residue to the test tube, shake it with a 10-mL portion of dichloromethane, and again filter the material on the Hirsch funnel. Add the filtrate to the 125-mL flask. Repeat this process twice more, then pour the combined filtrates into a separatory funnel. Add water and sodium chloride solution (which aids in the breaking of emulsions), and shake the funnel gently. This aqueous extraction will remove the acetone and any water-soluble components from the mixture, leaving the hydrocarbon carotenoids in the dichloromethane. Dry the colored organic layer over anhydrous calcium chloride, and filter the solution into a dry flask. Remove about 0.5 mL of this solution and store it under nitrogen in the dark until it can be analyzed by thin-layer chromatography. Evaporate the remainder of the dichloromethane solution to dryness under a stream of nitrogen or under vacuum on a rotary evaporator. This material will be used for column chromatography (*see* Chapter 10). If it is to be stored, fill the flask with nitrogen and store it in a dark place.

Air can be used for the evaporation, but nitrogen is better because these hydrocarbons air-oxidize with great rapidity.

Thin-Layer Chromatography

Spot the mixture on a TLC plate about 1 cm from the bottom and 8 mm from the edge. Make one spot concentrated by repeatedly touching the plate, but ensure that the spot is as small as possible, certainly less than 1 mm in diameter. The other spot can be of lower concentration. Develop the plate with 80:20 hexane:acetone. With other plates you could try cyclohexane and toluene as eluents and also hexane–ethanol mixtures of various compositions.

Many spots may be seen. There are two common carotene and chlorophyll isomers and four xanthophyll isomers.

The container in which the chromatography is carried out should be lined with filter paper that is wet with the solvent so that the atmosphere in the container will be saturated with solvent vapor. On completion of elution, mark the solvent front with a pencil, and outline the colored spots. Examine the plate under UV light. Also place the plate in an iodine chamber to visualize spots (see next experiment).

Cleaning Up   The aqueous saline filtrate containing acetone can be flushed down the drain. Recovered and unused dichloromethane should be placed in the halogenated organic waste container; the solvents used for TLC should be placed in the organic solvents container; and the drying agents, once free of solvents, can be placed in the nonhazardous solid waste container along with the used plant material and the TLC plates.

MICROSCALE AND MACROSCALE

Procedure

In a small mortar grind 2 g of green or brightly colored fall leaves (don't use ivy or waxy leaves) with 10 mL of ethanol, pour off the ethanol, which serves to break up and dehydrate the plant cells, and grind the leaves successively with three 1-mL portions of dichloromethane that are decanted or withdrawn with a Pasteur pipette and placed in a test tube. The pigments of interest are extracted by the dichloromethane. Alternatively, place 0.5 g of carrot paste (baby food) or tomato paste in a test tube, stir and shake the paste with 3 mL of ethanol until the paste has a somewhat dry or fluffy appearance, remove the ethanol, and extract the dehydrated paste with three 1-mL portions of dichloromethane. Stir and shake the plant material with the solvent in order to extract as much of the pigments as possible.

Fill the tube containing the dichloromethane extract from leaves or vegetable paste with a saturated sodium chloride solution, and shake the mixture. Remove the aqueous layer and to the dichloromethane solution add anhydrous calcium chloride pellets until the drying agent no longer clumps together. Shake the mixture with the drying agent for about 5 min, then withdraw the solvent with a Pasteur pipette and place it in a test tube. Add to the solvent a few pieces of Drierite to complete the drying process. Gently stir the mixture for about 5 min, transfer the solvent to a test tube, wash off the drying agent with more solvent, and then evaporate the combined dichloromethane solutions under a stream of nitrogen while warming the tube in the hand or in a beaker of warm water. Carry out this evaporation in the hood.

These hydrocarbons air-oxidize with great rapidity.

Immediately cork the tube filled with nitrogen, then add a drop or two of dichloromethane to dissolve the pigments for TLC analysis. Carry out the analysis without delay by spotting the mixture on a TLC plate about 1 cm from the bottom and 8 mm from the edge. Make one spot concentrated by repeatedly touching the plate, but ensure that the spot is as small as possible—less than 1.0 mm in diameter. The other spot can be of lower concentration. Develop the plate with 70:30 hexane:acetone. With other plates try cyclohexane and toluene as eluents and also hexane–ethanol mixtures of various compositions. The container in which the chromatography is carried out should be lined with filter paper that is wet with the solvent so the atmosphere in the container will be saturated with solvent vapor. On completion of elution, mark the solvent front with a pencil and outline the colored spots. Examine the plate under the UV light. Are any new spots seen? Report colors and R_f values for all of your spots and identify each as lycopene, carotene, chlorophyll, or xanthophyll.

Cleaning Up   The ethanol used for dehydration of the plant material can be flushed down the drain along with the saturated sodium chloride solution. Recovered and unused dichloromethane should be placed in the halogenated organic waste container. The solvents used for TLC should be placed in the organic solvents container. The drying agents, once free of solvents, can be placed in the nonhazardous solid waste container along with the used plant material and TLC plates.

3. For Further Investigation

Many of the pigments in plants are made up of compounds called *anthocyanins*. Grind about 4 g of colored plant tissue (flower petals, blueberries, strawberries, cranberries, apple skins, red cabbage, red or purple grapes, etc.) and a small amount of alumina or fine sand with about 4 mL of 99% methanol/1% hydrochloric acid. Spot the extract on cellulose TLC plates and elute with a solvent mixture of 20% concentrated hydrochloric acid, 40% water and 4% formic acid. Note the number and color of the spots. Look up the structures of the possible anthocyanins, of which many are glycosides of the aglycones delphinidin, peonidin, malvidin, cyanidin, and so on.

 MICROSCALE AND MACROSCALE

4. Colorless Compounds

You are now to apply the thin-layer technique to a group of colorless compounds. The spots can be visualized under an ultraviolet light if the plates have been coated with a fluorescent indicator, or chromatograms can be developed in a 4-oz bottle containing crystals of iodine. During development, spots appear rapidly, but remember that they also disappear rapidly. Therefore, outline each spot with a pencil immediately on withdrawal of the plate from the iodine chamber. Suggested solvents are as follows:

Cyclohexane	Toluene (3 mL)–dichloromethane (1 mL)
Toluene	9:1 Toluene–methanol (use 4 mL)

Make your own selections.

Compounds for trial are to be selected from the following list (all 1% solutions in toluene):

Except for tetraphenylthiophene, the structures for all of these molecules will be found in this book.

1. Anthracene*
2. Cholesterol
3. 2,7-Dimethyl-3,5-octadiyne-2,7-diol
4. Diphenylacetylene
5. *trans,trans*-1,4-Diphenyl-1,3-butadiene*
6. *p*-Di-*t*-butylbenzene
7. 1,4-Di-*t*-butyl-2,5-dimethoxybenzene
8. *trans*-Stilbene
9. 1,2,3,4-Tetraphenylnaphthalene*
10. Tetraphenylthiophene
11. *p*-Terphenyl*
12. Triphenylmethanol
13. Triptycene

*Fluorescent under UV light.

Preliminary trials on used plates

It is up to you to make selections and to plan your own experiments. Do as many as time permits. One plan would be to select a pair of compounds estimated to be separable and that have R_f values determinable with the same solvent. One can assume that a hydroxyl compound will travel less rapidly with a hydrocarbon solvent than a hydroxyl-free compound; you will therefore know

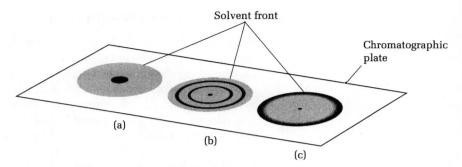

FIG. 9.6 Fast method for determining the correct solvent for TLC. See text for procedure.

what to expect if the solvent contains a hydroxylic component. An aliphatic solvent should carry along an aromatic compound with aliphatic substituents better than one without such groups. However, instead of relying on assumptions, you can do brief preliminary experiments on used plates upon which previous spots are visible or outlined. If you spot a pair of compounds on such a plate and let the solvent rise about 3 cm from the starting line before development, you might be able to tell if a certain solvent is appropriate for a given sample. Alternatively, make some spots on a plate (new or used) and then touch each spot with a different solvent held in a capillary. In Fig. 9.6(a), the mixture did not move away from the point of origin; in Fig. 9.6(b), two concentric rings are seen between the origin and the solvent front. This is how a good solvent behaves. In Fig. 9.6(c), the mixture of compounds traveled with the solvent front.

Once a solvent is chosen, run a complete chromatogram on the two compounds on a fresh plate. If separation of the two seems feasible, put two spots of one compound on a plate, let the solvent evaporate, and put spots of the second compound over the first ones. Run a chromatogram and see if you can detect two spots in either lane (with colorless compounds, it is advisable not to attempt a three-lane chromatogram until you have acquired considerable practice and skill).

Cleaning Up   Solvents should be placed in the organic solvents container, and dry, used chromatographic plates can be discarded in the nonhazardous solid waste container.

Discussion

If you have investigated hydroxylated compounds, you doubtless have found that it is reasonably easy to separate a hydroxylated from a nonhydroxylated compound, or a diol from a mono-ol. How, by a simple reaction followed by a thin-layer chromatogram, could you separate cholesterol from triphenylmethanol? Heating a sample of each with acetic anhydride-pyridine for 5 min on the steam bath, followed by chromatography, should do it. A first trial of a new reaction leaves questions about what has happened and how much, if any, starting material is present. A comparative chromatogram of reaction mixture with starting material may tell the story. How crude is a crude reaction product? How many components are present? The thin-layer technique may give the answers to these questions and suggest how best to process the product. A preparative column chromatogram may afford a large number of fractions of eluent (say, 1 to 30). Some fractions probably contain nothing and should be discarded, while others should be combined for evaporation and workup. How can you identify the good and the useless fractions? Take a few used plates and put numbered circles on clean places of each; spot samples of each of the fractions; and, without any chromatography, develop the plates with iodine. Negative fractions for discard will be obvious, and the pattern alone of positive fractions may allow you to infer which fractions can be combined. Thin-layer chromatograms of the first and last fractions of each suspected group would then show whether or not your inferences are correct.

Fluorescence

Never look into a UV lamp.

Four of the compounds listed in Experiment 3 are fluorescent under UV light. These compounds give colorless spots that can be picked up on a chromatogram by fluorescence (after removal from the UV-absorbing glass bottle). If a UV light source is available, spot the four compounds on a used plate and observe the fluorescence.

Take this opportunity to examine a white shirt or handkerchief under UV light to see if it contains a brightener, that is, a fluorescent white dye or optical bleach. These substances are added to counteract the yellow color that

Calcofluor White MR

7-Diethylamino-4-methylcoumarin

repeated washing gives to cloth. Brighteners of the type of Calcofluor White MR, a sulfonated *trans*-stilbene derivative, are commonly used in detergent formulations for cotton; the substituted coumarin derivative is typical of brighteners used for nylon, acetate, and wool. Detergents normally contain 0.1–0.2% of optical bleach. The amount of dye on a freshly laundered shirt is approximately 0.01% of the weight of the fabric.

Questions

1. Why might it be very difficult to visualize the separation of *cis*- and *trans*-2-butene by thin-layer chromatography?

2. What error is introduced into the determination of an R_f value if the top is left off of the developing chamber?

3. What problem will ensue if the level of the developing liquid is higher than the applied spot in a TLC analysis?

4. In what order (from top to bottom) would you expect to find naphthalene, butyric acid, and phenyl acetate on a silica gel TLC plate developed with dichloromethane?

5. In carrying out an analysis of a mixture, what do you expect to see when the TLC plate has been allowed to remain in the developing chamber too long, so that the solvent front has reached the top of the plate?

6. Arrange the following in order of increasing R_f on thin-layer chromatography: acetic acid, acetaldehyde, 2-octanone, decane, and 1-butanol.

7. What will be the result of applying too much compound to a TLC plate?

8. Why is it necessary to run TLC in a closed container and to have the interior vapor saturated with the solvent?

9. What will be the appearance of a TLC plate if a solvent of too low polarity is used for the development? too high polarity?

10. A TLC plate showed two spots of R_f 0.25 and 0.26. The plate was removed from the developing chamber, dried carefully, and returned to the developing chamber. What would you expect to see after the second development was complete?

11. One of the analgesics has a chiral center. Which compound is it? One of the two enantiomers is far more effective at reducing pain than the other.

12. Using a ruler to measure distances, calculate the R_f value for Substance B in Fig. 9.1.

CHAPTER
10

Column Chromatography: Acetylferrocene, Cholesteryl Acetate, and Fluorenone

Column chromatography is one of the most useful methods for the separation and purification of both solids and liquids when carrying out small-scale experiments. It becomes expensive and time consuming, however, when more than about 10 g of material must be purified.

The application in the present experiment is typical: A reaction is carried out, it does not go to completion, and so column chromatography is used to separate the product from starting material, reagents, and by-products.

The theory of column chromatography is analogous to that of thin-layer chromatography. The most common adsorbents—silica gel and alumina—are the same ones used in TLC. The sample is dissolved in a small quantity of solvent (the eluent) and applied to the top of the column. The eluent, instead of rising by capillary action up a thin layer, flows down through the column filled with the adsorbent. Just as in TLC, there is an equilibrium established between the solute adsorbed on the silica gel or alumina and the eluting solvent flowing down through the column. Under some conditions the solute may be partition-ing between an adsorbed solvent and the elution solvent; the partition coefficient, just as in the extraction process, determines the efficiency of separation in chromatography. The partition coefficient is determined by the solubility of the solute in the two phases, as was discussed in the extraction experiments (*see* Chapter 8).

Three mutual interactions must be considered in column chromatography: the polarity of the sample, the polarity of the eluting solvent, and the activity of the adsorbent.

Adsorbent

A large number of adsorbents have been used for column chromatography—cellulose, sugar, starch, inorganic carbonates—but most separations employ alumina (Al_2O_3) and silica gel (SiO_2). Alumina comes in three forms: acidic, neutral, and basic. The neutral form of Brockmann activity II or III, 150 mesh, is most commonly employed. The surface area of this alumina is about 150 m^2/g. Alumina as purchased will usually be activity I, meaning it will strongly adsorb solutes. It must be deactivated by adding water, shaking, and allowing the mixture to reach equilibrium over an hour or so. The amount of water needed to achieve certain activities is given in Table 10.1. The activity of the alumina on

TABLE 10.1 Alumina Activity

Brockmann activity	I	II	III	IV	V
Percent by weight of water	0	3	6	10	15

TLC plates is usually about III. Silica gel for column chromatography, 70–230 mesh, has a surface area of about 500 m^2/g and comes in only one activity.

Solvents

Petroleum ether: mostly isometric pentanes; ligroin: mostly isomeric hexanes

The elutropic series for a number of solvents is given in Table 10.2. The solvents are arranged in increasing polarity, with *n*-pentane being the least polar. This is the order of ability that these solvents possess to dissolve polar organic compounds and to dislodge a polar substance adsorbed onto either silica gel or alumina, with *n*-pentane having the lowest solvent power.

As a practical matter, the following sequence of solvents is recommended in an investigation of unknown mixtures: elute first with petroleum ether (pentanes); then ligroin (hexanes), followed by ligroin containing 1%, 2%, 5%, 10%, 25%, and 50% ether; pure ether; ether and dichloromethane mixtures; followed by dichloromethane and methanol mixtures. A sudden change in solvent polarity will cause heat evolution as the alumina or silica gel adsorbs the new solvent. This will cause undesirable vapor pockets and cracks in the column. Either diethyl ether or *t*-butyl methyl ether can be used. *t*-Butyl methyl ether is recommended.

TABLE 10.2 Elutropic Series for Solvents

n-Pentane (least polar)
Petroleum ether
Cyclohexane
Ligroin
Carbon disulfide
t-Butyl methyl ether
Dichloromethane
Tetrahydrofuran
Dioxane
Ethyl acetate
2-Propanol
Ethanol
Methanol
Acetic acid (most polar)

Solutes

The ease with which different classes of compounds elute from a column is indicated in Table 10.3. The order is similar to that of the eluting solvents—another application of "like dissolves like."

Sample and Column Size

TABLE 10.3 Elution Order for Solutes

Alkanes (first)
Alkenes
Dienes
Aromatic hydrocarbons
Ethers
Esters
Ketones
Aldehydes
Amines
Alcohols
Phenols
Acids (last)

The amount of alumina or silica gel used should generally weigh at least 30 times as much as the sample and the column, when packed, should have a height at least 10 times the diameter. The density of silica gel is 0.4 g/mL, and the density of alumina is 0.9 g/mL, so the optimum size for any column can be calculated. A microscale column for the chromatography of about 50 mg of material is shown in Fig. 10.1.

Packing the Chromatography Column

Uniform packing of the chromatography column is critical to the success of this technique. The sample is applied as a pure liquid or, if it is a solid, as a very concentrated solution in the solvent that will dissolve it best, regardless of polarity.

As elution takes place, this narrow band of sample will separate into several bands corresponding to the number of components in the mixture and their relative polarities and molecular weights. It is essential that the components move through the column as a narrow horizontal band in order to come off the column in the least volume of solvent and not overlap with other components of the mixture. The column should therefore be vertical, and the packing should be perfectly uniform, without voids caused by air bubbles.

The preferred method for packing silica gel and alumina columns is the slurry method, whereby a slurry of the adsorbent and the first eluting solvent is made and poured into the column. When nothing is known about the mixture being separated, thin-layer chromatography should be carried out first to acertain the best solvents to use in the column chromatography.

Microscale Procedure

27, N

Packing the Column. Assemble the column as depicted in Fig. 10.1. To measure the adsorbent, fill the column one-half to two-thirds full, then pour the powder into a 10-mL Erlenmeyer flask. Clamp the column in a vertical position and close the valve. Always grasp the valve with one hand while turning it with the other. Fill the apparatus with ligroin or hexane to the top of the glass column. Add about 8 mL hexane to the adsorbent in the flask, stir the mixture to eliminate air bubbles, then (this is the hard part) swirl the mixture to get the adsorbent suspended in the solvent and immediately pour the entire slurry into the funnel. Open the valve, drain some solvent into the flask that had the adsorbent in it, and finish transferring the slurry to the column. Place an empty flask under the column and allow the solvent to drain to about 5 mm above the top surface of the adsorbent. *Never allow the column to dry out*; this creates channels that will result in uneven bands and poor separation.

Adding the Sample and Eluting the Column. Dissolve the sample completely in the very minimum volume of dichloromethane (just a few drops) in an Erlenmeyer flask. Add to this solution 300 mg of the adsorbent, stir, and evaporate the solvent completely. Heat the flask *very gently* with *constant* stirring to avoid having the material bump. Remember that dichloromethane boils at 55°C. Pour this dry powder into the funnel of the chromatography column, wash it down onto the column with a few drops of hexane, and then tap the column to remove air bubbles from this layer of adsorbent-solute mixture just added. Open the valve and carefully add new solvent in such a manner that the top surface of the column is not disturbed. A thin layer of fine sand can be added to the column after the sample to avoid disturbance of the column surface when the solvent is being added. Run the solvent down near to the surface several times to apply the sample as a narrow band at the top of the column. Then fill the column with the solvent and elute the sample from the column.

Funnel

Glass column

Alumina

Micro Büchner funnel

Polyethylene frit

10-mL Erlenmeyer flask

FIG. 10.1 Microscale chromatographic column.

Macroscale Procedure

Extinguish all flames; work in laboratory hood.

The column can be prepared using a 50-mL burette such as the one shown in Fig. 10.2 or using the less expensive and equally satisfactory chromatographic tube shown in Fig. 10.3, in which the flow of solvent is controlled by a screw pinchclamp. Weigh out the required amount of silica gel (12.5 g in the first experiment), close the pinchclamp on the tube, and fill about half full with 90:10 ligroin:ether. With a wooden dowel or glass rod push a small plug of glass wool

Dry packing

through the liquid to the bottom of the tube, dust in through a funnel enough sand to form a 1-cm layer over the glass wool, and level the surface by tapping the tube. Unclamp the tube. With the right hand grasp both the top of the tube and the funnel so that the whole assembly can be shaken to dislodge silica gel that may stick to the walls, and with the left hand pour in the silica gel slowly (Fig. 10.4) while tapping the column with a rubber stopper fitted on the end of a pencil. If necessary, use a Pasteur pipette full of 90:10 ligroin:ether to wash down any silica gel that adheres to the walls of the column above the liquid. When the silica gel has settled, add a little sand to provide a protective layer at the top. Open the pinchclamp, let the solvent level fall until it is just a little above the upper layer of sand, and then stop the flow.

Slurry packing

Alternatively, the silica gel can be added to the column (half filled with ligroin) by slurrying the silica gel with 90:10 ligroin: ether in a beaker. The powder is stirred to suspend it in the solvent and immediately poured through

FIG. 10.2 Macroscale chromatographic column.

FIG. 10.3 Chromatographic tube on ring stand.

FIG. 10.4 A useful technique for filling a chromatographic tube with silica gel.

a wide-mouth funnel into the chromatographic tube. Rap the column with a rubber stopper to cause the silica gel to settle and to remove bubbles. Add a protective layer of sand to the top. The column is now ready for use.

Prepare several Erlenmeyer flasks as receivers by taring (weighing) each one carefully and marking them with numbers on the etched circle.

Cleaning Up   After use, the tube is conveniently emptied by pointing the open end into a beaker, opening the pinchclamp, and applying gentle air pressure to the tip. If the plug of glass wool remains in the tube after the alumina leaves, wet it with acetone and reapply air pressure. Allow the adsorbent to dry in the hood, and then dispose of it in the nonhazardous waste container.

Experiments

27, N

Ferrocene
MW 186.04
mp 172–174°C

CAUTION: Toxic.

Acetylferrocene
MW 228.08, mp 85–86°C

1. Chromatography of a Mixture of Ferrocene and Acetylferrocene

In this experiment a mixture of two compounds is separated by chromatography on alumina. The first compound to come down the column is ferrocene (a yellow band). The solvent polarity is changed so that acetylferrocene is eluted as an orange band. The solvents are evaporated from the collection flasks and the compounds recrystallized. Both these compounds are colored (*see* Chapter 44 for their preparation), so it is easy to follow the progress of the chromatographic separation.

Prepare the microscale alumina column exactly as described above. Then add a dry slurry of 90 mg of a 50:50 mixture of acetylferrocene (*Caution!* toxic) and ferrocene that has been adsorbed onto 300 mg of alumina following the above procedure for preparing and adding the sample.

Carefully add hexane to the column, open the valve (use both hands), and elute the two compounds. The first to be eluted, ferrocene, will be seen as a yellow band. Collect this in a 10-mL flask. Any crystalline material seen at the tip of the valve should be washed into the flask with a drop or two of ether. Without allowing the column to run dry, add a 50:50 mixture of hexane and ether, and elute the acetylferrocene, which will be seen as an orange band. Collect it in a 10-mL flask. Spot a thin-layer silica gel chromatography plate with these two solutions. Evaporate the solvents from the two flasks and determine the weights of the residues. An easy way to evaporate the solvent is to place it in a tared 25-mL filter flask and heat the flask in the hand under vacuum while swirling the contents (Fig. 10.5).

Recrystallize the products from the minimum quantities of hot hexane or ligroin. Isolate the crystals, dry them, and determine their weights and melting points. Calculate the percent recovery of the crude and recrystallized products based on the 45 mg of each in the original mixture.

The thin-layer chromatography plate is eluted with 30:1 toluene:absolute ethanol. Do you detect any contamination of one compound by the other?

MICROSCALE

Cleaning Up   Empty the chromatography column onto a piece of aluminum foil in the hood. After the solvent has evaporated, place the alumina and sand in the nonhazardous waste container. Evaporate the crystallization mother liquor to dryness, and place the residue in the hazardous waste container.

MICROSCALE AND MACROSCALE

2. Acetylation of Cholesterol

Cholesterol is a solid alcohol; the average human body contains about 200 g distributed in brain, spinal cord, and nerve tissue and occasionally clogging the arteries and the gall bladder.

In the present experiment, cholesterol is dissolved in acetic acid and allowed to react with acetic anhydride to form the ester cholesteryl acetate. The reaction does not take place rapidly and consequently does not go to completion under the conditions of this experiment. Thus, when the reaction is over, both unreacted cholesterol and the product, cholesteryl acetate, are present. Separating these by fractional crystallization would be extremely difficult; but because they differ in polarity (the hydroxyl group of the cholesterol is the more strongly adsorbed on alumina), they are easily separated by column chromatography. Both molecules are colorless and hence cannot be detected visually. Each fraction should be sampled for thin-layer chromatography. In that way not only the presence but also the purity of each fraction can be assessed. It is also possible to put a drop of each fraction on a watch glass and evaporate it to see if the fraction contains product. Solid will also appear on the tip of the column while a compound is being eluted.

FIG. 10.5 Evaporation of a low-boiling liquid under vacuum. Heat is supplied by the hand, the contents of the flask are swirled, and the vacuum is controlled with the thumb.

Cholesterol

$+ \ CH_3\overset{\overset{\displaystyle O}{\|}}{C}O\overset{\overset{\displaystyle O}{\|}}{C}CH_3 \longrightarrow$

Acetic anhydride

Cholesteryl acetate

$+ \ CH_3COOH$

Microscale Procedure

IN THIS EXPERIMENT cholesterol is refluxed with acetic acid and acetic anhydride. In the standard procedure the mixture is diluted with water, extracted with ether, and the ether dried and evaporated. The resulting mixture of cholesterol and cholesteryl acetate is separated by chromatography on silica gel, eluting with hexane and then hexane/ether mixtures. Cholesteryl acetate comes off first, followed by cholesterol.

In a reaction tube, add 0.5 mL of acetic acid to 50 mg of cholesterol, which can be material isolated from human gallstones. The initial thin slurry may set into a stiff paste of the molecular complex consisting of one molecule of cholesterol and one of acetic acid. Add 0.10 mL of acetic anhydride and a boiling chip, and gently reflux the reaction mixture on a hot sand bath for no more than 30 min (*see* Fig. 1.1).

27, N   While the reaction is taking place, prepare the microscale chromatography column as described above, using silica gel as the adsorbent. Cool the mixture, add 2 mL of water, and extract the product with three 2-mL portions of ether that are placed in the 15-mL centrifuge tube. Wash the ether extracts in the tube with two 2-mL portions of water and one 2.5-mL portion of 3 *M* sodium hydroxide (these three washes remove the acetic acid), and dry the ether by shaking it with 2.5 mL of saturated sodium chloride solution. Then complete the drying by adding enough anhydrous calcium chloride pellets to the solution so that it does not clump together.

Shake the ether solution with the drying agent for 10 min, then transfer it in portions to a tared reaction tube and evaporate to dryness. Use a drop of this ether solution to spot a TLC plate for later analysis. If the crude material weighs more than the theoretical weight, you will know it is not dry or that it contains acetic acid, which can be detected by its odor. Dissolve this crude cholesteryl acetate in the minimum quantity of ether, and apply it to the top of the chromatography column.

To prevent the solution from dribbling from the pipette, use a pipette pump to make the transfer. It also could be applied as a dry powder adsorbed on silica gel as in Experiment 1. Elute the column with ligroin or hexane, and collect two 5-mL fractions in tared 10-mL Erlenmeyer flasks or other suitable containers. Add a boiling stick to each flask, and evaporate the solvent under an aspirator tube on a steam bath or sand bath (Fig. 10.6). If the flask appears empty, it can be used to collect later fractions. Lower the solvent layer to the top of the sand and elute with 15 mL of 70:30 ligroin:ether, collecting five 3-mL fractions. Evaporate the ligroin under an aspirator tube (Fig. 10.6). The last traces of ligroin can be removed using reduced pressure as shown in Fig. 10.7. Follow the 70:30 mixture with 10 mL of 50:50 ligroin:ether, collecting four 2-mL fractions. Save any flask that has any visible residue. Analyze the original mixture and each fraction by thin-layer chromatography on silica gel plates using 1:1 ether:ligroin to develop the plates and either ultraviolet light or iodine vapor to visualize the spots.

Cholesteryl acetate (mp 115°C) and cholesterol (mp 149°C) should appear, respectively, in early and late fractions with a few empty fractions (no residue) in between. If so, combine consecutive fractions of early and late material and determine the weights and melting points. Calculate the percentage of the acetylated

FIG. 10.6 Aspirator tube in use. A boiling stick may be necessary to promote even boiling.

FIG. 10.7 Drying a solid by reduced air pressure.

material compared to the total recovered and calculate the percentage yield from cholesterol.

Cleaning Up   After neutralization, acetic acid, aqueous layers, and saturated sodium chloride layers from the extraction can be flushed down the drain with water. Ether, ligroin, and TLC solvents should be placed in the organic solvents container. The drying agent and chromatography adsorbent, once free of solvent, can be placed in the nonhazardous solid water container.

Macroscale Procedure

Carry out procedure in laboratory hood.

Cover 0.5 g of cholesterol with 5 mL of acetic acid in a small Erlenmeyer flask; swirl, and note that the initially thin slurry soon sets to a stiff paste of the molecular compound $C_{27}H_{45}OH \cdot CH_3CO_2H$. Add 1 mL of acetic anhydride, and heat the mixture on the steam bath for any convenient period of time from 15 min to 1 h; record the actual heating period. While the reaction takes place, prepare the chromatographic column. Cool the reaction mixture, add 20 mL of water, and extract with two 25-mL portions of ether. Wash the combined ethereal extracts twice with 15-mL portions of water and once with 25 mL of 3 M sodium hydroxide, dry by shaking the ether extracts with 25 mL saturated sodium chloride solution; then dry the ether over anhydrous calcium chloride pellets for 10 min in an Erlenmeyer flask, filter, and evaporate the ether. Save a few crystals of this material for TLC analysis. Dissolve the residue in 3 to 4 mL of ether, transfer the solution with a Pasteur pipette onto a column of 12.5 g of silica gel, and rinse the flask with another small portion of ether.[1]

In order to apply the ether solution to the top of the sand and avoid having it coat the interior of the column, pipette the solution down a 6-mm-diameter

---

1. Ideally, the material to be adsorbed is dissolved in ligroin, the solvent of least elutant power. The present mixture is not soluble enough in ligroin and so ether is used, but the volume is kept to a minimum.

glass tube that is resting on the top of the sand. Label a series of 50-mL Erlenmeyer flasks as fractions 1 to 10. Open the pinchclamp, run the eluant solution into a 50-mL Erlenmeyer flask, and as soon as the solvent in the column has fallen to the level of the upper layer of sand, fill the column with a part of a measured 125 mL of 70:30 ligroin:ether. When about 25 mL of eluant has collected in the flask (fraction 1), change to a fresh flask; add a boiling stone to the first flask, and evaporate the solution to dryness on the steam bath under an aspirator tube (Fig. 10.6). Evacuation using the aspirator helps to remove last traces of ligroin (Fig. 10.7). If this fraction 1 is negative (no residue), use the flask for collecting further fractions. Continue adding the ligroin–ether mixture until the 125-mL portion is exhausted, and then use 100 mL of a 1:1 ligroin:ether mixture. A convenient bubbler (Fig. 10.8) made from a 125-mL Erlenmeyer flask, a short piece of 10-mm-diameter glass tubing, and a cork will automatically add solvent. A separatory funnel with stopper and partially open stopcock serves the same purpose. Collect and evaporate successive 25-mL fractions of eluant. Save any flask that has any visible solid residue. The ideal method for removal of solvents involves the use of a rotary evaporator (Fig. 10.9). Analyze the original mixture and each fraction by TLC on silica gel plates

FIG. 10.8 Bubbler for adding solvent automatically.

FIG. 10.9 Rotary evaporator. The rate of evaporation with this apparatus is very fast due to the thin film of liquid spread over the entire inner surface of the rotating flask, which is heated under a vacuum. Foaming and bumping are also greatly reduced.

using 1:1 ether:ligroin to develop the plates and either ultraviolet light or iodine vapor to visualize the spots.

Cholesteryl acetate (mp 115°C) and cholesterol (mp 149°C) should appear, respectively, in early and late fractions with a few empty fractions (no residue) in between. If so, combine consecutive fractions of early and of late material, and determine the weights and melting points. Calculate the percentage of the acetylated material compared to the total recovered and compare your result with those of others in your class employing different reaction periods.

Cleaning Up   After neutralization, acetic acid, aqueous layers, and saturated sodium chloride layers from the extraction can be flushed down the drain with water. Ether, ligroin, and TLC solvents should be placed in the organic solvents container, and the drying agent, once free of solvent, can be placed in the non-hazardous solid waste container. Ligroin and ether from the chromatography go into the organic solvents container. If possible, spread out the silica gel in the hood to dry. It can then be placed in the nonhazardous solid waste container. If it is wet with organic solvents, it is a hazardous solid waste and must be disposed of, at great expense, in a secure landfill.

MICROSCALE AND MACROSCALE

3. Fluorene and Fluorenone

The 9-position of fluorene is unusually reactive for a hydrocarbon. The protons on this carbon atom are acidic by virtue of being doubly benzylic, and, consequently, this carbon can be oxidized by several reagents, including elemental oxygen. In the present experiment, the very powerful and versatile oxidizing agent Cr(VI), in the form of chromium trioxide, is used to carry out this oxidation. Cr(VI) in a variety of other forms is used to carry out about a dozen oxidation reactions in this text. The *dust* of Cr(VI) salts is reported to be a carcinogen, so avoid breathing it.

$$\xrightarrow[\text{CH}_3\text{COOH}]{\text{Na}_2\text{Cr}_2\text{O}_7}$$

Fluorene
mp 114°C
MW 166.22

Fluorenone
mp 83°C
MW 180.21

Microscale Procedure

IN THIS EXPERIMENT the hydrocarbon fluorene is oxidized to the ketone fluorenone with sodium dichromate in acetic acid by heating. The mixture is diluted with water, the crude product isolated by filtration, and then—in a standard procedure—it is dissolved in ether. The ether is dried and evaporated

FIG. 10.10 Spot each fraction on a chromatography plate. Examine under UV light to see which fractions contain compound.

to give a mixture of fluorene and fluorenone, which is separated by column chromatography.

In a reaction tube dissolve 50 mg of fluorene in 0.25 mL of acetic acid by heating, and add this hot solution to a solution of 0.15 g of sodium dichromate dihydrate in 0.5 mL of acetic acid. Heat the reaction mixture to 80°C for 15 min in a hot water bath; then cool it, and add 1.5 mL of water. Stir the mixture for 2 min, then filter it on the Hirsch funnel. Wash the product well with water, and press out as much water as possible. Return the product to the reaction tube, add 2 mL of ether, and add anhydrous calcium chloride pellets until it no longer clumps together. Cork and shake the tube, and allow the product to dry for 5 or 10 min before evaporating the ether in another tared reaction tube. Use ether to wash off the drying agent and to complete the transfer of product. Use this ether solution to spot a TLC plate. This crude mixture of fluorene and fluorenone will be separated by column chromatography.

27, N

The sample can also be applied to the column using the technique described on p. 173.

Ligroin = hexane = "hexanes."

Column Chromatography of the Fluorene-Fluorenone Mixture.
Prepare a microscale chromatographic column exactly as described at the beginning of this chapter. Dissolve the crude mixture of fluorene and fluorenone in 0.2 mL of warm toluene, and add this to the surface of the alumina. Be sure to add the sample as a solution; should any sample crystallize, add a drop more toluene. Run the ligroin down to the surface of the alumina, add a few drops more ligroin, and repeat the process until the sample is seen as a narrow band at the top of the column. Carefully add a 3-mm layer of sand, then fill the column with ligroin, and collect 5-mL fractions in tared 10-mL Erlenmeyer flasks. Sample each flask for thin-layer chromatography (Fig. 10.10), and evaporate each to dryness. Final drying can be done under vacuum using the technique shown in Fig. 10.7. You are to decide when all the product has been eluted from the column. The thin-layer plates can be developed using 20% dichloromethane in ligroin. Combine fractions that are identical, and determine the melting points of the two substances.

Macroscale Procedure

One-half hour unattended heating

Handle dichromate and acetic acid in laboratory hood; wear gloves.

In a 250-mL Erlenmeyer flask dissolve 5.0 g of practical grade fluorene in 25 mL of acetic acid by heating on the steam bath with occasional swirling. In a 125-mL Erlenmeyer flask dissolve 15 g of sodium dichromate dihydrate in 50 mL of acetic acid by swirling and heating on a hot plate. Adjust the temperature of the dichromate solution to 80°C, transfer the thermometer, adjust the fluorene–acetic acid solution to 80°C, then, **in the hood,** pour in the dichromate solution. Note the time and the temperature of the solution and heat on the steam bath for 30 min. Observe the maximum and final temperature, then cool the solution and add 150 mL of water. Swirl the mixture for a full 2 min to coagulate the product and so promote rapid filtration, then collect the yellow solid in an 8.5-cm Büchner funnel (in case filtration is slow, empty the funnel and flask into a beaker and stir vigorously for a few minutes). Wash the filter cake well with water and then suck the filter cake as dry as possible. Either let the product dry overnight, or dry it quickly as follows: Put the moist solid into a 50-mL Erlenmeyer flask, add ether (20 mL) and swirl to dissolve, and add anhydrous calcium chloride (10 g) to scavenge the water. Decant the ethereal solution through a cone of anhydrous calcium chloride in a funnel into a 125-mL Erlenmeyer flask then rinse the flask and funnel with ether. Evaporate on the steam bath under an aspirator, heat until all the ether is removed, and pour the hot oil into a 50-ml beaker to cool and solidify. Scrape out the yellow solid. Yield: 4.0 g.

Cleaning Up   The filtrate probably contains unreacted dichromate. To destroy it, add 3 *M* sulfuric acid until the pH is 1, then complete the reduction by adding solid sodium thiosulfate until the solution becomes cloudy and blue-colored. Neutralize with sodium carbonate, then filter the flocculent precipitate of $Cr(OH)_3$ through Celite in a Büchner funnel. The filtrate can be diluted with water and flushed down the drain, whereas the precipitate and Celite should be placed in the heavy metal hazardous waste container.

4. Separation of Fluorene and Fluorenone

N   Prepare a column of 12.5 g of alumina, run out excess solvent, and pour onto the column a solution of 0.5 g of fluorene–fluorenone mixture. Elute at first with ligroin and use tared 50-mL flasks as receivers. The yellow color of fluorenone provides one index of the course of the fractionation and the appearance of solid around the delivery tip provides another. Wash the solid on the tip frequently into the receiver with ether. When you believe that one component has been eluted completely, change to another receiver until you judge that the second component is beginning to appear. Then, when you are sure the second component is being eluted, change to a 1:1 ligroin:ether mixture and continue until the column is exhausted. It is possible to collect practically all of the two components in the two receiving flasks, with only a negligible intermediate fraction. After evaporation of solvent, evacuate each flask under vacuum (Fig. 10.7) and determine the weight and melting point of the products. A convenient method for evaporating fractions is to use a rotary evaporator (Fig. 10.9).

Cleaning Up   All organic material from this experiment can go in the organic solvents container. The alumina adsorbent, if free of organic solvents, can go in the nonhazardous solid waste container. If it is wet with organic solvents, it is a hazardous solid waste. Spread it in the hood to dry.

Questions

1. Predict the order of elution of a mixture of triphenylmethanol, biphenyl, benzoic acid, and methyl benzoate from an alumina column.

2. What would be the effect of collecting larger fractions when carrying out the experiments described?

3. What would have been the result if a large quantity of petroleum ether alone were used as the eluent in either of the experiments described?

4. Once the chromatographic column has been prepared, why is it important to allow the level of the liquid in the column to drop to the level of the alumina before applying the solution of the compound to be separated?

5. A chemist started to carry out column chromatography on a Friday afternoon, reached the point at which the two compounds being separated were about three-fourths of the way down the column, and then returned on Monday to find that the compounds came off the column as a mixture. Speculate on the reason for this. The column had not run dry over the weekend.

CHAPTER

11

Alkenes from Alcohols: Analysis of a Mixture by Gas Chromatography

PRELAB EXERCISE: If the dehydration of 2-methyl-2-butanol occurred on a purely statistical basis, what would be the relative proportions of 2-methyl-1-butene and 2-methyl-2-butene?

Separation of mixtures of volatile samples

Gas chromatography (GC), also called vapor phase chromatography (VPC) and gas-liquid chromatography (GLC), is a means of separating volatile mixtures, the components of which may differ in boiling points by only a few tenths of a degree. The GC process is similar to fractional distillation, but instead of a glass column 25 cm long packed with a stainless steel sponge, the GC column used is a 3–10 m long coiled metal tube (6-mm dia.), packed with ground firebrick. The firebrick serves as an inert support for a very high-boiling liquid (essentially nonvolatile), such as silicone oil and low molecular weight polymers like Carbowax. These are the *liquids* of gas-*liquid* chromatography and are referred to as the stationary phase. The sample (1–25 *micro*liters) is injected through a silicone rubber septum into the column, which is being swept with a current of helium (ca. 200 mL/min). The sample first dissolves in the high-boiling liquid phase, and then the more volatile components of the sample evaporate from the liquid and pass into the gas phase. Helium, the carrier gas, carries these components along the column a short distance where they again dissolve in the liquid phase before reevaporation (Fig. 11.1).

High-boiling liquid phase

The thermal conductivity detector

Eventually the carrier gas, which is a very good thermal conductor, and the sample reach the detector, an electrically heated tungsten wire. As long as pure helium is flowing over the detector, the temperature of the wire is relatively low and the wire has a low resistance to the flow of electric current. Organic molecules have lower thermal conductivities than helium. Hence, when a mixture of helium and an organic sample flows over the detector wire it is cooled less efficiently and heats up. When the wire is hot its electrical resistance becomes higher and offers higher resistance to the flow of current. The detector wire actually is one leg of a Wheatstone bridge connected to a chart recorder that records, as a peak, the amount of current necessary to again balance the bridge. The information produced by the recorder is called a chromatogram.

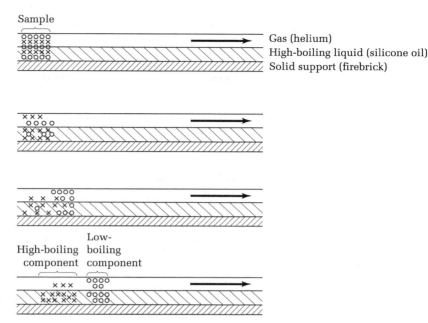

FIG. 11.1 Gas chromatography: Diagrammatic partition between gas and liquid phases.

The number and relative amounts of components in a mixture

A gas chromatogram is simply a recording of current versus time (which is equivalent to a certain volume of helium) (Fig. 11.2). In the illustration the smaller peak from component A has the shorter retention time, T_1, and so is a more volatile substance than component B (if the stationary phase is an inert liquid such as silicone oil). The areas under the two peaks are directly proportional to the molar amounts of A and B in the mixture (provided they are structurally similar). The retention time of a given component is a function of the column temperature, the helium flow rate, and the nature of the stationary phase. Hundreds of stationary phases are available; picking the correct one to carry out a given analysis is somewhat of an art, but widely used stationary phases are silicone oil and silicone rubber, both of which can be used at

FIG. 11.2 Gas chromatogram.

FIG. 11.3 Diagram of a gas chromatograph.

FIG. 11.4 One of the commercially available chromatographs.

Collecting a sample for an infrared spectrum

temperatures up to 300°C and separate mixtures on the basis of boiling point differences of the mixture's components. More specialized stationary phases will, for instance, allow alkanes to pass through readily (short retention time) while holding back (long retention time) alcohols by hydrogen bonding to the liquid phase.

A diagram of a typical gas chromatograph is shown in Fig. 11.3. The carrier gas, usually helium, enters the chromatograph at ca. 60 lb/sq in. The sample (1 to 25 microliters) is injected through a rubber septum using a small hypodermic syringe (Fig. 11.4). Handle the syringe with care. The syringe needles and plungers are thin and delicate; take care not to bend either one. Be wary of the injection port. It is very hot. The sample immediately passes through the column and then the detector. Injector, column, and detector are all enclosed in a thermostatically controlled oven, which can be maintained at any temperature up to 300°C. In this way samples that would not volatilize sufficiently at room temperature can be analyzed.

Gas chromatography determines the number of components and their relative amounts in a very small sample. The small sample size is an advantage in many cases, but it precludes isolating the separated components. Some specialized chromatographs can separate samples as large as 0.5 mL per injection and automatically collect each fraction in a separate container. At the other extreme, gas chromatographs equipped with flame ionization detectors can detect micrograms of sample, such as traces of pesticides in food or of drugs in blood and urine. Clearly a gas chromatogram gives little information about the chemical nature of the sample being detected. However, it is sometimes possible to collect enough sample at the exit port of the chromatograph to obtain an infrared spectrum. As the peak for the compound of interest appears on the chart paper, a 2-mm-dia. glass tube, 3 in. long and packed with glass wool, is inserted into the rubber septum at the exit port. The sample, if it is not too volatile, will condense in the cold glass tube. Subsequently, the sample is washed out with a drop or two of solvent and an infrared spectrum obtained. See Fig. 11.5 for another collection device.

Dehydration

1. 2-Methyl-1-butene and 2-Methyl-2-butene[1]

The dilute sulfuric acid catalyzed dehydration of 2-methyl-2-butanol (*t*-amyl alcohol) proceeds readily to give a mixture of alkenes that can be analyzed by gas chromatography. The mechanism of this reaction involves the intermediate formation of the relatively stable tertiary carbocation followed by loss of a proton either from a primary carbon atom to give the terminal olefin, 2-methyl-1-butene, or from a secondary carbon to give 2-methyl-2-butene.

MICROSCALE AND MACROSCALE

Polypropylene cup, fill with ice

1-mm Hole

Polypropylene microscale centrifuge tube, 5.3 × 47 mm

Outlet port of gas chromatograph

FIG. 11.5 Gas chromatographic collection device. Fill container with ice or dry ice–acetone mixture and attach to outlet port of GC. Available from Kontes.

$$
\begin{array}{ccc}
\text{OH} & & \overset{+}{\text{O}}\text{H}_2 \\
| & & | \\
\text{CH}_3\text{CH}_2\text{CCH}_3 + \text{H}_2\text{SO}_4 & \overset{\text{fast}}{\rightleftharpoons} & \text{CH}_3\text{CH}_2\text{CCH}_3 + \text{HSO}_4^- \\
| & & | \\
\text{CH}_3 & & \text{CH}_3
\end{array}
$$

2-Methyl-2-butanol
bp 102°C
den 0.805
MW 88.15

$$
\begin{array}{ccc}
\overset{+}{\text{O}}\text{H}_2 & & \\
| & & \\
\text{CH}_3\text{CH}_2\text{CCH}_3 & \overset{\text{slow}}{\rightleftharpoons} & \text{CH}_3\text{CH}_2\overset{+}{\text{C}}\text{CH}_3 + \text{H}_2\text{O} \\
| & & | \\
\text{CH}_3 & & \text{CH}_3
\end{array}
$$

$$
\text{CH}_3\text{CH}_2\overset{+}{\text{C}}\text{—CH}_2 \rightleftharpoons \text{CH}_3\text{CH}_2\text{C}=\text{CH}_2
$$

2-Methyl-1-butene
bp 31.16°, den 0.662
MW 70.14

$$
\text{CH}_3\text{CH—}\overset{+}{\text{C}}\text{CH}_3 \rightleftharpoons \text{CH}_3\text{CH}=\text{CCH}_3
$$

2-Methyl-2-butene
bp 38.57°C
den 0.662
MW 70.14

1. C.W. Schimelpfenig, *J. Chem. Ed.*, **39**, 310 (1962).

2-Methyl-2-butanol can also be dehydrated in high yield using iodine as a catalyst:

$$
\underset{\underset{CH_3}{|}}{\overset{\overset{OH}{|}}{CH_3CH_2CCH_3}} \xrightarrow{I_2 \text{ (trace)}} \underset{\underset{CH_3}{|}}{\overset{\overset{OI}{|}}{CH_3CH_2CCH_3}} \xrightarrow{-HOI}
$$

$$
\underset{\underset{CH_3}{|}}{CH_3CH_2C}{=}CH_2 + CH_3CH{=}\underset{\underset{CH_3}{|}}{CCH_3} + HI + HOI
$$

$$
HI + HOI \longrightarrow H_2O + I_2
$$

Each step of this E_1 elimination reaction is reversible and thus the reaction is driven to completion by removing one of the products, the alkene. In these reactions several alkenes can be produced. The Saytzeff rule states that the more substituted alkene is the more stable and thus the one formed in larger amount. And the *trans*-isomer is more stable than the *cis*-isomer. With this information it should be possible to deduce which peaks on the gas chromatogram correspond to a given alkene and to predict the ratios of the products.

In analyzing your results from this experiment, consider the fact that the carbocation can lose any of six primary hydrogen atoms but only two secondary hydrogen atoms to give the product olefins.

Microscale Dehydration Procedure

IN THIS EXPERIMENT a tertiary alcohol is dehydrated to a mixture of alkenes in a reaction catalyzed by sulfuric acid. The products are collected by simple distillation into an ice-cold vial. Cold aqueous base is added to remove acid and the organic layer dried with calcium chloride. The products are again distilled and then analyzed by gas chromatography.

Into a 5-mL long-necked, round-bottomed flask place 1 mL of water and then add dropwise with thorough mixing 0.5 mL of concentrated sulfuric acid. Cool the hot solution in an ice bath then add to the cold solution 1.00 mL (0.80 g) of 2-methyl-2-butanol. Mix the reactants thoroughly, add a boiling stone, and set up the apparatus for simple distillation as shown in Fig. 11.6. Hold the flask in a towel while connecting the apparatus to guard against spills or flask breakage. Cool the receiver (a vial) in ice to avoid losing the highly volatile products. Warm the flask on the sand bath to start the reaction and distill the products over the temperature range 30–45°C. After all the products have distilled, the rate of distillation will decrease markedly. Cease distillation at this point. After this, the temperature registered on the thermometer will rise rapidly as water and sulfuric acid begin to distill.

Keep the side arm down in the cold vial to avoid losing product.

— Air condenser

Ice

Receiver vial

Boiling chip

FIG. 11.6 Apparatus for dehydration of 2-methyl-2-butanol. Beaker can be clamped with large three-prong clamp.

To the distillate add 0.3 mL *cold* 3 *M* sodium hydroxide solution to neutralize sulfurous acid, mix well, draw off the aqueous layer, and dry the product over anhydrous calcium chloride pellets, adding the drying agent in small quantities until it no longer clumps together. Keep the vial cold. While the product is drying, rinse out the distillation apparatus with water, ethanol, and then a small amount of acetone and *dry* it thoroughly by drawing air through it using the aspirator. If this is not done carefully, the products will become contaminated with acetone. Carefully transfer the dry mixture of butenes to the distilling apparatus using a Pasteur pipette, add a boiling chip to the now dry products, and distill into a tared, cold receiver. Collect the portion boiling up to 43°C. The yield reported in the literature is 84% when the reaction is carried out on a much larger scale. Weigh the product, calculate the yield, and analyze it by gas chromatography. The average yield on a small scale is 50%. 2-Methyl-1-butene boils at 31.2°C, and 2-methyl-2-butene boils at 38.6°C.

Products are easily lost by evaporation. Store mixture in a spark-proof refrigerator if GC analysis must be postponed.

Cleaning Up The residue in the reaction tube should be diluted with water, neutralized with sodium carbonate, and then flushed down the drain.

Macroscale Dehydration Procedure

Pour 18 mL of water into a 100-mL round-bottomed flask and cool in an ice-water bath while slowly pouring in 9 mL of concentrated sulfuric acid. Cool this "1:2" acid further with swirling while slowly pouring in 18 mL (15 g) of 2-methyl-2-butanol. Shake the mixture thoroughly, then mount the flask for fractional distillation over a flask heater, as in Fig. 5.11, with the arrangement for ice cooling of the distillate seen in Fig. 19.2. Cooling is needed because the olefin is volatile. Use a long condenser and a rapid stream of cooling water. Heat the flask slowly with an electric flask heater until distillation of the hydrocarbon is complete. If the ice-cooled test tube will not hold 15 mL, be prepared to collect half of the distillate in another ice-cooled test tube. Transfer the distillate to a separatory funnel and shake it with about 5 mL of 3 *M* sodium hydroxide solution to remove any traces of sulfurous acid. The aqueous solution sinks to the bottom and is drawn off. Dry the hydrocarbon layer by adding sufficient anhydrous calcium chloride pellets until the drying agent no longer clumps together. After about 5 min remove the drying agent by gravity filtration or careful decantation into a *dry* 25-mL round-bottomed flask and distill the dried product through a fractionating column (*see* Fig. 19.2), taking the same precautions as before to avoid evaporation losses. Rinse the fractionating column with acetone and dry it with a stream of air to remove water from the first distillation. Collect in a tared bottle the portion boiling at 30–43°C. The yield reported in the literature is 84%; the average student yield is about 50%.

Cleaning Up   The pot residue from the reaction is combined with the sodium hydroxide wash and neutralized with sodium carbonate. The pot residue from the distillation of the product is combined with the acetone used to wash out the apparatus and placed in the organic solvents container. If the calcium chloride pellets are dry, they can be placed in the nonhazardous solid waste container. If they are wet with organic solvents, they must be placed in the hazardous solid waste container for solvent-contaminated drying agent.

2. Computational Chemistry

The steric energies of the two isomeric butenes produced in Experiment 1 can be calculated using a molecular mechanics program, but the results are not valid because the bonding type is not the same. It is possible to compare the steric energies of *cis*- and *trans*-isomers of alkenes, but not a 1,1-disubstituted alkene with a 1,2-disubstituted alkene.

Compare your yields of the two isomers to their heats of formation calculated using AM1 or a similar semi-empirical molecular orbital program. Do the calculated heats of formation correlate with relative percentages of the isomers? What does this correlation or lack thereof tell you about the mechanism of the reaction?

⊔ MICROSCALE

3. 1-Butene and *cis*- and *trans*-2-Butene[2]

$$
\underset{\substack{\text{2-Butanol}\\\text{MW 74.12}\\\text{bp 98°C}}}{CH_3CH_2\overset{\displaystyle OH}{\underset{\displaystyle |}{C}}HCH_3} \xrightarrow{H+} \underset{\substack{\text{1-Butene}\\\text{MW 56.11}\\\text{bp} -6.3°C}}{CH_3CH_2CH{=}CH_2} + \underset{\substack{\textit{cis}\text{-2-Butene}\\\text{MW 56.11}\\\text{bp 3.7°C}}}{\overset{\displaystyle CH_3 \quad CH_3}{\underset{\displaystyle H \qquad H}{C{=}C}}} + \underset{\substack{\textit{trans}\text{-2-Butene}\\\text{MW 56.11}\\\text{bp 0.9°C}}}{\overset{\displaystyle CH_3 \quad H}{\underset{\displaystyle H \qquad CH_3}{C{=}C}}}
$$

IN THIS EXPERIMENT 2-butanol is dehydrated with sulfuric acid to give a mixture of gaseous alkenes that are collected by the downward displacement of water. The gaseous mixture is analyzed by gas chromatography.

The quantities of alcohol and **O** *acid are not critical.*

33

Bend the polyethylene tubing to shape in hot sand or steam.

In a 10 × 100 mm reaction tube place 0.10 mL (81 mg) of 2-butanol and 0.05 mL (1 drop) of concentrated sulfuric acid. Mix the reactants well, and add a boiling chip. Stirring of the reaction mixture is not necessary because it is homogeneous. Insert a polyethylene tube through a septum (*see* Fig. 18.2), place this septum on the reaction tube, and lead the tubing into the mouth of the distilling column/collection tube, which is capped with a septum. The distilling column/collection tube is filled with water, capped with a finger, and inverted in the beaker of water and clamped for the collection of butene by the downward displacement of water (Fig. 11.7).

FIG. 11.7 Apparatus for dehydration of 2-butanol. Butenes are collected by the downward displacement of water.

Polyethylene tubing — Rubber septum — Butenes — 10-cm Column/collection tube — Rubber septum — Reaction tube — 2-Butanol + sulfuric acid — Hot sand bath

2. G.K. Helmkamp and H.W. Johnson, Jr. *Selected Experiments in Organic Chemistry,* 3d ed. (New York: Freeman, 1983), p. 99.

Lower the reaction tube into a hot (~ 100°C) sand bath, and increase the heat slowly to complete the reaction. Collect a few milliliters of butene, and *remove the polyethylene tube from the water bath.* If the polyethylene tube is not removed from the water bath, water will be sucked back into the reaction tube when it cools. Use about 0.5 mL of the gaseous butene mixture to carry out the GC analysis.

Cleaning Up   The residue in the reaction tube should be diluted with water, neutralized with sodium carbonate, and then flushed down the drain.

Gas Chromatographic Analysis

Be sure the helium cylinder is attached to a bench or wall.

Use care. The injection port is hot.

In your notebook record all information relevant to this analysis: column diameter and length, column packing, carrier gas and its flow rate, filament current, temperature of column, detector and injection port, sample size, attenuation, and chart speed.

Inject a few microliters of product into a gas chromatograph maintained at room temperature and equipped with a 6-mm-dia. × 3-m column packed with 10% SE-30 silicone rubber on Chromosorb-W or a similar inert packing. Mark the chart paper at the time of injection. In a few minutes two peaks should appear. After using the chromatograph, turn off the recorder and cap the pen. Make no unauthorized adjustments on the gas chromatograph. From your knowledge of the mechanisms of dehydration of secondary alcohols, which olefin should predominate? Does this agree with the boiling points? (In general, the compound with the shorter retention time has the lower boiling point.) Measure the relative areas under the two peaks. One way to perform this integration is to cut out the peaks with scissors and weigh the two pieces of paper separately on an analytical balance. Although time consuming, this method results in very precise results. If the peaks are symmetrical, their areas can be approximated by simply multiplying the height of the peak by its width at half-height.

Questions

1. Write the structure of the three olefins produced by the dehydration of 3-methyl-3-pentanol.

2. When 2-methylpropene is bubbled into dilute sulfuric acid at room temperature, it appears to dissolve. What new substance has been formed?

3. A student wished to prepare ethylene gas by dehydration of ethanol at 140°C using sulfuric acid as the dehydrating agent. A low-boiling liquid was obtained instead of ethylene. What was the liquid, and how might the reaction conditions be changed to give ethylene?

4. What would be the effect of increasing the carrier gas flow rate on the retention time?

5. What would be the effect of raising the column temperature on the retention time?

6. What would be the effect of raising the temperature or increasing the carrier gas flow rate on the ability to resolve two closely spaced peaks?

7. If you were to try a column one-half the length of the one you actually used, how do you think the retention times of the butenes would be affected? How do you think the separation of the peaks would be affected? How do you think the width of each peak would be affected?

8. From your knowledge of the dehydration of tertiary alcohols, which olefin should predominate in the product of the dehydration of 2-methyl-2-butanol, and why?

9. What is the maximum volume (at STP) of the butene mixture that could be obtained by the dehydration of 81 mg of 2-butanol?

10. What other gases are in the collection tube besides the three butenes at the end of the second reaction?

11. Using a molecular mechanics program (*see* Chapter 15), calculate the steric energies or heats of formation of the three isomeric butenes produced in the synthesis experiment. Do these energies correlate with the product distributions found? What does a correlation or lack thereof tell you about the mechanism of the reaction?

CHAPTER

12

Infrared Spectroscopy

PRELAB EXERCISE: When an infrared spectrum is run, there is a possibility that the chart paper is not properly placed or that the spectrometer is not mechanically adjusted. Describe how you could calibrate an infrared spectrum.

The presence and also the environment of functional groups in organic molecules can be identified by infrared (IR) spectroscopy. Like nuclear magnetic resonance (NMR) and ultraviolet (UV) spectroscopy, infrared spectroscopy is nondestructive. Moreover, the small quantity of sample needed, the speed with which a spectrum can be obtained, the relatively low cost of the spectrometer, and the wide applicability of the method combine to make infrared spectroscopy one of the most useful tools available to the organic chemist.

Infrared radiation consists of wavelengths that are longer than those of visible light. It is detected not with the eyes, but by a feeling of warmth on the skin. When absorbed by molecules, radiation of this wavelength (typically 2.5 to 25 μm) increases the amplitude of vibrations of the chemical bonds joining atoms.

2.5 to 25 μm equals 4000 to 400 cm⁻¹.

Wavenumbers, cm⁻¹, are proportional to frequency:

$$\bar{v}(cm^{-1}) = \frac{v}{c}$$

Infrared spectra are measured in units of frequency or wavelength. The wavelength is measured in micrometers or microns, μm ($1\ \mu m = 1 \times 10^{-4}$ cm). The positions of absorption bands are measured in frequency units by wavenumbers $\bar{v}$, which are expressed in reciprocal centimeters, cm⁻¹, corresponding to the number of cycles of the wave in each centimeter.

$$cm^{-1} = \frac{10,000}{\mu m}$$

Examine the scale carefully.

IR spectroscopy easily detects
Hydroxyl groups —OH

Amines —NH₂

Nitriles —C≡N

Nitro groups —NO₂

Unlike UV and NMR spectra, infrared spectra are inverted and are not always presented on the same scale. Some spectrometers record the spectra on an ordinate linear in microns, but this compresses the low-wavelength region. Other spectrometers present the spectra on a scale linear in reciprocal centimeters, but linear on two different scales: one between 4000 and 2000 cm⁻¹, which spreads out the low-wavelength region; and the other a smaller one between 2000 and 667 cm⁻¹. Consequently, spectra of the same compound run on two different spectrometers will not always look the same.

To picture the molecular vibrations that interact with infrared light, imagine a molecule as being made up of balls (atoms) connected by springs (bonds). The vibration can be described by Hooke's law from classical mechanics, which

194

says that the frequency of a stretching vibration is directly proportional to the strength of the spring (bond) and inversely proportional to the masses connected by the spring. Thus we find C—H, N—H, and O—H bond-stretching vibrations are high frequency (short wavelength) compared to those of C—C and C—O because of the low mass of hydrogen compared to that of carbon or oxygen. The bonds connecting carbon to bromine and iodine, atoms of large mass, vibrate so slowly that they are beyond the range of most common infrared spectrometers. A double bond can be regarded as a stiffer, stronger spring, so we find C=C and C=O vibrations at higher frequency than C—C and C—O stretching vibrations. And C≡C and C≡N stretch at even higher frequencies than C=C and C=O (but at lower frequencies than C—H, N—H, and O—H). These frequencies are in keeping with the bond strengths of single (~100 kcal/mol), double (~160 kcal/mol), and triple bonds (~220 kcal/mol).

IR spectroscopy is especially useful for detecting and distinguishing among all carbonyl-containing compounds:

$$
\text{Acids} \qquad -\overset{\overset{\displaystyle O}{\|}}{C}-OH
$$

$$
\text{Amides} \qquad -\overset{\overset{\displaystyle O}{\|}}{C}-NH_2
$$

$$
\text{Anhydrides} \qquad -\overset{\overset{\displaystyle O}{\|}}{C}-O-\overset{\overset{\displaystyle O}{\|}}{C}-
$$

$$
\text{Aldehydes} \qquad -\overset{\overset{\displaystyle O}{\|}}{C}-H
$$

$$
\text{Ketones} \qquad -\overset{\overset{\displaystyle O}{\|}}{C}-
$$

$$
\text{Esters} \qquad -\overset{\overset{\displaystyle O}{\|}}{C}-O-
$$

$$
\text{Lactones} \qquad \boxed{-\overset{\overset{\displaystyle O}{\|}}{C}-O-}
$$

The stretching vibrations noted above are intense and particularly easy to analyze. A nonlinear molecule of *n* atoms can undergo $3n - 6$ possible modes of vibration, which means cyclohexane with 18 atoms can undergo 48 possible modes of vibration. A single CH_2 group can vibrate in six different ways. Each vibrational mode produces a peak in the spectrum because it corresponds to the absorption of energy at a discrete frequency. These many modes of vibration create a complex spectrum that defies simple analysis, but even in very complex molecules, certain functional groups have characteristic frequencies that can easily be recognized. Within these functional groups are the above-mentioned atoms and bonds, C—H, N—H, O—H, C=C, C=O, C≡C, and C≡N. Their absorption frequencies are given in Table 12.1.

When the frequency of infrared light is the same as the natural vibrational frequency of an interatomic bond, light will be absorbed by the molecule and the amplitude of the bond vibration will increase. The intensity of infrared absorption bands is proportional to the change in dipole moment that a bond undergoes when it stretches. Thus the most intense bands (peaks) in an infrared spectrum are often from C=O and C—O stretching vibrations, whereas the C≡C stretching band for a symmetrical acetylene is almost nonexistent because the molecule undergoes no net change of dipole moment when it stretches:

$$
\overset{+}{\underset{\diagup}{\diagdown}}C=O \;\longleftrightarrow\; \overset{+}{\underset{\diagup}{\diagdown}}C=O \qquad H_3C-C\equiv C-CH_3 \;\longleftrightarrow\; H_2C-C\equiv C-CH_3
$$

Change in dipole moment   No change in dipole moment

Intensity of absorption is proportional to change in ✳ dipole moment.

Unlike proton NMR spectroscopy, where the area of the peaks is strictly proportional to the number of hydrogen atoms causing the peaks, the intensities of infrared peaks are not proportional to the numbers of atoms causing them. Given the chemical shifts and coupling constants, it is possible to calculate a theoretical NMR spectrum that is an exact match to the experimental one. It is not possible, except for very simple molecules, to do this for infrared spectra. Every peak or group of peaks in an NMR spectrum can be assigned to specific hydrogens in a

TABLE 12.1 Characteristic Infrared
Absorption Wavenumbers

Functional Group	Wavenumber (cm^{-1})
O—H	3600–3400
N—H	3400–3200
C—H	3080–2760
C≡N	2260–2215
C≡C	2150–2100
C=O	1815–1650
C=C	1660–1600
C—O	1200–1050

molecule, but the assignment of the majority of peaks in an infrared spectrum is usually not possible. Peaks to the right (longer wavelength) of 1250 cm^{-1} are the result of combinations of vibrations that are characteristic not of individual functional groups but of the molecule as a whole. This part of the spectrum is often referred to as the *fingerprint region* because it is uniquely characteristic of each molecule. Although two organic compounds can have the same melting points or boiling points and can have identical UV and NMR spectra, they cannot have identical infrared spectra (except, as usual, for enantiomers). Infrared spectroscopy is thus the final arbiter in deciding whether two compounds are identical.

Analysis of Infrared Spectra

Only a few simple equations or rules govern infrared spectroscopy. Since it is not practical to calculate theoretical spectra, the analysis is done almost entirely by correlation with other spectra. In printed form, these comparisons take the form of lengthy discussions, so detailed analysis of a spectrum is best done with a good reference book at hand.

In a modern analytical or research laboratory, a collection of many thousands of spectra is maintained on a computer. When the spectrum of an unknown compound is run, the analyst picks out five or six of the strongest peaks and asks the computer to list all compounds that have peaks within a few reciprocal centimeters of the listed peaks. From the printout of a dozen or so compounds, it is often possible to pinpoint all the functional groups in the molecule being analyzed. There may be a perfect match of all peaks, in which case the unknown will have been identified.

For relatively simple molecules, a computer search is hardly necessary. Much information can be gained about the functional groups in a molecule from relatively few correlations.

To carry out an analysis: (1) pay most attention to the strongest absorptions; (2) pay more attention to peaks to the left (shorter wavelength) of 1250 cm^{-1};

and (3) pay as much attention to the absence of certain peaks as to the presence of others. The absence of characteristic peaks will definitely exclude certain functional groups. Be wary of weak O—H peaks because water is a common contaminant of many samples. Because potassium bromide is hygroscopic, it is often found in the spectra of KBr pellets.

Step-by-Step Analysis of Infrared Spectra

1. Is there a peak between 1820 to 1625 cm^{-1}? If not, go to Step 2.
   (a) Is there also a strong, wide O—H peak between 3200 and 2500 cm^{-1}? If so, the compound is a carboxylic acid (Fig. 12.1, oleic acid). If not . . .
   (b) Is there a medium-to-weak N—H band between 3520 and 3070 cm^{-1}? If there are two peaks in this region, then it is a primary amide; if not, it is a secondary amide. If there is no peak in this region:
   (c) Are there two strong peaks, one in the region 1870 to 1800 cm^{-1} and the other in the region 1800 to 1740 cm^{-1}? If so, an acid anhydride is present. If not . . .
   (d) Is there a peak in the region of 2720 cm^{-1}? If so, is the carbonyl peak in the region 1715 to 1680 cm^{-1}? If so, it is a conjugated aldehyde; if not, it is an isolated aldehyde (Fig. 12.2, benzaldehyde). However, if there is no peak near 2720 cm^{-1}:
   (e) Does the strong carbonyl peak fall in the range 1815 to 1770 cm^{-1} and the molecule give a positive Beilstein test? If so, it is an acid halide. If not . . .
   (f) Does the strong carbonyl peak fall in the range 1690 to 1675 cm^{-1}? If so, it is a conjugated ketone. If not . . .
   (g) Does the strong carbonyl peak fall in the range 1670 to 1630 cm^{-1}? If so, it is a tertiary amide. If not . . .

FIG. 12.1   Infrared spectrum of oleic acid (thin film).

FIG. 12.2 Infrared spectrum of benzaldehyde (thin film).

(h) Does the molecule have a strong, wide peak in the range 1310 to 1100 cm^{-1}? If so, does the carbonyl peak fall in the range 1730 to 1715 cm^{-1}? If so, it is a conjugated ester; if not, the ester is not conjugated (Fig. 12.3, *n*-butyl acetate). If there is no strong, wide peak in the range 1310 to 1100 cm^{-1}, then:

(i) The molecule is an ordinary nonconjugated ketone.

2. If the molecule lacks a carbonyl peak in the range 1820 to 1625 cm^{-1}, does it have a broad band in the region 3650 to 3200 cm^{-1}? If so, does it also have a peak at about 1200 cm^{-1}, a C—H stretching peak to the left of 3000 cm^{-1}, and a peak in the region 1600 to 1470 cm^{-1}? If so, it is a

FIG. 12.3 Infrared spectrum of *n*-butyl acetate (thin film).

The effect of ring size on the carbonyl frequencies of lactones and esters

1727 cm^{-1}

FIG. 12.4   Infrared spectrum of cyclohexanol (thin film).

phenol. If it does not meet these latter three criteria, it is an alcohol (Fig. 12.4, cyclohexanol). However, if there is no broad band in the region 3650 to 3200 cm^{-1}, then:

(a) Is there a broad band in the region 3500 to 3300 cm^{-1}, does the molecule smell like an amine, or does it contain nitrogen? If so, are there two peaks in this region? If so, it is a primary amine; if not, it is a secondary amine. However, if there is no broad band in the region 3500 to 3300 cm^{-1}, then:

(b) Is there a sharp peak of medium-to-weak intensity at 2260 to 2100 cm^{-1}? If so, is there also a peak at 3320 to 3310 cm^{-1}? If so, the molecule is a terminal acetylene. If not, then the molecule is most likely a nitrile (Fig. 12.5, benzonitrile), although it might be an asymmetrically

1745 cm^{-1}

1740 cm^{-1}

1775 cm^{-1}

1832 cm^{-1}

FIG. 12.5   Infrared spectrum of benzonitrile (thin film).

The effect of ring size on the car-bonyl frequency ✳

1705 cm^{-1}

1715 cm^{-1}

O

1715 cm^{-1}

O

1745 cm^{-1}

O

1780 cm^{-1}

O

1815 cm^{-1}

FIG. 12.6   Infrared spectrum of 3-methylpentane (thin film).

substituted acetylene. If there is no sharp peak of medium-to-weak intensity at 2260 to 2100 cm^{-1}, then:

(c) Are there strong peaks in the region 1600 to 1540 cm^{-1} and 1380 to 1300 cm^{-1}? If so, the molecule contains a nitro group. If not . . .

(d) Is there a strong peak in the region 1270 to 1060 cm^{-1}? If so, the molecule is an ether. If not . . .

(e) The molecule is either a tertiary amine (odor?), a halogenated hydrocarbon (Beilstein test?), or just an ordinary hydrocarbon (Fig. 12.6, 3-methylpentane, and Fig. 12.7, *tert*-butylbenzene).

FIG. 12.7   Infrared spectrum of *tert*-butylbenzene (thin film).

TABLE 12.2 Characteristic Infrared Carbonyl Stretching Peaks (Chloroform Solutions)

	Carbonyl-Containing Compounds	Wavenumber (cm^{-1})
$\overset{\overset{\text{O}}{\|\|}}{\text{RCR}}$	Aliphatic ketones	1725–1705
$\overset{\overset{\text{O}}{\|\|}}{\text{RCCl}}$	Acid chlorides	1815–1785
$R-\overset{\|}{C}=\overset{\|}{C}-\overset{\overset{\text{O}}{\|\|}}{C}-R$	α,β-Unsaturated ketones	1685–1666
$\text{Ar}\overset{\overset{\text{O}}{\|\|}}{\text{CR}}$	Aryl ketones	1700–1680
=O (cyclohexanone)	Cyclohexanones	1725–1705
$-\overset{\overset{\text{O}}{\|\|}}{C}-CH_2-\overset{\overset{\text{O}}{\|\|}}{C}-$	β-Diketones	1640–1540
$\overset{\overset{\text{O}}{\|\|}}{\text{RCH}}$	Aliphatic aldehydes	1740–1720
$R-\overset{\|}{C}=\overset{\|}{C}-\overset{\overset{\text{O}}{\|\|}}{CH}$	α,β-Unsaturated aldehydes	1705–1685
$\text{Ar}\overset{\overset{\text{O}}{\|\|}}{\text{CH}}$	Aryl aldehydes	1715–1695
RCOOH	Aliphatic acids	1725–1700
$R-\overset{\|}{C}=\overset{\|}{C}-COOH$	α,β-Unsaturated acids	1700–1680
ArCOOH	Aryl acids	1700–1680
$\overset{\overset{\text{O}}{\|\|}}{\text{RCOR}'}$	Aliphatic esters	1740
$R-\overset{\|}{C}=\overset{\|}{C}-\overset{\overset{\text{O}}{\|\|}}{COR}'$	α,β-Unsaturated esters	1730–1715
$\text{Ar}\overset{\overset{\text{O}}{\|\|}}{\text{COR}}$	Aryl esters	1730–1715

(continued)

TABLE 12.2 *continued*

	Carbonyl-Containing Compounds	Wavenumber (cm^{-1})
$\overset{O}{\overset{\|}{HCOR}}$	Formate esters	1730–1715
$\overset{O}{\overset{\|}{CH_2=CHOCCH_3}}$ $\overset{O}{\overset{\|}{C_6H_5OCCH_3}}$	Vinyl and phenyl acetate	1776
$R-\overset{O}{\overset{\|}{C}}$ $R-\underset{\overset{\|}{O}}{C}{\overset{}{\diagdown}}O$	Acyclic anhydrides (two peaks)	1840–1800 1780–1740
$\overset{O}{\overset{\|}{RCNH_2}}$	Primary amides	1694–1650
$\overset{O}{\overset{\|}{RCNHR'}}$	Secondary amides	1700–1670
$\overset{O}{\overset{\|}{RCNR'_2}}$	Tertiary amides	1670–1630

FIG. 12.8 Band patterns of toluene and *o*-, *m*- and *p*-xylene. These peaks are *very weak*. They are characteristic of aromatic substitution patterns in general, not just for these four molecules. Try to find these patterns in other spectra throughout this text.

Many comments can be added to this bare outline. For example, dilute solutions of alcohols will show a sharp peak at about 3600 cm^{-1} for a nonhydrogen-bonded O—H in addition to the usual broad hydrogen-bonded O—H peak.

Aromatic hydrogens give peaks just to the left of 3000 cm^{-1}, whereas aliphatic hydrogens appear just to the right of 3000 cm^{-1}. However, NMR spectroscopy is the best method for identifying aromatic hydrogens.

The carbonyl frequencies listed earlier refer to the open chain or unstrained functional group in a nonconjugated system. If the carbonyl group is conjugated with a double bond or an aromatic ring, the peak will be displaced to the right by 30 cm^{-1} (see the margin notes). When the carbonyl group is in a ring smaller than six members or if there is oxygen substitution on the carbon adjacent to an aldehyde or ketone carbonyl, the peak will be moved to the left (see the margin notes and Table 12.2).

Methyl groups often give a peak near 1375 cm^{-1}, but NMR is a better method for detecting this group.

The pattern of substitution on an aromatic ring (mono-, *ortho*-, *meta*-, and *para*, di-, tri-, tetra-, and penta-) can be determined from C—H out-of-plane bending vibrations in the region 670–900 cm^{-1}. Much weaker peaks between 1650 and 2000 cm^{-1} are illustrated in Fig. 12.8.

Extensive correlation tables and discussions of characteristic group frequencies can be found in the specialized references listed at the end of this chapter.

The Fourier Transform Infrared (FTIR) Spectrometer

The double-beam infrared spectrometer is rapidly being supplanted by Fourier transform instruments. Like their NMR counterparts, they are computer based, can sum a number of scans to increase the signal-to-noise ratio, and being digitally oriented, allow enormous flexibility in the ways spectra can be analyzed and displayed. In addition, they are faster and more accurate than double-beam spectrometers.

A schematic diagram of a single-beam FTIR spectrometer is given in Fig. 12.9. Infrared radiation goes to a Michelson interferometer in which half the light beam passes through a partially coated mirror to a fixed mirror and half goes to a moving mirror. The combined beams pass through the sample and are then focused on the detector. The motion of the mirror gives a signal that varies sinusoidally. Depending on the mirror position, the different frequencies of light either reinforce or cancel each other, resulting in an interferogram. The mirror, the only moving part of the spectrometer, thus gives rise to a signal that encodes the very high optical frequencies as a low-frequency signal that changes as the mirror moves back and forth. The Fourier transform converts the digitized signal into a signal that is a function of frequency, i.e., a spectrum.

Like Fourier transform NMR spectroscopy, all infrared frequencies are sampled simultaneously instead of being scanned successively, so a spectrum is obtained in seconds. Because there is no slit to sort out the wavelengths, high resolution is possible without losing signal strength. Extremely small samples or very dilute solutions can be examined because it is easy to sum hundreds of scans in the computer. It is even possible to take a spectrum of an object seen

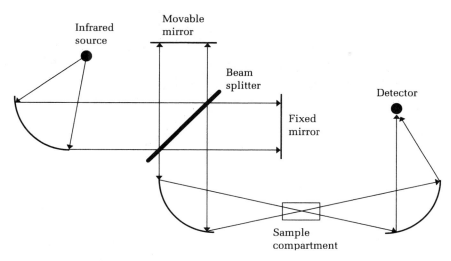

FIG. 12.9 Optical path diagram of an FTIR spectrometer.

under a microscope. The spectrum of one compound can be subtracted from, say, a binary mixture spectrum to reveal the nature of the other component. Data can be smoothed, added, resized, and so on because of the digital nature of the output from the spectrometer.

Experimental Aspects

*Sample, solvents, and equipment **must be dry.***

Infrared spectra can be determined on neat (undiluted) liquids, on solutions with an appropriate solvent, and on solids as mulls and KBr pellets. Glass is opaque to infrared radiation; therefore, the sample and reference cells used in infrared spectroscopy are sodium chloride plates. The sodium chloride plates are fragile and can be attacked by moisture. *Handle only by the edges.*

Spectra of Neat Liquids

To run a spectrum of a neat (free of water!) liquid, remove a demountable cell (Fig. 12.10) from the desiccator, place a drop of the liquid between the salt plates, press the plates together to remove any air bubbles, and add the top rubber gasket and metal top plate. Next, put on all four of the nuts and *gently* tighten them to apply an even pressure to the top plate. Place the cell in the sample compartment (nearest the front of the spectrometer), and run the spectrum.

Although running a spectrum on a neat liquid is convenient and results in no extraneous bands to interpret, it is not possible to control the path length of the light through the liquid in a demountable cell. A low-viscosity liquid when squeezed between the salt plates may be so thin that the short path length gives peaks that are too weak. A viscous liquid, on the other hand, may give peaks

FIG. 12.10 Exploded view of a demountable salt cell for analyzing the infrared spectra of neat liquids. Salt plates are fragile and expensive. Do not touch the surfaces. Use only dry solvents and samples.

FIG. 12.11 Demountable silver chloride cell.

that are too intense. A properly run spectrum will have the most intense peak with an absorbance of about 1.0.

Another demountable cell is pictured in Fig. 12.11. The plates are thin wafers of silver chloride, which is transparent to infrared radiation. This cell has advantages over the salt cell in that the silver chloride disks are more resistant to breakage than NaCl plates, less expensive, and not affected by water. Because silver chloride is photosensitive, the wafers must be stored in a dark place to prevent them from turning black. Because one side of each wafer is recessed, the thickness of the sample can be varied according to the manner in which the cell is assembled. In general, spectra of pure liquids are run as the thinnest possible films. Most of the spectra in this chapter have been obtained in this way. The disks are cleaned by rinsing them with an organic solvent such as acetone or ethanol and wiping dry with an absorbent paper towel.

A fast, simple alternative: Place a drop of the compound on a round salt plate, add a top plate, and mount the two on the holder pictured in Fig. 12.11.

A very simple "cell" consists of two circular sodium chloride disks (1" dia. $\times \frac{3}{16}$" thick, 25 mm $\times$ 4 mm). The sample, one drop of a pure liquid or solution, is applied to the center of a disk with a polyethylene pipette (to avoid scratching the sodium chloride). The other disk is added, the sample squeezed to a thin film, and the two disks placed on the V-shaped holder seen in Fig. 12.11.

Spectra of Solutions

Solvents: CHCl₃, CS₂, CCl₄

CAUTION: Chloroform, carbon tetrachloride, and carbon disulfide are toxic. The first two are carcinogens. Use laboratory hood. Avoid the use of these solvents if possible.

The most widely applicable method of running spectra of solutions involves dissolving an amount of the liquid or solid sample in an appropriate solvent to give a 10% solution. Just as in NMR spectroscopy, the best solvents to use are carbon disulfide and carbon tetrachloride, but because these compounds are not polar enough to dissolve many substances, chloroform is used as a compromise. Unlike NMR solvents, no solvent suitable in infrared spectroscopy is entirely free of absorption bands in the frequency range of interest (Figs. 12.12, 12.13,

FIG. 12.12 Infrared spectrum of chloroform (thin film).

FIG. 12.13 Infrared spectrum of carbon disulfide (thin film).

and 12.14). In chloroform, for instance, no light passes through the cell between 650 and 800 cm^{-1}. As can be seen from the figures, spectra obtained using carbon disulfide and chloroform cover the entire infrared frequency range. Carbon tetrachloride would appear to be a good choice because it has few interfering peaks, but it is a poor solvent for polar compounds. In practice, a baseline is run with the same solvent in both cells to ascertain if the cells are clean and matched. It is often necessary to obtain only one spectrum employing one solvent, depending on which region of the spectrum you need to use.

Three drops are needed to fill the cell.

Three large drops of solution will fill the usual sealed infrared cell (Fig. 12.15). A 10% solution of a liquid sample can be approximated by

FIG. 12.14 Infrared spectrum of carbon tetrachloride (thin film).

FIG. 12.15   Sealed infrared sample cell.

Solvent and sample must be dry. Do not touch or breathe on NaCl plates. Cells are very expensive.

Dispose of waste solvents in the container provided.

dilution of one drop of the liquid sample with nine drops of the solvent. Since weights are more difficult to estimate, solid samples should be weighed to obtain a 10% solution.

The infrared cell is filled by inclining it slightly and placing about three drops of the solution in the lower hypodermic port with a capillary dropper. The cell must be completely dry because the new sample will not enter if the cell contains solvent. The liquid can be seen rising between the salt plates by looking into the window. In the most common sealed cell, the salt plates are spaced 0.1 mm apart. Be sure that the cell is filled past the window and that no air bubbles are present. Then place the Teflon stopper lightly but firmly in the hypodermic port. Be particularly careful not to spill any of the sample on the outside of the cell windows.

Fill the reference cell from a clean hypodermic syringe in the same manner as the sample cell and place both cells in the spectrometer, with the sample cell toward the front of the instrument. After running the spectrum, force clean solvent through the sample cell using a syringe attached to the top port of the cell (Fig. 12.16). Finally, using the syringe, pull the last bit of solvent from both cells or suck clean dry air through the cells to dry them, and store them in a desiccator.

Cleaning Up   Discard halogenated liquids in the halogenated organic waste container. Other solutions should be placed in the organic solvents container.

Mulls

FIG. 12.16   Flushing the infrared sample cell. The solvent used to dissolve the sample is used in this process.

Solids insoluble in the usual solvents can be run as mulls. In preparing a mull, the sample is ground to a particle size less than that of the wavelength of light going through the sample (2.5 μm) in order to avoid scattering the light. About 15 to 20 mg of the sample is ground for 3 to 10 min in an agate mortar until it is spread over the entire inner surface of the mortar and has a caked and glassy appearance. Then, to make a mull, 1 or 2 drops of paraffin oil (Nujol) (Fig. 12.17) are added, and the sample ground 2 to 5 more minutes. The mull,

FIG. 12.17 Infrared spectrum of Nujol (paraffin oil).

Sample must be finely ground.

A fast, simple alternative: Grind a few milligrams of the solid with a drop of tetrachloroethylene between two round salt plates. Mount on the holder shown in Fig. 12.11.

which should have the consistency of thin margarine, is transferred to the bottom salt plate of a demountable cell (Fig. 12.10) using a rubber policeman, the top plate is added and twisted to distribute the sample evenly to eliminate all air pockets, and the spectrum is run. Since the bands from Nujol obscure certain frequency regions, running another mull using Fluorolube as the mulling agent will allow the entire infrared spectral region to be covered. If the sample has not been ground sufficiently fine, there will be marked loss of transmittance at the short-wavelength end of the spectrum. After running the spectrum, the salt plates are wiped clean with a cloth saturated with an appropriate solvent.

Potassium Bromide Disk

The spectrum of a solid sample can also be run by incorporating the sample in a potassium bromide (KBr) disk. This procedure needs only one disk to cover the entire spectral range because KBr is completely transparent to infrared radiation. Although very little sample is required, making the disk calls for special equipment and time to prepare it. Because KBr is hygroscopic, water is a problem.

Into a stainless steel capsule containing a ball bearing are weighed 1.5 to 2 mg of the compound and 200 mg of spectroscopic-grade potassium bromide (previously dried and stored in a desiccator). The capsule is shaken for 2 min on a Wig-L-Bug (the device used by dentists to mix silver amalgam). The sample is evenly distributed over the face of a 13-mm die and subjected to 14,000 to 16,000 lb/in.^{2} pressure for 3 to 6 min while under vacuum in a hydraulic press. A transparent disk is produced, which is removed from the die with tweezers and placed in a holder like that shown in Fig. 12.11 prior to running the spectrum.

Gas Phase Infrared Spectroscopy: The Williamson Gas Phase IR Cell

In the past it was difficult to obtain the infrared spectra of gases. A commercial gas cell costs hundreds of dollars and the cell must be evacuated and the dry gas carefully introduced—not a routine process. But we have found that a uniquely simple gas phase IR cell can be assembled at virtually no cost from a 105° microscale connecting adapter (Kontes 748001-1000).

To make the Williamson gas phase IR cell, attach a thin piece of polyethylene film from, for example, a sandwich bag to each end of the adapter with a small rubber band, fine wire, or thread. Place a loose wad of cotton in the side arm, and mount the IR cell in the beam of the spectrometer (Figs. 12.18 and 12.19).

The adapter can be supported on a V-block as shown in Fig. 12.19 or, temporarily, on a block of modeling clay. Be sure the beam, usually indicated by a red laser, strikes both ends of the cell. Run a background spectrum on the cell. The spectrum of polyethylene (Fig. 12.20) is very simple, so interfering bands will be few. This spectrum is automatically subtracted when you put a sample in the cell and run a spectrum.

A more permanent cell can be constructed by attaching two thin plates of silver chloride to ends of the adapter with epoxy glue. These silver chloride plates can be made in the press used for making potassium bromide discs or they can be purchased (Fisher 14-385-860). See the *Instructor's Guide*.

Obtaining a Spectrum

To run a gas phase spectrum, remove the cell from the spectrometer and spray onto the cotton a very short burst of a gas from an aerosol can. The nonvolatile components of the spray will stick to the cotton, and the propellant gas will diffuse into the cell. Run the spectrum in the usual way. The concentration of the

FIG. 12.18 The Williamson Gas Phase IR Cell utilizing the 105° adapter from the microscale kit.

FIG. 12.19 The Williamson Gas Phase IR Cell mounted in a cell holder.

gas is about the same as a thin film of liquid run between salt plates. If the concentration of the gas is too high, remove the cell from the spectrometer, remove the cotton, and "pour out" half the invisible gas by holding the cell in a vertical position.

   You may be fortunate in having in your institution's library a copy of *The Aldrich Library of FT-IR Spectra: Vapor Phase,* Volume 3 ($500). Most

FIG. 12.20 Infrared spectrum of polyethylene film.

libraries do not have it. This 2000-page book has more than 6500 gas phase spectra that will help you analyze the IR spectra of propellants in aerosol cans and any other gases you may encounter. Otherwise you may need to compare your spectra to the few in this text and in the *Instructor's Guide* and begin to assemble your own library of gas phase spectra. It is possible to make approximate calculations of IR spectra (vibrational spectra) using computational chemistry at the AM1 level, for example, with the program Spartan.

For Further Investigation

The Gas Phase IR Spectra of Aerosol Propellants

Acquire gas phase spectra from a number of aerosol cans. Some cans will be labeled with the name of the propellant gas, others will not. Analyze the spectra, bearing in mind that the gas will be a small molecule such as carbon dioxide (Fig. 12.21), methane (Fig. 12.22), nitrous oxide (Fig. 12.23), propane, butane, isobutane, or a fluorocarbon such as 1,1,1,2-tetrafluoroethane. A very old aerosol can may contain an illegal chlorofluorocarbon, now outlawed because these destroy the ozone layer. Some possibilities: hairsprays, lubricants (WD-40, Teflon), Freeze-It, inhalants for asthma, cigarette lighters, butane torches, natural gas from the lab.

FIG. 12.21   Infrared spectrum of carbon dioxide, gas phase.

FIG. 12.22 Infrared spectrum of methane, gas phase.

FIG. 12.23 Infrared spectrum of nitrous oxide, gas phase.

Other Gas Phase Spectral Research

You can deliberately generate hydrogen chloride (or deuterium chloride) and sulfur dioxide and then analyze the gas that is evolved from a thionyl chloride reaction. Can you detect carbon monoxide in automobile exhaust? How about "marsh gas" that you see bubbling out of ponds? With perhaps dozens of scans, can you record the spectra of vanillin over vanilla beans, of eugenol vapor over cloves, of anisaldehyde over anise seeds? What is the nature of the volatile components of chili peppers, orange peel, nail polish, and nail polish remover? Send me your results (williamson99@attbi.com), and I will post them on my Web page.

Running the Spectrum

Calibration with polystyrene

Satisfactory spectra are easily obtained with the lower-cost analog spectrometers, even those that have only a few controls and require few adjustments. To run a spectrum on these instruments, the paper must be positioned accurately, the pen set between 90 and 100% transmittance with the 100% control (0.0 and 0.05 absorbance), and the speed control set for a fast scan (usually one of about 3 min). The calibration of a given spectrum can be checked by backing up the pen and superimposing a spectrum of a thin polystyrene film. This film, mounted in a cardboard holder, will be found near most spectrometers. The film is held in the sample beam, and parts of the spectrum to be calibrated are rerun. See Fig. 12.24 for the spectrum of polystyrene. The spectrometer gain (amplification)

FIG. 12.24 Infrared spectrum of polystyrene film calibration standard.

should be checked frequently and adjusted when necessary. To check the gain, put the pen on the 90% transmittance line with the 100% control. Place your finger in the sample beam so that the pen goes down to 70% *T*. Then quickly remove your finger. The pen should overshoot the 90% *T* line by 2%.

Fourier transform spectrometers are faster, more sensitive, and can print out peak locations to at least four significant figures. They do not usually require routine calibration or gain adjustments, and the size of the most intense peak can be adjusted. A background spectrum (the empty cell, of whatever nature, or the cell plus a pure solvent) is run first and automatically stored in digital form in the spectrometer. The sample is introduced (a thin film, a solution, a mull, or a gas) and the background spectrum automatically subtracted, leaving only the spectrum of the sample.

Throughout the remainder of this book, representative infrared spectra of starting materials and products are presented and the important bands in each spectrum identified.

Experiment

Unknown Carbonyl Compound

Sample, solvents, and apparatus must be dry.

Run the infrared spectrum of an unknown carbonyl compound obtained from the laboratory instructor. Be particularly careful that all apparatus and solvents are completely free of water, which will damage the sodium chloride cell plates. The spectrum can be calibrated by positioning the spectrometer pen at a wavelength of about 1610 cm^{-1} without disturbing the paper and rerunning the spectrum in the region from 1610 to 1575 cm^{-1} while holding the polystyrene calibration film in the sample beam (Fig. 12.24). This will superimpose a sharp calibration peak at 1601 cm^{-1} and a less intense peak at 1583 cm^{-1} on the spectrum. Fourier transform spectrometers do not need frequent calibration. Determine the frequency of the carbonyl peak in the unknown, *and* list the possible types of compounds that could correspond to this frequency (Table 12.2).

Surfing the Web

http://www.cc.columbia.edu/cu/chemistry/irtutor/Edison.html
An excellent demo of an infrared spectroscopy tutorial is available from this Columbia University site. The infrared spectrum of 1-hexene can, for example, be expanded and each of the 11 major peaks can be selected, giving animations of the molecular motions responsible for each peak.

References

J. W. Cooper, *Spectroscopic Techniques for Organic Chemists,* John Wiley, New York, 1980.

Charles J. Pouchert, *The Aldrich Library of FT-IR Spectra,* 1st ed., Aldrich Chemical Co., Milwaukee, WI, 1985.

Norman B. Colthup, Lawrence H. Daly, and Stephen E. Wiberley, *Introduction to Infrared and Raman Spectroscopy,* 3rd ed., Academic Press, New York, 1990.

The Handbook of Infrared and Raman Characteristic Frequencies of Organic Molecules, Academic Press, Boston, 1991.

Noel P. G. Roeges, *A Guide to the Complete Interpretation of Infrared Spectra of Organic Structures,* John Wiley, New York, 1994.

Infrared and Raman Spectroscopy: Methods and Applications, VCH, New York, 1995.

CHAPTER
13
Nuclear Magnetic Resonance Spectroscopy

PRELAB EXERCISE: Outline the preliminary solubility experiments you would carry out on an unknown using inexpensive solvents, before preparing a solution of a compound for nuclear magnetic resonance spectroscopy.

Proton Nuclear Magnetic Resonance (NMR) Spectroscopy

NMR: Determination of the number, kind, and relative locations of hydrogen atoms (protons) in a molecule

Nuclear magnetic resonance (NMR) spectroscopy is a means of determining the number, kind, and relative locations of certain atoms, principally hydrogen, in molecules. The number of peaks or groups of coupled peaks indicate the number of chemically and magnetically distinct hydrogen atoms in a molecule. The *integral* indicates the relative number of protons within a peak or group of peaks. The separation between the lines within a group of peaks, called the *coupling constant, J,* can give information about the locations of the protons relative to other nearby protons and thus, the geometry of the molecule. And the location of a peak in the spectrum, called the *chemical shift, δ,* indicates which kind of proton gave rise to the peak, be it a methyl group, an alkene, or an aromatic ring.

Chemical shift, δ

Integration: The area under a peak or group of peaks

In the process of analyzing a sample, it is possible to expand portions of the spectrum so that patterns of peaks become clear, to *integrate* all peaks, which is the process of determining the relative areas of the peaks numerically or graphically and printing out the frequency of every peak. The integral indicates how many of each type of proton are present. If one or more sets of peaks are well resolved, then the coupling pattern can be analyzed to determine how many protons are adjacent to the proton or protons giving rise to that peak. Measurement of the magnitude of the coupling constant can give information about the geometry of the molecule.

Spectral Analysis: Proton Chemical Shifts

The first place to turn in analyzing a spectrum is a table of chemical shifts. Table 13.1 in this text and in similar general organic chemistry texts is just barely adequate for the task. In books devoted to NMR spectroscopy, such as the one by Friebolin (see the references at the end of this chapter), dozens of detailed tables are supplied for all types of functional groups. Many of the tables

TABLE 13.1 Proton Chemical Shifts

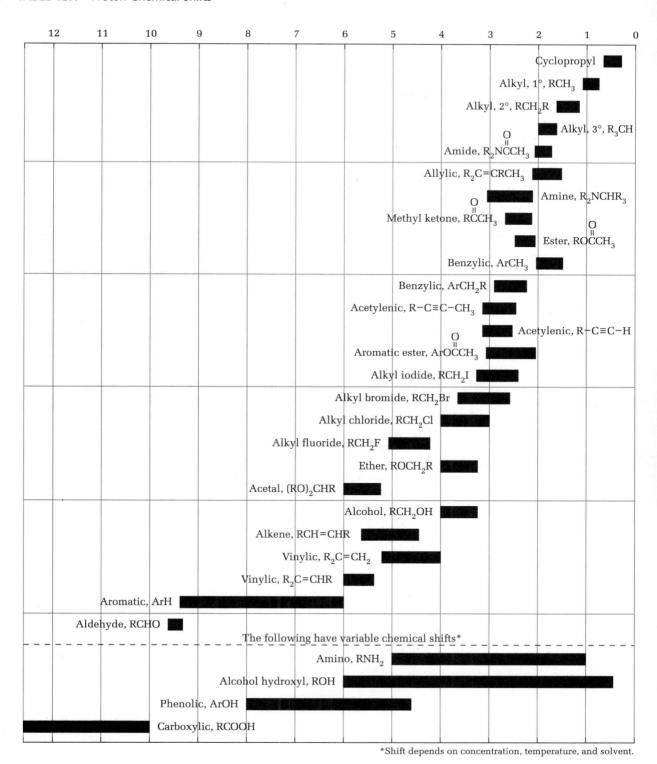

*Shift depends on concentration, temperature, and solvent.

FIG. 13.1 Proton NMR spectrum of ethyl iodide. The staircaselike line is the integral. In the integral mode of operation, the recorder pen moves from left to right and moves vertically a distance proportional to the areas of the peaks over which it passes. Hence the relative area of the quartet of peaks at 3.20 PPM to the triplet of peaks at 1.83 PPM is given by the relative heights of the integral (4 cm is to 6 cm as 2 is to 3). The relative numbers of hydrogen atoms are proportional to the peak areas (2H and 3H) (60-MHz spectrum).

contain additivity parameters that allow the approximate calculation of chemical shifts for, say, the protons in a 1,4-disubstituted aromatic ring containing a bromine atom and a methyl group.

A spectrum of ethyl iodide, typical of those obtained in an older low-field spectrometer operating at 60 MHz, is seen in Fig. 13.1. Fig. 13.2 shows a spectrum for the same compound obtained at 250 MHz. The information contained in these two spectra is identical. The chemical shifts reported in parts per million (δ) are identical and expansion of the pattern of lines in Fig. 13.2 shows that the coupling is exactly the same.

FIG. 13.2 Proton NMR spectrum of ethyl iodide (250 MHz). Compare this spectrum to Fig. 13.1, run at 60 MHz.

Every proton and carbon spectrum contains tetramethylsilane (TMS), which serves as the zero reference point. Chemical shifts are measured in dimensionless parts per million (PPM) downfield from the reference TMS according to the equation

$$\delta(\text{PPM}) = \frac{\text{Shift of peak downfield from TMS (measured in Hz)}}{\text{Spectrometer frequency (measured in MHz)}}$$

An NMR spectrum is characterized completely by the chemical shifts and coupling constants of the nuclei; this is the only information reported in research reports. Using just this information, one can calculate NMR spectra using programs such as gNMR (see the "Surfing the Web" section at the end of this chapter).

The Coupling Constant, J

Coupling Constants.

In an open-chain molecule with free rotation about the bonds and no chiral centers, protons couple with each other over three chemical bonds to give characteristic patterns of lines. If one or more equivalent protons couple to one adjacent proton, then the coupling hydrogen(s) appears as a doublet of equal intensity lines separated by the coupling constant, *J*, measured in hertz. If the coupling proton or protons couple equally to two protons three chemical bonds away, they appear as a triplet of lines with relative intensities of 1:2:1, again separated by the coupling constant, *J*. In general, chemically equivalent protons give a pattern of lines containing one more line than the number of protons being coupled to, and the intensities of the peaks follow the binomial expansion, conveniently represented by Pascal's triangle. Thus an ethyl group, as in ethyl iodide (Figs. 13.1 and 13.2), appears as a quartet of lines at 3.20 PPM with relative intensities of 1:3:3:1 because the two methylene protons have coupled to the three equivalent methyl protons. The methyl peak is split into a 1:2:1 triplet centered at 1.83 PPM because the methyl protons have coupled to the two adjacent methylene protons.

Pascal's triangle

			1			*singlet, s*
		1		1		*doublet, d*
	1		2		1	*triplet, t*
1		3		3	1	*quartet, q*
1	4		6	4	1	*pentet*
1	5	10	10	5	1	*sextet*

Other characteristic proton coupling constants are given in Table 13.2. In alkenes *trans* coupling is larger than *cis* coupling, and both are much larger than geminal coupling. *Ortho, meta,* and *para* couplings in aromatic rings range from 9 to 0 Hz. The couplings in a rigid system of saturated bonds are strongly dependent on the dihedral angle between the coupling protons as seen in cyclohexane.

The Integral.

The relative numbers of hydrogen atoms (protons) in the molecule of ethyl iodide are determined from the *integral,* the stair-step line over the peaks. The height of the step is proportional to the area under the NMR peak or group of peaks. In NMR spectroscopy (contrasted with infrared spectroscopy, for instance) the area of each group of peaks is directly proportional to the number of hydrogen atoms causing the peaks. Integrators are part of all NMR spectrometers; running the integral takes little more time than running the spectrum. Most spectrometers print out a numerical value for the integral (with many more significant figures than are justified!).

TABLE 13.2 Spin–Spin Coupling Constants for Various Geometries

Fragment	*J* (Hz)	Fragment	*J* (Hz)
(cis) H–C=C–H	7–12	(geminal) H–C–H	12–15
(trans) H–C=C–H	13–18	H–C–C–H	0–10
H–C=C–H	0.5–3	aromatic ring *ortho*	6–9
		meta	1–3
		para	0–1
H–C=C–C–H	0.5–2.5	H–C=C–C—H	0
H–C=C–C=C–H	9–13	CH_3—CH_2—	6.5–7.5
—C(H)—C(H)=O	1–3	$(CH_3)_2CH$—	5.5–7
H–C=C–C—H	4–10	cyclohexane H–H	5–9
			2–4

A more complex spectrum

Some NMR spectra are not as easily analyzed as the spectrum for ethyl iodide. Consider the spectra shown in Fig. 13.3. The proton spectrum of this unsaturated chloroester has been run at 500 MHz. Each chemically and magnetically nonequivalent proton is well resolved so that all of the couplings can be seen. Only the quartet of peaks at 4.1 PPM (relative area 2) and the triplet at 1.2 PPM (relative area 3) follow the simple first-order coupling rules outlined above. This quartet/triplet pattern is very characteristic of the commonly encountered ethyl group.

FIG. 13.3 The 500-MHz ^{1}H and 75-MHz ^{13}C NMR spectra of ethyl (3-chloromethyl)-4-pentenoate.* *I. ^{13}C DEPT spectrum. The CH$_3$ and CH peaks are upright and the CH$_2$ peaks inverted. The quaternary carbon (the carbonyl carbon) does not appear. II. The normal 75-MHz noise-decoupled ^{13}C spectrum. Note the small size of the carbonyl peak. III. Expansions of each group of proton NMR peaks. Protons E and F as well as protons H and I are not equivalent to each other. These pairs of protons are diastereotopic because they are on a carbon adjacent to a chiral carbon atom. The frequencies of all peaks are found in the Instructor's Guide. IV. The integral. The height of the integral is proportional to the number of protons under it. V. The 500-MHz ^{1}H spectrum.*

*Spectra courtesy of Professor Scott Virgil.

Because of the chiral carbon (marked with an asterisk), the protons on carbons D and E are diastereotopic, have different chemical shifts, and couple with each other and with adjacent protons to give the patterns seen in the spectrum. Many of the peaks can be assigned to specific hydrogens based simply on their chemical shifts. The coupling patterns then confirm these assignments.

Carbon-13 Spectroscopy

The element carbon consists of 98.9% carbon with mass 12 and spin 0 (NMR inactive) and only 1.1% ^{13}C with spin 1/2 (NMR active). Carbon, with such a low concentration of spin 1/2 nuclei, gives a very small signal when run under the same conditions as a proton spectrum. Carbon resonates at 75 MHz in a spectrometer where protons resonate at 300 MHz. Because only 1 in 100 carbon atoms has mass 13, the chances of a molecule having two ^{13}C atoms adjacent to one another are small. Consequently, coupling of one carbon with another is not observed.

Each ^{13}C atom couples to hydrogen atoms over one, two, and three bonds. Because the coupling constants are large there is a high frequency of peak overlap. To simplify the spectra as well as to increase the signal-to-noise ratio, a special technique is routinely used in obtaining ^{13}C spectra: *broadband noise decoupling*. Decoupling has the effect of collapsing all multiplets (quartets, triplets, etc.) into a single peak. Further, the energy put into decoupling the protons can be looked on as appearing in the carbon spectrum in the form of an enhanced peak. This nuclear Overhauser enhancement (NOE) effect makes the peak appear three times larger than it would otherwise be. The result of decoupling is that every chemically and magnetically distinct carbon atom will appear as a single sharp line in the spectrum. Because the NOE effect is somewhat variable and does not affect carbons bearing no protons, one cannot obtain reliable information about peak areas by integration of the carbon spectrum.

^{13}C spectra: Broadband noise decoupling gives a single line for each carbon.

Carbon Chemical Shifts

The range of carbon chemical shifts is 200 PPM compared to the 10-PPM range for protons. It is not common to have accidental overlap of carbon peaks. In the unsaturated chloroester seen in Fig. 13.3 there are eight sharp peaks corresponding to the eight carbon atoms in the molecule.

The generalities governing carbon chemical shifts are very similar to those governing proton shifts, as seen by comparing Table 13.1 to Table 13.3. Most of the downfield peaks are due to those carbon atoms near electron-withdrawing groups. In Fig. 13.3 the most downfield peak is that from the carbonyl carbon of the ester. The attached electronegative oxygen makes the peak appear at about 172 PPM. The peak is smaller than any other in the spectrum because it does not have an attached proton and thus does not benefit from a full NOE effect.

The ^{13}C spectrum of sucrose seen in Fig. 13.4 displays a single line for each carbon atom, and in Fig. 20.3 a single line is seen for each of the 27 carbon atoms in cholesterol.

TABLE 13.3 Carbon Chemical Shifts

FIG. 13.4 ^{13}C NMR spectrum of sucrose (22.6 MHz). Not all lines have been assigned to individual carbon atoms.

Fourier Transform Spectroscopy

The Fourier transform spectrometer

Even with broadband decoupling, the signal from ^{13}C spectra can get lost in the random noise produced by the spectrometer. Similarly, dilute solutions of samples give very noisy proton spectra. To increase the signal-to-noise ratio, the data for a number of spectra are averaged in the spectrometer computer. Because noise is random and the signal coherent, the signal will increase in size and the noise decrease as many spectra are averaged together. The improvement in the signal-to-noise ratio is proportional to the square root of the number of scans.

Spectra are accumulated rapidly by applying a very short pulse of radio-frequency energy to the sample and then storing the resulting free induction decay (FID) signal in digital form in the computer. The FID signal, which takes seconds to acquire, contains frequency information about all the signals in the spectrum. In a few minutes several hundred FID signals can be obtained and averaged in the computer. The FID signal is converted to a spectrum of conventional appearance by carrying out a Fourier transform computation on the signal using the spectrometer's computer.

Because the spectral information is in digital form, a large number of operations can be performed on it. The spectrum can be smoothed at the expense of resolution, or the resolution can be enhanced at the expense of noise. As indicated earlier, the spectrum can be numerically integrated and the position of each peak, in hertz or parts per million, printed above the peak. The spectra can be expanded both vertically and horizontally to clarify complex couplings, and all the parameters used to acquire the spectrum can be printed as well.

Protons with Variable Chemical Shifts

Protons attached to oxygen and nitrogen form hydrogen bonds with each other and with protonic solvents. As a result the chemical shifts of these protons depend

Labile Protons	δ (PPM)
ROH	0.5–6
ArOH	4.5–8
RCOOH	10–12
Enols	10–17
RNH_2	1–5
Amides	5–6.5

on solvent, temperature, and concentration and can appear almost anywhere in a spectrum. They will exchange with each other, a process catalyzed by small concentrations of acid or base. If this exchange is rapid (a common occurrence in alcohols, for example), only a single sharp line for the hydroxyl proton will be seen. At intermediate rates of exchange the line becomes broad; at slow rates of exchange it couples to other protons within three chemical bonds.

Protons bound to nitrogen often give a broad line because of the nonuniform distribution of charge on the nucleus of ^{14}N. Obviously NMR spectroscopy is a poor means for detecting hydroxylic, amine, and amide protons; infrared spectroscopy, on the other hand, is an excellent means.

Deuterium exchange

Because labile protons can undergo rapid exchange with each other they can also exchange with deuterium. If a drop of D_2O is added to a $CDCl_3$ solution of an NMR sample of a compound that contains such protons and gently mixed, the protons will exchange for deuterium atoms. The water will, of course, float on top of the denser chloroform. The peak for the labile proton will disappear, thus simplifying the spectrum and allowing for assignment of the peak.

Shift Reagents

Some spectra can be simplified by addition of shift reagents to the sample. The resulting spectrum is similar to that one might obtain in a high-field spectrometer.

Addition of a few milligrams of a hexacoordinate complex of europium {tris(dipivaloylmethanato)europium(III), [Eu(dpm)$_3$]} to an NMR sample that contains a Lewis base center (an amine or basic oxygen, such as a hydroxyl group) has a dramatic effect on the spectrum. This lanthanide (soluble in $CDCl_3$) causes large shifts in the positions of peaks arising from the protons near the metal atom in this molecule and is therefore referred to as a *shift reagent*. It produces the shifts by complexing with the unshared electrons of the hydroxyl oxygen, the amine nitrogen, or other Lewis base center.

With no shift reagent present, the NMR spectrum of 2-methyl-3-pentanol [Fig. 13.5(a)] is not readily analyzed. Addition of 10-mg portions of the shift reagent to the sample causes very large downfield shifts of peaks owing to protons near the coordination site [Figs. 13.5(b)–(g)].[1] The two protons on C-4 and the two methyls on C-2 are diastereotopic and thus magnetically nonequivalent because they are adjacent to a chiral center C-3; each gives a separate set of peaks. When enough shift reagent is added, this spectrum can be analyzed by inspection (Fig. 13.6).

Quantitative information about molecular geometry can be obtained from shifted spectra. The shift induced by the shift reagent is related to the distance and the angle that the proton bears to the europium atom.

Chiral shift reagents

Chiral shift reagents (derivatives of camphor) will cause differential shifts of the protons or carbon atoms in enantiomers. The separated peaks can be integrated to determine enantiomeric purity. A chiral shift reagent is used in

---

1. K.L. Williamson, D.R. Clutter, R. Emch, M. Alexander, A.E. Burroughs, C. Chua, and M.E. Bogel, *J. Am. Chem. Soc.*, **96**, 1471 (1974).

FIG. 13.5 The 60-MHz ^{1}H NMR spectrum of 2-methyl-3-pentanol (0.4 *M* in CS$_2$) with various amounts of shift reagent present. (A) No shift reagent present. All methyl peaks are superimposed. The peak for the proton adjacent to the hydroxyl group is downfield from the others because it is adjacent to the electonegative oxygen atom. (B) 2-Methyl-3-pentanol + Eu(dpm)$_3$. Mole ratio of Eu(dpm)$_3$ to alcohol = 0.05. The hydroxyl proton peak at 1.6 PPM in spectrum A appears at 6.2 PPM in spectrum B because it is closest to the Eu in the complex formed between Eu(dpm)$_3$ and the alcohol. The next closest proton, the one on the hydroxyl-bearing carbon atom, gives a peak at 4.4 PPM. Peaks due to the three different methyl groups at 1.1 to 1.5 PPM begin to differentiate. (C) Mole ration of Eu(dpm)$_3$ to alcohol = 0.1. The hydroxyl proton does not appear in this spectrum because its chemical shift is greater than 8.6 PPM with this much shift reagent present. (D) Mole ratio of Eu(dpm)$_3$ to alcohol = 0.25. Further differentiation of methyl peaks (2.3 to 3.0 PPM) is evident. (E) Mole ratio of Eu(dpm)$_3$ to alcohol = 0.5. Separate groups of peaks begin to appear in the region 4.2 to 6.2 PPM. (F) Mole ratio of Eu(dpm)$_3$ to alcohol = 0.7. Three groups of peaks (at 6.8, 7.7, and 8.1 PPM) due to the protons on C-2 and C-4 are evident, and three different methyls are now apparent. (G) Mole ratio of Eu(dpm)$_3$ to alcohol = 0.9. Only the methyl peaks appear on the spectrum. The two doublets come from the methyls attached to C-2, and the triplet comes from the terminal methyl at C-5.

Tris(dipivaloylmethanato)europium(III), Eu(dpm)$_3$
MW 701.78, mp 188–189°C

FIG. 13.6 Proton NMR spectrum of 2-methyl-3-pentanol containing Eu(dpm)$_3$ (60 MHz). Mole ratio of Eu(dpm)$_3$ to alcohol = 1.0. Compare this spectrum with those shown in Fig. 13.5. Protons nearest the hydroxyl group are shifted most. Methyl groups are recorded at reduced spectrum amplitude. Note the large chemical shift difference between the two diastereotopic protons on C-4.

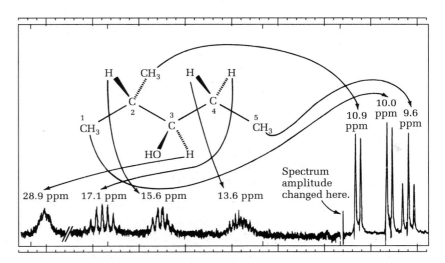

Chapter 66 to determine the enantiomeric purity of a chiral alcohol made by enzymatic reduction of a ketone.

Experiments

1. Running an NMR Spectrum

Sample Preparation

A typical ^{1}H NMR sample consists of about 10–50 mg of sample disolved in about 0.9 mL of deuterochloroform, CDCl$_3$, that contains a very small percentage of TMS, the reference compound. Because the tiniest particles of dust, especially metal particles, can adversely affect resolution, it is best to filter every sample routinely through a wad of cotton or glass wool in a Pasteur pipette (Fig. 13.7).

If very high resolution spectra (all lines very sharp) are desired, oxygen, a paramagnetic impurity, must be removed by bubbling a fine stream of pure nitrogen through the sample for 60 sec. Routine samples do not require this treatment.

It is most convenient if all tubes in a laboratory are filled to exactly the same height with the CDCl$_3$ solution; this will greatly facilitate tuning of the spectrometer. High-quality NMR tubes give the best spectra, free of spinning side bands. A good tube should roll at a slow, even rate down a very slightly inclined piece of plate glass.

Chemical shifts of protons and carbon are measured relative to the sharp peak in the TMS (taken as 0.0 PPM). Because the deuterochloroform is not 100% pure there will always be a very small peak at 7.27 PPM in the proton spectrum that arises from the tiny amount of residual ordinary chloroform, CHCl$_3$, in the sample. In the carbon spectrum three lines of equal intensity appear at 77 PPM due to coupling of the deuterium atom with the carbon in CDCl$_3$.

FIG. 13.7 Microfilter for NMR samples. Solution to be filtered is placed in the top of the Pasteur pipette, the rubber bulb is put in place, and pressure is applied to force the sample through the cotton or glass wool into an NMR sample tube.

FIG. 13.8 Effect of too rapid spinning or insufficient sample. The active volume is the only part of the sample detected by the spectrometer.

If the sample does not dissolve in deuterochloroform, a number of other deuterated solvents are available including deuteroacetone (CD_3COCD_3), deuterodimethylsulfoxide (DMSO-d_6), and deuterobenzene (C_6D_6). All of these solvents are expensive, so the solubility of the sample should first be checked in nondeuterated solvents. For highly polar samples, a mixture of the more expensive deuterodimethylsulfoxide with the less expensive deuterochloroform is often satisfactory. If it is necessary to use D_2O as the solvent, then a special water-soluble reference, sodium 2,2-dimethyl-2-silapentane-5-sulfonate [$(CH_3)_3$ $Si(CH_2)_3SO_3^-Na^+$ (DSS)], must be used. The protons on the three methyl groups bound to the silicon in this salt absorb at 0.0 PPM.

The usual NMR sample has a volume of about 0.9 mL, even though the volume sensed by the spectrometer receiver coils (referred to as the *active volume*) is much smaller. To average the magnetic fields produced by the spectrometer within the sample, the tube is spun by an air turbine at about 30 revolutions per second while taking the spectrum. Spinning that is too rapid or an insufficient amount of solution will cause the vortex produced by the spinning to penetrate the active volume, giving erratic nonreproducible spectra (Fig. 13.8).

Cleaning Up   Place halogenated solvents and compounds in the halogenated organic waste container. All others go into the organic solvents container.

Adjusting the Spectrometer

To be certain the spectrometer is correctly adjusted and working properly, record the spectrum of the standard sample of chloroform and TMS usually found with the instrument.

Small peaks symmetrically placed on each side of a principal peak are artifacts called *spinning side bands*. They are recognized as such by changing the spin speed, which causes the spinning side bands to change positions. They can be minimized by proper adjustment of the homogeneity controls.

Since Fourier transform (FT) spectrometers lock on the resonance of deuterium to achieve field/frequency stabilization, all samples must be dissolved in a solvent containing deuterium. Confirmation that the lock is obtained is registered on a meter or oscilloscope. The Z and Z^2 controls are used to maximize the field homogeneity and achieve the highest resolution. This adjustment is needed for virtually every sample, but, as noted earlier, if all sample tubes in a laboratory are filled to exactly the same height, these adjustments will be minimized.

Two-Dimensional NMR Spectroscopy

The fast computers associated with FT spectrometers allow for a series of precisely timed pulses and data accumulations to give a large data matrix that can be subjected to Fourier transformation in two dimensions to produce a two-dimensional (2D) NMR spectrum.

FIG. 13.9 The 2D COSY NMR spectrum of citronellol.

One of the most common and useful of these is the COSY (correlated spectroscopy) spectrum (Fig. 13.9). In this spectrum, two ordinary one-dimensional (1D) spectra are correlated with each other through spin–spin coupling. The 2D spectrum is a topographic representation, where spots represent peaks. The 1D spectra at the top and side are projections of these peaks. Along the diagonal of the 2D spectrum is a spot for each group of peaks in the molecule.

Fig. 13.9 shows the 2D spectrum of citronellol. (See Fig. 13.10 for the 1D spectrum of this compound.) Consider spot A (Fig. 13.9) on the diagonal of the 2D spectrum. From a table of chemical shifts we know that this is a vinyl proton, the single proton on the double bond. From the structure of citronellol, we can expect this proton to have a small coupling over four bonds to the methyl groups, and a stronger coupling to the protons on carbon-6. In the absence of a 2D spectrum, it is not obvious which group of peaks belongs to carbon-6, but the spot at B correlates with spot C on the diagonal, which is directly below the peak labeled 6 on the spectrum.

The diagonal spot C, which we have just assigned to carbon-6, correlates through the off-diagonal spot D with the diagonal spot E, which lies just below

FIG. 13.10 ¹H NMR spectrum of citronellol (250 MHz).

the group of peaks labeled 5. Spot A on the diagonal also correlates through spots F and G with spots H and I on the diagonal, which lie directly below methyl peaks 8 and 9. In this way we can determine the complete connectivity pattern of the molecule, seeing which protons are coupled to other protons.

Other 2D experiments allow proton spectra on one axis to be correlated with carbon spectra on the other axis. NOESY (nuclear Overhauser effect spectroscopy) experiments give cross-peaks for protons that are near to each other in space but not spin coupled to each other.

2. Identification of Unknown Alcohol or Amine by ¹H NMR

Prepare a solution of the unknown in deuterochloroform, and run a spectrum in the normal way. To the unknown solution add about 5 mg of Eu(dpm)₃ (the shift reagent), shake thoroughly to dissolve, and run another spectrum. Continue adding Eu(dpm)₃ in 5- to 10-mg portions until the spectrum is shifted enough for easy analysis. Integrate peaks and groups of peaks if in doubt about their relative areas. To protect the Eu(dpm)₃ from moisture, store it in a desiccator.

Shift reagents are expensive.

Cleaning Up   All samples containing shift reagents go into a hazardous waste container for heavy metals.

Questions

1. Propose a structure or structures consistent with the proton NMR spectrum of Fig. 13.11. Numbers adjacent to groups of peaks refer to relative peak areas. Account for missing lines.

2. Propose a structure or structures consistent with the proton NMR spectrum of Fig. 13.12. Numbers adjacent to groups of peaks refer to relative peak areas.

3. Propose a structure or structures consistent with the proton NMR spectrum of Fig. 13.13.

4. Propose structures for (a), (b), and (c) consistent with the ^{1}H NMR spectrum of Fig. 13.14 and the ^{13}C NMR spectra of Figs. 13.15, and 13.16. These are isomeric alcohols with the empirical formula $C_4H_{10}O$.

FIG. 13.11   Proton NMR spectrum (60 MHz), Question 1.

FIG. 13.12   Proton NMR spectrum (60 MHz), Question 2.

FIG. 13.13 Proton NMR
spectrum (60 MHz),
Question 3.

FIG. 13.14 ^{1}H NMR
spectrum $C_4H_{10}O$ (60 MHz),
Question 4(a).

FIG. 13.15 ^{13}C NMR
spectrum $C_4H_{10}O$ (22.6 MHz),
Question 4(b).

FIG. 13.16 ^{13}C NMR spectrum $C_4H_{10}O$ (22.6 MHz), Question 4(c).

Surfing the Web

The digital nature of modern NMR spectroscopy naturally lends itself to the graphical and computer-intensive material available on the Internet. From this wealth of material the following sites have been chosen:

http://www.aist.go.jp/RIODB/SDBS/menu-e.html

This Japanese site (in English) is produced by the National Institute of Advanced Industrial Science and Technology. Carbon and proton NMR spectra and numerical data are produced by entering the names of compounds. Alternatively upon entering up to five line frequencies (chemical shifts of individual lines) from either carbon or proton spectra a list of possible compounds is produced. The database includes thousands of compounds.

http://www.chem.wisc.edu/areas/reich.plt.windmnr.htm

WINDNMR-Pro is a Windows program for the simulation of NMR spectra. It will calculate spectra resulting from 3 to 8 coupled spins given the chemical shifts and coupling constants of the nuclei. Hans Reich of the University of Wisconsin produced the program.

http://www.chem.vt.edu/chem-dept/hbell/simulation/VTNMR.html

This very useful site, produced by Harold Bell of Virginia Tech, also allows the calculation of NMR spectra by closely simulating the operation of a spectrometer. Eight other Windows programs will calculate various 2D spectral patterns, generate free induction decays, etc.

http://www.chem.uni-potsdam.de/tools/

Stefen Thomas at the University of Potsdam has created a site in which a single proton or carbon chemical shift can be entered to produce a list of possible compounds. In addition, the carbon spectra of substituted benzenes are very easily calculated.

References

R. J. Abraham, J. Fisher, and P. Loftus, *Introduction to NMR Spectroscopy,* John Wiley & Sons, Chichester, 1988.

J. K. M. Sanders and B. K. Hunter, *Modern NMR Spectroscopy,* 2d ed., Oxford University Press, Oxford, 1993.

H. Friebolin, *Basic One- and Two-Dimensional NMR Spectroscopy,* 2d ed., VCH, New York, 1993.

W. R. Croasmun and R. M. K. Carlson, *Two-Dimensional NMR Spectroscopy. Applications for Chemists and Biochemists,* 2d ed., VCH Publishers, New York, 1994.

D. G. Gadian, *NMR and Its Applications to Living Systems,* Oxford University Press, Oxford, 1996.

I. R. Young, D. M. Grant, and R. K. Harris (eds.), and K. Harris, *Methods in Biomedical Magnetic Resonance Imaging and Spectroscopy,* 2 vol., John Wiley & Sons, New York, 2000.

CHAPTER

14

Ultraviolet Spectroscopy and Mass Spectrometry

PRELAB EXERCISE: Predict the appearance of the ultraviolet spectrum of 1-butylamine in acid, of methoxybenzene in acid and base, and of benzoic acid in acid and base. Predict the mass spectrum of ethanol, benzyl bromide, and 1-methyl cyclohexene.

1. Ultraviolet Spectroscopy

UV: Electronic transitions within molecules

Ultraviolet (UV) spectroscopy produces data about electronic transitions within molecules. Whereas absorption of low-energy infrared radiation causes bonds in a molecule to stretch and bend, the absorption of short-wavelength, high-energy UV radiation causes electrons to move from one energy level to another with energies that are often capable of breaking chemical bonds.

We shall be most concerned with transitions of π-electrons in conjugated and aromatic ring systems. These transitions occur in the wavelength region of 200 to 800 nm (nanometers, 10^{-9} meters, formerly known as mμ, millimicrons). Most common UV spectrometers cover the region of 200 to 400 nm as well as the visible spectral region of 400 to 800 nm. Below 200 nm air (oxygen) absorbs UV radiation; spectra in that region must therefore be obtained in a vacuum or in an atmosphere of pure nitrogen.

Consider ethylene, even though it absorbs UV radiation in the normally inaccessible region at 163 nm. The double bond in ethylene has two *s* electrons in a σ-molecular orbital and two, less tightly held, *p* electrons in a π-molecular orbital. Two unoccupied, high-energy-level, antibonding orbitals are associated with these orbitals. When ethylene absorbs UV radiation, one electron moves up from the bonding π-molecular orbital to the antibonding π^*-molecular orbital (Fig. 14.1). As the diagram indicates, this change requires less energy than the excitation of an electron from the σ to the σ^* orbital.

By comparison of infrared spectra and NMR spectra, UV spectra are fairly featureless (Fig. 14.2). This condition results as molecules in a number of different vibrational states undergo the same electronic transition to produce a band spectrum instead of a line spectrum.

Band spectra

Unlike IR spectroscopy, UV spectroscopy lends itself to precise quantitative analysis of substances. The intensity of an absorption band is usually given by the molar extinction coefficient, ε, which, according to the Beer–Lambert

Beer–Lambert law

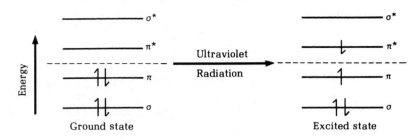

FIG. 14.1 Electronic energy levels of ethylene.

law, is equal to the absorbance, A, divided by the product of the molar concentration, c, and the path length, l, in centimeters.

$$\varepsilon = \frac{A}{cl}$$

λ_{max}, wavelength of maximum absorption

The wavelength of maximum absorption (the tip of the peak) is given by λ_{max}. Because UV spectra are so featureless, it is common practice to describe a spectrum like that of cholesta-3,5-diene (Fig. 14.2) as λ_{max} 234 nm ($\varepsilon = 20{,}000$) and not bother to reproduce the actual spectrum.

The extinction coefficients of conjugated dienes and enones are in the range of 10,000–20,000, so only very dilute solutions are needed for spectra. In the example of Fig. 14.2 the absorbance at the tip of the peak, A, is 1.2, and the path length is the usual 1 cm; so the molar concentration needed for this spectrum is 6×10^{-5} mole per liter,

ε, extinction coefficient

$$c = \frac{A}{l\varepsilon} = \frac{1.2}{20{,}000} = 6 \times 10^{-5} \text{ mole per liter}$$

which is 0.221 mg per 10 mL of solvent.

Spectro grade solvents

The usual solvents for UV spectroscopy are 95% ethanol, methanol, water, and saturated hydrocarbons such as hexane, trimethylpentane, and isooctane; the three hydrocarbons are often especially purified to remove impurities that absorb in the UV region. Any transparent solvent can be used for spectra in the visible region.

Sample cells for spectra in the visible region are made of glass, but UV cells must be composed of the more expensive fused quartz, since glass absorbs

FIG. 14.2 The ultraviolet spectrum of cholesta-3,5-diene in ethanol.

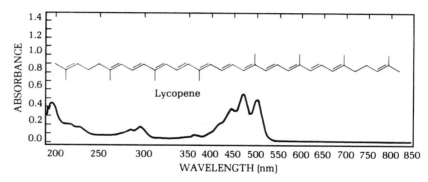

FIG. 14.3 The ultraviolet–visible spectrum of lycopene in isooctane.

UV cells are expensive; handle with care.

UV radiation. The cells and solvents must be clean and pure, since very little of a substance produces a UV spectrum. A single fingerprint will give a spectrum!

Ethylene has λ_{max} 163 nm ($\varepsilon = 15{,}000$), and butadiene has λ_{max} 217 nm ($\varepsilon = 20{,}900$). As the conjugated system is extended, the wavelength of maximum absorption moves to longer wavelengths (toward the visible region). For example, lycopene with 11 conjugated double bonds has λ_{max} 470 nm ($\varepsilon = 185{,}000$; Fig. 14.3). Because lycopene absorbs blue visible light at 470 nm, the substance appears bright red. It is responsible for the color of tomatoes; its isolation is described in Chapter 9.

Woodward and Fieser rules for dienes and dienones

The wavelengths of maximum absorption of conjugated dienes and polyenes and conjugated enones and dienones are given by the Woodward and Fieser rules, Tables 14.1 and 14.2. The application of the rules in these tables is demonstrated by the spectra of pulegone (1) and carvone (2) in Fig. 14.4. The solvent correction is given in Table 14.3. The calculations are given in Tables 14.4 and 14.5.

These rules will be applied in a later experiment in which cholesterol is converted into an α,β-unsaturated ketone.

TABLE 14.1 Rules for the Prediction of λ_{max} for Conjugated Dienes and Polyenes

	Increment (nm)
Parent acyclic diene (butadiene)	217
Parent heteroannular diene	214
Double bond extending the conjugation	30
Alkyl substituent or ring residue	5
Exocyclic location of double bond to any ring	5
Groups: OAc, OR	0
	0
Solvent correction, see Table 14.3 ( )	
λ_{max}^{EtOH} = Total	

TABLE 14.2 Rules for the Prediction of λ_{max} for Conjugated Enones and Dienones

$$\overset{\beta}{|}\ \overset{\alpha}{|}\ \overset{R}{|} \qquad \overset{\delta}{|}\ \overset{\gamma}{|}\ \overset{\beta}{|}\ \overset{\alpha}{|}\ \overset{R}{|}$$
$$\beta-C=C-C=O \ \text{and} \ \delta-C=C-C=C-C=O$$

	Increment (nm)
Parent α,β-unsaturated system	215
Double bond extending the conjugation	30
R (alkyl or ring residue), OR, OCOCH$_3$ α	10
$\qquad\qquad\qquad\qquad\qquad\qquad\qquad\qquad\beta$	12
$\qquad\qquad\qquad\qquad\qquad\lambda, \delta,$ and higher	18
α-Hydroxyl, enolic	35
α-Cl	15
α-Br	23
exo-Location of double bond to any ring	5
Homoannular diene component	39

Solvent correction, see Table 14.3 ( )

$$\lambda_{max}^{EtOH} = \text{Total}$$

TABLE 14.3 Solvent Correction

Solvent	Factor for Correction to Ethanol
Hexane	+11
Ether	+7
Dioxane	+5
Chloroform	+1
Methanol	0
Ethanol	0
Water	−8

FIG. 14.4 Ultraviolet spectra of (1) pulegone and (2) carvone in hexane.

TABLE 14.4   Calculation of λ_{max} for Pulegone (See Fig. 14.4)

Parent α,β-unsaturated system	215 nm
α-Ring residue, R	10
β-Alkyl group (two methyls)	24
Exocyclic double bond	5
Solvent correction (hexane)	-11

Calcd λ_{max} 245 nm; found 244 nm

TABLE 14.5   Calculation of λ_{max} for Carvone (See Fig. 14.4)

Parent α,β-unsaturated system	215 nm
α-Alkyl group (methyl)	10
β-Ring residue	12
Solvent correction (hexane)	-11

Calcd λ_{max} 226 nm; found 229 nm

No simple rules exist for calculation of aromatic ring spectra, but several generalizations can be made. From Fig. 14.5 it is obvious that as polynuclear aromatic rings are extended linearly, λ_{max} shifts to longer wavelengths.

As alkyl groups are added to benzene, λ_{max} shifts from 255 nm for benzene to 261 nm for toluene to 272 nm for hexamethylbenzene. Substituents bearing nonbonding electrons also cause shifts of λ_{max} to longer wavelengths, i.e. from 255 nm for benzene to 257 nm for chlorobenzene, 270 nm for phenol, and 280 nm for aniline ($\varepsilon = 6200–8600$). That these effects are the result of interaction of the π-electron system with the nonbonded electrons is seen dramatically in the spectra of vanillin and the derived anion (Fig. 14.6). Addition of two more nonbonding electrons in the anion causes λ_{max} to shift from 279 to

Effect of acid and base on λ_{max}

FIG. 14.5   The ultraviolet spectra of (1) naphthalene, (2) anthracene, and (3) tetracene.

FIG. 14.6 The ultraviolet spectra of (1) neutral vanillin, (2) the anion of vanillin.

FIG. 14.7 The ultraviolet spectra of (1) aniline and (2) aniline hydrochloride.

351 nm and ε to increase. Removing the electrons from the nitrogen of aniline by making the anilinium cation causes λ_{max} to decrease from 280 to 254 nm (Fig. 14.7). These changes of λ_{max} as a function of pH have obvious analytical applications.

Intense bands result from $\pi-\pi$ conjugation of double bonds and carbonyl groups with the aromatic ring. Styrene, for example, has λ_{max} 244 nm ($\varepsilon = 12,000$) and benzaldehyde λ_{max} 244 nm ($\varepsilon = 15,000$).

Experiment

UV Spectrum of Unknown Acid, Base, or Neutral Compound

Determine whether an unknown compound obtained from the instructor is acidic, basic, or neutral from the UV spectra in the presence of acid and base as well as in neutral media.

Cleaning Up   Because UV samples are extremely dilute solutions in ethanol, they can normally be flushed down the drain.

2. Mass Spectrometry

Mass spectrometry is the oldest of the spectroscopic methods. The principles were discovered by Wien in 1898 and J.J. Thomson, who discovered the electron, and built a spectrometer during the first decade of the last century. Aston and Dempster improved upon it in 1918. Wien, Thomson, and Aston all were Nobel laureates. A gigantic mass spectrometer three stories tall was used to separate ^{235}U from ^{238}U for the first atomic bomb.

The absorption of electromagnetic radiation characterizes IR, visible, UV, and NMR spectroscopy. A source of radiation is detected, processed, often by Fourier transform methods, and displayed as a spectrum. Mass spectrometry is rather different. The spectrum consists of a record of ion currents as a function of molecular mass. This spectral data can be generated in many different ways.

The magnetic sector spectrometer described in this chapter is the oldest and perhaps the easiest to understand. The ions can also be dispersed in time-of-flight, double focusing, ion cyclotron resonance, and quadrupole spectrometers. In addition to electron impact, the most common way to generate ions, there are a host of other methods—field ionization, field desorption, chemical ionization, electrospray, and matrix-assisted laser desorption/ionization (MALDI). The quadrupole mass spectrometer is the most common instrument because it is compact and relatively inexpensive. It is the basis for most benchtop units coupled to a gas chromatograph.

A mass spectrum is usually presented as a bar graph of an ionized molecule and fragments of that molecule arranged in increasing order of mass. On the y-axis is plotted the relative abundances of the ions. The relative abundance is normalized to the largest peak, which is given a value of 100%.

A mass spectrometer (Fig. 14.8) consists of a sample inlet system in which an extremely small sample of a substance is admitted to a region where it is ionized. The ions are accelerated and proceed through an analyzer (a magnetic field) were they are sorted according to mass before being detected, usually

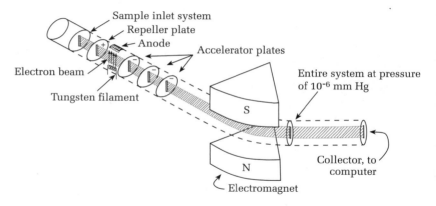

FIG. 14.8   Schematic of mass spectrometer.

electrically (formerly photographically). The entire operation occurs in a very high vacuum (10^{-6} mm Hg) so there is no interaction between ions once they are formed.

The sample inlet system allows for a liquid sample to be vaporized in a hot chamber and then diffuse into the high vacuum system of the spectrometer. Alternatively it is possible to insert a capillary with a sample inside into the inlet. The capillary is then heated electrically to volatilize the sample. Using new electrospray and MALDI systems it is now possible to introduce proteins and DNA into a mass spectrometer.

The sample once volatilized passes through an orthogonal electron beam generated by a tungsten filament. This beam of 70 electron volt (eV) electrons will knock one or more (usually one) electrons out of the molecule to generate a positive ion. In many but not all cases the original molecule having a positive charge will make it through the spectrometer to give the *molecular ion peak* or the *parent ion peak*. The easiest electrons to remove are the unshared electrons on an element such as oxygen, nitrogen, or one of the halogens.

$$\langle\!\!\!\bigcirc\!\!\!\rangle\!\!-\!CH_2\!:\!\ddot{O}\!:\!CH_3 + e^- \longrightarrow \left[\langle\!\!\!\bigcirc\!\!\!\rangle\!\!-\!CH_2\!:\!\dot{\ddot{O}}\!:\!CH_3\right]^+ + 2e^-$$

Molecular ion or
parent ion M+

The next easiest electrons to remove are the π–electrons followed by the σ-electrons. The 70 eV bombardment also transfers an enormous amount of energy to the molecule. This vibrational energy causes the molecule to fragment in various ways to produce smaller positive ions. This group of ions passes through a series of accelerator plates the first one of which is maintained at a potential difference of some 4000 to 10,000 volts with respect to the repeller plate.

These ions, of different mass, but all having a single positive charge, enter a magnetic field (Fig. 14.9) where their paths are bent along circular paths. The heavy

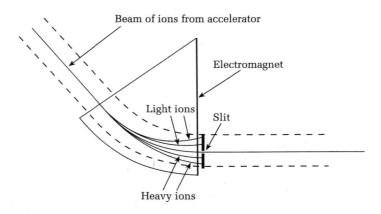

FIG. 14.9 Selection of positive ions according to mass.

ones tend to go straighter than the light ones under the influence of the magnetic field. Only a very narrow range (one mass unit or less) of ions can go through the slit to the detector. To obtain the entire spectrum the magnetic field strength is increased so that first the light ions pass through followed by those of increasing mass. The whole process is governed by this equation from classical mechanics

$$\frac{m}{z} = \frac{H^2 R^2}{2V}$$

where m is the mass of the ion, z is its charge, H is the magnetic field strength, R is the radius of curvature of the ion path, and V is the applied acceleration voltage.

The parent ion peak is very useful because it allows the exact molecular weight to be determined. A high resolution spectrometer, such as a double focusing instrument, will give masses to as many as six significant figures. This allows not only the molecular weight but also the determination of the molecular formula. For example, at least three compounds have a nominal MW of 44. These are carbon dioxide, propane, and acetaldehyde. The exact atomic weights of the component elements are

$$^1\text{H} \quad 1.0078$$
$$^{12}\text{C} \quad 12.0000$$
$$^{16}\text{O} \quad 15.9949$$

so carbon dioxide would have a MW of 43.9898, propane 44.0624, and acetaldehyde 44.0261. A high resolution spectrometer can distinguish among these, and thus allow identification of the molecule.

Sometimes the molecular ion does not appear in the spectrum because all of the ionized molecules fragment before reaching the accelerator plates. The techniques of field ionization and chemical ionization are gentle methods for making ions; the molecular ions usually appear when these methods are employed, for example with 1,4-dioxane (Fig. 14.10).

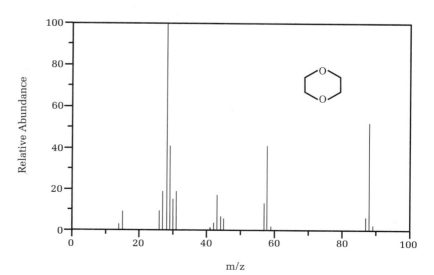

FIG. 14.10   Mass spectrum of 1,4-dioxane.

In addition to giving the molecular weight or perhaps even the molecular formula, an analysis of the fragment ions can give much information regarding the structure of the molecule.

Isotopes

Most of the elements in the periodic table are made of mixtures of isotopes. Some of these are familiar through their use in NMR spectroscopy, such as deuterium, the isotope of hydrogen with mass 2 that gives no signal in the proton region of the spectrum and ^{13}C, the isotope that has a spin of 1/2 and is therefore detectable by NMR. A few elements have only one isotope, ^{19}F, ^{31}P and ^{127}I being the most important to the organic chemist. A list of the most important ones is given in Table 14.6. By definition the exact mass of the most common isotope of carbon is taken to be 12.00000. All other masses are relative to this.

Deuterium is not listed because it has a natural abundance of only 0.015% and so is not usually observed. The ability of the mass spectrometer to distinguish differences of mass of one unit makes isotopic labeling very useful in determining the mechanism of organic reactions, for example, in studying the hydrolysis of esters or the structure of benzyne. But almost every mass spectrum will be influenced by the isotopic distribution.

It is easy to spot a molecule containing one bromine atom because the molecular ion region will have two peaks of almost equal intensity (note the abundances of ^{79}Br and ^{81}Br). If the molecule contains two bromines the molecular ion region will have three peaks of relative intensities 1:2:1. Similarly, a molecule with one chlorine atom will show two peaks of relative intensity 3:1.

TABLE 14.6 Exact masses and percent natural abundance for elements important to organic mass spectrometry

Nuclide	Atomic mass	Natural abundance, %
^{1}H	1.007825	99.985
^{12}C	12.00000	98.9
^{13}C	13.00335	1.11
^{14}N	14.00307	99.63
^{16}O	15.994914	99.80
^{19}F	18.998405	100.00
^{28}Si	27.976927	92.21
^{31}P	30.973763	100.00
^{32}S	31.972074	94.62
^{34}S	33.96786	4.2
^{35}Cl	34.968855	75.5
^{37}Cl	36.9658	24.5
^{79}Br	78.918348	49.5
^{81}Br	80.983	50.5
^{127}I	126.904352	100.00

If the molecule has two chlorine atoms the peaks at the molecular ion position will have relative intensities of 9:6:1.

The 1.1% ^{13}C can cause complications. A molecule with 10 carbons will show an M + 1 peak with an intensity of 10% that of the M (molecular ion) peak. As the number of carbons increases, this peak grows to the point where it can be confused with the molecular ion peak.

The Nitrogen Rule

A molecule is known to contain just one nitrogen atom. A chemist reports the molecular weight of the molecule as 178. What is wrong? The answer is found in the nitrogen rule: a molecule having an odd number of nitrogen atoms will have an odd molecular weight, a consequence of the trivalent nature of nitrogen. Molecules containing just C, H, O, S, P, and the halogens, as well as molecules with an even number of nitrogens, will always have an even numbered molecular ion peak.

Fragmentation

The energy supplied by the 70 eV electron beam in the source region of the spectrometer not only knocks out an electron to generate the molecular ion, it also imparts an enormous amount of vibrational energy to the molecule. During the 10^{-5} secs between the generation of the ion and its entry into the accelerator region the ion can fragment. This fragmentation is a unimolecular gas-phase reaction; the probability of ion-molecule reactions at 10^{-6} torr is not large, although some do occur.

The fragments produced in greatest abundance are the most stable thermodynamically and are, in general, quite logical. For example, alkanes fragment to produce preferentially tertiary carbocations if possible, followed by secondary and finally primary ions:

$$\left[\begin{array}{c} CH_3CH_2CHCH_3 \\ | \\ CH_3 \end{array} \right]^{\overset{\cdot}{+}} \longrightarrow CH_3CH_2\overset{+}{C}HCH_3 \; + \; \cdot CH_3$$

Ketones and aldehydes fragment next to the carbonyl group to give the resonance stabilized acylium ion:

$$CH_3\overset{\overset{\displaystyle :O:}{::}}{C}:CH_3 \xrightarrow{70\,eV} \left[CH_3\overset{\overset{\displaystyle :O\cdot}{::}}{C}:CH_3 \right]^{+}$$

$$\cdot CH_3 \; + \; \left[\overset{+}{\ddot{O}}:::C:CH_3 \longleftrightarrow \ddot{O}::\overset{+}{C}:CH_3 \right]$$

If the molecule contains a hetero atom with unshared electrons such as oxygen, nitrogen, or sulfur the adjacent carbon-carbon bond is cleaved because the resulting ion is stabilized by resonance.

Benzylic substituted compounds have a great tendency to lose a substituent radical to form the tropylium ion (*see* Chapter 31). Toluene will lose a hydrogen radical and xylene will lose a methyl radical to form the same ion, with m/z 91.

Tropylium ion, m/z 91

Ketones and esters with a hydrogen atom on the γ-carbon atom can undergo the McLafferty rearrangement.

R=OR′, H, alkyl, aryl

Cyclohexenes can undergo a retro-Diels-Alder reaction to give an alkene and a diene. The charge will reside on the diene component.

$$\left[\begin{array}{c} \bigcirc \end{array}\right]^{\ddot{+}} \longrightarrow \left[\begin{array}{c} \diagup\diagdown \end{array}\right]^{\ddot{+}} + \begin{array}{c} CH_2 \\ \| \\ CH_2 \end{array}$$

Other small neutral molecules can be eliminated from molecular ions. Perhaps the most important is the elimination of water from alcohols, but CO, NH_3, ROH, H_2, HCN, H_2S, ethylene, and acetic acid are also eliminated. One fragment that is not eliminated from the molecular ion is CH_2.

Like infrared spectroscopy there are large libraries of mass spectra available so that relatively common materials can easily be identified simply by comparison. In addition, computer programs are available that can calculate the intensities of the M, M + 1, M + 2, etc. peaks for a given elemental composition.

Mass spectrometers have become more reliable and less complex and expensive in recent years.

Sample Preparation

The amount of sample needed for a mass spectrum is exceedingly small. MS is the most sensitive analytical instrument; it is possible to detect a single ion with an electron-multiplier detector. But MS is also capable of detecting impurities which can make analysis of the spectrum difficult. Any organic liquid that comes in contact with flexible plastic, e.g. Tygon tubing, will be contaminated with plasticizers such as dioctyl phthalate. Contamination with grease from stopcocks and joints is also common. Samples recovered from NMR analysis are often contaminated with deuterated solvents which can also confuse MS analysis.

Questions _____

1. Calculate the UV absorption maximum for 2-cyclohexene-1-one.

2. Calculate the UV absorption maximum for 3,4,4-trimethyl-2-cyclohexene-1-one.

3. Calculate the UV absorption maximum for

4. What concentration, in g/mL, of a substance with MW 200 should be prepared in order to give an absorbance value A equal to 0.8 if the substance has $\varepsilon = 16,000$ and a cell with a path length of 1 cm is employed?

5. Propose a structure or structures consistent with the mass spectrum of Fig. 14.11.

6. Propose a structure or structures consistent with the mass spectrum of Fig. 14.12.

7. Propose a structure or structures consistent with the mass spectrum of Fig. 14.13.

FIG. 14.11   Mass spectrum, Question 5.

FIG. 14.12   Mass spectrum, Question 6.

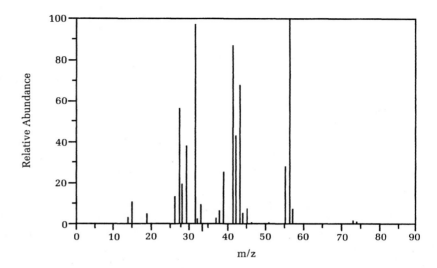

FIG. 14.13   Mass spectrum, Question 7.

References

H. H. Jaffe and M. Orchin, *Theory and Application of Ultraviolet Spectroscopy,* John Wiley, New York, 1962.

A. E. Gillam and E. S. Stern, *An Introduction to Electronic Absorption Spectroscopy in Organic Chemistry,* Edward Arnold, London, 1967.

C. N. R. Rao, *Ultraviolet and Visible Spectroscopy,* 2d ed., Butterworths, London, 1967.

R. M. Silverstein, C. G. Bassler, and T. C. Morrill, *Spectrometric Identification of Organic Compounds,* 4th ed., John Wiley, New York, 1981. (Includes IR, UV, and NMR.)

D. H. Williams and I. Fleming, *Spectroscopic Methods in Organic Chemistry,* 5th ed., McGraw-Hill, 1995.

F. G. Kitson, B. S. Larsen, and C. N. McEwen, *Gas Chromatography and Mass Spectrometry, A Practical Guide,* Academic Press, 1996.

G. Siuzdak, *Mass Spectrometry for Biotechnology,* Academic Press, 1996.

J. Throck Watson, *Introduction to Mass Spectrometry,* 3d ed., Lippincott Williams and Wilkins, 1997.

J. B. Lambert, H.F. Shurvell, D. Lightner, and R. G. Cooks, *Organic Structural Spectroscopy,* Prentice-Hall, 1998.

R. M. Silverstein and F. X. Webster, *Spectrometric Identification of Organic Compounds*, 6th ed., Wiley, 1998.

Proteome Research: Mass Spectrometry (Principles and Practice), P. James, ed, Springer Verlag, 2000.

CHAPTER

38

Grignard Synthesis of Triphenylmethanol and Benzoic Acid

PRELAB EXERCISE: Prepare a flow sheet for the preparation of triphenyl-methanol. Through a knowledge of the physical properties of the solvents, reactants, and products, show how the products are purified. Indicate which layer in separations should contain the product.

In 1912 Victor Grignard received the Nobel prize in chemistry for his work on the reaction that bears his name, a carbon–carbon bond-forming reaction by which almost any alcohol may be formed from appropriate alkyl halides and carbonyl compounds. The Grignard reagent is easily formed by reaction of an alkyl halide, in particular a bromide, with magnesium metal in anhydrous diethyl ether. Although the reaction can be written and thought of as simply

$$R\text{---}Br + Mg \longrightarrow R\text{---}Mg\text{---}Br$$

it appears that the structure of the material in solution is rather more complex. There is evidence that dialkylmagnesium is present

$$2\ R\text{---}Mg\text{---}Br \rightleftharpoons R\text{---}Mg\text{---}R + MgBr_2$$

Structure of the Grignard reagent

and that the magnesium atoms, which have the capacity to accept two electron pairs from donor molecules to achieve a four-coordinated state, are solvated by the unshared pairs of electrons on diethyl ether:

$$
\begin{array}{c}
Et\diagdown\ \ \ \diagup Et \\
\ddot{O} \\
R\text{---}\overset{..}{\underset{..}{Mg}}\text{---}Br \\
\ddot{O} \\
Et\diagup\ \ \ \diagdown Et
\end{array}
$$

A strong base and strong nucleophile

The Grignard reagent is both a strong base and a strong nucleophile. As a base it will react with all protons that are more acidic than those found on alkenes and alkanes. Thus, Grignard reagents react readily with water, alcohols, amines, thiols, and so on, to regenerate the alkane:

461

$$R—Mg—Br + H_2O \longrightarrow R—H + MgBrOH$$

$$R—Mg—Br + R'OH \longrightarrow R—H + MgBrOR'$$

$$R—Mg—Br + R'NH_2 \longrightarrow R—H + MgBrNHR'$$

$$R—Mg—Br + R'C \equiv C—H \longrightarrow R—H + R'C \equiv CMgBr$$
(an acetylenic Grignard reagent)

The starting material for preparing the Grignard reagent can contain no acidic protons. The reactants and apparatus must all be completely dry; otherwise the reaction will not start. If proper precautions are taken, however, the reaction proceeds smoothly.

The magnesium metal, in the form of a coarse powder, has a coat of oxide on the outside. A fresh surface can be exposed by crushing the powder under the absolutely dry ether in the presence of the organic halide. Reaction will begin at exposed surfaces, as evidenced by a slight turbidity in the solution and evolution of bubbles. Once the exothermic reaction starts it proceeds easily, the magnesium dissolves, and a solution of the Grignard reagent is formed. The solution is often turbid and gray due to impurities in the magnesium. The reagent is not isolated but reacted immediately with, most often, an appropriate carbonyl compound

$$R — Mg — Br + R' — \overset{\displaystyle \overset{..}{O}:}{\underset{}{\overset{\|}{C}}} — R'' \longrightarrow R' — \overset{\displaystyle :\overset{..}{O}:^- MgBr^+}{\underset{\displaystyle R}{\overset{|}{C}}} — R''$$

to give, in another exothermic reaction, the magnesium alkoxide, a salt insoluble in ether. In a simple acid–base reaction this alkoxide is reacted with acidified ice water to give the covalent, ether-soluble alcohol and the ionic water-soluble magnesium salt:

$$R' — \overset{\displaystyle :\overset{..}{O}:^- MgBr^+}{\underset{\displaystyle R}{\overset{|}{C}}} — R'' \;\; + \; H^+Cl^- \longrightarrow R' — \overset{\displaystyle :\overset{..}{O} — H}{\underset{\displaystyle R}{\overset{|}{C}}} — R'' \; + \; Mg^{2+}Br^-Cl^-$$

The great versatility of this reaction lies in the wide range of reactants that undergo the reaction. Thirteen representative reactions are shown on the following page.

A versatile reagent

In every case except reaction 1 the intermediate alkoxide must be hydrolyzed to give the product. The reaction with oxygen (reaction 2) is usually not a problem because the ether vapor over the reagent protects it from attack by oxygen, but this reaction is one reason why the reagent cannot usually be stored without special precautions. Reactions 6 and 7 with ketones and aldehydes giving, respectively, tertiary and secondary alcohols are among the most common. Reactions 8–13 are not nearly so common.

In the present experiment we shall carry out another common type of Grignard reaction, the formation of a tertiary alcohol from 2 moles of the reagent and one of an ester. The ester employed is the methyl benzoate synthesized in Chapter 40. The initially formed product is unstable and decomposes to a ketone, which, being more reactive than an ester, immediately reacts with more Grignard reagent:

Biphenyl has a characteristic odor. Triphenylmethanol is odorless.

The primary impurity in the present experiment is biphenyl, formed by the reaction of phenylmagnesium bromide with unreacted bromobenzene.[1] The most effective way to lessen this side reaction is to add the bromobenzene slowly to the reaction mixture so it will react with the magnesium and not be present in high concentration to react with previously formed Grignard reagent. The impurity is easily eliminated because it is much more soluble in hydrocarbon solvents than triphenylmethanol.

---

1. See Fig. 38.7 at the end of the chapter for the ^{13}C NMR spectrum.

Biphenyl
mp 72°C

Triphenylmethanol can also be prepared from benzophenone.

Phenylmagnesium bromide

Benzophenone
MW 182.22
mp 48°C

Triphenylmethanol
MW 260.34
mp 164.2°C

Experiments

MICROSCALE

1. Phenylmagnesium Bromide (Phenyl Grignard Reagent)

Bromobenzene
MW 157.02
bp 156°C
den. 1.491

Magnesium
At. Wt
24.31

Phenylmagnesium bromide
not isolated, used *in situ*

anhydrous
ether

Advance Preparation

It is imperative that all equipment and reagents be absolutely dry. The glassware to be used—two reaction tubes, two 1-dram vials, and a stirring rod—can be dried in a 110°C oven for at least 30 min, along with the magnesium. Alternatively, if the glassware, syringe, septa, and magnesium appear to be perfectly dry, they can be used without special drying. The plastic and rubber ware should be rinsed with acetone if it appears to be either dirty or wet with water and then placed in a desiccator for at least 12 h. Do not place plastic ware in the oven. New, sealed packages of syringes can be used without prior drying. The ether used throughout this reaction must be absolutely dry (absolute ether). To prepare the Grignard reagent, absolute diethyl ether must be used; elsewhere, ordinary ether (diethyl or *t*-butyl methyl) can be used; for example, ether extractions of aqueous solutions do not need to be carried out with dry ether. It is strongly recommended that *t*-butyl methyl ether be used in all cases except the preparation of the Grignard reagent itself (*see* Chapter 8).

A very convenient container for absolute diethyl ether is a 50-mL septum-capped bottle. This method of dispensing the solvent has three advantages: the ether is kept anhydrous, the exposure to oxygen is minimized, and there is little possibility of its catching fire. Ether is extremely flammable; do not work with this solvent near flames.

R1

43

44

To remove ether from a septum-capped bottle, inject a volume of air into the bottle equal to the amount of ether being removed. Pull more ether than needed into the syringe, then push the excess back into the bottle before removing the syringe. In this way there will be no air bubbles in the syringe, and it will not dribble (Fig. 38.1).

Procedure

29

IN THIS EXPERIMENT magnesium and absolutely dry diethyl ether in a dry, septum-capped tube is reacted with an aromatic halide to give phenylmagnesium bromide. The exothermic reaction is started by crushing the magnesium. If the reaction does not start in under a minute it will be necessary to start again, using equipment that was not used in the first try.

Remove a reaction tube from the oven and immediately cap it with a septum. In the operations that follow, keep the tube capped except when it is necessary to open it. After it cools to room temperature, add about 2 mmol (about 50 mg) of magnesium powder. Record the weight of magnesium used to the nearest milligram. We will make it the limiting reagent by using a 5% molar excess of bromobenzene (about 2.1 mmol).

*Diethyl ether can be made and kept anhydrous by storing over Linde 5A molecular sieves. Discard diethyl ether within 90 days because of peroxide formation. *tert-*Butyl methyl ether does not have this problem.*

Using a dry syringe, add to the magnesium by injection through the septum 0.5 mL of anhydrous diethyl ether. Your laboratory instructor will demonstrate transfer from the storage container used in your laboratory.

Into an oven-dried vial weigh about 2.1 mmol (about 330 mg) of dry (stored over molecular sieves) bromobenzene. Using a syringe, add to this vial 0.7 mL anhydrous diethyl ether, and *immediately,* with the same syringe, remove all the solution from the vial. This can be done virtually quantitatively so you do not need to rinse the vial. Immediately cap the empty vial to keep it dry for later use. Inject about 0.1 mL of the bromobenzene–ether mixture into the reaction tube and mix the contents by flicking the tube. Pierce the septum with another syringe needle for pressure relief (Fig. 38.2).

It takes much force to crush the magnesium. Place the tube on a hard surface and bear down with the stirring rod while twisting the reaction tube. Do not pound the magnesium.

The reaction will not ordinarily start at this point, so remove the septum, syringe, and empty syringe needle and crush the magnesium with a dry stirring rod. You can do this easily in the confines of the 10-mm-diameter reaction tube

FIG. 38.1 Polypropylene syringe (1 mL, with 0.01-mL graduations). The needle is blunt. When there are no air bubbles in the syringe, it will not dribble ether.

Read volume here

FIG. 38.2 Once the reaction has started, bromobenzene in ether is added slowly from the syringe. The empty needle is for pressure relief, but if condensation is complete (aided by the damp pipe cleaner), it will not be needed. Once the reaction slows down, stir it with the magnetic stirring bar.

FIG. 38.3 To start the Grignard reaction, remove the septum and apply pressure to the stirring rod while rotating the reaction tube on a hard surface that will not scratch the tube, such as a book.

R2

while it is placed on a hard surface. There is little danger of poking the stirring rod through the bottom of the tube (Fig. 38.3). Immediately replace the septum, syringe, and empty syringe needle (for pressure relief). The reaction should start within seconds. The formerly clear solution becomes cloudy and soon begins to boil as the magnesium metal reacts with the bromobenzene to form the Grignard reagent, phenylmagnesium bromide.

If the reaction does not start within 1 min, begin again with completely different, dry equipment (syringe, syringe needle, reaction tube, etc.). Once the

Grignard reaction begins, it will continue. To prevent the ether from boiling away, wrap a pipe cleaner around the top part of the reaction tube. Dampen this with water or, if the room temperature is very hot, with alcohol.

R3   To the refluxing mixture add slowly and dropwise over a period of several minutes the remainder of the solution of bromobenzene in ether at a rate such that the reaction remains under control at all times. After all the bromobenzene solution is added, spontaneous boiling of the diluted mixture may be slow or become slow. At this point, add a magnetic stirring bar to the reaction tube and stir the reaction mixture with a magnetic stirrer. If the rate of reaction is too fast, slow down the stirrer. The reaction is complete when none or a very small quantity of the metal remains. Check to see that the volume of ether has not decreased. If it has, add more anhydrous diethyl ether. Since the solution of the Grignard reagent deteriorates on standing, the next step should be started at once. The phenylmagnesium bromide can be converted to triphenylmethanol or to benzoic acid.

▯ MICROSCALE   ▭ 2. Triphenylmethanol

| Phenylmagnesium bromide | Benzophenone MW 182.22 mp 48°C | Triphenylmethanol MW 260.34 mp 164.2°C |

IN THIS EXPERIMENT the Grignard reagent prepared in the previous reaction is added to a dry ether solution of benzophenone. Very thorough mixing is required. When the red color disappears the salt is hydrolyzed by adding hydrochloric acid. More ether is added, the layers separated, and the ether dried and evaporated to give crude product. An impurity, biphenyl, is removed by dissolving it in ligroin and the product recrystallized from 2-propanol. It crystallizes very slowly, so do not collect the product immediately.

Make t-butyl methyl ether anhydrous by storing it over molecular sieves.

In an oven-dried vial dissolve 2.0 mmol (0.364 g) of benzophenone in 1.0 mL of anhydrous ether by capping the vial and mixing the contents thoroughly. With a dry syringe, remove all the solution from the vial and add it dropwise with *thorough* mixing (magnetic stirring, flicking of the tube, or stirring with a stirring rod near the end of the addition) after each drop to the solution

R4   of the Grignard reagent. Add the benzophenone at a rate such as to maintain the

R5   ether at a gentle reflux. Rinse the vial with a few drops of anhydrous ether after all the first solution has been added, and add this rinse to the reaction tube.

Mixing the reaction mixture is very important.

R6   After all the benzophenone has been added, the mixture should be homogeneous. If not, mix it again, using a stirring rod if necessary. The syringe can be removed, but leave the pressure-relief needle in place. Allow the reaction mixture to stand at room temperature. The reaction apparently is complete

R7   when the red color disappears.

R8   At the end of the reaction period, cool the tube in ice and add to it dropwise with stirring (use a glass rod or a spatula) 2 mL of 3 M hydrochloric acid. A creamy-white precipitate of triphenylmethanol will separate between the layers. Add more ether (it need not be anhydrous) to the reaction tube and shake

R9   the contents to dissolve all the triphenylmethanol. The result should be two perfectly clear layers. Remove a drop of the ether layer for TLC analysis. Any bubbling seen at the interface or in the lower layer is leftover magnesium reacting with the hydrochloric acid. Remove the aqueous layer and shake the ether layer

R10   with an equal volume of saturated aqueous sodium chloride solution in order to remove water and any remaining acid. Carefully remove all of the aqueous layer; then dry the ether layer by adding anhydrous calcium chloride pellets to the reaction tube until the drying agent no longer clumps together. Cork the tube and shake it from time to time over a 5- or 10-min period to complete the drying.

Using a Pasteur pipette, remove the ether from the drying agent and place it in another tared, dry reaction tube or the centrifuge tube. Use more ether to wash off the drying agent and combine these ether extracts. Evaporate the ether in a hood by blowing nitrogen or air onto the surface of the solution while warming the tube in a beaker of water or in the hand.

After all the solvent has been removed, determine the weight of the crude product. Note the odor of biphenyl, the product of the side reaction that takes place between bromobenzene and phenylmagnesium bromide during the first reaction.

R11   Trituration (grinding) of the crude product with petroleum ether will remove the biphenyl. Stir the crystals with 0.5 mL of petroleum ether in the ice bath, remove the solvent as thoroughly as possible, add a boiling stick, and recrystallize the residue from boiling 2-propanol (no more than 2 mL). Allow the solution to cool slowly to room temperature then cool it thoroughly in ice. Triphenylmethanol crystallizes slowly, so allow the mixture to remain in the ice as long as possible. Stir the ice-cold mixture well and collect the product by

F   vacuum filtration on the Hirsch funnel. Save the filtrate. Concentration may give a second crop of crystals.

An alternative method for purification of the triphenylmethanol utilizes a mixed solvent. Dissolve the crystals in the smallest possible quantity of warm ether and add to the solution 1.5 mL of ligroin. Add a boiling stick to the solution and boil off some of the ether until the solution becomes slightly cloudy, indicating it is saturated. Allow the solution to cool slowly to room temperature. Triphenylmethanol is deposited slowly as large, thick prisms. Cool the solution in ice and, after allowing time for complete crystallization to occur, remove the ether with a

FIG. 38.4 Apparatus for drying crystals in reaction tube under vacuum.

FIG. 38.5 Semimicroscale, research-type apparatus for Grignard reaction, with provision for a motor-driven stirrer and an inlet and outlet for dry nitrogen.

4, G   Pasteur pipette and wash the crystals once with a few drops of a cold 1:4 ether–ligroin mixture. Dry the crystals in the tube under vacuum (Fig. 38.4).

Determine the weight, melting point, and percentage yield of the triphenylmethanol. Analyze the crude and recrystallized product by TLC on silica gel (*see* Chapter 10), developing the plate with dichloromethane–petroleum ether, 1:5. An IR spectrum can be determined in chloroform solution or by preparing a mull or KBr disk (*see* Chapter 13). Compare the apparatus used in this experiment with the research-type apparatus shown in Fig. 38.5.

Cleaning Up   The acidic aqueous layer and the saturated sodium chloride layer are combined, diluted with water, neutralized with sodium carbonate, and flushed down the drain. Ether is allowed to evaporate from the drying agent in the hood, and is then discarded in the nonhazardous solid waste container. The petroleum ether and 2-propanol or ether–ligroin mother liquor are placed in the organic solvents container.

MICROSCALE   ## 3. Benzoic Acid

IN THIS EXPERIMENT the Grignard reagent prepared in Experiment 1 is squirted onto a piece of dry ice. The resulting white carboxylate salt is hydrolyzed with hydrochloric acid, releasing benzoic acid, which is extracted into the ether present. The ether solution could be dried and evaporated to give the product, but better product is obtained by adding base to make the benzoate salt and then adding acid to this basic solution to cause benzoic acid to crystallize. It can be recrystallized from hot water.

Phenylmagnesium bromide + Carbon dioxide (MW 44.01, mp −78.5°C (sublimes)) → → $\xrightarrow{HCl}$ Benzoic acid (MW 122.12, mp 123°C) + MgBrCl

CAUTION: Handle dry ice with a towel or gloves. Contact with the skin can cause frostbite because dry ice sublimes at −78.5°C.

Prepare 2 mmol of phenylmagnesium bromide exactly as described in Experiment 1. Wipe off the surface of a small piece of dry ice (solid carbon dioxide) with a dry towel to remove frost and place it in a dry 30-mL beaker. Remove the pressure-relief needle from the reaction tube; then insert a syringe through the septum, turn the tube upside down, and draw into the syringe as much of the reagent solution as possible. Squirt this solution onto the piece of dry ice, and then, using a clean needle, rinse out the reaction tube with a milliliter of anhydrous diethyl ether and squirt this onto the dry ice. Allow excess dry ice to sublime; then hydrolyze the salt by the addition of 2 mL of 3 M hydrochloric acid.

V

Transfer the mixture from the beaker to a reaction tube and shake it thoroughly. Two homogeneous layers should result. Add 1 to 2 mL of acid or of ordinary (not anhydrous) ether if necessary. Remove the aqueous layer and shake the ether layer with 1 mL of water, which is removed and discarded. Then extract the benzoic acid by adding to the ether layer 0.7 mL of 3 M sodium hydroxide solution, shaking the mixture thoroughly, and withdrawing the aqueous layer, which is placed in a very small beaker or vial. The extraction is repeated with another 0.5-mL portion of base and finally 0.5 mL of water. Now that the extraction is complete, the ether, which can be discarded, contains primarily biphenyl, the by-product formed during the preparation of the phenylmagnesium bromide.

F

The combined aqueous extracts are heated briefly to about 50°C to drive off dissolved ether from the aqueous solution and then made acidic by the addition of concentrated hydrochloric acid (test with indicator paper). Cool the mixture thoroughly in an ice bath. Collect the benzoic acid on the Hirsch funnel, and wash it with about 1 mL of ice water while on the funnel. A few crystals of this crude material are saved for a melting-point determination; the remainder of the product is recrystallized from boiling water.

The solubility of benzoic acid in water is 68 g/L at 95°C and 1.7 g/L at 0°C. Dissolve the acid in very hot water. Let the solution cool slowly to room temperature; then cool it in ice for several minutes before collecting the product by vacuum filtration on the Hirsch funnel. Use the ice-cold filtrate in the filter flask to complete the transfer of benzoic acid from the reaction tube. Turn the product out onto a piece of filter paper, squeeze out excess water, and allow it to dry thoroughly. Once dry, weigh it, calculate the percentage yield, and determine the melting point along with the melting point of the crude material.

The IR spectrum may be determined as a solution in chloroform (1 g of benzoic acid dissolves in 4.5 mL of chloroform) or as a mull or KBr disk (*see* Chapter 12).

Cleaning Up   Combine all aqueous layers, dilute with a large quantity of water, and flush the slightly acidic solution down the drain.

MACROSCALE

4. Phenylmagnesium Bromide (Phenyl Grignard Reagent)

Bromobenzene	Magnesium	Phenylmagnesium bromide
MW 157.02	At. Wt	not isolated, used in situ
bp 156°C	24.31	
den. 1.491		

All equipment and reagents must be *absolutely dry*. The Grignard reagent is prepared in a dry 100-mL round-bottomed flask fitted with a long reflux condenser. A calcium chloride drying tube inserted in a cork that will fit either the flask or the top of the condenser is also made ready [Fig. 38.6(a) Fig. 38.5.] The flask, condenser, and magnesium (2 g = 0.082 mol of magnesium turnings) should be as dry as possible to begin with, and then should be further dried in a 110°C oven for at least 35 min. Alternatively, the magnesium is placed in the flask, the calcium chloride tube is attached directly, and the flask is heated gently but thoroughly with a cool luminous flame. Do not overheat the magnesium. It will become deactivated through oxidation or, if strongly overheated, can burn. The flask on cooling pulls dry air through the calcium chloride. Cool to room temperature before proceeding! **Extinguish all flames!** Ether vapor is denser than air and can travel along bench tops and into sinks. Use care.

Make an ice bath ready in case control of the reaction becomes necessary, although this is usually not the case. Remove the drying tube and fit it to the top of the condenser. Then pour into the flask through the condenser 15 mL of *absolute* ether (absolutely dry, anhydrous) and 9 mL (13.5 g = 0.086 mol) of bromobenzene. Be sure the graduated cylinders used to measure the ether and bromobenzene are absolutely dry. (More ether is to be added as soon as the reaction starts, but at the outset the concentration of bromobenzene is kept high to promote easy starting.) If there is no immediate sign of reaction, insert a *dry* stirring rod with a flattened end and crush a piece of magnesium firmly against the bottom of the flask under the surface of the liquid, giving a twisting motion to the rod. When this is done properly the liquid becomes slightly cloudy and

CAUTION: Ether is extremely flammable. Extinguish all flames before using ether.

Specially dried ether is required.

Cotton
or glass wool

8 Mesh
CaCl$_2$

Cotton

(a)

Calcium
chloride tube

Water out

Water in

Distilling
flask

Thermowell

(b)

FIG. 38.6 (a) Calcium chloride drying tube fitted with a rubber stopper. Store for future use with cork in top, pipette bulb on bottom. (b) Apparatus for refluxing Grignard reaction.

ebullition commences at the surface of the compressed metal. Be careful not to punch a hole in the bottom of the flask. Attach the condenser at once, swirl the flask to provide fresh surfaces for contact and, as soon as you are sure that the reaction has started, add 25 mL more absolute ether through the top of the condenser before spontaneous boiling becomes too vigorous (replace the drying tube). Note the volume of ether in the flask. Cool in ice if necessary to slow the reaction, but do not overcool the mixture; the reaction can be stopped by too much cooling. Any difficulty in initiating the reaction can be dealt with by trying the following expedients in succession.

Starting the Grignard reaction

1. Warm the flask with your hands or a beaker of warm water. Then see if boiling continues when the flask (condenser attached) is removed from the warmth.

Diethyl ether can be kept anhydrous by storing over Linde 5A molecular sieves.

Discard the ether after 90 days because of peroxide formation.

Use minimum steam to avoid condensation on outside of the condenser.

2. Try further mashing of the metal with a dry stirring rod.
3. Add a tiny crystal of iodine as a starter (in this case the ethereal solution of the final reaction product should be washed with sodium bisulfite solution to remove the yellow color).
4. Add a few drops of a solution of phenylmagnesium bromide or of methyl-magnesium iodide (which can be made in a test tube).
5. Start afresh, taking greater care with the dryness of apparatus, measuring tools, and reagents, and sublime a crystal or two of iodine on the surface of the magnesium to generate Gattermann's "activated magnesium" before beginning the reaction again.

Once the reaction begins, spontaneous boiling in the diluted mixture may be slow or become slow. If so, mount the flask and condenser on the steam bath (one clamp supporting the condenser suffices) and reflux gently until the magnesium has disintegrated and the solution has acquired a cloudy or brownish appearance [Fig. 38.6(b)]. The reaction is complete when only a few remnants of metal (or metal contaminants) remain. Check to see that the volume of ether has not decreased. If it has, add more anhydrous ether. Since the solution of Grignard reagent deteriorates on standing, the next step should be started at once.

MACROSCALE

5. Triphenylmethanol from Methyl Benzoate

Phenylmagnesium bromide

Methyl benzoate
MW 136.15
bp 198–199°C

Triphenylmethanol
MW 260.34
mp 164.2°C

Mix 5 g (0.037 mol) of methyl benzoate and 15 mL of absolute ether in a separatory funnel, cool the flask containing phenylmagnesium bromide solution briefly in an ice bath, remove the drying tube, and insert the stem of the separatory funnel into the top of the condenser. Run in the methyl benzoate solution *slowly* with only such cooling as is required to control the mildly exothermic reaction, which affords an intermediate salt that separates as a white solid. Replace the calcium chloride tube; swirl the flask until it is at room temperature and the reaction has subsided. Go to Experiment 7.

🜶 MACROSCALE

6. Triphenylmethanol from Benzophenone

| **Phenylmagnesium bromide** | **Benzophenone** MW 182.22 mp 48°C | | **Triphenylmethanol** MW 260.34 mp 164.2°C |

Dissolve 6.75 g (0.037 mol) of benzophenone in 25 mL of absolute ether in a separatory funnel and cool the flask containing *half* the phenylmagnesium bromide solution (0.041 mol) briefly in an ice bath. (The other half can be used to make benzoic acid.) Remove the drying tube and insert the stem of the separatory funnel into the top of the condenser. Add the benzophenone solution *slowly* with swirling and only such cooling as is required to control the mildly exothermic reaction, which gives a bright-red solution and then precipitates a white salt. Replace the calcium chloride tube; swirl the flask until it is at room temperature and the reaction has subsided. Go to Experiment 7.

7. Completion of Grignard Reaction

This is a suitable stopping point.

The reaction is then completed by either refluxing the mixture for one-half hour, or stoppering the flask with the calcium chloride tube and letting the mixture stand overnight (subsequent refluxing is then unnecessary).[2]

In this part of the experiment, ordinary (not anhydrous) diethyl ether or t-butyl methyl ether may be used.

Pour the reaction mixture into a 250-mL Erlenmeyer flask containing 50 mL of 10% sulfuric acid and about 25 g of ice, and use both ordinary ether and 10% sulfuric acid to rinse the flask. Swirl well to promote hydrolysis of the addition compound; basic magnesium salts are converted into water-soluble neutral salts; triphenylmethanol is distributed into the ether layer. An additional amount of ether (ordinary) may be required. Pour the mixture into a separatory funnel (rinse the flask with ether), shake, and draw off the aqueous layer. Shake the ether solution with 10% sulfuric acid to further remove magnesium salts and wash with saturated sodium chloride solution to remove water that has dissolved in the ether. The amounts of liquid used in these washing operations are not critical. In general, an amount of wash liquid equal to one-third of the ether volume is adequate.

Saturated aqueous sodium chloride solution removes water from ether.

---

2. A rule of thumb for organic reactions: A 10°C rise in temperature will double the rate of the reaction.

To effect final drying of the ether solution, pour the ether layer out of the neck of the separatory funnel into an Erlenmeyer flask, add about 5 g of calcium chloride pellets, swirl the flask intermittently, and after 5 min remove the drying agent by gravity filtration (using a filter paper and funnel) into a tared Erlenmeyer flask. Rinse the drying agent with a small amount of ether. Add 25 mL of 66–77°C ligroin, and concentrate the ether-ligroin solutions (steam bath) in an Erlenmeyer flask under an aspirator tube (*see* Fig. 8.5). Evaporate slowly until crystals of triphenylcarbinol just begin to separate, then let crystallization proceed, first at room temperature and then at 0°C. The product should be colorless and should melt no lower than 160°C. Concentration of the mother liquor may yield a second crop of crystals. A typical student yield is 5.0 g. Evaporate the mother liquors to dryness and save the residue for later isolation of the components by chromatography.

Analyze the first crop of triphenylmethanol and the residue from the evaporation of the mother liquors by thin-layer chromatography. Dissolve equal quantities of the two solids (a few crystals) and also biphenyl in equal quantities of dichloromethane (1 or 2 drops). Using a microcapillary, spot equal quantities of material on silica gel TLC plates, and develop the plates in an appropriate solvent system. Try 1:3 dichloromethane–petroleum ether first, and adjust the relative quantities of solvent as needed. The spots can be seen by examining the TLC plate under a fluorescent lamp or by treating the TLC plate with iodine vapor. From this analysis decide how pure each of the solids is and whether it would be worthwhile to attempt to isolate more triphenylmethanol from the mother liquors.

Dispose of recovered and waste solvents in the appropriate containers.

Turn in the product in a vial labeled with your name, the name of the compound, its melting point, and the overall percent yield from benzoic acid.

 MACROSCALE   ## 8. Benzoic Acid

Wipe the frost from a piece of dry ice, transfer the ice to a cloth towel, and crush it with a hammer. Without delay (so moisture will not condense on the cold solid) transfer about 10 g of dry ice to a 250-mL beaker. Cautiously pour one-half of the solution of phenylmagnesium bromide prepared in Experiment 1 onto the dry ice. A vigorous reaction will ensue. Allow the mixture to warm up; stir it until the dry ice has evaporated. To the beaker add 20 mL of 3 *M* hydrochloric acid; then heat the mixture over a steam bath in the hood to boil off the ether. Cool the beaker thoroughly in an ice bath and collect the solid product by vacuum filtration on a Büchner funnel.

Transfer the solid back to the beaker and dissolve it in the minimum quantity of saturated sodium bicarbonate solution (2.8 *M*). Note that a small quantity of a by-product remains suspended and floating on the surface of the solution. Note the odor of the mixture. Transfer it to a separatory funnel and shake it briefly with about 15 mL of ether. Discard the ether layer, place the clear aqueous layer in the beaker, and heat it briefly to drive off dissolved ether. Carefully add 3 *M* hydrochloric acid to the mixture until the solution tests acid to pH paper. Cool the mixture in ice and collect the product on a Büchner funnel. Recrystallize it from the minimum quantity of hot water and isolate it in the usual manner. Determine the melting point and the weight of the benzoic acid, and calculate its yield based on the weight of magnesium used to prepare the Grignard reagent.

Cleaning Up Combine all aqueous layers, dilute with a large quantity of water, and flush the slightly acidic solution down the drain. The ether–ligroin mother liquor from the crystallization goes in the organic solvents container. The thin-layer chromatography developer, which contains dichloromethane, is placed in the halogenated organic waste container. Calcium chloride from the drying tube should be dissolved in water and flushed down the drain.

Questions

1. Triphenylmethanol also can be prepared from the reaction of ethyl benzoate with phenylmagnesium bromide and by the reaction of diethylcarbonate

with phenylmagnesium bromide. Write stepwise reaction mechanisms for these two reactions.

2. If the ethyl benzoate used to prepare triphenylmethanol is wet, what by-product is formed?

3. Exactly what weight of dry ice is needed to react with 2 mmol of phenylmagnesium bromide?

4. In the synthesis of benzoic acid, benzene is often detected as an impurity. How does this come about?

5. The benzoic acid could have been extracted from the ether layer using sodium bicarbonate solution. Give equations showing how this might be done and how the benzoic acid would be regenerated. What practical reason makes this extraction method less desirable than sodium hydroxide extraction?

6. What is the weight of frost (ice) on the dry ice that will react with all of Grignard reagent used in Experiment 8?

7. How many moles of carbon dioxide are contained in 10 g of dry ice?

8. Just after the dry ice has evaporated from the beaker, what is the white solid remaining?

9. Write an equation for the reaction of the white solid with 3 *M* hydrochloric acid.

FIG. 38.7 ^{13}C NMR spectrum of bromobenzene (22.6 MHz).

10. Write an equation for the reaction of the product with sodium bicarbonate.

11. Would you expect sodium benzoate to have an odor? Why or why not?

12. What odor do you detect after the product has dissolved in sodium bicarbonate solution?

13. What is the purpose of the ether extraction?

14. What is meant by the sentence "Isolate the product in the usual way"?

Surfing the Web

http://ull.chemistry.uakron.edu/organic_lab/grignard/
The synthesis of phenylmagnesium bromide (Experiment 1) is shown in 10 good close-up color photos at this University of Akron site. A further 15 photos show the synthesis of triphenylmethanol from benzophenone. The synthesis of benzoic acid, with three photos, remains, as it is here, as an open-ended experiment.

PRELAB EXERCISE: Account for the fact that the Wittig–Horner reaction of cinnamaldehyde gives almost exclusively the *E,E*-butadiene with very little contaminating *E,Z*-product.

$(C_6H_5)_3P$ + ClH_2C—⟨benzene ring⟩ ⟶ $(C_6H_5)_3\overset{+}{P}CH_2$—⟨benzene ring⟩ Cl^- $\xrightarrow[\text{(50\% NaOH)}]{\text{Base}}$

Triphenylphosphine
(1)

Benzyl chloride
(2)

Benzyltriphenylphosphonium
chloride
(3)

$(C_6H_5)_3P{=}CH$—⟨benzene ring⟩ ⟷ $(C_6H_5)_3\overset{+}{P}{-}\overset{-}{CH}$—⟨benzene ring⟩ ⟶

The Wittig reagent,
an ylide
(4)

$O{=}C$ with H

9-Anthraldehyde
(5)

$(C_6H_5)_3P{-}CH$—⟨benzene ring⟩ ⟶ $(C_6H_5)_3P$ + ⟨structure⟩
with $O{-}C$ H ⟨anthracene⟩

$\overset{\|}{O}$

Triphenylphosphine
oxide
(7)

$H{-}C$

4-Anthranyl-2,2,2,3-tetraphenyl-
1,2-oxaphosphetane
(6)

trans-**9-(2-Phenylethenyl)anthracene**
(8)

The Wittig reaction affords an invaluable method for the conversion of a carbonyl compound to an olefin; for example, the conversion of 9-anthraldehyde (**5**) and benzyl chloride (**2**), by means of the Wittig reagent (**4**), through a four-centered intermediate to the product (**8**). Because the active reagent, an ylide, is unstable, it is generated in the presence of the carbonyl compound by dehydrohalogenation of the phosphonium chloride (**3**) with base. Usually a very strong base, like phenyllithium in dry ether, is employed, but in this experiment, 50% sodium hydroxide is employed. The existence of the four-membered ring intermediate was proved by NMR in 1984.[1] The phenylethenylanthracene product produces a green fluorescence with the chemiluminescent substance, Cyalume, in the "light stick" reaction (*see* Chapter 62).

The light stick reaction

When the halogen compound employed in the first step has an activated halogen atom ($RCH=CHCH_2X$, $C_6H_5CH_2X$, XCH_2CO_2H), a simpler procedure known as the *Horner phosphonate modification* of the Wittig reaction is applicable. When benzyl chloride is heated with triethyl phosphite, chloroethane is eliminated from the initially formed phosphonium chloride with the production of diethyl benzylphosphonate. This phosphonate is stable, but in the presence of a strong base, such as the sodium methoxide used here, it condenses with a carbonyl component in the same way that a Wittig ylide condenses. Thus it reacts with benzaldehyde to give *E*-stilbene and with cinnamaldehyde to give *E,E*-1,4-diphenyl-1,3-butadiene.

Simplified Wittig reaction

Benzyl chloride
bp 179°C, MW 126.59
den. 1.10, n_D^{20} 1.5380

Triethyl phosphite
bp 156°C, MW 166.16
den. 0.94, n_D^{20} 1.4130

Benzyltriethylphosphonium chloride

Diethyl benzylphosphonate
bp 156°C/9 torr
MW 228.23, den. 1.045
n_D^{20} 1.4970

Chloroethane
bp 12.3°C
MW 64.52, den. 0.891

1. B. E. Maryanoff, A. B. Reitz, and M. S. Mutter, *J. Am. Chem. Soc.* **106,** 1873 (1984).

Diethyl benzylphosphonate + CH$_3$O$^-$Na$^+$ ⟶

Na$^+$

$\bar{C}$H—P—OCH$_2$CH$_3$ + CH$_3$OH

O—CH$_2$CH$_3$

Ylide

Sodium methoxide
MW 52.02

Ylide +

H   H
C═C
| |
H   O

Cinnamaldehyde
MW 132.16, den. 1.11
bp 248°C

⟶

H   H
C═C—C═C
| |
H   H

E,E-1,4-Diphenyl-1,3-butadiene
mp 153°C, MW 206.27

+ Na$^+$$\bar{O}$—P—OCH$_2CH_3$

O—CH$_2$CH$_3$

The energy-minimized conformation of E,E-1,4-diphenyl-1,3-butadiene. Because of steric hindrance, the molecule is not flat.

Experiments

1. Synthesis of *trans*-9-(2-Phenylethenyl)anthracene[2]

Microscale Procedure

IN THIS EXPERIMENT a phosphonium chloride is reacted with base to form the Wittig reagent. An aldehyde in the same solution reacts with the Wittig reagent to give the alkene product. The solvent, dichloromethane, is dried and evaporated to give the product that is, in turn, recrystallized from 1-propanol.

To a reaction tube add 200 mg of benzyltriphenylphosphonium chloride, 115 mg of 9-anthraldehyde, 0.6 mL of dichloromethane, and a magnetic stirring bar. With rapid stirring, 0.26 mL of 50% sodium hydroxide solution is added dropwise from a Pasteur pipette. After stirring vigorously for one-half hour, 1.5 mL of dichloromethane and 1.5 mL of water are added, then the tube is capped and shaken. The organic layer is removed and placed in another reaction

2. For macroscale syntheses see H.-D. Becker and K. Andersson, *J. Org. Chem.* **48**, 4552, 1983; G. Merkl and A. Merz, *Synthesis,* 295, 1973; E. F. Silversmith, *J. Chem. Ed.* **63**, 645, 1986.

tube, and the aqueous layer is extracted with 1 mL of dichloromethane. The combined dichloromethane extracts are dried over calcium chloride pellets, the dichloromethane is removed, the drying agent is washed with more solvent, and the solvent is removed under vacuum in the filter flask (Fig. 39.1). To the solid remaining in the filter flask add 3 mL of 1-propanol, and transfer the hot solution to an Erlenmeyer flask to crystallize. After cooling spontaneously to room temperature, cool the flask in ice and collect the product on the Hirsch funnel. The triphenylphosphine oxide remains in the propanol solution. The reported melting point of the product is 131–132°C.

Macroscale Procedure

Into a 10-mL round-bottomed flask place 0.97 g of benzyltriphenylphosphonium chloride, 0.57 g of 9-anthraldehyde, 3 mL of dichloromethane, and a stirring bar. Clamp the flask over a magnetic stirrer and stir the mixture at high speed while adding 1.3 mL of 50% sodium hydroxide solution dropwise from a Pasteur pipette. After the addition is complete, continue the stirring for 30 min; then transfer the contents of the flask to a 50-mL separatory funnel using 10 mL of water and 10 mL of dichloromethane to complete the transfer. Shake the mixture, remove the organic layer, then extract the aqueous layer once more with 5 mL of dichloromethane. Dry the combined organic layers with anhydrous calcium chloride pellets, transfer the solution to a 50-mL Erlenmeyer flask, evaporate it to dryness on a steam bath, and recrystallize the yellow partially crystalline residue from 15 mL of 2-propanol. The product crystallizes as thin yellow plates, mp 131–132°C. Save the product for use as a fluorescer in the Cyalume chemiluminescence experiment (*see* Chapter 62). Examine a dilute ethanol solution of the product under an ultraviolet lamp.

FIG. 39.1 Apparatus for removal of a solvent under a vacuum.

To aspirator

MICROSCALE

2. Synthesis of 1,4-Diphenyl-1,3-butadiene

IN THIS EXPERIMENT benzyl chloride and triethyl phosphite are reacted with each other to give a phosphonate salt. This salt, on reaction with the strong base, sodium methoxide, gives a Wittig reagent-like ylide that reacts with an aldehyde to give the product alkene, diphenylbutadiene. It is isolated by filtration and can be recrystallized if necessary from methylcyclohexane.

CAUTION: Take care to keep organophosphorus compounds off the skin.

Use freshly prepared sodium methoxide. Commercial material is often inactive.

The success of this reaction is strongly dependent on the purity of the starting materials.[3] Benzyl chloride and triethyl phosphite are usually pure enough as received from the supplier. Cinnamaldehyde from a new, previously unopened bottle should be satisfactory, but because it oxidizes in air extremely rapidly, it should be distilled, preferably under nitrogen or at reduced pressure, if there is any doubt about its quality. Sodium methoxide, direct from reputable suppliers, has been found on occasion to be completely inactive. No

---

3. The instructor should try out this experiment before assigning it to a class.

Cool part
of tube

Refluxing liquid
(Air condenser)

Sand

Heated
area

Boiling
liquid

Boiling
chip

Electric
flask heater

FIG. 39.2 Microscale reflux
apparatus.

*CAUTION: Handle benzyl
chloride in the hood. Severe
lachrymator and irritant of the
respiratory tract.*

$$\underset{H}{\overset{O}{\parallel}}C-N\underset{CH_3}{\overset{CH_3}{}}$$

***N,N*-Dimethylformamide (DMF)**
MW 73.10, bp 153°C
n_D^{20} 1.4310

easy method exists for determining its activity; therefore, it is best prepared
following the procedure of *Organic Syntheses,* Col. Vol. IV, 651, 1963.[4]

To a 10 mm × 100 mm reaction tube add 316 mg (0.0025 mol) of benzyl
chloride (α-chlorotoluene), 415 mg (0.44 mL, 0.0025 mol) of triethyl phosphite,
and a boiling chip (Fig. 39.2). Because the triethyl phosphite has an offensive odor,
obtain this material from the dispenser that has been calibrated to deliver the correct quantity. Place the reaction tube to a depth of about 1 cm in a sand bath that
has been preheated to 210 to 220°C. Reflux the reaction mixture for 1 h. The vapors
condense on the cool upper portion of the reaction tube, so a condenser is not necessary. At an internal temperature of about 140°C (which you need not monitor),
ethyl chloride is evolved and, by the end of the reflux period, the temperature of
the reaction mixture will be 200 to 220°C. At the end of the reaction period, remove

---

4. For enough sodium methoxide for 50 microscale or 2 macroscale reactions, add 3.5 g of sodium
spheres to 50 mL of anhydrous methanol in a 100-mL flask equipped with a condenser. Add the
sodium a few pieces at a time through the top of the condenser at a rate such as to keep the reaction under control. It is safest to wait for complete reaction of one portion of sodium before adding
the next. After all the sodium has reacted, remove the methanol on a rotary evaporator, first over a
steam bath and then over a bath heated to 150°C. The sodium methoxide will be a free-flowing
white powder that should keep for several weeks in a desiccator. Yield: 8.2 g.

A highly polar solvent capable of dissolving ionic compounds such as sodium methoxide yet miscible with water—avoid skin contact.

Filter paper, 12 mm dia.

Polyethylene filter disk (frit), 10 mm dia.   **F**

Hirsch funnel

To aspirator

25-mL Filter flask

FIG. 39.3   Hirsch funnel for filtration.

the tube from the sand bath, cool it to room temperature, then add the contents to 160 mg (0.003 mol) of sodium methoxide in a 10-mL Erlenmeyer flask using 1 mL of dry dimethylformamide to complete the transfer. Cool the mixture in ice, mix the contents of the flask thoroughly, then add 330 mg (0.0025 mol) of freshly distilled cinnamaldehyde in 1 mL of dry dimethylformamide dropwise with thorough mixing in the ice bath. Allow the mixture to come to room temperature. Note the changes that take place over the next few minutes.

After a *minimum* of 10 min, add 2 mL of methanol to the Erlenmeyer flask with thorough stirring. Then almost fill the flask with water and stir the mixture until it is homogeneous in color. The hydrocarbon precipitates from the reaction mixture upon the addition of the methanol and water. Collect the product by vacuum filtration on the Hirsch funnel (Fig. 39.3) and wash the crystals: first with water to remove the red color, then with ice-cold methanol to remove the yellow color. The hydrocarbon is completely insoluble in water and only sparingly soluble in methanol. Weigh the dry product, which should be faint yellow in color, determine its melting point, and calculate the crude yield. If the melting point is below 150°C, recrystallize the product from methylcyclohexane (10 mL/g), and again determine the melting point and yield. Hand in the product, giving crude and recrystallized weights, melting points, and yields.

Cleaning Up   The filtrate and washings from this reaction are dark, oily, and smell bad. The mixture contains dimethylformamide and could contain traces of all starting materials. Keep the volume as small as possible and place it in the hazardous waste container for organophosphorus compounds. If methylcyclohexane was used for recrystallization, place the mother liquor in the organic solvents container.

3. Synthesis of 1,4-Diphenyl-1,3-butadiene

 MACROSCALE

CAUTION: Keep organophosphorus compounds off the skin. Handle benzyl chloride in the hood. It is a severe lachrymator and respiratory tract irritant.

Use freshly prepared or opened sodium methoxide; keep bottle closed.

Avoid skin contact with dimethylformamide.

The success of this reaction is strongly dependent upon the purity of the starting materials.

With the aid of pipettes and a pipetter, measure into a 25 × 150-mm test tube 5 mL of benzyl chloride (α-chlorotoluene) and 7.7 mL of triethyl phosphite. Add a boiling stone, insert a cold finger condenser and, with a flask heater, reflux the liquid gently for 1 h. Alternatively, carry out the reaction in a 25-mL round-bottomed flask equipped with a reflux condenser. (Elimination of ethyl chloride starts at about 130°C and, in the time period specified, the temperature of the liquid rises to 190–200°C.) Let the phosphonate ester cool to room temperature, pour it into a 125-mL Erlenmeyer flask containing 2.4 g of sodium methoxide, and add 40 mL of dimethylformamide, using a part of this solvent to rinse the test tube. Swirl the flask vigorously in a water–ice bath to thoroughly chill the contents and continue swirling while running in 5 mL of cinnamaldehyde by pipette. The mixture soon turns deep red; then crystalline hydrocarbon starts to separate. When there is no further change (about 2 min), remove the flask from the cooling bath and let it stand at room temperature for about 10 min. Then add 20 mL of water and 10 mL of methanol, swirl vigorously to dislodge crystals, and finally collect the product on a suction funnel using the red mother liquor to wash the flask.

N,N-Dimethylformamide (DMF)
MW 73.10, bp 153°C
n_D^{20} 1.4310

A highly polar solvent capable of dissolving ionic compounds such as sodium methoxide yet miscible with water

Wash the product with water until the red color of the product is completely replaced by yellow. Then wash with methanol to remove the yellow impurity, and continue until the wash liquor is colorless. The yield of the crude, faintly yellow hydrocarbon (mp 150–151°C) should be about 5.7 g. This material is satisfactory for use in Chapter 51 (1.5 g required). A good solvent for crystallization of the remaining product is methylcyclohexane (bp 101°C, 10 mL/g; use more if the solution requires filtration). Pure *E,E*-1,4-diphenyl-1,3-butadiene melts at 153°C.

Cleaning Up   The filtrate and washings from this reaction are dark, oily, and smell bad. The mixture contains dimethylformamide and could contain traces of all starting materials. Keep the volume as small as possible and place it in the hazardous waste container for organophosphorus compounds. If methylcyclohexane was used for recrystallization, place the mother liquor in the organic solvents container.

Questions

1. Show how 1,4-diphenyl-1,3-butadiene might be synthesized from benzaldehyde and an appropriate halogenated compound.

2. Explain why the methyl groups of trimethyl phosphite give two peaks in the ^{1}H NMR spectrum (Fig. 39.4).

3. Write the equation for the reaction between sodium methoxide and moist air.

4. The Wittig reaction usually gives a mixture of *cis* and *trans* isomers. Using a molecular mechanics program, calculate the steric energies or heats of formation of both possible products in Experiments 2 and 4. Are these compounds planar? Are the most stable molecules produced in these two experiments? If not, why not?

FIG. 39.4 ^{1}H NMR spectrum of trimethyl phosphite (90 MHz).

CHAPTER
40

Esterification and Hydrolysis

PRELAB EXERCISE: Give the detailed mechanism for the acid-catalyzed hydrolysis of methyl benzoate.

$$O$$
$$\|$$
$$R-C-O-R'$$

The ester group

Flavors and fragrances

Fischer esterification

The ester group is an important functional group that can be synthesized in a number of different ways. The low molecular weight esters have very pleasant odors and indeed comprise the major flavor and odor components of a number of fruits. Although the natural flavor may contain nearly a hundred different compounds, single esters approximate the natural odors and are often used in the food industry for artificial flavors and fragrances (Table 40.1).

Esters can be prepared by the reaction of a carboxylic acid with an alcohol in the presence of a catalyst such as concentrated sulfuric acid, hydrogen chloride, *p*-toluenesulfonic acid, or the acid form of an ion exchange resin:

$$CH_3C-OH + CH_3OH \underset{}{\overset{H^+}{\rightleftharpoons}} CH_3C-OCH_3 + H_2O$$

Acetic acid   **Methanol**   **Methyl acetate**

This Fischer esterification reaction reaches equilibrium after a few hours of refluxing. The position of the equilibrium can be shifted by adding more of the acid or of the alcohol, depending on cost or availability. The mechanism of the reaction involves initial protonation of the carboxyl group, attack by the nucleophilic hydroxyl, a proton transfer, and loss of water followed by loss of the catalyzing proton to give the ester. Each of these steps is completely reversible, so this process is also, in reverse, the mechanism for the hydrolysis of an ester:

TABLE 40.1   Fragrances and Boiling Points of Esters

Ester	Formula	bp (°C)	Fragrance
2-Methylpropyl formate	$\overset{O}{\overset{\|}{H C}}-OCH_2\overset{CH_3}{\overset{\|}{C}}HCH_3$	98.4	Raspberry
1-Propyl acetate	$CH_3\overset{O}{\overset{\|}{C}}-OCH_2CH_2CH_3$	101.7	Pear
Methyl butyrate	$CH_3CH_2CH_2\overset{O}{\overset{\|}{C}}-OCH_3$	102.3	Apple
Ethyl butyrate	$CH_3CH_2CH_2\overset{O}{\overset{\|}{C}}-OCH_2CH_3$	121	Pineapple
2-Methylpropyl propionate	$CH_3CH_2\overset{O}{\overset{\|}{C}}-OCH_2\overset{CH_3}{\overset{\|}{C}}HCH_3$	136.8	Rum
3-Methylbutyl acetate	$CH_3\overset{O}{\overset{\|}{C}}-OCH_2CH_2\overset{CH_3}{\overset{\|}{C}}HCH_3$	142	Banana
Benzyl acetate	$CH_3\overset{O}{\overset{\|}{C}}-OCH_2-\bigcirc$	213.5	Peach
Octyl acetate	$CH_3\overset{O}{\overset{\|}{C}}-OCH_2(CH_2)_6CH_3$	210	Orange
Methyl salicylate	$\bigcirc\overset{\overset{O}{\overset{\|}{C}}-OCH_3}{}_{OH}$	222	Wintergreen

Other methods are available for the synthesis of esters, most of which are more expensive but readily carried out on a small scale. For example, alcohols react with anhydrides and with acid chlorides:

$$CH_3CH_2OH + CH_3\overset{O}{\overset{\|}{C}}-O-\overset{O}{\overset{\|}{C}}CH_3 \longrightarrow CH_3\overset{O}{\overset{\|}{C}}-OCH_2CH_3 + CH_3\overset{O}{\overset{\|}{C}}-OH$$

Ethanol   **Acetic anhydride**   **Ethyl acetate**   **Acetic acid**

$$CH_3CH_2CH_2OH + CH_3\overset{O}{\overset{\|}{C}}-Cl \longrightarrow CH_3\overset{O}{\overset{\|}{C}}-OCH_2CH_2CH_3 + HCl$$

1-Propanol   **Acetyl chloride**   **n-Propyl acetate**

In the latter reaction, an organic base such as pyridine is usually added to react with the hydrogen chloride.

A number of other methods can be used to synthesize the ester group. Among these are the addition of 2-methylpropene to an acid to form *t*-butyl esters, the addition of ketene to make acetates, and the reaction of a silver salt with an alkyl halide:

Other ester syntheses

2-Methylpropene   **Propionic acid**   ***t*-Butyl propionate**
(isobutylene)

Ketene   **Benzyl alcohol**   **Benzyl acetate**

Silver acetate   **1-Bromo-3-methylbutane**   **3-Methylbutyl acetate**

As noted above, Fischer esterification is an equilibrium process. Consider the reaction of acetic acid with 1-butanol to give *n*-butyl acetate:

The equilibrium constant is:

$$K_{eq} = \frac{[n\text{-BuOAc}][H_2O]}{[n\text{-BuOH}][HOAc]}$$

For primary alcohols reacting with unhindered carboxylic acids, $K_{eq} \approx 4$. If equal quantities of 1-butanol and acetic acid are allowed to react, at equilibrium the theoretical yield of ester is only 67%. To upset the equilibrium we can, by Le Châtelier's principle, increase the concentration of either the alcohol or acid, as noted above. If either one is doubled, the theoretical yield increases to 85%. When one is tripled it goes to 90%. But note that in the example cited the boiling point of the relatively nonpolar ester is only about 8°C higher than the boiling points of the polar acetic acid and 1-butanol, so a difficult separation

E 40.2   The Ternary Azeotrope of Boiling Point 90.7°C

Compound	Boiling Point of Pure Compound (°C)	Percentage Composition of Azeotrope		
		Vapor Phase	*Upper Layer*	*Lower Layer*
1-Butanol	117.7	8.0	11.0	2.0
n-Butyl acetate	126.7	63.0	86.0	1.0
Water	100.0	29.0	3.0	97.0

Azeotropic distillation

problem exists if either starting material is increased in concentration and the product isolated by distillation.

Another way to upset the equilibrium is to remove water. This can be done by adding to the reaction mixture molecular sieves (an artificial zeolite), which preferentially adsorb water. Most other drying agents, such as anhydrous sodium sulfate or calcium chloride pellets, will not remove water at the temperatures used to make esters.

A third way to upset the equilibrium is to preferentially remove the water as an azeotrope (a constant-boiling mixture of water and an organic liquid). The information in Table 40.2 can be found in a chemistry handbook table of ternary (three-component) azeotropes.

These data tell us that vapor that distills from a mixture of 1-butanol, *n*-butyl acetate, and water will boil at 90.7°C and that the vapor contains 8% alcohol, 63% ester, and 29% water. The vapor is homogeneous, but when it condenses, it separates into two layers. The upper layer is composed of 11% alcohol, 86% ester, and 3% water, but the lower layer consists of 97% water with only traces of alcohol and ester. If some ingenious way to remove the lower layer from the condensate and still return the upper layer to the reaction mixture can be devised, then the equilibrium can be upset and nearly 100% of the ester can be produced in the reaction flask.

Microscale Dean–Stark apparatus

A cork is used instead of a septum so that layer separation can be observed clearly.

The apparatus shown in Fig. 40.1, modeled after that of Dean and Stark, achieves the desired separation of the two layers. The mixture of equimolar quantities of 1-butanol and acetic acid is placed in the flask along with an acid catalyst. Stirring reduces bumping. The vapor, the temperature of which is 90.7°C, condenses and runs down to the sidearm, which is closed with a cork. The layers separate, with the denser water layer remaining in the sidearm while the lighter ester plus alcohol layer runs down into the reaction flask. As soon as the theoretical quantity of water has collected, the reaction is over and the product in the flask should contain ester of high purity. The macroscale apparatus is illustrated in Fig. 40.2.

Esterification using a carboxylic acid and an alcohol requires an acid catalyst. In the first experiment, the acid form of an ion-exchange resin is used. This resin, in the form of small beads, is a cross-linked polystyrene that bears sulfonic acid groups on some of the phenyl groups. It is essentially an immobilized form of *p*-toluenesulfonic acid, an organic-substituted sulfuric acid.

FIG. 40.1   Microscale azeotropic esterification apparatus.

FIG. 40.2   Macroscale azeotropic distillation apparatus, with Dean-Stark trap where water collects.

An ion exchange catalyst

This catalyst has the distinct advantage that at the end of the reaction it can be removed simply by filtration. Immobilized catalysts of this type are becoming more and more common in organic synthesis.

If concentrated sulfuric acid were used as the catalyst, it would be necessary to dilute the reaction mixture with ether; wash the ether layer successively with water, sodium carbonate solution, and saturated sodium chloride solution; then dry the ether layer with anhydrous calcium chloride pellets before evaporating the ether.

Experiments

☐ MICRORSCALE   ### 1. *n*-Butyl Acetate by Azeotropic Distillation of Water

$$
\underset{\substack{\textbf{Acetic acid}\\ \text{MW 60.05}\\ \text{bp 117.9°C, den 1.049}\\ n_\text{D}^{20}\ 1.3720}}{CH_3\overset{\displaystyle O}{\overset{\|}{C}}{-}OH}
\;+\;
\underset{\substack{\textbf{1-Butanol}\\ \text{MW 74.12}\\ \text{bp 117.7°C, den 0.810}\\ n_\text{D}^{20}\ 1.3990}}{HOCH_2CH_2CH_2CH_3}
\;\overset{H^+}{\rightleftharpoons}\;
\underset{\substack{\textit{n}\textbf{-Butyl acetate}\\ \text{MW 116.16}\\ \text{bp 126.5°C, den 0.882}\\ n_\text{D}^{20}\ 1.3940}}{CH_3\overset{\displaystyle O}{\overset{\|}{C}}{-}OCH_2CH_2CH_2CH_3}
\;+\; \underset{\substack{\\ \text{MW 18}}}{H_2O}
$$

IN THIS EXPERIMENT acetic acid is esterified with butanol in the presence of an acid catalyst attached to very small polystyrene beads. Since esterification is an equilibrium reaction the equilibrium is upset by removal of the water formed in a unique apparatus patterned after the Dean–Stark water separator. The product is isolated simply by withdrawing it from the reaction flask with a Pasteur pipette, leaving the catalyst behind. It can be further purified by simple distillation.

Ion-exchange resin catalyst

A cork instead of a septum allows the accumulation of water to be observed.

S

In a 5-mL short-necked, round-bottomed flask, place 0.2 g of Dowex 50X2-100 ion-exchange resin,[1] 0.60 g (0.58 mL) of acetic acid (0.01 mole), 0.74 g (0.91 mL) of 1-butanol (0.01 mole), and a stirring bar. Attach the addition port with the sidearm corked and an empty distilling column as shown in Fig. 40.1, and clamp the apparatus at the angle shown. Heat the flask while stirring on a hot sand bath and bring the reaction mixture to a boil. Stirring the mixture prevents it from bumping. As an option, you might hold a thermometer just above the boiling liquid and note a temperature of about 91°C. Remove the thermometer and allow the reaction mixture to reflux in a manner such that the vapors condense about one-third of the way up the empty distilling column, which is functioning as an air condenser. Note that the material that condenses is not homogeneous, since droplets of water begin to collect in the upper part of the apparatus. As the sidearm fills with condensate, it is cloudy at first, and then two layers separate. When the volume of the lower aqueous layer does not appear to increase, the reaction is over. This will take about 20 to 30 min. Carefully remove the apparatus from the heat, allow it to cool, and then tip the apparatus very carefully to allow all the upper layer in the sidearm to run back into the reaction flask. Disconnect the apparatus.

Remove the product from the reaction flask with a Pasteur pipette, determine its weight and boiling point, and assess its purity by thin-layer chromatography and IR spectroscopy. The product can be analyzed by gas chromatography on a 10-ft (3-m) Carbowax column. At 152°C, the 1-butanol has a retention time of 2.1 min, the *n*-butyl acetate 2.5 min, and the acetic acid 7.5 min. Look for the

---

1. The Dowex resin as received should be washed with water by decantation to remove much of the yellow color. It is then collected by vacuum filtration on a Büchner funnel and returned, in a slightly damp state, to the reagent bottle.

presence of hydroxyl and carboxyl absorption bands in the IR spectrum. The product can easily be purified by simple distillation (*see* Figure 5.7).

Cleaning Up   Place the catalyst in the solid hazardous waste container.

MICROSCALE

2. Isobutyl Propionate by Fischer Esterification

IN THIS EXPERIMENT a propionate ester is prepared by reacting excess propanoic acid with an alcohol in the presence of an acid catalyst on polystyrene beads (Dowex 50X). The excess acid serves to drive the equilibrium reaction toward formation of the product. The excess propanoic acid is removed by reaction with potassium carbonate, and the water is adsorbed by silica gel when the reaction mixture is chromatographed.

Wet pipe cleaner

FIG. 40.3 Esterification apparatus.

$$CH_3CH_2\overset{O}{\overset{\|}{C}}OH \;+\; HOCH_2\overset{CH_3}{\overset{|}{C}}HCH_3 \;\underset{\longleftarrow}{\overset{H^+}{\rightleftharpoons}}\; CH_3CH_2\overset{O}{\overset{\|}{C}}OCH_2\overset{CH_3}{\overset{|}{C}}HCH_3 \;+\; H_2O$$

Propanoic acid
MW 74.08
bp 141°C

2-Methyl-1-propanol
MW 74.12
bp 108°C

Isobutyl propionate
MW 130.19
bp 136.8°C

Procedure

To a reaction tube add 112 mg of 2-methyl-1-propanol (isobutyl alcohol), 148 mg of propanoic acid (propionic acid), 50 mg of Dowex 50X2-100 ion-exchange resin, and a boiling chip. Attach the empty distilling column as an air condenser (Fig. 40.3). Reflux the resulting mixture for 1 h or more, cool it to room temperature, remove the product mixture from the resin with a Pasteur pipette, and chromatograph the product (2-methyl-1-propyl propanoate) on a silica-gel column.

G

Chromatography Procedure

Carry out this part of the experiment in a hood. Dichloromethane is a suspected carcinogen.

27, N

Assemble the column as depicted in Fig. 40.4 being sure it is clamped in a vertical position. Close the valve and fill the column with dichloromethane to the bottom of the funnel. In a small beaker prepare a slurry of 1 g of silica gel in 4 mL of dichloromethane. Stir the slurry gently to remove air bubbles and gently swirl, pour, and scrape the slurry into the funnel, which has a capacity of 10 mL. After some of the silica gel has been added to the column, open the stopcock and allow solvent to drain slowly into an Erlenmeyer flask. Use this dichloromethane to rinse the beaker containing the silica gel. As the silica gel is being added, tap the column with a glass rod or pencil so the adsorbent will pack tightly into the column. Continue to tap the column while cycling the dichloromethane through the column once more; then add 1 g of anhydrous potassium carbonate to the top of the silica gel. The potassium carbonate will remove water from the esterification mixture as well as react with any

Funnel

Glass
column

Anhydrous
potassium
carbonate

Silica gel

Micro
Büchner
funnel

Polyethylene
frit

10-mL
Erlenmeyer
flask

FIG. 40.4 Chromatographic
column for esters.

carboxylic acid present. Allow the solvent to flow until it reaches the top of the
potassium carbonate layer.

Adding the Sample.   The solvent is drained just to the surface of the
potassium carbonate. Using a Pasteur pipette, add sample to the column and
let it run into the adsorbent, stopping when the solution reaches the top of the

potassium carbonate. The flask and ion-exchange resin are rinsed twice with 0.5-mL portions of dichloromethane that are run into the column, with the eluent being collected in a tared reaction tube. The elution is completed with 1 mL more dichloromethane.

Analysis of the Product. Evaporate the dichloromethane under a stream of air or nitrogen in the hood and remove the last traces by connecting the reaction tube to the water aspirator. Because the dichloromethane boils at 40°C and the product at 137°C, separation of the two is easily accomplished. Determine the weight of the product and its boiling point and calculate the yield. The ester should be a perfectly clear, homogeneous liquid. Obtain an IR spectrum and analyze it for the presence of unreacted alcohol and carboxylic acid. Check the purity of the product by thin-layer and/or gas chromatography.

Cleaning Up   Place the catalyst in the hazardous waste container. Any dichloromethane should be placed in the halogenated organic waste container. The contents of the chromatography column, if free of solvent, can be placed in the nonhazardous solid waste container; otherwise, this material is classified as a hazardous waste and must go in the container so designated.

MICROSCALE

3. Benzyl Acetate from Acetic Anhydride

Benzyl alcohol	Acetic anhydride	Benzyl acetate	Acetic acid
MW 108.14	MW 102.09	MW 150.18	MW 60.06
bp 205°C	bp 138–140°C	bp 213.5°C	bp 117–118°C
n_D^{20} 1.5400	n_D^{20} 1.3900	n_D^{20} 1.5020	n_D^{20} 1.3720

To a reaction tube add 108 mg of benzyl alcohol, 102 mg of acetic anhydride, and a boiling chip. Reflux the mixture for at least 1 h, cool the mixture to room temperature, and chromatograph the liquid in exactly the same manner described immediately above. Analyze the product by thin-layer chromatography and by IR spectroscopy as a thin film between salt or silver chloride plates. Note the presence or absence of hydroxyl and carboxyl bands.

    This ester cannot be prepared by Fischer esterification using Dowex. Polymerization seems to occur.

Cleaning Up   Place the catalyst in the hazardous waste container. Any dichloromethane should be placed in the halogenated organic waste container. The contents of the chromatography column, if free of solvent, can be placed in the nonhazardous solid waste container; otherwise, this material is classified as a hazardous waste and must go in the container so designated.

MICROSCALE

4. Other Esterifications

This experiment lends itself to wide-ranging experimentation. All three methods of esterification described above can, in principle, be applied to any unhindered primary or secondary alcohol. These methods work well for most of the esters in Table 40.1 and for hundreds of others as well.

MACROSCALE

5. Methyl Benzoate by Fischer Esterification

Benzoic acid	Methanol	Methyl benzoate
mp 122°C,	bp 64.6°C,	bp 198–199°C,
MW 122.12	den. 0.791	den. 1.094
	MW 32.04	MW 136.15

IN THIS EXPERIMENT benzoic acid and excess methanol are refluxed in the presence of a catalytic amount of sulfuric acid. Water and ether are added, the water layer withdrawn, and the ether layer washed with water, bicarbonate, and saturated salt solutions. After drying over calcium chloride the ether is evaporated and finally the product, ethyl benzoate, is distilled.

Place 10.0 g of benzoic acid and 25 mL of methanol in a 125-mL round-bottomed flask, cool the mixture in ice, pour 3 mL of concentrated sulfuric acid *slowly and carefully down the walls of the flask,* then swirl to mix the components. Attach a reflux condenser, add a boiling chip, and reflux the mixture gently for 1 h (Fig. 40.5 illustrates this apparatus). Cool the solution, decant it into a separatory funnel containing 50 mL of water, and rinse the flask with 35 mL of ether. Add this ether to the separatory funnel, shake thoroughly, and drain off the water layer, which contains the sulfuric acid and the bulk of the methanol. Wash the ether in the separatory funnel with 25 mL of water followed by 25 mL of 0.5 *M* sodium bicarbonate to remove unreacted benzoic acid. Again shake, with frequent release of pressure by inverting the separatory funnel and opening the stopcock, until no further reaction is apparent; then drain off the bicarbonate layer into a beaker. If this aqueous material is made strongly acidic with hydrochloric acid, unreacted benzoic acid may be observed. Wash the ether layer in the separatory funnel with saturated sodium chloride solution and dry the solution over anhydrous calcium chloride in an Erlenmeyer flask. Add sufficient calcium chloride pellets so that it no longer clumps together on the

Water out

Water in

FIG. 40.5 Apparatus for refluxing a reaction mixture.

bottom of the flask. After 10 min decant the dry ether solution into a flask, wash the drying agent with an additional 5 mL of ether, and decant again.

   Remove the ether by simple distillation or by evaporation on the steam bath under an aspirator tube. Use the methods illustrated in Fig. 3.22, 5.10, or use a rotary evaporator (*see* Fig. 10.9). When evaporation ceases, add 2–3 g of anydrous calcium chloride pellets to the residual oil and heat for about 5 min longer. Then decant the methyl benzoate into a 50-mL round-bottomed flask, attach a stillhead, dry out the ordinary condenser and use it without water circulating in the jacket, and distill. The boiling point of the ester is so high

Tared: previously weighed

(199°C) that a water-cooled condenser is liable to crack. Use a tared 25-mL Erlenmeyer as the receiver to collect material boiling above 190°C. A typical student yield is about 7 g. See Chapter 28 for the nitration of methyl benzoate and Chapter 38 for its use in the Grignard synthesis of triphenylmethanol.

   IR and NMR spectra of benzoic acid and methyl benzoate are found at the end of the chapter (Figs. 40.6 to 40.11).

Cleaning Up   Pour the sulfuric acid layer into water, combining it with the bicarbonate layer, neutralize it with sodium carbonate, and flush the solution down the drain with much water. The saturated sodium chloride layer can also be flushed down the drain. If the calcium chloride is free of ether and methyl benzoate, it can be placed in the nonhazardous solid waste container; otherwise it must go into the hazardous waste container. Ether goes into the organic solvents container, along with the pot residues from the final distillation.

6. Hydrolysis (Saponification): The Synthesis of Soap

In general, the reversal of esterification is called *hydrolysis*. In the case of hydrolysis of a fatty acid ester, it is called *saponification*. In this experiment, the saturated fat made from hydrogenated olive oil in Chapter 25 will be saponified to give a soap, which, in this case, will be primarily sodium stearate.

Glycerol tristearate   **Glycerol**   **Sodium stearate (soap)**

Microscale Procedure

IN THIS EXPERIMENT a saturated fat is heated with sodium hydroxide in water–ethanol. The resulting soap is precipitated in salt solution, and collected on the Hirsch funnel where it is washed free of base and salt.

Place 0.18 g of the saturated triglyceride made in Chapter 25, Experiment 4, in a 5-mL short-necked, round-bottomed flask. Add 1.5 mL of a 50:50 water–ethanol solution that contains 0.18 g of sodium hydroxide. Add an air condenser and gently reflux the mixture on the sand bath for 30 min, taking care not to boil away the ethanol. At the end of the reaction period, some of the soap will have precipitated. Transfer the mixture to a 10-mL Erlenmeyer flask containing a solution of 0.8 g of sodium chloride in 3 mL of water. Collect **F** the precipitated soap on the Hirsch funnel and wash it free of excess sodium hydroxide and salt using 4 mL of distilled ice water.

Test the soap by adding a very small piece (about 5–15 mg) to a centrifuge or test tube along with 3 or 4 mL of distilled water. Cap the tube and shake it vigorously. Note the height and stability of the bubbles. Add a crystal of magnesium chloride or calcium chloride to the tube. Shake the tube again, and note the results. For comparison, do these same tests with a few grains of a detergent instead of the soap.

Macroscale Procedure

In a 100-mL round-bottomed flask, place 5 g of hydrogenated olive oil (Chapter 25) or lard or solid shortening (e.g., Crisco). Add 20 mL of ethanol and a hot solution of 5 g of sodium hydroxide in 20 mL of water. This solution, prepared in a beaker, will become very hot as the sodium hydroxide dissolves. Fit the flask with a water-cooled condenser and reflux the mixture on the sand bath for 30 min. At the end of the reaction period some of the soap may precipitate from the reaction mixture. Transfer the mixture to a 250-mL Erlenmeyer flask containing an ice-cold solution of 25 g of sodium chloride in 90 mL of distilled water. Collect the precipitated soap on a Büchner funnel, and wash it free of excess sodium hydroxide and salt using no more than 100 mL of distilled ice water.

Test the soap by adding a small piece to a test tube along with about 5 mL of water. Cap the tube and shake it vigorously. Note the height and stability of the bubbles formed. Add a few crystals of magnesium chloride or calcium chloride to the tube. Shake the tube again and note the results. For comparison, do these same tests with an amount of detergent equal to that of the soap used.

Questions _____

1. In the preparation of methyl benzoate, what is the purpose of: (a) Washing the organic layer with sodium bicarbonate solution? (b) Washing the organic layer with saturated sodium chloride solution? (c) Treating the organic layer with anhydrous calcium chloride pellets?

2. Assign the resonances in Fig. 40.8 to specific protons in methyl benzoate.

3. Figs. 40.9 and 40.10 each have two resonances that are very small. What do the carbons causing these peaks have in common?

FIG. 40.6 Infrared spectrum of benzoic acid in CS_2 (KBr disk).

FIG. 40.7 ^{1}H NMR spectrum of benzoic acid (250 MHz).

FIG. 40.8 ^{1}H NMR spectrum of methyl benzoate (250 MHz).

FIG. 40.9 ^{13}C NMR spectrum of benzoic acid (22.6 MHz).

FIG. 40.10 ^{13}C NMR spectrum of methyl benzoate (22.6 MHz).

FIG. 40.11 IR spectrum of methyl benzoate.

CHAPTER
70

Qualitative Organic Analysis

PRELAB EXERCISE: In the identification of an unknown organic compound, certain procedures are more valuable than others. For example, far more information is obtained from an IR spectrum than from a refractive index measurement. Outline, in order of priority, the steps you will employ in identifying your unknown.

Identification and characterization of the structures of unknown substances are an important part of organic chemistry. It is often, of necessity, a micro process, for example, in drug analyses. It is sometimes possible to establish the structure of a compound on the basis of spectra alone (IR, UV, and NMR), but these spectra must usually be supplemented with other information about the unknown: physical state, elementary analysis, solubility, and confirmatory tests for functional groups. Conversion of the unknown to a solid derivative of known melting point will often provide final confirmation of structure.

However, before spectra are run, other information about the sample must be obtained. Is it homogeneous (test by thin-layer, gas, or liquid chromatography)? What are its physical properties (melting point, boiling point, color, solubility in various solvents)? Is it soluble in a common NMR solvent? It might also be necessary to determine which elements are present in the sample and its percentage elemental composition (mass spectroscopy).

Nevertheless, an organic chemist can often identify a sample in a very short time by performing solubility tests and some simple tests for functional groups, coupled with spectra that have not been compared to a database. Conversion of the unknown to a solid derivative of known melting point will often provide final confirmation of structure. This chapter provides the information needed to carry out this type of qualitative analysis of an organic compound.

Procedures

All experiments in this chapter can, if necessary, be run on two to three times the indicated quantities of material.

Physical State

Check for Sample Purity

Distill or recrystallize as necessary. Constant boiling point and sharp melting point are indicators, but beware of azeotropes and eutectics. Check homogeneity by TLC, gas, HPLC, or paper chromatography.

Note the Color

Common colored compounds include nitro and nitroso compounds (yellow), α-diketones (yellow), quinones (yellow to red), azo compounds (yellow to red), and polyconjugated olefins and ketones (yellow to red). Phenols and amines are often brown to dark-purple because of traces of air oxidation products.

CAUTION: Do not taste an unknown compound. To note the odor, cautiously smell the cap of the container and do it only once.

Note the Odor

Some liquid and solid amines are recognizable by their fishy odors; esters are often pleasantly fragrant. Alcohols, ketones, aromatic hydrocarbons, and aliphatic olefins have characteristic odors. On the unpleasant side are thiols, isonitriles, and low-molecular weight carboxylic acids.

Make an Ignition Test

Heat a small sample on a spatula; first hold the sample near the side of a microburner to see if it melts normally and then burns. Heat it in the flame. If a large ashy residue is left after ignition, the unknown is probably a metal salt. Aromatic compounds often burn with a smoky flame.

Spectra

Obtain infrared and nuclear magnetic resonance spectra following the procedures of Chapters 12 and 13. If these spectra indicate the presence of conjugated double bonds, aromatic rings, or conjugated carbonyl compounds, obtain the UV spectrum following the procedures of Chapter 14. Interpret the spectra as fully as possible by reference to the sources cited at the end of the various spectroscopy chapters.

Explanation

Elementary Analysis, Sodium Fusion

This method for detection of nitrogen, sulfur, and halogen in organic compounds depends on the fact that fusion of substances containing these elements with sodium yields NaCN, Na_2S, and NaX (X = Cl, Br, I). These products can, in turn, be readily identified. The method has the advantage that the most usual elements other than C, H, and O present in organic compounds can all be detected following a single fusion, although the presence of sulfur sometimes

˙ *Rarely performed by*
professional chemists

interferes with the test for nitrogen. Unfortunately, even in the absence of sulfur, the test for nitrogen is sometimes unsatisfactory (nitro compounds in particular). Practicing organic chemists rarely perform this test. Either they know which elements their unknowns contain, or they have access to a mass spectrometer or atomic absorption instrument.

Place a 3-mm cube of sodium[1] (30 mg, no more)[2] in a 10 × 75-mm Pyrex test tube, and support the tube in a vertical position (Fig. 70.1). Have a microburner with small flame ready to move under the tube, place an estimated 20 mg of solid on a spatula or knife blade, put the burner in place, and heat until the sodium first melts and then vapor rises 1.5–2.0 cm in the tube. Remove the burner, and at once drop the sample onto the hot sodium. If the substance is a liquid add 2 drops of it. If there is a flash or small explosion the fusion is complete; if not, heat briefly to produce a flash or a charring. Then let the tube cool to room temperature, be sure it is cold, add a drop of methanol, and let it react. Repeat until 10 drops have been added. With a stirring rod break up the char to uncover sodium. When you are sure that all sodium has reacted, empty the tube into a 13 × 100-mm test tube, hold the small tube pointing away from you or a neighbor, and pipette into it 1 mL of water. Boil and stir the mixture, and pour the water into the larger tube; repeat with 1 mL more water. Then transfer the solution with a Pasteur pipette to a 2.5-cm funnel (fitted with a fluted filter paper) resting in a second 13 × 100-mm test tube. Portions of the alkaline filtrate are used for the tests that follow.

CAUTION: Manipulate sodium with a knife and forceps; never touch it with the fingers. Wipe it free of kerosene with a dry towel or filter paper; return scraps to the bottle or destroy scraps with methyl or ethyl alcohol, never with water. Safety glasses! Hood!

Do not use CHCl₃ or CCl₄ as samples in sodium fusion. They react extremely violently.

(a) Nitrogen

Run each test on a known and an unknown.

The test is done by boiling a portion of the alkaline solution from the solution fusion with iron(II) sulfate and then acidifying. Sodium cyanide reacts with iron(II) sulfate to produce ferrocyanide, which combines with iron(III) salts, inevitably formed by air oxidation in the alkaline solution, to give insoluble Prussian Blue, $NaFe[Fe(CN)_6]$. Iron(II) and iron(III) hydroxide precipitate along with the blue pigment but dissolve on acidification.

Place 50 mg of powdered iron(II) sulfate (this is a large excess) in a 10 × 75-mm test tube, add 0.5 mL of the alkaline solution from the fusion, heat the mixture gently with shaking to the boiling point, and then—without cooling—acidify with dilute sulfuric acid (hydrochloric acid is unsatisfactory). A deep-blue precipitate indicates the presence of nitrogen. If the coloration is dubious, filter through a 2.5-cm funnel and see if the paper shows blue pigment.

Cleaning Up   Dilute the test solution with water and flush down the drain.

Notes for the instructor

---

1. Sodium spheres $\frac{1}{16}''$ to $\frac{1}{4}''$ are convenient.

2. A dummy 3-mm cube of rubber can be attached to the sodium bottle to indicate the correct amount.

10x75-mm Pyrex—
test tube

1.5 - 2 cm

Dark, metallic
sodium vapor

Globule of sodium

FIG. 70.1   Sodium fusion, just prior to addition of sample.

(b) Sulfur

1. Dilute 1 drop of the alkaline solution with 1 mL of water, and add a drop of sodium nitroprusside; a purple coloration indicates the presence of sulfur.
2. Prepare a fresh solution of sodium plumbite by adding 10% sodium hydroxide solution to 0.2 mL of 0.1 *M* lead acetate solution until the precipitate just dissolves, and add 0.5 mL of the alkaline test solution. A black precipitate or a colloidal brown suspension indicates the presence of sulfur.

$$Na_2(NO)Fe(CN)_6 \cdot 2H_2O$$

Sodium nitroprusside

Cleaning Up   Dilute the test solution with water and flush down the drain.

(c) Halogen

Differentiation of the halogens

Do not waste silver nitrate.

Acidify 0.5 mL of the alkaline solution from the fusion with dilute nitric acid (indicator paper) and, if nitrogen or sulfur has been found present, boil the solution (hood) to expel HCN or H_2S. On addition of a few drops of silver nitrate solution, halide ion is precipitated as silver halide. Filter with minimum exposure to light on a 2.5-cm funnel, wash with water, and then with 1 mL of concentrated ammonia solution. If the precipitate is white and readily soluble in ammonium hydroxide solution it is AgCl; if it is pale yellow and not readily soluble it is AgBr; if it is yellow and insoluble it is AgI. Fluorine is not detected in this test since silver fluoride is soluble in water.

Cleaning Up   Dilute the test solution with water and flush down the drain.

> Run tests on knowns in parallel with unknowns for all qualitative
> organic reactions. In this way, interpretations of positive reactions are
> clarified and defective test reagents can be identified and replaced.

Beilstein Test for Halogens

A fast, easy, reliable test

Heat the tip of a copper wire in a burner flame until no further coloration of
the flame is noticed. Allow the wire to cool slightly, then dip it into the
unknown (solid or liquid), and again heat it in the flame. A green flash is indicative of chlorine, blue-green of bromine, and blue of iodine; fluorine is not
detected because copper fluoride is not volatile. The Beilstein test is very sensitive; halogen-containing impurities may give misleading results. Run the test
on a compound known to contain halogen for comparison to your unknown.[3]

Solubility Tests

*Like dissolves like; a substance is most soluble in that solvent to which it is most
closely related in structure.* This statement serves as a useful classification scheme
for all organic molecules. The solubility measurements are done at room temperature with 1 drop of a liquid, or 5 mg of a solid (finely crushed), and 0.2 mL of
solvent. The mixture should be rubbed with a rounded stirring rod and shaken
vigorously. Lower members of a homologous series are easily classified; higher
members become more like the hydrocarbons from which they are derived.

*Weigh and measure
carefully.*

   If a very small amount of the sample fails to dissolve when added to some of
the solvent, it can be considered insoluble; and, conversely, if several portions dissolve readily in a small amount of the solvent, the substance is obviously soluble.

   If an unknown seems to be more soluble in dilute acid or base than in
water, the observation can be confirmed by neutralization of the solution; the
original material will precipitate if it is less soluble in a neutral medium.

   If both acidic and basic groups are present, the substance may be amphoteric and therefore soluble in both acid and base. Aromatic aminocarboxylic
acids are amphoteric, like aliphatic ones, but they do not exist as zwitterions.
They are soluble in both dilute hydrochloric acid and sodium hydroxide, but not
in bicarbonate solution. Aminosulfonic acids exist as zwitterions; they are soluble in alkali but not in acid.

   The solubility tests are not infallible and many borderline cases are known.
Carry out the tests according to the scheme of Fig. 70.2 and the following "Notes
to Solubility Tests," and tentatively assign the unknown to one of the groups I–X.

---

3. http://odin.chemistry.uakron.edu/organic_lab/beil/
With seven very good color photos from the University of Akron, the Beilstein test is clearly
demonstrated on this Web site. The dramatic differences among chlorine (green), bromine (blue-
green), and iodine (blue) are quite clearly seen.

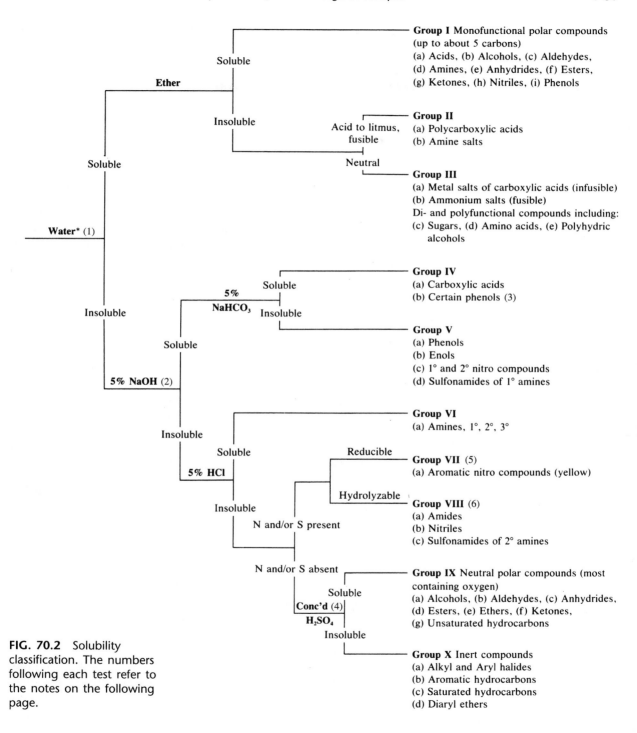

FIG. 70.2 Solubility classification. The numbers following each test refer to the notes on the following page.

Cleaning Up Because the quantities of material used in these tests are extremely small, and because no hazardous substances are handed out as unknowns, it is possible to dilute the material with a large quantity of water and flush it down the drain.

Notes to Solubility Tests

See Fig. 70.2.

1. Groups I, II, III (soluble in water). Test the solution with pH paper. If the compound is not easily soluble in cold water, treat it as water insoluble but test with indicator paper.
2. If the substance is insoluble in water but dissolves partially in 5% sodium hydroxide, add more water; the sodium salts of some phenols are less soluble in alkali than in water. If the unknown is colored, be careful to distinguish between the *dissolving* and the *reacting* of the sample. Some quinones (colored) *react* with alkali and give highly colored solutions. Some phenols (colorless) *dissolve and then* become oxidized to give colored solutions. Some compounds (e.g., benzamide) are hydrolyzed with such ease that careful observation is required to distinguish them from acidic substances.
3. Nitrophenols (yellow), aldehydophenols, and polyhalophenols are sufficiently strongly acidic to react with sodium bicarbonate.
4. Oxygen- and nitrogen-containing compounds form oxonium and ammonium ions in concentrated sulfuric acid and dissolve.
5. On reduction in the presence of hydrochloric acid, these compounds form water-soluble amine hydrochlorides. Dissolve 250 mg of tin(II) chloride in 0.5 mL of concentrated hydrochloric acid, add 50 mg of the unknown, and warm. The material should dissolve with the disappearance of the color and give a clear solution when diluted with water.
6. Most amides can be hydrolyzed by short boiling with 10% sodium hydroxide solution; the acid dissolves with evolution of ammonia. Reflux 100 mg of the sample and 10% sodium hydroxide solution for 15–20 min. Test for the evolution of ammonia, which confirms the elementary analysis for nitrogen and establishes the presence of a nitrile or amide.

Classification Tests

After the unknown is assigned to one of the solubility groups (Fig. 70.2) on the basis of solubility tests, the possible type should be further narrowed by application of classification tests; for example, for alcohols, or methyl ketones, or esters.

Complete Identification—Preparation of Derivatives

Once the unknown has been classified by functional group, the physical properties should be compared with those of representative members of the group (see tables at the end of this chapter). Usually, several possibilities present themselves, and the choice can be narrowed by preparation of derivatives. Select derivatives that distinguish most clearly among the possibilities.

Classification Tests

Group I. Monofunctional Polar Compounds (up to ca. 5 carbons)

(a) Acids

(Table 70.1, page 784; Derivatives, page 779)
No classification test is necessary. Carboxylic and sulfonic acids are detected by testing aqueous solutions with litmus. Acyl halides may hydrolyze during the solubility test.

(b) Alcohols

(Table 70.2, page 786; Derivatives, pages 779–780)

Jones' Oxidation. Dissolve 5 mg of the unknown in 0.5 mL of pure acetone in a test tube, and add to this solution 1 small drop of Jones' reagent (chromic acid in sulfuric acid). A positive test is formation of a green color within 5 sec upon addition of the orange-yellow reagent to a primary or secondary alcohol. Aldehydes also give positive tests, but tertiary alcohols do not.

CAUTION: Cr^{+6} dust is toxic.

    Reagent: Dissolve/suspend 13.4 g of chromium trioxide in 11.5 mL of concentrated sulfuric acid, and add this carefully with stirring to enough water to bring the volume to 50 mL.

Cleaning Up Place the test solution in the hazardous waste container.

Handle dioxane with care. It is a suspected carcinogen.

Cerium(IV) Nitrate Test [Ammonium Hexanitratocerium(IV) Test]. Dissolve 15 mg of the unknown in a few drops of water or dioxane in a reaction tube. Add to this solution 0.25 mL of the reagent, and mix thoroughly. Alcohols cause the reagent to change from yellow to red.
    Reagent: Dissolve 22.5 g of ammonium hexanitratocerium(IV), $Ce(NH_4)_2(NO_3)_6$, in 56 mL of 2 N nitric acid.

Cleaning Up Dilute the solution with water and flush down the drain.

(c) Aldehydes

(Table 70.3, page 787; Derivatives, pages 442 and 444; ch. 36)

2,4-Dinitrophenylhydrazones. All aldehydes and ketones readily form bright-yellow to dark-red 2,4-dinitrophenylhydrazones. Yellow derivatives are formed from isolated carbonyl groups and orange-red to red derivatives from aldehydes or ketones conjugated with double bonds or aromatic rings.
    Dissolve 10 mg of the unknown in 0.5 mL of ethanol, and then add 0.75 mL of 2,4-dinitrophenylhydrazine reagent. Mix thoroughly and let sit for a few minutes. A yellow to red precipitate is a positive test.

Reagent: Dissolve 1.5 g of 2,4-dinitrophenylhydrazine in 7.5 mL of concentrated sulfuric acid. Add this solution, with stirring, to a mixture of 10 mL of water and 35 mL of ethanol.

Cleaning Up   Place the test solution in the hazardous waste container.

Schiff Test.   Add 1 drop (30 mg) of the unknown to 1 mL of Schiff's reagent. A magenta color will appear within 10 min with aldehydes. Compare the color of your unknown with that of a known aldehyde.

Reagent: Prepare 50 mL of a 0.1% aqueous solution of *p*-rosaniline hydrochloride (fuchsin). Add 2 mL of a saturated aqueous solution of sodium bisulfite. After 1 h add 1 mL of concentrated hydrochloric acid.

Bisulfite Test.   Follow the procedure in Chapter 36. Nearly all aldehydes and most methyl ketones form solid, water-soluble bisulfite addition products.

Destroy used Tollens' reagent promptly with nitric acid. It can form explosive fulminates.

Tollens' Test.   Follow the procedure in Chapter 36. A positive test, deposition of a silver mirror, is given by most aldehydes, but not by ketones.

(d) Amides and Amines

(Tables 70.4, 70.5, and 70.6, pages 788–791; Derivatives of amines, pages 780–781)

Hinsberg Test.   Follow the procedure in Chapter 43, using benzenesulfonyl chloride to distinguish between primary, secondary, and tertiary amines.

(e) Anhydrides and Acid Halides

(Table 70.7, page 791; Derivatives, page 781–782) Anhydrides and acid halides will react with water to give acidic solutions, detectable with litmus paper. They easily form benzamides and acetamides.

Acidic Iron(III) Hydroxamate Test.   With iron(III) chloride alone a number of substances give a color that can interfere with this test. Dissolve 2 drops (or about 30 mg) of the unknown in 1 mL of ethanol, and add 1 mL of 1 N hydrochloric acid followed by 1 drop of 10% aqueous iron(III) chloride solution. If any color except yellow appears you will find it difficult to interpret the results from the following test.

Add 2 drops (or about 30 mg) of the unknown to 0.5 mL of a 1 N solution of hydroxylamine hydrochloride in alcohol. Add 2 drops of 6 M hydrochloric acid to the mixture, warm it slightly for 2 min, and boil it for a few seconds. Cool the solution, and add 1 drop of 10% ferric chloride solution. A red-blue color is a positive test.

Cleaning Up   Neutralize the reaction mixture with sodium carbonate, dilute with water, and flush down the drain.

(f) Esters

(Table 70.8, page 792. Derivatives are prepared from component acid and alcohol obtained on hydrolysis.)

Esters, unlike anhydrides and acid halides, do not react with water to give acidic solutions and do not react with acidic hydroxylamine hydrochloride. They do, however, react with alkaline hydroxylamine.

Alkaline Iron(III) Hydroxamate Test.   First test the unknown with iron(III) chloride alone. [See under Group I(e), Acidic Iron(III) Hydroxamate Test.]

To a solution of 1 drop (30 mg) of the unknown in 0.5 mL of 0.5 N hydroxylamine hydrochloride in ethanol, add 2 drops of 20% sodium hydroxide solution. Heat the solution to boiling, cool slightly, and add 1 mL of 1 N hydrochloric acid. If cloudiness develops add up to 1 mL of ethanol. Add 10% iron(III) chloride solution dropwise with thorough mixing. A red-blue color is a positive test. Compare your unknown with a known ester.

Cleaning Up   Neutralize the solutions with sodium carbonate, dilute with water, and flush down the drain.

(g) Ketones

(Table 70.14, page 796; Derivatives, pages 442 and 444)

2,4-Dinitrophenylhydrazone.   See under Group I(c), Aldehydes. All ketones react with 2,4-dinitrophenylhydrazine reagent.

Iodoform Test for Methyl Ketones.   Follow the procedure in Chapter 36.

A positive iodoform test is given by substances containing the $CH_3\overset{\displaystyle O}{\overset{\displaystyle \|}{C}}-$ group or by compounds easily oxidized to this group, e.g., CH_3COR, CH_3CHOHR, CH_3CH_2OH, CH_3CHO, $RCOCH_2COR$. The test is negative for compounds of the structure CH_3COOR, CH_3CONHR, and other compounds of similar structure that give acetic acid on hydrolysis. It is also negative for $CH_3COCH_2CO_2R$, CH_3COCH_2CN, $CH_3COCH_2NO_2$.

Bisulfite Test.   Follow the procedure in Chapter 36. Aliphatic methyl ketones and unhindered cyclic ketones form bisulfite addition products. Methyl aryl ketones, such as acetophenone, $C_6H_5COCH_3$, fail to react.

(h) Nitriles

(Table 70.15, page 797. Derivatives prepared from the carboxylic acid obtained by hydrolysis.)

At high temperature nitriles (and amides) are converted to hydroxamic acids by hydroxylamine:

$$RCN + 2\ H_2NOH \longrightarrow RCONHOH + NH_3$$

The hydroxamic acid forms a red-blue complex with iron(III) ion. The unknown must first give a negative test with hydroxylamine at lower temperature [Group I(f), Alkaline Iron(III) Hydroxamate Test] before trying this test.

Hydroxamic Acid Test for Nitriles (and Amides).

To 1 mL of a 1 *M* hydroxylamine hydrochloride solution in propylene glycol add 15 mg of the unknown dissolved in the minimum amount of propylene glycol. Then add 0.5 mL of 1 *N* potassium hydroxide in propylene glycol, and boil the mixture for 2 min. Cool the mixture, and add 0.1 to 0.25 mL of 10% iron(III) chloride solution. A red-blue color is a positive test for almost all nitrile and amide groups, although benzanilide fails to give a positive test.

Cleaning Up   Because the quantity of material is extremely small, the test solution can be diluted with water and flushed down the drain.

(i) Phenols

(Table 70.17, page 798; Derivatives, page 783)

Iron(III) Chloride Test.

Dissolve 15 mg of the unknown compound in 0.5 mL of water or water-alcohol mixture, and add 1–2 drops of 1% iron(III) chloride solution. A red, blue, green, or purple color is a positive test.

Cleaning Up   Because the quantity of material is extremely small, the test solution can be diluted with water and flushed down the drain.

A more sensitive test for phenols consists of dissolving or suspending 15 mg of the unknown in 0.5 mL of chloroform and adding 1 drop of a solution made by dissolving 0.1 g of iron(III) chloride in 10 mL of chloroform. Addition of a drop of pyridine, with stirring, will produce a color if phenols or enols are present.

CAUTION: CHCl₃ is a carcinogen.

Group II. Water-Soluble Acidic Salts, Insoluble in Ether

Amine Salts

[Table 70.5 (1° and 2° amines), pages 789–790; Table 70.6 (3° amines), page 791]

The free amine can be liberated by addition of base and extraction into ether. Following evaporation of the ether, the Hinsberg test, Group I(d), can be applied to determine if the compound is a primary, secondary, or tertiary amine.

The acid iron(III) hydroxamate test, Group I(d), can be applied directly to the amine salt (see the Hinsburg test, page 770).

Group III. Water-Soluble Neutral Compounds, Insoluble in Ether

(a) Metal Salts of Carboxylic Acids

(Table 70.1, carboxylic acids, page 784; Derivatives, page 779)

The free acid can be liberated by addition of acid and extraction into an appropriate solvent, after which the carboxylic acid can be characterized by mp or bp before proceeding to prepare a derivative.

(b) Ammonium Salts

(Table 70.1, carboxylic acids, page 784; Derivatives, page 779)

Ammonium salts on treatment with alkali liberate ammonia, which can be detected by its odor and the fact that it will turn red litmus to blue. A more sensitive test utilizes the copper(II) ion, which is blue in the presence of ammonia [see Group VIII a(i)]. Ammonium salts will not give a positive hydroxamic acid test (Ih) as given by amides.

(c) Sugars

See Chapter 36 for Tollens' test and Chapter 63 for phenylosazone formation.

(d) Amino Acids

Add 2 mg of the suspected amino acid to 1 mL of ninhydrin reagent, boil for 20 sec, and note the color. A blue color is a positive test.

Reagent: Dissolve 0.2 g of ninhydrin in 50 mL of water.

Cleaning Up   Because the quantity of material is extremely small, the test solution can be diluted with water and flushed down the drain.

(e) Polyhydric Alcohols

(Table 70.2, page 786; Derivatives, pages 779–780)

Periodic Acid Test for vic-Glycols.[4]

Vicinal glycols (hydroxyl groups on adjacent carbon atoms) can be detected by reaction with periodic acid. In addition to 1,2-glycols, a positive test is given by α-hydroxy aldehydes, α-hydroxy ketones, α-hydroxy acids, and α-amino alcohols, as well as 1,2-diketones.

To 2 mL of periodic acid reagent add 1 drop (no more) of concentrated nitric acid and shake. Then add 1 drop or a small crystal of the unknown. Shake

---

4. R. L. Shriner, R. C. Fuson, D. Y. Curtin, and T. C. Morill. *The Systematic Identification of Organic Compounds,* 6th ed., JohnWiley & Sons, Inc., New York, 1980.

for 15 sec, and add 1–2 drops of 5% aqueous silver nitrate solution. Instantaneous formation of a white precipitate is a positive test.

    Reagent: Dissolve 0.25 g of paraperiodic acid (H_5IO_6) in 50 mL of water.

Cleaning Up   Because the quantity of material is extremely small, dilute the test solution with water and flush down the drain.

Group IV. Certain Carboxylic Acids, Certain Phenols, and Sulfonamides of 1° Amines

(a) Carboxylic Acids

Solubility in both 5% sodium hydroxide and sodium bicarbonate is usually sufficient to characterize this class of compounds. Addition of mineral acid should regenerate the carboxylic acid. The neutralization equivalent can be obtained by titrating a known quantity of the acid (ca. 50 mg) dissolved in water-ethanol with 0.1 *N* sodium hydroxide to a phenolphthalein end point.

(b) Phenols

Negatively substituted phenols such as nitrophenols, aldehydrophenols, and polyhalophenols are sufficiently acidic to dissolve in 5% sodium bicarbonate. See Group I(i) for the iron(III) chloride test for phenols; however, this test is not completely reliable for these acidic phenols.

Group V. Acidic Compounds, Insoluble in Bicarbonate

(a) Phenols

See Group I(i).

(b) Enols

See Group I(i).

(c) 1° and 2° Nitro Compounds

(Table 70.16, page 797; Derivatives, page 780)

Iron(II) Hydroxide Test.   To a small vial (capacity (1–2 mL) add 5 mg of the unknown to 0.5 mL of freshly prepared ferrous sulfate solution. Add 0.4 mL of a 2 *N* solution of potassium hydroxide in methanol, cap the vial, and shake it. The appearance of a red-brown precipitate of iron(III) hydroxide within 1 min is a positive test. Almost all nitro compounds give a positive test within 30 sec.

    Reagents: Dissolve 2.5 g of ferrous ammonium sulfate in 50 mL of deoxygenated (by boiling) water. Add 0.2 mL of concentrated sulfuric acid and a piece of iron to prevent oxidation of the ferrous ion. Keep the bottle tightly stoppered. The potassium hydroxide solution is prepared by dissolving 5.6 g of potassium hydroxide in 50 mL of methanol.

Cleaning Up   Because the quantity of material is extremely small, the test solution can be diluted with water and flushed down the drain after neutralization with dilute hydrochloric acid.

(d) Sulfonamides of 1° Amines

An extremely sensitive test for sulfonamides (Feigl, *Spot Tests in Organic Analysis*) consists of placing a drop of a suspension or solution of the unknown on sulfonamide test paper followed by a drop of 0.5% hydrochloric acid. A red color is a positive test for sulfonamides.

CAUTION: Handle N,N-dimethyl-1-naphthylamine with care. As a class, aromatic amines are quite toxic and many are carcinogenic. Handle them all with care—in a hood if possible.

The test paper is prepared by dipping filter paper into a mixture of equal volumes of a 1% aqueous solution of sodium nitrite and a 1% methanolic solution of *N,N*-dimethyl-1-naphthylamine. Allow the filter paper to dry in the dark.

Cleaning Up   Place the test paper in the solid hazardous waste container.

Group VI. Basic Compounds, Insoluble in Water, Soluble in Acid

Amines

See Group I(d).

Group VII. Reducible, Neutral *N*- and *S*-Containing Compounds

Aromatic Nitro Compounds

See Group V(c).

Group VIII. Hydrolyzable, Neutral *N*- and *S*-Containing Compounds (identified through the acid and amine obtained on hydrolysis)

(a) Amides

Unsubstituted amides are detected by the hydroxamic acid test, Group I(h).

(1) Unsubstituted Amides.   Upon hydrolysis, unsubstituted amides liberate ammonia, which can be detected by reaction with cupric ion [Group III(b)].

To 1 mL of 20% sodium hydroxide solution, add 25 mg of the unknown. Cover the mouth of the reaction tube with a piece of filter paper moistened with a few drops of 10% copper(II) sulfate solution. Boil for 1 min. A blue color on the filter paper is a positive test for ammonia.

Cleaning Up   Neutralize the test solution with 10% hydrochloric acid, dilute with water, and flush down the drain.

(2) Substituted Amides.

The identification of substituted amides is not easy. There are no completely general tests for the substituted amide groups and hydrolysis is often difficult.

Hot sodium hydroxide solution is corrosive; use care.

Hydrolyze the amide by refluxing 250 mg with 2.5 mL of 20% sodium hydroxide for 20 min. Isolate the primary or secondary amine produced, by extraction into ether, and identify as described under Group I(d). Liberate the acid by acidification of the residue, isolate by filtration or extraction, and characterize by bp or mp and the mp of an appropriate derivative.

Use care in shaking concentrated sulfuric acid.

Cleaning Up   Dilute the test solution with water and flush down the drain.

(3) Anilides.

Add 50 mg of the unknown to 1.5 mL of concentrated sulfuric acid. Carefully stopper the reaction tube with a rubber stopper, and shake vigorously. (*Caution!*) Add 25 mg of finely powdered potassium dichromate. A blue-pink color is a positive test for an anilide that does not have substituents on the ring (e.g., acetanilide).

Dichromate dust is carcinogenic, when inhaled. Cr^{+6} is not a carcinogen when applied to the skin or ingested.

Cleaning Up   Carefully add the solution to water, neutralize with sodium carbonate, and flush down the drain.

(b) Nitriles

See Group I(h).

(c) Sulfonamides

See Group V(d).

Group IX. Neutral Polar Compounds, Insoluble in Dilute Hydrochloric Acid, Soluble in Concentrated Sulfuric Acid (most compounds containing oxygen)

(a) Alcohols

See Group I(b).

(b) Aldehydes

See Group I(c).

(c) Anhydrides

See Group I(e).

(d) Esters

See Group I(f).

(e) Ethers

(Table 70.9, page 793)

Ethers are very unreactive. Care must be used to distinguish ethers from those hydrocarbons that are soluble in concentrated sulfuric acid.

$Fe[Fe(SCN)_6]$

Iron(III) hexathiocyanato-ferrate(III)

Ferrox Test.   In a dry test tube grind together, with a stirring rod, a crystal of iron(III) ammonium sulfate (or iron(III) chloride) and a crystal of potassium thiocyanate. Iron(III) hexathiocyanatoferrate(III) will adhere to the stirring rod. In a clean tube place 3 drops of a liquid unknown or a saturated toluene solution of a solid unknown, and stir with the rod. The salt will dissolve if the unknown contains oxygen to give a red-purple color, but it will not dissolve in hydrocarbons or halocarbons. Diphenyl ether does not give a positive test.

Alkyl ethers are generally soluble in concentrated sulfuric acid; alkyl aryl and diaryl ethers are not soluble.

Cleaning Up   Place the mixture in the hazardous waste container.

(f) Ketones

(Table 70.14, page 796; Derivatives, pages 442 and 444).

(g) Unsaturated Hydrocarbons

(Table 70.12, page 794)

Use care in working with the bromine solution

Bromine in Carbon Tetrachloride.   Dissolve 1 drop (20 mg) of the unknown in 0.5 mL of carbon tetrachloride. Add a 2% solution of bromine in carbon tetrachloride dropwise with shaking. If more than 2 drops of bromine solution are required to give a permanent red color, unsaturation is indicated. The bromine solution must be fresh.

Cleaning Up   Place the mixture in the halogenated solvents container.

Potassium Permanganate Solution.   Dissolve 1 drop (20 mg) of the unknown in reagent grade acetone and add a 1% aqueous solution of potassium permanganate dropwise with shaking. If more than one drop of reagent is required to give a purple color to the solution, unsaturation or an easily oxidized functional group is present. Run parallel tests on pure acetone and, as usual, a compound known to be an alkene.

Cleaning Up Dilute the solution with water and flush down the drain.

Group X. Inert Compounds. Insoluble in Concentrated Sulfuric Acid

(a) Alkyl and Aryl Halides

Alkyl Halides (Table 70.10, page 793)
Aryl Halides (Table 70.11, page 794)

Do not waste silver nitrate.

Alcoholic Silver Nitrate. Add 1 drop of the unknown (or saturated solution of 10 mg of unknown in ethanol) to 0.2 mL of a saturated solution of silver nitrate. A precipitate that forms within 2 min is a positive test for an alkyl bromide, or iodide, or a tertiary alkyl chloride, as well as alkyl halides.

If no precipitate forms within 2 min, heat the solution to boiling. A precipitate of silver chloride will form from primary and secondary alkyl chlorides. Aryl halides and vinyl halides will not react.

Cleaning Up Because the quantity of material is extremely small, it can be diluted with water and flushed down the drain.

(b) Aromatic Hydrocarbons

(Table 70.13, page 795; Derivatives, pages 780 and 782)
Aromatic hydrocarbons are best identified and characterized by UV and NMR spectroscopy, but the Friedel–Crafts reaction produces a characteristic color with certain aromatic hydrocarbons.

Keep moisture away from aluminum chloride.
CAUTION: Chloroform is carcinogenic. Carry out this test in a hood.

Friedel–Crafts Test. Heat a test tube containing about 50 mg of anhydrous aluminum chloride in a hot flame to sublime the salt up onto the sides of the tube. Add a solution of about 10 mg of the unknown dissolved in a drop of chloroform to the cool tube in such a way that it comes into contact with the sublimed aluminum chloride. Note the color that appears.

Nonaromatic compounds fail to give a color with aluminum chloride, benzene and its derivatives give orange or red colors, naphthalenes a blue or purple color, biphenyls a purple color, phenanthrene a purple color, and anthracene a green color.

Cleaning Up Place the test mixture in the halogenated organic solvents container.

(c) Saturated Hydrocarbons

Saturated hydrocarbons are best characterized by NMR and IR spectroscopy, but they can be distinguished from aromatic hydrocarbons by the Friedel–Crafts test [Group X(b)].

(d) Diaryl Ethers

Because they are so inert, diaryl ethers are difficult to detect and may be mistaken for aromatic hydrocarbons. They do not give a positive Ferrox test (see p. 777) for ethers and do not dissolve in concentrated sulfuric acid. Their infrared spectra, however, are characterized by an intense C—O single-bond, stretching vibration in the region 1270–1230 cm^{-1}.

Derivatives

1. Acids

(Table 70.1)

p-Toluidides and Anilides.   Reflux a mixture of the acid (100 mg) and thionyl chloride (0.5 mL) in a reaction tube for 0.5 h. Cool the reaction mixture, and add 0.25 g of aniline or *p*-toluidine in 3 mL of toluene. Warm the mixture on the steam bath for 2 min, and then wash with 1-mL portions of water, 5% hydrochloric acid, 5% sodium hydroxide, and water. The toluene is dried briefly over anhydrous calcium chloride pellets and evaporated in the hood; the derivative is recrystallized from water or ethanol–water.

CAUTION: p-Toluidine is a highly toxic irritant.

Cleaning Up   Dilute the aqueous layers with water and flush down the drain. Place the drying agent in the hazardous waste container.

Amides.   Reflux a mixture of the acid (100 mg) and thionyl chloride (0.5 mL) for 0.5 h. Transfer the cool reaction mixture into 1.4 mL of ice-cold concentrated ammonia. Stir until reaction is complete, collect the product by filtration, and recrystallize it from water or water–ethanol.

Thionyl chloride is an irritant. Use it in a hood.

Cleaning Up   Neutralize the aqueous filtrate with 10% hydrochloric acid, dilute with water, and flush down the drain.

2. Alcohols

(Table 70.2)

3,5-Dinitrobenzoates.   Gently boil 100 mg of 3,5-dinitrobenzoyl chloride and 25 mg of the alcohol for 5 min. Cool the mixture, pulverize any solid that forms, and add 2 mL of 2% sodium carbonate solution. Continue to grind and stir the solid with the sodium carbonate solution (to remove 3,5-dinitrobenzoic acid) for about a minute, filter, and wash the crystals with water. Dissolve the product in about 2.5–3 mL of hot ethanol, add water to the cloud point, and allow crystallization to proceed. Wash the 3,5-dinitrobenzoate with water–alcohol and dry.

Note to instructor: Check to ascertain that the 3,5-dinitrobenzoyl chloride has not hydrolyzed. The mp should be >65°C. Reported mp is 68–69°C.

Phenyl isocyanate

CAUTION: *Lachrymator*

Cleaning Up   Dilute the aqueous filtrate with water and flush down the drain.

Phenylurethanes.   Mix 100 mg of anhydrous alcohol (or phenol) and 100 mg of phenyl isocyanate (or α-naphthylurethane), and heat on the steam bath for 5 min. (If the unknown is a phenol add a drop of pyridine to the reaction mixture.) Cool, add about 1 mL of ligroin, heat to dissolve the product, filter hot to remove a small amount of diphenylurea which usually forms, and cool the filtrate in ice, with scratching, to induce crystallization.

Cleaning Up   Place the ligroin filtrate in the organic solvents container.

3. Aldehydes

(Table 70.3)

Semicarbazones.   See Chapter 36. Use 0.5 mL of the stock solution and an estimated 1 mmol of the unknown aldehyde (or ketone).

2,4-Dinitrophenylhydrazones.   See Chapter 36. Use 1 mL of the stock solution of 0.1 M 2,4-dinitrophenylhydrazine and an estimated 0.1 mmol of the unknown aldehyde (or ketone).

4. Primary and Secondary Amines

(Table 70.5)

Benzamides.   Add about 0.25 g of benzoyl chloride in small portions with vigorous shaking and cooling to a suspension of 0.5 mmol of the unknown amine in 0.5 mL of 10% aqueous sodium hydroxide solution. After about 10 min of shaking the mixture is made pH 8 (pH paper) with dilute hydrochloric acid. The lumpy product is removed by filtration, washed thoroughly with water, and recrystallized from ethanol–water.

Cleaning Up   Dilute the filtrate with water and flush down the drain.

**Picric acid
(2,4,6-Trinitrophenol)**

Handle pure acid with care (explosive). It is sold as a moist solid. Do not allow to dry out.

Picrates.   Add a solution of 30 mg of the unknown in 1 mL of ethanol (or 1 mL of a saturated solution of the unknown) to 1 mL of a saturated solution of picric acid (2,4,6-trinitrophenol, a strong acid) in ethanol, and heat the solution to boiling. Cool slowly, remove the picrate by filtration, and wash with a small amount of ethanol. Recrystallization is not usually necessary; in the case of hydrocarbon picrates the product is often too unstable to be recrystallized.

Cleaning Up   See page 523 for the treatment of solutions containing picric acid.

Acetamides.   Reflux about 0.5 mmol of the unknown with 0.2 mL of acetic anhydride for 5 min, cool, and dilute the reaction mixture with 2.5 mL of water.

Acetic anhydride is corrosive. Work with this in a hood.

Initiate crystallization by scratching, if necessary. Remove the crystals by filtration, and wash thoroughly with dilute hydrochloric acid to remove unreacted amine. Recrystallize the derivative from alcohol–water. Amines of low basicity, e.g., *p*-nitroaniline, should be refluxed for 30–60 min with 1 mL of pyridine as a solvent. The pyridine is removed by shaking the reaction mixture with 5 mL of 2% sulfuric acid solution; the product is isolated by filtration and recrystallized.

Cleaning Up   Neutralize the filtrate from the usual reaction with sodium carbonate. Then dilute it with water and flush down the drain. If pyridine is used as the solvent, neutralize the filtrate with sodium carbonate and extract it with ligroin. Place the ligroin/pyridine in the organic solvents container; dilute the aqueous layer with water and flush down the drain.

5. Tertiary Amines

(Table 70.6)

Picrates.   See under Primary and Secondary Amines.

$$R_3N + CH_3I$$
$$\downarrow$$
$$R_3\overset{+}{N}CH_3I^-$$

Methyl iodide is a suspected carcinogen.

Methiodides.   Reflux 100 mg of the amine and 100 mg of methyl iodide for 5 min on the steam bath. Cool, scratch to induce crystallization, and recrystallize the product from ethyl alcohol or ethyl acetate.

Cleaning Up   Because the filtrate may contain some methyl iodide, place it in the halogenated solvents container.

6. Anhydrides and Acid Chlorides

(Table 70.7)

Acids.   Reflux 40 mg of the acid chloride or anhydride with 1 mL of 5% sodium carbonate solution for 20 min or less. Extract unreacted starting material with 1 mL of ether, if necessary, and acidify the reaction mixture with dilute sulfuric acid to liberate the carboxylic acid.

Cleaning Up   Place the ether in the organic solvents container; dilute the aqueous layer with water and flush it down the drain.

Amides.   Because the acid chloride (or anhydride) is already present, simply mix the unknown (50 mg) and 0.7 mL of ice-cold concentrated ammonia until reaction is complete, collect the product by filtration, and recrystallize it from water or ethanol–water.

Cleaning Up   Neutralize the filtrate with dilute hydrochloric acid and flush it down the drain.

Anilides.   Reflux 40 mg of the acid halide or anhydride with 100 mg of aniline in 2 mL of toluene for 10 min. Wash the toluene solution with 5-mL portions each of water, 5% hydrochloric acid, 5% sodium hydroxide, and again with water. The toluene solution is dried over anhydrous calcium chloride and evaporated; the anilide is recrystallized from water or ethanol–water.

Cleaning Up   Dilute the combined aqueous layers with water and flush down the drain. Place the soldium sulfate in the aromatic amines hazardous waste container.

7. Aryl Halides

(Table 70.11)

Nitration.   Add 0.4 mL of concentrated sulfuric acid to 100 mg of the aryl halide (or aromatic compound) and stir. Add 0.4 mL of concentrated nitric acid dropwise with stirring and shaking while cooling the reaction mixture in water. Then heat and shake the reaction mixture in a water bath at about 50°C for 15 min, pour into 2 mL of cold water, and collect the product by filtration. Recrystallize from methanol to constant melting point.

Use great care when working with fuming nitric acid.   To nitrate unreactive compounds, use fuming nitric acid in place of concentrated nitric acid.

Cleaning Up   Dilute the filtrate with water, neutralize with sodium carbonate, and flush the solution down the drain.

Sidechain Oxidation Products.   Dissolve 0.2 g of sodium dichromate in 0.6 mL of water, and add 0.4 mL of concentrated sulfuric acid. Add 50 mg of the unknown and boil for 30 min. Cool, add 0.4–0.6 mL of water, and then remove the carboxylic acid by filtration. Wash the crystals with water and recrystallize from methanol–water.

Cleaning Up   Place the filtrate from the reaction, after neutralization with sodium carbonate, in the hazardous waste container.

8. Hydrocarbons: Aromatic

(Table 70.13)

Nitration.   See preceding, under Aryl Halides.

Picrates.   See preceding, under Primary and Secondary Amines.

9. Ketones

(Table 70.14)

Semicarbazones and 2,4-dinitrophenylhydrazones.   See preceding directions under Aldehydes.

10. Nitro Compounds

(Table 70.16)

Reduction to Amines.   Place 100 mg of the unknown in a reaction tube, add 0.2 g of tin, and then—in portions—2 mL of 10% hydrochloric acid. Reflux for 30 min, add 1 mL of water, then add slowly, with good cooling, sufficient 40% sodium hydroxide solution to dissolve the tin hydroxide. Extract the reaction mixture with three 1-mL portions of *t*-butyl methyl ether, dry the ether extract over anhydrous calcium chloride pellets, wash the drying agent with ether, and evaporate the ether to leave the amine. Determine the boiling point or melting point of the amine and then convert it into a benzamide or acetamide as described under the section on Primary and Secondary Amines.

Cleaning Up   Neutralize the aqueous layer with 10% hydrochloric acid, remove the tin hydroxide by filtration, and discard it in the nonhazardous solid waste container. Dilute the filtrate with water and flush down the drain. After the ether evaporates from the calcium chloride, place it in the nonhazardous waste container.

11. Phenols

(Table 70.17)

α-Naphthylurethane.   Follow the procedure for preparation of a phenylurethane under the Alcohols section.

Use great care when working with bromine. Should any touch the skin wash it off with copious quantities of water. Work in a hood and wear disposable gloves.

Bromo Derivative.   In a reaction tube dissolve 160 mg of potassium bromide in 1 mL of water. *Carefully* add 100 mg of bromine. In a separate flask dissolve 20 mg of the phenol in 0.2 mL of methanol, and add 0.2 mL of water. Add about 0.3 mL of the bromine solution with swirling (hood); continue the addition of bromine until the yellow color of unreacted bromine persists. Add 0.6–0.8 mL of water to the reaction mixture, and shake vigorously. Remove the product by filtration, and wash well with water. Recrystallize from methanol-water.

Cleaning Up   Destroy any unreacted bromine by adding sodium bisulfite solution dropwise until the color dissipates. Then dilute the solution with water and flush it down the drain.

TABLE 70.1 Acids

bp	mp	Compound	p-*Toluidide*[a] mp	*Anilide*[b] mp	*Amide*[c] mp
101		Formic acid	53	47	43
118		Acetic acid	126	106	79
139		Acrylic acid	141	104	85
141		Propionic acid	124	103	81
162		*n*-Butyric acid	72	95	115
163		Methacrylic acid		87	102
163		Trimethylacetic acid		127	178
165		Pyruvic acid	109	104	124
185		Valeric acid	70	63	106
186		2-Methylvaleric acid	80	95	79
194		Dichloroacetic acid	153	118	98
202–203		Hexanoic acid	75	95	101
237		Octanoic acid	70	57	107
254		Nonanoic acid	84	57	99
	31–32	Decanoic acid	78	70	108
	43–45	Lauric acid	87	78	100
	47–49	Bromoacetic acid		131	91
	47–49	Hydrocinnamic acid	135	92	105
	54–55	Myristic acid	93	84	103
	54–58	Trichloroacetic acid	113	97	141
	61–62	Chloroacetic acid	162	137	121
	61–62.5	Palmitic acid	98	90	106
	67–69	Stearic acid	102	95	109
	68–69	3,3-Dimethylacrylic acid		126	107
	71–73	Crotonic acid	132	118	158
	77–78.5	Phenylacetic acid	136	118	156
	101–102	Oxalic acid dihydrate		257	400 (dec)
	98–102	Azelaic acid (nonanedioic)	164 (di)	107 (mono) 186 (di)	93 (mono) 175 (di)
	103–105	*o*-Toluic acid	144	125	142
	108–110	*m*-Toluic acid	118	126	94
	119–121	DL-Mandelic acid	172	151	133
	122–123	Benzoic acid	158	163	130
	127–128	2-Benzoylbenzoic acid		195	165
	129–130	2-Furoic acid	107	123	143
	131–133	DL-Malic acid	178 (mono) 207 (di)	155 (mono) 198 (di)	163 (di)
	131–134	Sebacic acid	201	122 (mono) 200 (di)	170 (mono) 210 (di)

(continued)

a. For preparation, see page 779.
b. For preparation, see page 779.
c. For preparation, see page 779.

TABLE 70.1   *continued*

			Derivatives		
			p-*Toluidide*[a]	*Anilide*[b]	*Amide*[c]
bp	mp	Compound	mp	mp	mp
	134–135	*E*-Cinnamic acid	168	153	147
	134–136	Maleic acid	142 (di)	198 (mono)	260 (di)
				187 (di)	
	135–137	Malonic acid	86 (mono)	132 (mono)	
			253 (di)	230 (di)	
	138–140	2-Chlorobenzoic acid	131	118	139
	140–142	3-Nitrobenzoic acid	162	155	143
	144–148	Anthranilic acid	151	131	109
	147–149	Diphenylacetic acid	172	180	167
	152–153	Adipic acid	239	151 (mono)	125 (mono)
				241 (di)	220 (di)
	153–154	Citric acid	189 (tri)	199 (tri)	210 (tri)
	157–159	4-Chlorophenoxyacetic acid		125	133
	158–160	Salicylic acid	156	136	142
	164–166	5-Bromosalicylic acid		222	232
	166–167	Itaconic acid		190	191 (di)
	171–174	D-Tartaric acid		180 (mono)	171 (mono)
				264 (di)	196 (di)
	179–182	3,4-Dimethoxybenzoic acid		154	164
	180–182	4-Toluic acid	160	145	160
	182–185	4-Anisic acid	186	169	167
	187–190	Succinic acid	180 (mono)	143 (mono)	157 (mono)
			255 (di)	230 (di)	260 (di)
	201–203	3-Hydroxybenzoic acid	163	157	170
	203–206	3,5-Dinitrobenzoic acid		234	183
	210–211	Phthalic acid	150 (mono)	169 (mono)	149 (mono)
			201 (di)	253 (di)	220 (di)
	214–215	4-Hydroxybenzoic acid	204	197	162
	225–227	2,4-Dihydroxybenzoic acid		126	228
	236–239	Nicotinic acid	150	132	128
	239–241	4-Nitrobenzoic acid	204	211	201
	299–300	Fumaric acid		233 (mono)	270 (mono)
				314 (di)	266 (di)
	>300	Terephthalic acid		334	

a. For preparation, see page 779.
b. For preparation, see page 779.
c. For preparation, see page 779.

TABLE 70.2   Alcohols

		Derivatives	
		3,5-Dinitrobenzoate[a]	Phenylurethane[b]
bp	mp	Compound	mp	mp
---	---	---	---	---
65		Methanol	108	47
78		Ethanol	93	52
82		2-Propanol	123	88
83		*t*-Butyl alcohol	142	136
96–98		Allyl alcohol	49	70
97		1-Propanol	74	57
98		2-Butanol	76	65
102		2-Methyl-2-butanol	116	42
104		2-Methyl-3-butyn-2-ol	112	
108		2-Methyl-1-propanol	87	86
114–115		Propargyl alcohol		63
114–115		3-Pentanol	101	48
118		1-Butanol	64	61
118–119		2-Pentanol	62	oil
123		3-Methyl-3-pentanol	96(62)	43
129		2-Chloroethanol	95	51
130		2-Methyl-1-butanol	70	31
132		4-Methyl-2-pentanol	65	143
136–138		1-Pentanol	46	46
139–140		Cyclopentanol	115	132
140		2,4-Dimethyl-3-pentanol	75	95
146		2-Ethyl-1-butanol	51	
151		2,2,2-Trichloroethanol	142	87
157		1-Hexanol	58	42
160–161		Cyclohexanol	113	82
170		Furfuryl alcohol	80	45
176		1-Heptanol	47	60(68)
178		2-Octanol	32	oil
178		Tetrahydrofurfuryl alcohol	83	61
183–184		2,3-Butanediol		201 (di)
183–186		2-Ethyl-1-hexanol		34
187		1,2-Propanediol		153 (di)
194–197		Linaloöl		66
195		1-Octanol	61	74
196–198		Ethylene glycol	169	157 (di)
204		1,3-Butanediol		122
203–205		Benzyl alcohol	113	77
204		1-Phenylethanol	95	92
219–221		2-Phenylethanol	108	78
230		1,4-Butanediol		183 (mono)
231		1-Decanol	57	59

(continued)

a. For preparation, see page 779.
b. For preparation, see page 780.

TABLE 70.2   *continued*

			Derivatives	
			3,5-Dinitrobenzoate[a]	*Phenylurethane*[b]
bp	mp	Compound	mp	mp
259		4-Methoxybenzyl alcohol		92
	33–35	Cinnamyl alcohol	121	90
	38–40	1-Tetradecanol	67	74
	48–50	1-Hexadecanol	66	73
	58–60	1-Octadecanol	77(66)	79
	66–67	Benzhydrol	141	139
	147	Cholesterol	195	168

a. For preparation, see page 779.
b. For preparation, see page 780.

TABLE 70.3   Aldehydes

			Derivatives	
			Semicarbazone[a]	*2,4-Dinitrophenylhydrazone*[b]
bp	mp	Compound	mp	mp
21		Acetaldehyde	162	168
46–50		Propionaldehyde	89(154)	148
63		Isobutyraldehyde	125(119)	187(183)
75		Butyraldehyde	95(106)	123
90–92		3-Methylbutanal	107	123
98		Chloral	90	131
104		Crotonaldehyde	199	190
117		2-Ethylbutanal	99	95(130)
153		Heptaldehyde	109	108
162		2-Furaldehyde	202	212(230)
163		2-Ethylhexanal	254	114(120)
179		Benzaldehyde	222	237
195		Phenylacetaldehyde	153	121(110)
197		Salicylaldehyde	231	248
204–205		4-Tolualdehyde	234(215)	232
209–215		2-Chlorobenzaldehyde	146(229)	213
247		2-Ethoxybenzaldehyde	219	
248		4-Anisaldehyde	210	253

(continued)

a. For preparation, see page 444.
b. For preparation, see page 442.

TABLE 70.3   *continued*

bp	mp	Compound	Derivatives	
			Semicarbazone[a]	2,4-Dinitrophenylhydrazone[b]
			mp	mp
250–252		*E*-Cinnamaldehyde	215	255
	33–34	1-Naphthaldehyde	221	254
	37–39	2-Anisaldehyde	215	254
	42–45	3,4-Dimethoxybenzaldehyde	177	261
	44–47	4-Chlorobenzaldehyde	230	254
	57–59	3-Nitrobenzaldehyde	246	293
	81–83	Vanillin	230	271

a. For preparation, see page 444.
b. For preparation, see page 442.

TABLE 70.4   Amides

bp	mp	Name of Compound	mp	Name of Compound
153		*N,N*-Dimethylformamide	127–129	Isobutyramide
164–166		*N,N*-Dimethylacetamide	128–129	Benzamide
210		Formamide	130–133	Nicotinamide
243–244		*N*-Methylformanilide	177–179	4-Chloroacetanilide
	26–28	*N*-Methylacetamide		
	79–81	Acetamide		
	109–111	Methacrylamide		
	113–115	Acetanilide		
	116–118	2-Chloroacetamide		

TABLE 70.5   Primary and Secondary Amines

			Derivatives		
			Benzamide[a]	*Picrate*[b]	*Acetamide*[c]
bp	mp	Compound	mp	mp	mp
33–34		Isopropylamine	71	165	
46		*t*-Butylamine	134	198	
48		*n*-Propylamine	84	135	
53		Allylamine		140	
55		Diethylamine	42	155	
63		*s*-Butylamine	76	139	
64–71		Isobutylamine	57	150	
78		*n*-Butylamine	42	151	
84		Diisopropylamine		140	
87–88		Pyrrolidine	oil	112	
106		Piperidine	48	152	
111		Di-*n*-propylamine	oil	75	
118		Ethylenediamine	244 (di)	233	172 (di)
129		Morpholine	75	146	
137–139		Diisobutylamine		121	86
145–146		Furfurylamine		150	
149		*N*-Methylcyclohexylamine	85	170	
159		Di-*n*-butylamine	oil	59	
182–185		Benzylamine	105	199	60
184		Aniline	163	198	114
196		*N*-Methylaniline	63	145	102
199–200		2-Toluidine	144	213	110
203–204		3-Toluidine	125	200	65
205		*N*-Ethylaniline	60	138(132)	54
208–210		2-Chloroaniline	99	134	87
210		2-Ethylaniline	147	194	111
216		2,6-Dimethylaniline	168	180	177
218		2,4-Dimethylaniline	192	209	133
218		2,5-Dimethylaniline	140	171	139
221		*N*-Ethyl-*m*-toluidine	72		
225		2-Anisidine	60(84)	200	85
230		3-Chloroaniline	120	177	72(78)
231–233		2-Phenetidine	104		79
241		4-Chloro-2-methylaniline	142		140
242		3-Chloro-4-methylaniline	122		105
250		4-Phenetidine	173	69	137
256		Dicyclohexylamine	153(57)	173	103

(continued)

a. For preparation, see page 780.
b. For preparation, see page 780.
c. For preparation, see page 780.

TABLE 70.5 *continued*

bp	mp	Compound	Benzamide[a] mp	Picrate[b] mp	Acetamide[c] mp
	35–38	*N*-Phenylbenzylamine	107	48	58
	41–44	4-Toluidine	158	182	147
	49–51	2,5-Dichloroaniline	120	86	132
	52–54	Diphenylamine	180	182	101
	57–60	4-Anisidine	154	170	130
	57–60	2-Aminopyridine	165 (di)	216(223)	
	60–62	*N*-Phenyl-1-naphthylamine	152		115
	62–65	2,4,5-Trimethylaniline	167		162
	64–66	1,3-Phenylenediamine	125 (mono) 240 (di)	184	87 (mono) 191 (di)
	66	4-Bromoaniline	204	180	168
	68–71	4-Chloroaniline	192	178	179(172)
	71–73	2-Nitroaniline	110(98)	73	92
	97–99	2,4-Diaminotoluene	224 (di)		224 (di)
	100–102	1,2-Phenylenediamine	301	208	185
	104–107	2-Methyl-5-nitroaniline	186		151
	107–109	2-Chloro-4-nitroaniline	161		139
	112–114	3-Nitroaniline	157(150)	143	155(76)
	115–116	4-Methyl-2-nitroaniline	148		99
	117–119	4-Chloro-2-nitroaniline			104
	120–122	2,4,6-Tribromoaniline	198(204)		232
	131–133	2-Methyl-4-nitroaniline			202
	138–140	2-Methoxy-4-nitroaniline	149		
	138–142	1,4-Phenylenediamine	128 (mono) 300 (di)		162 (mono) 304 (di)
	148–149	4-Nitroaniline	199	100	215
	162–164	4-Aminoacetanilide			304
	176–178	2,4-Dinitroaniline	202(220)		120

a. For preparation, see page 780.
b. For preparation, see page 780.
c. For preparation, see page 780.

TABLE 70.6 Tertiary Amines

| | | Derivatives | |
| | | *Picrate*[a] | *Methiodide*[b] |
bp	Compound	mp	mp
85–91	Triethylamine	173	280
115	Pyridine	167	117
128–129	2-Picoline	169	230
143–145	2,6-Lutidine	168(161)	233
144	3-Picoline	150	92(36)
145	4-Picoline	167	149
155–158	Tri-*n*-propylamine	116	207
159	2,4-Lutidine	180	113
183–184	*N,N*-Dimethylbenzylamine	93	179
216	Tri-*n*-butylamine	105	186
217	*N,N*-Diethylaniline	142	102
237	Quinoline	203	133(72)

a. For preparation, see page 780.
b. For preparation, see page 781.

TABLE 70.7 Anhydrides and Acid Halides

| | | | Derivatives | | | |
| | | | *Acid*[a] | | *Amide*[b] | *Anilide*[c] |
bp	mp	Compound	bp	mp	mp	mp
52		Acetyl chloride	118		82	114
77–79		Propionyl chloride	141		81	106
102		Butyryl chloride	162		115	96
138–140		Acetic anhydride	118		82	114
167		Propionic anhydride	141		81	106
198–199		Butyric anhydride	162		115	96
198		Benzoyl chloride		122	130	163
225		3-Chlorobenzoyl chloride		158	134	122
238		2-Chlorobenzoyl chloride		142	142	118
	32–34	*cis*-1,2-Cyclohexanedicarboxylic anhydride		192		
	35–37	Cinnamoyl chloride		133	147	151
	39–40	Benzoic anhydride		122	130	163
	54–56	Maleic anhydride		130	181 (mono) 266 (di)	173 (mono) 187

(continued)

a. For preparation, see page 781.
b. For preparation, see page 781.
c. For preparation, see page 782.

TABLE 70.7 *continued*

			Derivatives				
			Acid[a]		Amide[b]	Anilide[c]	
bp	mp	Compound	bp	mp	mp	mp	
	72–74	4-Nitrobenzoyl chloride		241	201	211	
	119–120	Succinic anhydride		186	157 (mono)	148 (mono)	
					260 (di)	230 (di)	
	131–133	Phthalic anhydride		206	149 (mono)	170 (mono)	
					220 (di)	253 (di)	
	254–258	Tetrachlorophthalic anhydride		250			
	267–269	1,8-Naphthalic anhydride		274		250–282 (di)	

a. For preparation, see page 781.
b. For preparation, see page 781.
c. For preparation, see page 782.

TABLE 70.8 Esters

bp	mp	Compound	bp	mp	Compound
34		Methyl formate	169–170		Methyl acetoacetate
52–54		Ethyl formate	180–181		Dimethyl malonate
72–73		Vinyl acetate	181		Ethyl acetoacetate
77		Ethyl acetate	185		Diethyl oxalate
79		Methyl propionate	198–199		Methyl benzoate
80		Methyl acrylate	206–208		Ethyl caprylate
85		Isopropyl acetate	208–210		Ethyl cyanoacetate
93		Ethyl chloroformate	212		Ethyl benzoate
94		Isopropenyl acetate	217		Diethyl succinate
98		Isobutyl formate	218		Methyl phenylacetate
98		t-Butyl acetate	218–219		Diethyl fumarate
99		Ethyl propionate	222		Methyl salicylate
99		Ethyl acrylate	225		Dimethyl maleate
100		Methyl methacrylate	229		Ethyl phenylacetate
101		Methyl trimethylacetate	234		Ethyl salicylate
102		n-Propyl acetate	268		Diethyl suberate
106–113		s-Butyl acetate	271		Ethyl cinnamate
120		Ethyl butyrate	282		Dimethyl phthalate
127		n-Butyl acetate	298–299		Diethyl phthalate
128		Methyl valerate	298–299		Phenyl benzoate
130		Methyl chloroacetate	340		Dibutyl phthalate
131–133		Ethyl isovalerate		56–58	Ethyl p-nitrobenzoate
142		n-Amyl acetate		88–90	Ethyl p-aminobenzoate
142		Isoamyl acetate		94–96	Methyl p-nitrobenzoate
143		Ethyl chloroacetate		95–98	n-Propyl p-hydroxybenzoate
154		Ethyl lactate		116–118	Ethyl p-hydroxybenzoate
168		Ethyl caproate (ethyl hexanoate)		126–128	Methyl p-hydroxybenzoate

TABLE 70.9 Ethers

bp	mp	Compound	bp	mp	Compound
32		Furan	215		4-Bromoanisole
33		Ethyl vinyl ether	234–237		Anethole
65–67		Tetrahydrofuran	259		Diphenyl ether
94		n-Butyl vinyl ether	273		2-Nitroanisole
154		Anisole	298		Dibenzyl ether
174		4-Methylanisole		50–52	4-Nitroanisole
175–176		3-Methylanisole		56–60	1,4-Dimethoxybenzene
198–203		4-Chloroanisole		73–75	2-Methoxynaphthalene
206–207		1,2-Dimethoxybenzene			

TABLE 70.10 Halides

bp	Compound	bp	Compound
34–36	2-Chloropropane	100–105	1-Bromobutane
40–41	Dichloromethane	105	Bromotrichloromethane
44–46	Allyl chloride	110–115	1,1,2-Trichloroethane
57	1,1-Dichloroethane	120–121	1-Bromo-3-methylbutane
59	2-Bromopropane	121	Tetrachloroethylene
68	Bromochloromethane	123	3,4-Dichloro-1-butene
68–70	2-Chlorobutane	125	1,3-Dichloro-2-butene
69–73	Iodoethane	131–132	1,2-Dibromoethane
70–71	Allyl bromide	140–142	1,2-Dibromopropane
71	1-Bromopropane	142–145	1-Bromo-3-chloropropane
72–74	2-Bromo-2-methylpropane	146–150	Bromoform
74–76	1,1,1-Trichloroethane	147	1,1,2,2-Tetrachloroethane
81–85	1,2-Dichloroethane	156	1,2,3-Trichloropropane
87	Trichloroethylene	161–163	1,4-Dichlorobutane
88–90	2-Iodopropane	167	1,3-Dibromopropane
90–92	1-Bromo-2-methylpropane	177–181	Benzyl chloride
91	2-Bromobutane	197	(2-Chloroethyl)benzene
94	2,3-Dichloro-1-propene	219–223	Benzotrichloride
95–96	1,2-Dichloropropane	238	1-Bromodecane
96–98	Dibromomethane		

TABLE 70.11 Aryl Halides

			Derivatives			
			Nitration Product[a]		Oxidation Product[b]	
bp	mp	Compound	Position	mp	Name	mp
132		Chlorobenzene	2, 4	52		
156		Bromobenzene	2, 4	70		
157–159		2-Chlorotoluene	3, 5	63	2-Chlorobenzoic acid	141
162		4-Chlorotoluene	2	38	4-Chlorobenzoic acid	240
172–173		1,3-Dichlorobenzene	4, 6	103		
178		1,2-Dichlorobenzene	4, 5	110		
196–203		2,4-Dichlorotoluene	3, 5	104	2,4-Dichlorobenzoic acid	164
201		3,4-Dichlorotoluene	6	63	3,4-Dichlorobenzoic acid	206
214		1,2,4-Trichlorobenzene	5	56		
279–281		1-Bromonaphthalene	4	85		
	51–53	1,2,3-Trichlorobenzene	4	56		
	54–56	1,4-Dichlorobenzene	2	54		
	66–68	1,4-Bromochlorobenzene	2	72		
	87–89	1,4-Dibromobenzene	2, 5	84		
	138–140	1,2,4,5-Tetrachlorobenzene	3	99		
			3, 6	227		

a. For preparation, see page 782.
b. For preparation, see page 782.

TABLE 70.12 Hydrocarbons: Alkenes

bp	Compound	bp	Compound
34	Isoprene	149–150	1,5-Cyclooctadiene
83	Cyclohexene	152	DL-α-Pinene
116	5-Methyl-2-norbornene	160	Bicyclo[4.3.0]nona-3,7-diene
122–123	1-Octene	165–167	(−)-β-Pinene
126–127	4-Vinyl-1-cyclohexene	165–169	α-Methylstyrene
132–134	2,5-Dimethyl-2,4-hexadiene	181	1-Decene
141	5-Vinyl-2-norbornene	181	Indene
143	1,3-Cyclooctadiene	251	1-Tetradecene
145	4-Butylstyrene	274	1-Hexadecene
145–146	Cyclooctene	349	1-Octadecene
145–146	Styrene		

TABLE 70.13   Hydrocarbons: Aromatic

bp	mp	Compound	Nitro[a] Position	Nitro[a] mp	Picrate[b] mp
80		Benzene	1, 3	89	84
111		Toluene	2, 4	70	88
136		Ethylbenzene	2, 4, 6	37	96
138		*p*-Xylene	2, 3, 5	139	90
138–139		*m*-Xylene	2, 4, 6	183	91
143–145		*o*-Xylene	4, 5	118	88
145		4-*t*-Butylstyrene	2, 4	62	
145–146		Styrene			
152–154		Cumene	2, 4, 6	109	
163–166		Mesitylene	2, 4	86	97
			2, 4, 6	235	
165–169		α-Methylstyrene			
168		1,2,4-Trimethylbenzene	3, 5, 6	185	97
176–178		*p*-Cymene	2, 6	54	
189–192		4-*t*-Butyltoluene			
197–199		1,2,3,5-Tetramethylbenzene	4, 6	181(157)	
203		*p*-Diisopropylbenzene			
204–205		1,2,3,4-Tetramethylbenzene	5, 6	176	92
207		1,2,3,4-Tetrahydronaphthalene	5, 7	95	
240–243		1-Methylnaphthalene	4	71	142
	34–36	2-Methylnaphthalene	1	81	116
	50–51	Pentamethylbenzene	6	154	131
	69–72	Biphenyl	4, 4'	237(229)	
	80–82	1,2,4,5-Tetramethylbenzene	3, 6	205	
	80–82	Naphthalene	1	61(57)	149
	90–95	Acenaphthene	5	101	161
	99–101	Phenanthrene			144(133)
	112–115	Fluorene	2	156	87(77)
			2, 7	199	
	214–217	Anthracene			138

a. For preparation, see page 782.
b. For preparation, see page 780.

TABLE 70.14   Ketones

			Derivatives	
			Semicarbazone[a]	2,4-Dinitrophenylhydrazone[b]
bp	mp	Compound	mp	mp
56		Acetone	187	126
80		2-Butanone	136, 186	117
88		2,3-Butanedione	278	315
100–101		2-Pentanone	112	143
102		3-Pentanone	138	156
106		Pinacolone	157	125
114–116		4-Methyl-2-pentanone	132	95
124		2,4-Dimethyl-3-pentanone	160	88, 95
128–129		5-Hexen-2-one	102	108
129		4-Methyl-3-penten-2-one	164	205
130–131		Cyclopentanone	210	146
133–135		2,3-Pentanedione	122 (mono) 209 (di)	209
145		4-Heptanone	132	75
145		5-Methyl-2-hexanone	147	95
145–147		2-Heptanone	123	89
146–149		3-Heptanone	101	81
156		Cyclohexanone	166	162
162–163		2-Methylcyclohexanone	195	137
169		2,6-Dimethyl-4-heptanone	122	66, 92
169–170		3-Methylcyclohexanone	180	155
173		2-Octanone	122	58
191		Acetonylacetone	185 (mono) 224 (di)	257 (di)
202		Acetophenone	198	238
216		Phenylacetone	198	156
217		Isobutyrophenone	181	163
218		Propiophenone	182	191
226		4-Methylacetophenone	205	258
231–232		2-Undecanone	122	63
232		n-Butyrophenone	188	191
232		4-Chloroacetophenone	204	236
235		Benzylacetone	142	127
	35–37	4-Chloropropiophenone	176	223
	35–39	4-Phenyl-3-buten-2-one	187	227
	36–38	4-Methoxyacetophenone	198	228
	48–49	Benzophenone	167	238
	53–55	2-Acetonaphthone	235	262
	60	Desoxybenzoin	148	204
	76–78	3-Nitroacetophenone	257	228
	78–80	4-Nitroacetophenone		257
	82–85	9-Fluorenone	234	283
	134–136	Benzoin	206	245
	147–148	4-Hydroxypropiophenone		240

a. For preparation see page 444.

TABLE 70.15   Nitriles

bp	mp	Compound	bp	mp	Compound
77		Acrylonitrile	212		3-Tolunitrile
83–84		Trichloroacetonitrile	217		4-Tolunitrile
97		Propionitrile	233–234		Benzyl cyanide
107–108		Isobutyronitrile	295		Adiponitrile
115–117		*n*-Butyronitrile		30.5	4-Chlorobenzyl cyanide
174–176		3-Chloropropionitrile		32–34	Malononitrile
191		Benzonitrile		38–40	Stearonitrile
205		2-Tolunitrile		46–48	Succinonitrile
				71–73	Diphenylacetonitrile

TABLE 70.16   Nitro Compounds

bp	mp	Compound	bp	mp	Amine Obtained by Reduction of Nitro Groups — Acetamide[a] mp	Benzamide[b] mp
210–211		Nitrobenzene	184		114	160
225		2-Nitrotoluene	200		110	146
225		2-Nitro-*m*-xylene	215		177	168
230–231		3-Nitrotoluene	203		65	125
245		3-Nitro-*o*-xylene	221		135	189
245–246		4-Ethylnitrobenzene	216		94	151
	34–36	2-Chloro-6-nitrotoluene	245		157(136)	173
	36–38	4-Chloro-2-nitrotoluene		21	139(131)	
	40–42	3,4-Dichloronitrobenzene		72	121	
	43–50	1-Chloro-2,4-dinitrobenzene		91	242 (di)	178 (di)
	52–54	4-Nitrotoluene		45	147	158
	55–56	1-Nitronaphthalene		50	159	160
	83–84	1-Chloro-4-nitrobenzene		72	179	192
	88–90	*m*-Dinitrobenzene		63	87 (mono)	125 (mono)
					191 (di)	240 (di)

a. For preparation, see page 780.
b. For preparation, see page 780.

TABLE 70.17 Phenols

| | | | Derivatives | |
| | | | α-Naphthylurethane[a] | Bromo[b] |
bp	mp	Compound	mp	mp
175–176		2-Chlorophenol	120	48 (mono)
				76 (di)
181	42	Phenol	133	95 (tri)
202	32–34	*p*-Cresol	146	49 (di)
				108 (tetra)
203		*m*-Cresol	128	84 (tri)
228–229		3,4-Dimethylphenol	141	171 (tri)
	32–33	*o*-Cresol	142	56 (di)
	42–43	2,4-Dichlorophenol		68
	42–45	4-Ethylphenol	128	
	43–45	4-Chlorophenol	166	90 (di)
	44–46	2,6-Dimethylphenol	176	79
	44–46	2-Nitrophenol	113	117 (di)
	49–51	Thymol	160	55
	62–64	3,5-Dimethylphenol		166 (tri)
	64–68	4-Bromophenol	169	95 (tri)
	74	2,5-Dimethylphenol	173	178 (tri)
	92–95	2,3,5-Trimethylphenol	174	
	95–96	1-Naphthol	152	105 (di)
	98–101	4-*t*-Butylphenol	110	50 (mono)
				67 (di)
	104–105	Catechol	175	192 (tetra)
	109–110	Resorcinol	275	112 (tri)
	112–114	4-Nitrophenol	150	142 (di)
	121–124	2-Naphthol	157	84
	133–134	Pyrogallol	173	158 (di)

a. For preparation, see page 783.
b. For preparation, see page 783.

CHAPTER
71

Searching the Chemical Literature

In planning a synthesis or investigating the properties of compounds, the organic chemist is faced with the problem of locating information on the chemical and physical properties of substances that have been previously prepared as well as the best methods and reagents for carrying out a synthesis. With tens of millions of compounds known and new ones being reported at the rate of more than 700,000 per year, this task might seem formidable. However, the field of chemistry has developed one of the best information retrieval systems of all the sciences. In a university chemistry library or over the Internet (at an academic institution that has subscribed to the proper databases), it is possible to locate information on almost any known compound in a few minutes. Even a modest library will have information on several million different substances in printed form.

The ultimate source of information is the primary literature: articles written by individual chemists and published in journals. The secondary literature consists of compilations of information taken from these primary sources. For example, to find the melting point of benzoic acid, one would naturally turn to a secondary reference containing a table of physical constants of organic compounds. If, on the other hand, one wished to have information about the phase changes of benzoic acid under high pressure, one would need to consult the primary literature. If the piece of information, such as a melting point, is crucial to an investigation, the primary literature should be consulted because, for instance, transcription errors can occur in the preparation of secondary references.

In this chapter we will consider first the traditional chemistry library and then the resources available on the Internet, although a distinction between the real and virtual library is becoming less clear each day.

Handbooks

For rapid access to information such as mp, bp, density, solubility, optical rotation, λ max, and crystal form, one turns first to the *Handbook of Chemistry and Physics,* now in its 81st edition. This book contains information on some 15,000 organic compounds, including the Beilstein reference (see below) to each compound. The compounds presented are well known and completely characterized. Most are commercially available. The *Merck Index,* 13th ed., 2001, contains information on more than 10,000 compounds, especially those of pharmaceutical interest. In addition to the usual physical properties, information and literature references to synthesis, isolation, and medicinal properties, such as toxicity data, are found. The last third of the *Merck Index* is devoted to such items as a long cross index of names (which is very useful for looking up drugs), a table of organic name reactions, an excellent section on first-aid for poisons, a list of chemical poisons, and a listing of the locations of many poison control centers. It too is available online for a fee.

In every organic chemistry laboratory throughout the world can be found a copy of the *Aldrich Handbook of Fine Chemicals and Laboratory Equipment*, available without charge from the Aldrich Company (see "Surfing the Web" at the end of this chapter). Not only does this catalog list the prices of the more than 48,000 chemicals (primarily organic) as well as their molecular weights, melting points, boiling points, and optical rotations, it also gives references to IR and NMR spectral data and to Beilstein, *Merck Index,* and Fiesers's *Reagents.* In addition, for each chemical the catalog provides the reference to the *Registry of Toxic Effects of Chemical Substances* (RTECS #) and, if appropriate, the reference to Sax, *Dangerous Properties of Industrial Materials.* Special hazards are noted ("severe poison," "lachrymator," "corrosive"). The Aldrich catalog also provides pertinent information (uses, physiological effects, etc.) with literature references for many compounds. Material Safety Data Sheets (MSDS) are also available. The catalog is online; it can be searched and orders placed on the Internet.

A complete list of all chemicals sold commercially and the addresses of the companies making them is found in *Chem Sources,* published yearly.

After consulting these three single-volume references, one would turn to more comprehensive multi-volume sources such as the *Dictionary of Organic Compounds,* 6th edition. This dictionary, still known as "Heilbron," the name of its former editor, now comprises seven volumes of specific information, with primary literature references, on the syntheses, reactions, and derivatives of more than 50,000 compounds. Rodd's *Chemistry of Carbon Compounds,* another valuable multi-volume work with primary literature references, is organized by functional group rather than in dictionary form.

The ultimate reference for chemistry as a whole, including articles on individual substances, environmental aspects, industrial processes, pharmaceuticals, polymers, food additives, etc. is the 25-volume Kirk-Othmer *Encyclopedia of Chemical Technology.* It is also available, for a fee, at *Kirk-Othmer Online.*

Beilstein's *Handbüch der organischen Chemie* is certainly not a "handbook" in the American sense—it can occupy an entire alcove of a chemistry library! This reference covers every well-characterized organic compound that has been reported in the literature up to 1979—synthesis, properties, and reactions. Included with the main reference set come three supplements covering the periods 1910–1919, 1920–1929, 1930–1949 with later supplements. Although written in German, this reference can provide much information even to those who possess no knowledge of the language. Physical constants and primary literature references are easy to pick out. A German–English dictionary for Beilstein is available on the Internet as well as a number of guides and leading references to its use.

Beilstein is organized around a complex classification scheme that is explained on the Internet and in *The Beilstein Guide* by O. Weissback, but the casual user can gain access through the *Handbook of Chemistry and Physics* and the Aldrich catalog. In the *Handbüch* the reference for 2-iodobenzoic acid is listed as **B9**^{2}, 239, which means the reference will be found on p. 239 of Vol. (Band) 9 of the second supplement (Zweites Ergänzungwerk, EII). In the Aldrich catalog the reference is given as Beil **9,** 363, which indicates information can be found in the main series on p. 363, Vol. 9. The System Number assigned to each compound can be traced through the supplements. The easiest access to Beilstein itself is through the formula index (General Formel register) of the second supplement. A rudimentary knowledge of German will enable one to pick out iodo (Jod) benzoic acid (Saure), for example.

Beilstein, in English, is available, for a fee, on the Internet (see below). Some 100 properties of 8 million compounds and 5 million reactions are available for searching.

Chemical Abstracts

Secondary references are incomplete, some suffer from transcription errors, and the best—Beilstein—is not completely up-to-date in its survey of the organic literature, so one must often turn to the primary chemical literature. However, there are more than 14,000 periodicals where chemical information might appear. Chemists are fortunate to have an index, *Chemical Abstracts* (CA), that covers this huge volume of literature very promptly and publishes biweekly abstracts of each article. The information in each abstract is then compiled into author, chemical substance, general subject, formula, and patent indexes.

Chemical Abstracts Service (CAS) and STN International, a database vendor, are owned by the American Chemical Society. Since publication of CA began in 1907, nomenclature has changed. Now no trivial names are used, so acetone appears as 2-propanone and *o*-cresol as benzene, 1-methyl, 2-hydroxy. It takes some experience to adapt to these changing names, and, even now, *Chemical Abstracts* does not exactly follow the rules of the International Union of Pure and Applied Chemistry (IUPAC). The formula index is useful because it provides not only reference to specific abstracts but also a correct name that can be found in the chemical substances index.

Current Contents

As long as a year can elapse between the time a paper appears and the time an abstract is published. *Current Contents* and *Chemical Titles* help fill the gap by providing much of the information found in an abstract: a list of the titles, authors, and keywords that appear in titles of papers recently published—or, in some cases, papers about to be published.

Science Citation Index

Science Citation Index is unique in that it allows for a type of search not possible with any other index—a search forward in time. For example, if one wanted to learn what recent applications have been made of the coupling reaction first reported by Stansbury and Proops in 1962, one would look up their paper [*J. Org.* Chem., **27,** 320 (1962)] in a current volume, say 1998, of Science Citation Index and find there a list of those articles published in 1998 in which an author cited the 1962 work of Stansbury and Proops in a footnote. This database is available, by subscription, on the Internet where it is known as *The Web of Science.*

Planning a Synthesis

In planning a synthesis the organic chemist is faced with at least three overlapping considerations: the chemical reactions, the reagents, and the experimental procedure to be employed. For students an advanced textbook such as Carey and Sundberg, *Advanced Organic Chemistry,* Parts A and B, 4th ed., 2001, or Smith and March's *Advanced Organic Chemistry,* 5th ed., 2001, which have literature references, might be a place to start. Often a good lead is through named reactions, for which Mundy and Ellerd's *Name Reactions and Reagents in Organic Chemistry,* 1988, is a useful reference.

It is instructive for the beginning synthetic chemist to read about some elegant and classical syntheses that have been carried out in the past. For this purpose see Anand, Bindra, and Ranganathan, *Art in Organic Synthesis,* 2nd ed., 1988, for some of the most elegant syntheses carried out in recent years. Similarly, Bindra and Bindra, *Creativity in Organic Synthesis,* Vol. 1, and Fleming, *Selected Organic Syntheses,* are compendia of elegant syntheses. At a more advanced level see Corey and Cheng, *The Logic of Chemical Synthesis,* 1995. For natural product synthesis see the excellent series edited by ApSimon, *The Total Synthesis of Natural Products,* in nine volumes, the latest published in 1992. House's *Modern Synthetic Reactions,* 2nd ed., 1972, is a more comprehensive source of information with several thousand references to the original literature. It is brought further up-to-date at about the same level by Carruthers in *Some Modern Methods of Organic Synthesis,* 3rd ed., 1987.

An extremely useful reference is the *Compendium of Organic Synthetic Methods,* presently in eight volumes, the latest published in 1995. The material is organized by reaction type. In addition, *Organic Reactions,* published annually, should be consulted. Over 100 preparative reactions, with examples of experimental details, are covered in great detail in some 30 volumes. *Annual Reports in Organic Synthesis* is an excellent review of new reactions in a given year, organized by reaction type. *Stereoselective Synthesis* by Robert S. Atkinson, published in 1995, treats one of the newest and most important areas of organic chemistry.

The late Mary Fieser was responsible for publishing the first 17 volumes of *Reagents for Organic Synthesis.* The last three volumes have been edited by Tse-Lok Ho. Begun in 1967, this series critically surveys the reagents employed to carry out organic synthesis. Included are references to the original literature and suppliers of reagents, and to *Organic Syntheses* (see below), as well as the critical reviews that have been written about various reagents. The index of reagents according to type of reaction is very useful when planning a synthesis. On a much larger scale is the comprehensive *Encyclopedia of Reagents for Organic*

Synthesis, 1995, edited by Leo Paquette. It contains 3500 articles, giving a critical assessment of most of the reagents one would use in carrying out a synthesis.

To carry out a reaction on one functional group without affecting another functional group it is often necessary to put on a protective group. This rather specialized subject is admirably covered in Greene and Wuts's *Protective Groups in Organic Synthesis,* 3rd ed., 1999.

Before carrying out the synthesis itself one should consult *Organic Syntheses,* an annual series since 1921, which is grouped in nine collective volumes with reaction and reagent indexes. *Organic Syntheses* gives detailed laboratory procedures for carrying out more than 1000 different reactions. Each synthesis is submitted for review and then the procedure is sent to an independent laboratory to be checked. The reactions, unlike many that are reported in the primary literature, are carried out a number of times and can therefore be relied on to work. This valuable series is available at no cost on the Internet (see "Surfing the Web").

Laboratory techniques are covered in the 14 volumes of Weissberger et al., *Techniques of Organic Chemistry,* an uneven, multi-authored compendium, outdated in many respects. An excellent advanced text on the detailed mechanisms of many representative reactions is Lowry and Richardson's *Mechanism and Theory in Organic Chemistry,* 3rd ed., 1987.

Methoden der Organischen Chemie (Methods of Organic Chemistry, often called Houben-Weyl) is a multi-volume work, published in English since 1990. Detailed experimental procedures are presented for the syntheses of thousands of compounds, making this a valuable resource. *Organic Reactions,* as the name implies, has long chapters or even an entire volume devoted to one reaction. Each article of this 59-volume series is written by an authority.

The Modern Chemistry Library

Although there will probably always be a chemistry library, more and more of the resources of the traditional library are becoming available on the Internet. All 2.5 million pages (a stack of paper 81 stories high) of all the journals published by the American Chemical Society (ACS) since it began in 1879 are now online and searchable. No longer will it be necessary to go to the library stacks and pull off volume 26 of the *Journal of Organic Chemistry,* turn to page 4563, and write down the details of the syntheses of steroidal α acetoxyketones. You can simply go to a computer terminal and get the same information in a fraction of the time, if your institution subscribes to the ACS database.

All of the ACS journals are published both on paper and electronically. The subscription to the database might seem expensive until you consider how many cubic feet those volumes occupy in a library and what it costs to build and maintain that space. There are a number of commercial vendors of databases, of which the ACS is but one. STN International, owned by the American Chemical Society, is connected to more than 200 of these databases. The *Chemical Abstracts* (CA) database is available only on STN; you can carry out structural searches on the 40 million substances in this index. *CrossFire Beilstein* is the Web version of this comprehensive database of organic compounds.

Many journals are now available by electronic subscription. Most of the American Chemical Society journals and even secondary references are now available on the Web. Very little of this information is free to the outsider, but the economics and usefulness of computer literature searching and retrieval make it extremely attractive for the institution. The chemical information available to the casual surfer of the Net is of varying quality, but certain governmentally supported sites, such as the *Protein Data Bank,* are invaluable.

Using a computer it is now possible to conduct substructure searches of a database that are impossible through the printed page. For example, one can ask for a list of all three-membered rings bearing a single hydroxyl group, even if the ring is buried in a large, complex molecule.

STN International is a vendor with access to more than 200 databases, including all of Chemical Abstracts and the ACS journals. It is not always easy to navigate this wealth of information for an online search, especially a structure search. The command language has a steep learning curve; searches are often the province of the trained professional librarian. *SciFinder Scholar,* a free STN International product, eases this searching problem for the novice.

While the journals may disappear from the shelves, the books, monographs and treatises, and many of the secondary references will remain in the chemistry libraries of the future.

Surfing the Web

http://www.sigmaaldrich.com/Brands/Aldrich.html
The Aldrich catalog online. A free, printed copy of this 2,900-page book is available from the Aldrich Chemical Co., 1001 West Saint Paul Ave., Milwaukee, WI, 53233.

http://www.beilstein.com/products/xfire/quick_ref/
CrossFire Quick Reference Guide Version 4.0, the tool for using Beilstein online (fee).

http://stneasy.cas.org/html/english/login1.html
A free demo for searching 80 of the STN databases. The prices per title found are given ($2.50 and up).

http://www.mdli.com/downloads/isis.draw/isisdraw.html
A free, fully-functional chemical drawing program from MDL (Molecular Design Limited). For entering structures in databases and for general use.

http://www.mdlchime.com./chime
The free molecular visualization program needed for many organic chemistry sites. From MDL.

http://products.cambridgesoft.com/ProdInfo.cfm?PID=252
A trial version of the most popular chemical structure drawing program, ChemDraw, from CambridgeSoft. Expires two weeks after downloading.

http://products.cambridgesoft.com/ProdInfo.cfm?PID=260
A free version of ChemDraw without print/save/copy/paste abilities. Does not expire.

http://www.cas.org/SCIFINDER/SCHOLAR/
Provides access to the CAS databases.

http://www.orgsyn.org/
Free access to *Organic Syntheses*. Sponsored by Wiley, CambridgeSoft, and DataTrace.

INDEX

Ab initio calculations, 251
Abbé refractometer, 78
Abortifacient, 361
ABS rubber, 742
Absolute ethyl alcohol, reactant, 509
Absorbance, UV, 235
Acenaphthene, 795
Acetaldehyde, 440, 699, 700, 787
Acetamide, preparation, 780, 788
4-Acetamidophenol (Acetaminophen), TLC, 160
p-Acetaminobenzenesulfonamide, see
    sulfanilamide, 544, 547
p-Acetaminobenzenesulfonyl chloride,
    547, 553
Acetaminophen, 502
  separation of, 527
  TLC of, 61
Acetanilide, 521, 546, 788
  ^{1}H NMR, 559
  IR, 559,
  preparation of, 552
Acetate rayon, 562
Acetic acid, 491, 784
Acetic acid, solvent, 40, 494, 503, 585, 791
Acetic anhydride, amide formation, 521
Acetic anhydride, for esters, 487
2-Acetonaphthone, 796
Acetone, 796
Acetone, solvent, 40
Acetonedicarboxylic acid, 728
Acetonide synthesis, 646
Acetonylacetone, 796
Acetophenone, 796
Acetyl chloride, 487, 791
2-Acetylamino-1,4-naphthoquinone, 586
Acetylation
  of DL-alanine, 715
  of aniline, 546, 552
  of benzil, 649-653
  of cholesterol, 176
N-Acetylcaprolactam, 750
N-Acetyl-D-alanine, 715
N-Acetyl-DL-alanine, 715
Acetylene, IR, 200
Acetyleugenol, 107
Acetylferrocene, synthesis, 420
Acetylide group, as explosive, 27
Acetylsalicylic acid (aspirin), synthesis, 503;
  ^{1}H NMR, 491; IR, 505,
Acetylsalicylic acid (aspirin), TLC, 161
Acid anhydrides, IR, 197
Acid chlorides
  derivatives, 781
  IR, 197
Acid halides, tests for, 770
Acid/base extraction, 133
Acid-base indicators, 568

Acids, derivatives, 779
  tests for, 769
Acrylic acid, 784
Acrylonitrile, 742, 797
Activated charcoal, 43
Acylase, 715
Adenosine triphosphate, 674, 701
Adipic acid, 743, 785
  synthesis of, 311-324;
  ^{13}C NMR, 324
Adiponitrile, 797
ADP, 701
Adsorbents, for thin-layer chromatography, 157
Aerosol propellants, gas phase IR, 211
Aflatoxin, safety, 30
Air condenser, 3, 10
L-Alanine, 715
  ^{13}C NMR, 722
DL-Alanine, enzymatic resolution, 715
Alcoholic fermentation, 699
Alcohols
  derivatives, 779
  IR, 199
  tests for, 769
Aldehydes
  derivatives, 780
  IR, 197
  peroxide hazard, 28
  reactions, tests for, 435-453, 769
Alder, Kurt, 589
Aldol condensation, 454
Aldolase, 701
Aldrich Catalog Handbook of Fine
    Chemicals, 800
Aleve, 502
Alizarin, 571
Alka-Seltzer, 502
Alkaline cleavage, benzopinacol, 687
Alkanes and alkenes, tests for, 282
Alkenes from alcohols, 287-293
Alkenes, tests for, 282
Alkyl halides, reactions of, 267-273
Alkylation of mesitylene, 386-392
Alkyne
  IR, 200
  synthesis, 654-663
Allinger, Norman, 251
Allyl alcobol, 786
Allyl bromide, 793
Allyl carbocation, 270
Allyl chloride, 793
Allylamine, 789
Allylic compounds, peroxide hazard, 28
Alumina, 157
  activity of, 171
  disposal of, 36
Aluminum chloride, 372, 407

AM1 (Austin method 1) calculations, 737
American Chemical Society, 803
American Cyanamid Co., 674
Amides, basicity, 517
  IR, 197
  preparation of, 779
  tests for, 775
Amine picrate, 521
Amine salts, test for, 772
Amines, 516-526
  aromatic, basicity, 517
  derivatives, 781
  IR, 199
  solubility, 517
  spectra, NMR, IR, UV, 523
Amino acids, tests for, 773
4-Amino-1,2-naphthoquinone, 587
2-Amino-1,4-naphthoquinone, 586
2-Amino-1,4-naphthoquinonimine
    diacetate, 585
2-Amino-1,4-naphthoquinonimine
    hydrochloride, 585
2-Amino-6-methoxybenzothiazole, 576
4-Aminoacetanilide, 790
p-Aminobenzenesulfonamide, 544
2-Aminobenzoic acid, 539
p-Aminobenzoic acid, 545
3-Aminophthalhydrazide, 678
2-Aminopyridine, 790
Ammonia, basicity, 516
Ammonical silver nitrate solution, 440
Ammonium formate, as hydrogen donor, 351
Ammonium hydroxide, safety, 30
Ammonium ion, 516
Ammonium salts, test for, 773
Amobarbital, 508
Ampule, 686
n-Amyl acetate, 792
Amylases, 699
Anabolic steriods, 360
Anacin, 502
Analgesic tablets, analysis of, 527
Analgesics, 502
Analgesics, TLC of, 160
Anand, et al., *Art in Organic Synthesis,* 802
Anesthetics, 507
Anethole, 793
Anhydrides, derivatives, 781, 792
Anhydrides, IR, 197
Anhydrides, tests for, 770
Anilides, preparation, 779, 782
Anilides, test for, 776
Aniline, 518, 524, 789
  extraction of, 135
  ^{1}H NMR, 524
  IR, 524
  safety, 30

Aniline, synthesis, 548
 ¹H NMR, 558
 IR, 558
Aniline, UV, 240
Anilinium chloride, extraction, 135
Anilinium ion, 546
Anilinium ion, UV, 240
Anionic polymerization, 750
2-Anisaldehyde, 787
4-Anisaldehyde, 788
4-Anisic acid, 785
2-Anisidine, 789
4-Anisidine, 790
Anisole, 793
Annual Reports in Organic Synthesis, 802
Anthracene, 795
Anthracene, as reactant, 430
 ¹H NMR, 434
Anthracene, crystallization, 57
Anthracene, isolation by steam distillation, 104
Anthracene, mp standard, 70
Anthracene, synthesis, 416
Anthracene, UV, 239
Anthrahydroquinone anion, 408
Anthrahydroquinone diradical dianion, 408
9-Anthraldehyde, 479
Anthranilic acid, 430, 539, 785
9-Anthranyl-2,2,2,4-tetraphenyl-1,2-
 oxaphosphetane, 479
Anthraquinone synthesis, 412
Anthrone, synthesis, 414
Anticonvulsants, 508
Antipyretic, 502
APC, 502
Apple odor, 487
Aprotic solvents, 272
ApSimon, *The Total Synthesis of Natural
 Products,* 802
Arabinose, 691
Aromatic compounds
 IR, 202
 test for, 778
 UV, 239
Aromatic solvents, safety, 30
Arteriosclerosis, 349
Arthritis, 502
Aryl halides, derivatives, 782
 test for, 778
Aspartame, 691
L-Aspartyl-L-phenylalanine methyl ester, 691
Aspirator tube, 48
Aspirin, separation from caffeine, 527
Aspirin, synthesis, 501–506
Aspirin, TLC of, 161
Aston, 241
Atkinson, *Stereoselective Syntheses,* 802
ATP, 699
Atropine, 727
Auschwitz, 502
Azelaic acid (nonanedioic acid), 784
Azeotropes, 83, 489
Azeotropic distillation, 489
Azide group, as explosive, 27
Azo dyes, 563
2,2'(-Azobis-(2-methylpropionitrile) [AIBN], 277

Backwashing, 139
Badische Anilin und Sodafabrik (BASF), 502
Baekeland, Leo, 739

Bakelite, 739, 742, 747
Baker's yeast, 708
Balance, electronic, top-loading, 15
Balance, top-loading, electronic, 13
Banana odor, 487
Band spectra, 235
Barbituate, synthesis, 507
Barbituric acid, 507
Barfoed's test, 695
Basic fuchsin, 441
Basicity constant, 516
Bayberry, 101
Bayer aspirin, 502
Bayer, A. G., 502
Bayer, Friedrich, 501
Beer, 699
Beer-Lambert law, 235
Beilstein test for halogens, 766
Beilstein, 800
Benzalacetone, 455
Benzaldehyde, 632, 787
Benzaldehyde, as reactant, 454, 664
Benzaldehyde, ¹H NMR, 452; IR, 453;
Benzamides, 788
 preparation of, 780
1,4-Benzene dicarboxylic acid, 743
Benzene sulfonyl chloride, ¹³C NMR, 525
Benzene, 239, 795
 alkylation of, 372
 as reactant, 407
Benzenediazonium chloride, 534
Benzenediazonium-2-carboxylate, 430
Benzenesulfonyl chloride, 519
Benzhydrol, 687, 787
Benzil quinoxaline, synthesis, 639; UV, 641
Benzil
 acetylation of, 649–653
 reactant, 618
 synthesis, 636
 ¹H NMR, 642
 IR, 641
 UV, 645
Benzoic acid, 495, 784
 extraction of, 132
Benzoic acid
 ¹³C NMR, 499
 ¹H NMR, 498
 IR, 498
Benzoic acid, partition coefficient of, 132
Benzoic acid, synthesis, 470, 476,
Benzoic anhydride, 791
Benzoin, 796
 oxidation, 796
 synthesis, 632–634
 ¹H NMR, 635
 IR, 637
 UV, 637
Benzoin condensation, 630–635,
 condensation, cyanide ion-catalyzed, 632
 condensation, thiamine-catalyzed, 633
Benzonitrile, 797
Benzophenone, 796
 as reactant, 468, 475
 ¹H NMR, 690
 IR, 690
Benzopinacol, synthesis, 683–689
Benzopinacolone, 688
Benzotrichloride, 793
Benzoyl chloride, 791

Benzoyl chloride, ¹³C NMR, 524
Benzoyl peroxide, 752
2-Benzoylbenzoic acid, 784
2-Benzoylbenzoic acid, synthesis, 407, 410
Benzoyloxy radical, 752
Benzyl acetate, 487, 494
Benzyl alcohol, 488, 494, 786
Benzyl chloride, 51, 479, 512, 793
Benzyl cyanide, 797
Benzylacetone, 796
Benzylamine, 789
Benzylic compounds, peroxide hazard, 28
Benzyltriethylammonium chloride, 307
Benzyltriethylammonium hydroxide, 307
Benzyltriethylphosphonium chloride, 479
Benzyltrimethylammonium hydroxide,
 catalyst, 618
Benzyne, 424, 430
Bial test, 696
Bicyclo[4.3.0]nona-3,7-diene, 794
Bimolecular nucleophilic substitution, 259
Bindra, *Creativity in Organic Synthesis,* 802
Biomimetic synthesis, pseudopellitierene, 728
Biphenyl, 465, 795
Bis(cyclopentadienyl)iron, 606
Bis(2,4,6-triphenyl)oxalate, 675
Bisulfite addition products, 437
Bisulfite test, 447
Black, Joseph, 698
Blankophor B, 580
Bleach, 317
Blood, as catalyst, 682
Bluing, 580
Boiling points, 72
 as a function of pressure, 73
 composition diagram, for cyclohexane-toluene
 mixtures, 83
 composition diagram, for ethanol-water
 mixtures, 84
 determination of, by distillation, 74
 determination of, in a 3-5 mm tube, 75
 determination of, in a reaction tube, 74
 relation to structure, 73
 using digital thermometer, 74
 variation with pressure, 85
 vs pressure curves, 117
Boiling sticks, 41
Bond angle bending energy, 252
Bond energies, 253
Bond stretching energy, 252
Bond torsion energy, 252
Borneol, 731
Bornyl acetate, 731
Boron trifluoride etherate, 504
Breslow, Ronald, 631
Brockmann activity of alumina, 171
Bromination, of cholesterol, 294
Bromination, of stilbene, 658
Bromination, stereochemistry, 294
Bromine, 294
Bromine, in carbon tetrachloride, test for
 unsaturation, 777
Bromine, in nonaqueous solution, test for
 alkenes, 283
Bromine water, test for alkenes, 283
Bromo derivatives of phenols, 783
1-Bromo-2-methylpropane, 793
2-Bromo-2-methylpropane, 793
1-Bromo-3-chloropropane, 793

1-Bromo-3-methylbutane, 488
1-Bromo-4-chlorobenzene, 536
Bromoacetic acid, 784
4-Bromoaniline, 535, 790
4-Bromoanisole, 793
Bromobenzene, 272, 794
  as reactant, 464, 472
  ^{13}C NMR, 478
4-Bromobenzenediazonium chloride, 535
2-Bromobutane, 272, 793
1-Bromobutane, 793
  ^{13}C NMR, 264
  reactant, 509
  synthesis, 259–266
1,4-Bromochlorobenzene, 794
Bromochloromethane, 793
1-Bromodecane, 793
Bromoform, 793
Bromohydrin formation, 283
1-Bromonaphthalene, 794
4-Bromophenol, 798
1-Bromopropane, 793
2-Bromopropane, 793
5-Bromosalicylic acid, 785
N-Bromosuccinimide, test for alkenes, 282, 285
Bromotrichloromethane, 793
Brown sugar, decolorizing, 59
Brown, H. C., 643
Brown hydrogenation, 347
Bubble cap column, 82
Bubbler, 179
Büchner, Eduard, 698
Büchner funnel, 5
  for macroscale filtration, 55
  micro, 46
  microscale, 529
Bufferin, 502
Bulb-to-bulb distillation apparatus, 122
Bumping, 41
Buna, 742
Bunsen, 403
Butadiene, 742
1,3-Butadiene, in Diels–Alder reaction, 589
Butadiene, UV, 237
Butane, minimum energy calculation, 254
1,3-Butanediol, 786
1,4-Butanediol, 786
2,3-Butanediol, 786
2,3-Butanedione, 795
2-Butanol, 191, 786
1-Butanol, 488, 491, 786
  as reactant, 259
  ^{13}C NMR, 265
  ^{1}HNMR, 265
2-Butanone, 796
  ^{13}C NMR, 451
  ^{1}H NMR, 450
  solvent, 40
1-Butene, 191, 260
2-Butene, 191
Butter Yellow, 163
n-Butyl acetate, 488, 491, 792
s-Butyl acetate, 792
t-Butyl acetate, 792
t-Butyl alcohol, 786
t-Butyl alcohol, as reactant, 379
n-Butyl bromide, 259
t-Butyl chloride, as reactant, 373
t-Butyl methyl ether, advantages of, 29

t-Butyl methyl ether, extraction solvent, 127
t-Butyl methyl ether, solvent, 41
t-Butyl propionate, 488
n-Butyl vinyl ether, 793
n-Butylamine, 789
s-Butylamine, 789
t-Butylamine, 789
n-Butylbarbituric acid, 509
4-t-Butylcatechol, 753
n-Butyllithium, as reactant, 401
4-t-Butylphenol, 139, 798
4-Butylstyrene, 794
4-t-Butylstyrene, 795
4-t-Butyltoluene, 795
Butyraldehyde, 787
n-Butyric acid, 784
Butyric anhydride, 791
n-Butyronitrile, 797
n-Butyrophenone, 796
Butyryl chloride, 791

Cadaverine, 517
Caffeine
  from cola syrup, extraction, 151
  from tea, sublimation of, 148
  ^{1}H NMR of, 153
  mp standard, 70
  salicylate, 153
  separation from aspirin, 527
  TLC of, 161
Calcium chloride, drying agent, 137
Calcofluor White MR, fluorescent dye, 169
Camphene to camphor, 731–738
Camphor, 101, 731
  ^{1}H NMR, 736
  synthesis of, 727
Cantharidin, 591
Capillary for vacuum distillation, 110
Capillary, sealed, for melting point, 611
Caprolactam, 750
Caraway seeds, 101
Carbocation, 394
Carbocations, stability, 267
Carbohydrates, 690; analysis, 691
Carbon dioxide, as reactant, 471, 476,
Carbon dioxide, gas phase IR, 211
Carbon monoxide, 607
Carbon tetrachloride, safety, 30
Carbon tetrachloride, synthesis, 277
Carbon-13 chemical shifts, table, 223
Carbon-13 NMR spectra, 222
Carbonyl group, reactions of, 435
Carbonyl group, stretching frequencies, IR,
  table, 201
Carboxylic acids
  IR, 197
  test for, 774
Carcinogenic compounds, 163
Carcinogens, 31
Carey and Sundberg, *Advanced Organic
  Chemistry,* 802
β-Carotene, TLC of, 162
Carotene, 723
Carotenes, TLC of, 163
Carotenoid, 723
Carothers, Wallace, 742
Carrot paste (baby food), 725
Carrot, 723
Carrots, TLC of pigments, 163

Carruthers, *Some Modern Methods of Organic
  Synthesis,* 802
Carvone, 101
  UV, 238
CAS (Chemical Abstracts Service), 805
Castor oil, 757
Catalyst, radical, 277
Catalytic hydrogenation, 340–353
Catechol, 798
Cedarwood, 106
Celite filter aid, 704, 710
Celliton Fast Blue B, 576
Celluloid, 739
Cellulose acetate, 739
Cellulose, 562, 739
Central nervous system depressants, 507
Centrifuge tube, 10
Cerium(IV) nitrate test, for alcohols, 769
Chain reactions, 275
Changing fractions, vacuum distillation, 113
Charcoal, 43
Charge density, 737
Chaser, for distillation, 263
ChemDraw, 804
Chemical Abstracts, 801
Chemical ionization MS, 241
Chemical shifts, NMR, definition of, 219
Chemical shifts, ^{1}H NMR, table of, 217
Chemical Sources, 800
Chemical Titles, 801
Chemiluminescence, 674–682
Chemiluminescent reaction, 679
Chemotherapy, 544
Cheng and Corey, *The Logic of Chemical
  Synthesis,* 802
Chiral alcohol, synthesis, 708
Chloral, 388, 787
Chloral hydrate, 436
Chlorination of 1-chlorobutane, 274–282
Chlorine radicals, 274
1-Chloro-2,4-dinitrobenzene, 797
2-Chloro-2-butene, 272, 273
1-Chloro-2-butene, 272
1-Chloro-2-methylpropane, 272
2-Chloro-2-methylpropane, 272
2-Chloro-2-methylpropane, as reactant, 373
4-Chloro-2-nitroaniline, 790
4-Chloro-2-nitrotoluene, 797
2-Chloro-4-nitroaniline, 790
1-Chloro-4-nitrobenzene, 797
2-Chloro-6-nitrotoluene, 797
2-Chloroacetamide, 788
4-Chloroacetanilide, 762
Chloroacetic acid, 784
Chloroacetic acid, as reactant, 406
4-Chloroacetophenone, 796
1-Chloroadamantane, 273
2-Chloroaniline, 789
3-Chloroaniline, 789
4-Chloroaniline, extraction of, 141
4-Chloroanisole, 793
2-Chlorobenzaidehyde, 787
4-Chlorobenzaidehyde, 788
Chlorobenzene, 794
2-Chlorobenzoic acid, 785
4-Chlorobenzoic acid, 794
2-Chlorobenzoic acid, extraction of, 140
2-Chlorobenzoyl chloride, 791

3-Chlorobenzoyl chloride, 791
4-Chlorobenzyl cyanide, 797
1-Chlorobutane, 272
2-Chlorobutane, 272, 793
1-Chlorobutane, chlorination of, 278
1-Chlorobutane, radical chlorination, 274
Chloroethane, 479
2-Chloroethanol, 786
(2-Chloroethyl)benzene, 793
Chloroform, for IR, 205
Chloroform, synthesis, 277
Chloromethane, 277
3-Chloroperoxybenzoic acid, 363
2-Chlorophenol, 798
4-Chlorophenol, 798
4-Chlorophenoxyacetic acid, 785
Chlorophyll, TLC of, 163
2-Chloropropane, 793
3-Chloropropionitrile, 797
4-Chloropropiophenone, 796
Chlorosulfonation, 553
Chlorosulfonic acid, 547, 553
Chlorotin Light Blue 8G, 579
2-Chlorotoluene, 794
4-Chlorotoluene, 794
α-Chlorotoluene, as reactant, 479
4-Chlorotoluene, synthesis, 536, 541
    ^{13}C NMR, 543
    ^{1}H NMR, 542
    IR, 542
Cholesta-3,5-diene, UV, 236
5,7-Cholestadien-3β-ol,
5-Cholesten-3β-ol, 294
7-Cholesten-3βol,
3β-Cholestanol, 294
Cholesterol, 176, 787
    biosynthesis, 364
    bromination, 294
    epoxidation, 360
    ^{13}C NMR, 300
    ^{1}H NMR, 299
    IR, 300
Cholesteryl acetate, synthesis and column
    chromatography of, 176
Chore Boy, distillation column packing, 83
4-Choroaniline, 790
Chromatic adjustment of refractomer, 79
Chromatogram, visualization, 158
Chromatography column, packing, 172
Chromatography of esters, column, 493
Chromatography solvents, 158
Chromatography, column, 7, 10
Chromic acid, safety, 29
Chromium trioxide, 325
1,8-Cineole, 101
E-Cinnamaldehyde, 788
Cinnamaldehyde, as reactant, 481
E-Cinnamic acid, 785
Cinnamic acid, melting point, and mixed melting
    point, 71
Cinnamon, 106
Cinnamoyl chloride, 791
Cinnamyl alcohol, 787
cis-Fatty acids, 349
Citral, isolation of, 103
Citral, steam distillation, 100
Citric acid, 785
Citronellal, 328
    ^{1}H NMR, 333

Citronellol, 327
    2D NMR spectra of, 229
Citronellol, oxidation, 325
    ^{1}H NMR, 323
Claisen-Schmidt reaction, 454
Classification tests, 768
Cleaning Up, discussion of, 35–37
Clorox, as oxidant, 317
Clove oil, 107
Cloves, steam distillation of, 107
Cobalt acetate, 760
Coca-Cola, 727
Cocaine, 727
Cola syrup, extraction of caffeine, 151
Collins' reagent, 325
Color of organic compounds, 763
Column chromatography, 171–183
Column chromatography, ferrocene and
    acetylferrocene, 421
Column packing, for distillation, 83
Compendium of Organic Synthetic Methods, 802
Competitive inhibitor, 545
Compound X
    synthesis, 599
    ^{1}H NMR, 605
    IR, 605
Compressed gas cylinders, working with, 33
Computational chemistry, 250
    azocarboxylate isomers, benzyne, 433
    camphene to camphor, 737
    dibenzalacetone isomers, 457
    isopulegols, isopulegones, pulegone, 332
    α-phenylcinnamic acids, 668
    stilbene diacetates, 653
    stilbene dibromide, 673
Computer search of literature, 803
Concerted reaction, 591
Condensation polymerization, 747
Conformational analysis problem, 354
Congo Red, 571
Conjugated diene, in Diels–Alder reaction, 589
Conjugated diene, UV, 236
Connecting adapter, Viton (black), Santoprene
    (white), 10
Connector with support rod, 4, 10
Contact lenses, 25
Copper chromite, 669
Copper wire, 764
Copper(I) chloride, synthesis, 537
Corey, E. J., 325
Coricidin, 502
Corn oil, 349
Correlated spectroscopy, NMR, 229
Cortisone, 591
COSY, 2D NMR, 229
Cotton, 562
Coupling constant, NMR, dihedral angle
    dependence, 356
Coupling constants, NMR, table of, 220
Cracking of dicyclopentadiene, micro and
    macroscale, 592–594
Creslan, 562
o-Cresol, 798
p-Cresol, 798
m-Cresol, 798
CrossFire Beilstein, 804
Crotonaldehyde, 787
    ^{13}C NMR, 452
    ^{1}H NMR, 451

Crotonic acid, 784
Crude oil, distillation, 82
Crystal Violet, 572
Crystallites, in polyethylene, 741
Crystallization
    from a solvent pair, 60
    induction of, 62
    in reaction tube, 5
    process, 48
    purification of unknown, 61
    the seven steps, 38
    solvent, choosing, 39
    summary, the seven steps, 63
Current Contents, 801
Cyalume synthesis, 674–682
Cyanide ion, catalyst, 630
Cyanohydrin formation, 438
Cycloaddition reaction, 589
Cyclooctene, 794
Cyclodeca-1,2,6,7-tetraene, 303
Cyclodecapentaene, conformation of, 251
Cyclodehydration, 412
Cycloheptatriene, 399
Cycloheptatrienide carbocation, 399
Cyclohexane
    solvent, 41
    vapor pressure of, 80
1,2-Cyclohexanedicarboxylic anhydride, 791
Cyclohexane-toluene distillation, 89
Cyclohexanol, 786
    ^{13}C NMR, 293
    dehydration of, 287–293
    IR, 314
    oxidation of 301
Cyclohexanone, 796
    synthesis, 313
    ^{13}C NMR, 323
    ^{1}H NMR, 323
    IR, 324
Cyclohexene and palladium on carbon, 341
Cyclohexene
    ^{13}C NMR, 293
    ^{1}H NMR, 292
    as hydrogen donor, 350
    precautions, 29
    synthesis, 287–293
1,5-Cyclooctadiene, 293, 774 in 7E
1,3-Cyclooctadiene, 794
1,5-Cyclooctadiene, 794
Cyclopentadiene, 606, 609
    synthesis of, 592
Cyclopentadienone, 618
Cyclopentadienylmagnesium bromide, 607
Cyclopentanol, 786
Cyclopentanone, 796
Cymene, 795
p-Cymene, 795

Dacron, 562, 743
Dalton's law, 82
DDT, synthesis, 387
Dean-Stark apparatus, 489, 490,
Debromination, zinc dust, 294
Decanedioic acid, 744
Decanoic acid, 784
1-Decanol, 786
Decantation, 46
Decarboxylation, 669
1-Decene, 794

Decolorizing solutions, 43
  procedure, 59
Dehydration of cyclohexanol, 287–293
Dehydration, of alcohols, 187
Dehydrobromination, 660
Denim, 574
Density, definition, 15
Depolymerization, 755
DEPT NMR spectrum, 221
Desoxybenzoin, 796
Desyl chloride, 655
Detergents, 580
  fluorescent dyes in, 169
Deuteroacetone, NMR solvent, 228
Deuterobenzene, NMR solvent, 228
Deuterochloroform, NMR solvent, 228
Deuterodimethylsulfoxide, NMR solvent, 228
Developed dyes, 572
Dewar flasks, 33
Di(2-ethylhexyl)phthalate, 740
N,N-Dimethylacetamide, 788
2,4-Diacetylamino-1-naphthol, 585
2,4-Diamino-1-naphthol, 581, 584
2,4-Diaminotoluene, 790
Diaphragm valve, 34
Diaryl ethers, test for, 779
Diatomaceous earth, 704
Diazo compound, 534
Diazonium group, as explosive, 27
Diazonium ion, 534
Diazotization
  of 4-bromoaniline, 535
  of p-toluidine, 541
  of sulfanilic acid, 563
Dibenzalacetone
  ^{1}H NMR, 459
  IR, 459
  synthesis, 454
Dibenzocyclobutadiene, 433
Dibenzyl ether, 793
1,4-Dibromobenzene, 794
Dibromocarbene, 303
5α,6β-Dibromocholestan-3β-ol, 294–296
1,2-Dibromoethane, 793
Dibromomethane, 793
1,2-Dibromopropane, 793
1,3-Dibromopropane, 793
Dibutyl ether, 260
Dibutyl phthalate, 792
3,4-Dichloro-1-butene, 793
2,3-Dichloro-1-propene, 793
1,3-Dichloro-2-butene, 793
Dichloroacetic acid, 784
2,5-Dichloroaniline, 790
1,2-Dichlorobenzene, 794
1,3-Dichlorobenzene, 794
1,4-Dichlorobenzene, 794
1,4-Dichlorobenzene, extraction of, 141
1,2-Dichlorobenzene, solvent, 622
2,4-Dichlorobenzoic acid, 794
3, 4-Dichlorobenzoic acid, 794
7,7-Dichlorobicyclo[4.1.0]heptane
  synthesis, 307
  ^{1}H NMR, 310
1,4-Dichlorobutane, 793
Dichlorocarbene, 301
1,1-Dichloroethane, 793
1,2-Dichloroethane, 793
Dichloromethane, solvent, 40, 793

synthesis of, 277
3,4-Dichloronitrobenzene, 797
2,4-Dichlorophenol, 798
1,2-Dichloropropane, 793
2,4-Dichlorotoluene, 794
3,4-Dichlorotoluene, 794
Dichromate oxidation, 311
Dicyclohexylamine, 789
Dicyclopentadiene
  cracking, microscale, 592–594
  ^{1}H NMR 584;
  IR, 601
  macroscale, 595
Diels, Otto, 589
Diels–Alder reaction, 424, 431, 589–605
  used in synthesis, 622–627
Diene, 590
Dienophile, 590
Diethyl benzylphosphonate, 479
Diethyl ether
  explosion hazard, 28
  flammability of, 26
  solvent, 41
Diethyl fumarate, 792
Diethyl maleate, 792
Diethyl malonate, 508
Diethyl n-butylmalonate, 509
Diethyl oxalate, 792
Diethyl phthalate, 792
Diethyl succinate, 792
Diethylamine, 789
7-Diethylamino-4-methylcoumarin, fluorescent
  dye, 169
Diethylaminoethanol, 758
Diethylbenzyl malonate, 512
Diethylene glycol dimethyl ether, 301
Diethylene glycol, 755
RT-Diformazan, 695
Digital thermometer, with surface probe
  for boiling points, 74
  for melting points, 68
Diglyme, 304
Dihedral driver, molecular mechanics, 255
3,4-Dihydro-2-ethoxy-2H-pyran, 728
Dihydroteroate synthetase, 545
Dihydroxyacetone phosphate, 701
2,4-Dihydroxybenzoic acid, 785
Diisobutylamine, 789
Diisopropylamine, 789
p-Diisopropylbenzene, 795
Diisopropylether, safety, 29
Dimesitylmethane, synthesis, 389–390;
  ^{1}H NMR, 392; ^{13}C NMR, 393
3,4-Dimetboxybenzaldehyde, 788
1,2-Dimethoxybenzene, 793
1,4-Dimethoxybenzene, 793
Dimethoxybenzene, alkylation, 372
1,4-Dimethoxybenzene
  as reactant, 379
  extraction, 138
  ^{1}H NMR, 382
  IR, 381
p-Dimethoxybenzene, extraction, 138
3,4-Dimethoxybenzoic acid, 785
Dimethoxyethane, 432
  as solvent, 608
Dimethyl acetylenedicarboxylate, 614
Dimethyl acetylenedicarboxylate, reactant, 622
Dimethyl malonate, 792

Dimethyl phthalate, 792
Dimethyl suberate, 792
Dimethyl sulfoxide, solvent, 40
Dimethyl tetraphenylphthalate, synthesis,
  622–627
Dimethyl-1,4-diphenyl-1,4-dihydrophthalate, 615
2,5-Dimethyl-2,4-hexadiene, 794
2,7-dimethyl-3,5-octadiyn-2,7-diol, synthesis, 335
2,4-Dimethyl-3-pentanol, 786
2,4-Dimethyl-3-pentanone, 796
3,3-Dimethylacrylic acid, 784
N,N-Dimethylaniline, 567
2,4-Dimethylaniline, 789
2,5-Dimethylaniline, 789
2,6-Dimethylaniline, 789
N,N-Dimethylaniline, as reactant, 535
Dimethylbenzylamine, 791
N,N-Dimethylformamide, 483
N,N-Dimethylformamide, 788
Dimethylmaleic anhydride, 592
2,5-Dimethylphenol, 798
2,6-Dimethylphenol, 798
3,4-Dimethylphenol, 798
3,5-Dimethylphenol, 798
Dimethylsulfoxide, as solvent, 609
2,4-Dinitro-1-naphthol, 581, 583
2,4-Dinitroaniline, 790
m-Dinitrobenzene, 797
3,5-Dinitrobenzoates, 714
3,5-Dinitrobenzoates, 779
3,5-Dinitrobenzoic acid, 785
3,5-Dinitrobenzoyl chloride, 714
2,4-Dinitrophenylhydrazine, 440, 442, 769
2,4-Dinitrophenylhydrazones, 769
Dioctyl phthalate, 740
1,4-Dioxane, mass spectrum, 243
Dioxane
  peroxide hazard, 28
  solvent, 41
Diphenyl ether, 793
1,4-Diphenyl-1,3-butadiene, synthesis, 481, 614
1,5-Diphenyl-1,4-pentadien-3-one, 454
Diphenylacetic acid, 785
1,3-Diphenylacetone, reactant, 618
Diphenylacetonitrile, 797
Diphenylacetylene, 624
  synthesis of, 660
  UV, 663
Diphenylamine, 790
1,2-Diphenylethane, derivatives of, a multistep
  synthesis, 628
Diphenyliodonium carboxylate, 424
9,10-Diphenylanthracene, fluorescer, 675
1,3-Diphosphoglyceric acid, 700
Dipole-dipole attraction, and melting point, 65
Direct dyes, 570
Disaccharides, 692
Disodium hydrogen phosphate, 703
Disperse dyes, 576
Disperse Red, 576
Disposal guides for chemicals, 37
Disposal of waste, 36
Distillation, 80–97
  apparatus, micro and macro, 9
  apparatus, microscale, 490
  head, vacuum, 114
  instant microscale, 384
  instant microscale, 519
Distilling adapter, 7

Distilling column, 4
1,4-Di-*t*-Butyl-2,5-dimethoxybenzene,
    synthesis, 379
1,4-Di-*t*-butylbenzene
    synthesis, 373
    ¹H NMR, 376
    IR, 375
DMSO, 609
Dowex 50X 2-100, 491
Drierite, drying agent, 137
Drying crystals, under vacuum, macroscale, 178
Drying, of crystals, 56
    under vacuum, 154, 456
Drying of organic liquids, 131
DSS, NMR reference, 228
Duisberg, Carl, 502
Dyes and dyeing, 561–580
    dyeing with detergents, 580

Eastman Kodak, 502
Eastman, George, 739
Ehrlich, Paul, 544
Elastomer, 742
Electrocyclic reaction, 591
Electronic energy levels, 684
Electronic transitions, UV spectra, 235
Electrospray MS, 241
Elution order for solutes, 172
Elutropic series for solvents, 172
Emden-Meyerhof-Parnas scheme, 699
Emulsion polymerization, 741
Emulsions, in extraction, 136
Enantiomeric excess, 709
Enantiomeric excess, determination of, 713
Energy minimization calculations, 251
Enzymatic reactions, tests on, 706
Enzymatic reduction, 708
Enzymatic resolution of *N*-acetyl-DL-alanine, 720
Enzymatic resolution, 708–722
Enzymes, 699
Eosin, 571, 577
Epileptic seizures, 508
Epoxidation, of cholesterol, 360
5α,6βEpoxycholestan-3β-ol, 360
Equilibrium constant, 488
Ergosterol, 362
Erlenmeyer flask, 5
Escher, H. R., 163
Ester interchange, 758
Ester interchange reaction, 743
Esterification, 486–500,
Esters, IR, 198
Esters, test for, 771
Estrone, 361
Ethanol, 700, 786
    absolute, reactant, 512
    azeotrope, 84
    biosynthesis, 698–707
    solvent, 40
Ether, diethyl, solvent, 41
Ethers, IR, 200
Ethers, test for, 777
2-Ethoxybenzaidehyde, 787
Ethyl (3-chloromethyl)-4-pentenoate, NMR
    spectra, 221
Ethyl 3-hydroxybutanoate, 708
Ethyl acetate, 792
Ethyl acetate, solvent, 40
Ethyl acetoacetate, 708, 792

Ethyl acrylate, 792
Ethyl benzoate, 792
Ethyl butyrate, 487, 792
Ethyl caproate (ethyl hexanoate), 792
Ethyl caprylate, 792
Ethyl chloroacetate, 792
Ethyl chloroformate, 792
Ethyl cinnamate, 792
Ethyl cyanoacetate, 792
Ethyl formate, 792
Ethyl group, NMR, 218
Ethyl iodide, NMR, 218
Ethyl isovalerate, 792
Ethyl lactate, 792
4-Ethyl nitrobenzene, 797
Ethyl *p*-aminobenzoate, 792
Ethyl phenylacetate, 792
Ethyl *p*-hydroxybenzoate, 792
Ethyl *p*-nitrobenzoate, 792
Ethyl propionate, 792
Ethyl salicylate, 792
Ethyl vinyl ether, 793
2-Ethyl-1-butanol, 786
2-Ethyl-1-hexanol, 786
Ethyl-4-aminobenzoate, extraction of, 141
N-Ethylaniline, 789
2-Ethylaniline, 789
Ethylbenzene, 795
2-Ethylbutanal, 787
Ethylene glycol, 743, 754, 786
Ethylene, UV, 235
Ethylenediamine, 789
2-Ethylhexanal, 787
N-Ethyl-*m*-toluidine, 789
4-Ethylphenol, 798
Ethyltestosterone, 361
Eu(dpm)³, NMR shift reagent, 225
Eucalyptus, 101
Eugenol, isolation from cloves, 106
Europium shift reagent, 713
Eutectic, 66
Evaporation of solvents, 145
    in a reaction tube, 50
    micro, under vacuum, 50
    microscale, 131
Excedrin, 502
    separation of components, 528
Explosive substances, 27
Extinction coefficient, 236
Extraction, 133
    acid/base, 133
    caffeine from coffee, 151
    caffeine from cola syrup, 149
    caffeine from tea, 145
Extraction solvents, properties of, 127
Eye protection, 25

Fat, analysis, 343
    synthesis, 349
Fatty acids, saturated and unsaturated, 349
Fermentation of sucrose, 703
Fermentation, apparatus, 698
Ferrocene, acylation, 420
    apparatus for synthesis, macroscale, 612
    apparatus for synthesis, microscale, 612
    synthesis, 606–613
    structure, 607
Ferrocene/acetylferrocene chromato-graphy, 175
Ferrous ammonium sulfate, 774

Ferrox test, for ethers, 777
Fever reducer, 502
Fiber reactive dyes, 579
Fiberglass, 758
Field desorption MS, 241
Field ionization MS, 241
Fieser rules, for UV spectra, 237–238
Fieser, Louis, 2, 581, 678
Fieser, *Reagents for Organic Synthesis,* 800
Fieser's solution, 408
Filter adapter (Filtervac), 5
Filter flask, micro, 10
Filter paper, 47
Filtervac, 12
Filtrate, 49
Filtration, 38
    gravity, 46
    in a Pasteur pipette, 342
    pipette method, in reaction tube, 4, 5
    pressure, 45
    using micro Büchner funnel, 45
    using the Hirsch funnel, 50
    with a Pasteur pipette, 45
    with Wilfilter, 51–52
Fingerprint region of infrared spectrum, 196
Fire extinguisher, dry chemical, 27
Firefly, 674
Fischer, Emil, 507
Fischer esterification, 486, 495
Flammable substances, working with, 26
Flash chromatography, 421
Flash points, 26
Flask heater, 3, 14
Flask heater, electric, 13
Fleming, *Selected Organic Syntheses,* 802
Flow sheet, for extraction 135
Fluoboric acid, 399
Fluorene, 795
    column chromatography of, 180–181
    ¹H NMR, 449
    IR, 445
9-Fluorenone, 796
Fluorenone
    ¹H NMR, 450
    IR, 449
    synthesis and column chromatography of,
        171–183
Fluorescein, 577, 578
Fluorescence, 169, 578, 675, 684
Fluorescent anthracene, synthesis, 416
o-Fluorobromobenzene, 430
Fluorocortisone, 362
Fluorolube, for IR mulls, 208
Fluting a filter paper, 47
Folic acid, 545
Food and Drug Administration, 502
Force field calculations, 251
Formaldehyde, 747
    as reactant, 388
Formamide, 788
Formic acid, 415, 416, 417, 784
    as reactant, 388
Fourier transform IR (FTIR) spectrometer, 203
Fourier transform NMR spectrometer, 224;
    spectroscopy, 224
Fractional crystallization, 649
Fractional distillation, 82
Fractional distillation experiment, microscale, 90;
    macroscale, 93

Fractionating column, 9, 82
Fragmentation, MS, 245
Free radical, 403
    polymerization, 752
Freeze drying, 122
Friedel–Crafts
    acylation of, 420
    alkylation of benzene, 372
    alkylation of mesitylene, 386–393
    test for aromatic hydrocarbons, 778
Fructose, 691
Fructose-1,6-diphosphate, 699
Fructose-6-phosphate, 700
Fuchsin, 441
Fufurylamine, 789
Fumaric acid, 785
Funnel, for filtration, 47
Funnel, micro, 16
2-Furaldehyde, 787
Furan, 793
Furfuryl alcohol, 786
2-Furoic acid, 784

Galactose, 691
Gas chromatographic collection device, 187
Gas chromatography, 184–192
    analysis of chlorinated hydrocarbons, 281
Gas collection, microscale, 191
Gas cylinder cart, 34
Gas cylinders, safety, 34
Gas phase infrared spectroscopy, 209
Gas pressure regulator, 34
Gas trap, 554
    micro, 279
    macro, 279
Gas-liquid chromatography, 184–192
Gay-Lussac, Joseph L., 403, 698
General anesthetic, 508
Geranium oil, 327
Gerhardt, Charles, 501
Glaser reaction, 335
Glass scorer, 12
Glasses, 26
GlaxoSmithKline, 502
Glenbrook laboratories, 502
Gloves, *warning,* 32
Glucokinase, 701
Glucose, 691, 699
Glucose, as hemiacetal, 437
Glucose phenylhydrazone, 697
Glucose phenylosazone, 697
Glucose-6-phosphate, 700
Glutaraldehyde, 728
Glyceraldehyde-3-phosphate, 700
Glycerol trioleate, hydrogenation, 350
Glycerol tristearate, 496
    synthesis of, 350
Glycerol, 496
vic-Glycols, test for, 773
Glycolysis, 758
Gomberg, Moses, 403
Goodyear, Charles, 740
Graduated pipette, 12
Greene and Wuts, *Protective Groups in Organic
        Synthesis,* 803
Grignard synthesis, 461
    apparatus, 467, 470, 473
    starting, 466
Grignard, Victor, 461

Ground state, 684
Gum benzoin, 106

Halides, test for, 778
Halogen, test for, 765
Halogenated organic solvents, waste, 36
Handbook of Chemistry and Physics, 799, 800
Handbuch der Organichen Chemie, 800
Hazardous wastes, treatment, 36
HDL (high-density lipoproteins), 349
Heat of combustion, calculation of, 251
Heating baths, for vacuum distillation, 112
Heating mantle, 3
Heating organic reactions, 14
Height equivalent to a theoretical plate (HETP),
        83
Heilbron, *Dictionary of Organic Compounds,* 800
Helium, 184
Hemiacetal, 436
Heptaldehyde, 786
1-Heptanol, 786
2-Heptanone, 796
3-Heptanone, 796
4-Heptanone, 796
HETP, 83
Hexachlorocyclopropane, 301
1-Hexadecanol, 787
1-Hexadecene, 794
Hexamethylbenzene, UV, 239
Hexamethylenediamine, 743
Hexane, solvent, 41
Hexane-1,6-diamine, 743
Hexanoic acid, 784
1-Hexanol, 786
Hexaphenylbenzene, synthesis, 622–627
Hexaphenylethane, 403
5-Hexen-2-one, 796
High resolution mass spectrometer, 243
High-density polyethylene, HDPE, 754
Hinsberg test, 519
Hirsch filtration assembly, 53
Hirsch funnel
    for macroscale filtration, 54
    with polyethylene frit, 5
    with polyethylene frit, micro, 10
Hoechst, 502
Hoffmann, Felix, 501
Hoffmann, Roald, 592
Hooke's Law, 194, 252
Hops, 699
Horner reaction, 479
Host-guest chemistry, 372–376
Houben-Weyl, *Methods of Organic
        Chemistry,* 803
House, *Modern Synthetic Reactions,* 802
Hückel rule, 607
Hydrazine, 678
Hydrides, safety, 30
Hydriodic acid, as reactant, 398
Hydrobenzoin(1 R,2R) and (1S, 2S)-
        Hydrobenzoin, synthesis, 643
Hydrobenzoin(1 R,2S)-*meso*-Hydrobenzoin,
        synthesis, 643
Hydrobenzoin, 636
    configuration, 646
Hydrobromic acid, 259
    as reactant, 398
Hydrocinnamic acid, 784
Hydrofluoric acid, safety, 29

Hydrogen bonds, and melting point, 65
Hydrogen chloride trap, 374, 409
Hydrogen, generation, 345
Hydrogen peroxide, 678, 682
    safety, 29
Hydrogenation
    apparatus, microscale, 345
    apparatus for quantitative, 346
    catalytic, 340–353
Hydrolysis, of an ester, 496
Hydroquinone dimethyl ether, as reactant, 379
Hydroquinone dimethyl ether, extraction, 138
Hydroxamic acid test for nitriles and
        amides, 772
p-Hydroxyacetanilide, 527
3-Hydroxybenzoic acid, 785
4-Hydroxybenzoic acid, 785
Hydroxyl group, IR, 197
Hydroxylamine, 439
4-Hydroxypropiophenone, 796
Hypnotic drugs, 507
Hypnotics, 436
Hypochlorite oxidation, 317

I. G. Farbenindustrie, 502
Ibuprofen, 502
    TLC of, 161
Ignition test, of unknown, 763
Immunology, 544
Implosion, 33
Inclusion complex, thiourea, 373, 376
Indene, 794
Indigo, 574
    synthesis of, 335
Inflammation, 502
Infrared absorption frequencies of functional
        groups, 194
Infrared cell, filling, 207
Infrared spectra
    of gases, 209
    of solutions, 205
    of carbonyls, 195
Infrared spectrometer, FTIR, 203
Infrared spectroscopy, 194–215
Infrared spectroscopy, running the spectrum, 213
Instant coffee, extraction of caffeine from, 151
Instant microscale distillation, 87, 384
Integration of NMR spectra, 216
Integration, NMR, 219
Interfacial polymerization, 744
Intersystem crossing, 684
Inversion of configuration, S_N2 reaction, 269
Iodine, 441
    as catalyst, 188
Iodobenzoic acid, as reactant, 424
2-Iodobenzoic acid, synthesis, 539
Iodoethane, 273
Iodoform test, 441
2-Iodopropane, 793
Ion exchange catalyst, 489
Ion exchange resin, 486
Ionic attraction, and melting point, 65
IR spectra, analysis of, 196
IR, out-of-plane bending vibrations, for
        substituted benzenes, 383
Iron pentacarbonyl, 607
Iron(II) chloride, 606
Iron(II) hydroxide test, for nitro compounds, 774

Iron(III) chloride
catalyst, 382
test for phenols, 772
Iron(III) chloride, test for phenols, 772
Iron(III) hydroxamate test for anhydrides, 770
for esters, 771
Iron, in ferrocene, 607
Isoamyl acetate, 488, 792
Isoamyl nitrite, 430
Isoborneol, 731
Isobornyl acetate, 731
Isobutyl alcohol, 492
Isobutyl amine, 789
Isobutyl formate, 792
Isobutyl propionate, 492
Isobutylene, 488
2-(4-Isobutylphenyl)propionic acid (Ibuprofen),
TLC, 160
Isobutyraldehyde, 787
Isobutyramide, 788
Isobutyronitrile, 797
Isobutyrophenone, 796
Isocyanate, 755
Isopentenyl pyrophosphate, 101
Isoprene, 101, 327
Isoprene rule, 102
Isopropenyl acetate 733, 792
Isopropyl acetate, 792
Isopropylamine, 789
Isopulegone, 328–330
Isotopes, MS, 244
Itaconic acid, 785

Jasmine oil, 107
Jones' oxidation of alcohols, 769
Jones reagent, 325, 734

KBr disk, for IR, 208
Keck clamp, 11
in use, 9
Ketene, 488
Ketones
IR, 197
peroxide hazard, 28
reactions, tests for, 435–453
Knockout drops, 436
Kola nuts, 151
Kolbe electrolysis, 403
Kolbe synthesis, 501
Kugelrohr, 122
Kutzing, 698

Lab pack, 36
Laboratory hood, use of, 32
Laboratory notebook, 16–24
Laboratory record, preparing, 18
Lactic acid, 700
Lactones, IR, 199
Lactose, 692
Latex paint, 741
Lauric acid, 784
Lavender, 100
Lavoisier, 698
LDL (low-density lipoproteins), 349
Le Chatelier's principle, 488
Lead acetate, 765
Leaving groups, 270
Leeuwenhock, Anton van, 698
Lemongrass oil, 102

Lemons, 101
Leur tip, 10
Lewis acid catalyst, 372
Liebig, 698
Light sticks, 674
Light-producing reaction, 682
Ligroin, solvent, 41
Limonene, 101
Linalool, 786
Liquid/liquid extraction, 126–133
Literature of chemistry, searching, 779–783
Lithium triphenylmethide, 401
Local minimum problem, molecular
mechanics, 254
Long-necked flask, micro, 10
Low-density polyethylene, LDPE, 754
Lowry and Richardson, *Mechanism and Theory
in Organic Chemistry,* 803
Luciferase, 674
Luciferin, 674
Luminol, synthesis, 677–682
LUMO (lowest unoccupied molecular
orbital), 737
LUMO, lowest unoccupied molecular orbital,
calculations, 737
2,4-Lutidine, 791
2,6-Lutidine, 791
Lycopene, 723
TLC, 163
UV, 237
Lyophilization, 122

Macroscale apparatus kit, 11
Magnesium sulfate, drying agent, 137
Magnesium, 461, 466
Magnetic sector mass spectrometer, 241
Magnetic stirring bar, 13
Malachite Green, 572
Malcic acid, 785
MALDI MS, 241
Maleic anhydride, 311
Maleic anhydride, 760, 791
Maleic anhydride, reactant, 431
DL-Malic acid, 784
Mallory sublimator, 121
Malonic acid, 785
as reactant, 405
ester synthesis of, 507
Malononitrile, 797
Malt, 699
Maltose, 692
Mammoth cave, 577
DL-Mandelic acid, 784
Mandelonitrile, 630
Manganese dioxide, 312
Manganese ion, as catalyst, 756
Mannich condensation, 727
Mannose, 691
Manometer, 113
Manometric gasometer, 707
March, *Advanced Organic Chemistry,* 802
Martius Yellow, 570, 581–588
Mass spectrometer, schematic, 241
Mass spectrometry (MS), 241–249
McLafferty rearrangement, 246
McLeod gauge, 116
MDL (Molecular Design Limited), 804
Melamine, 740
Mel-Temp melting point apparatus, 68

Melting points, 65
apparatus, 67
capillaries, filling, 68
capillaries, sealed, 68
capillary, sealed, 611
composition diagrams, 66
depression, 66
determination, 69
unknowns, 72
Menthol, 100
Merck Index, 799
Mercury diffusion pump, 117
Mercury manometer, 113
Mercury spills, cleaning up, 35
Mesitylene, 795
as reactant, 389
Metallocene, 607
Methacrylamide, 788
Methacrylic acid, 784
Methane, gas phase IR, 212
Methanol, 786
solvent, 40
Methiodides, 781
Methoden der Organischen Chemie (Methods of
Organic Chemistry), 803
2-Methoxy-4-nitroaniline, 790
4-Methoxyacetophenone, 796
4-Methoxybenzyl alcohol, 787
2-Methoxynaphthalene, 793
Methyl acetoacetate, 792
Methyl acrylate, 792
Methyl amine, 728
Methyl benzoate, 495
as reactant, 367, 464, 474
^{13}C NMR, 500
^{1}H NMR, 499
IR, 500
nitration, 367
Methyl butyrate, 487
Methyl chloride, synthesis, 277
Methyl chloroacetate, 792
Methyl ethyl ketone peroxide, 760
Methyl ethyl ketone, as solvent, 40
Methyl formate, 792
Methyl group, IR, 202
Methyl iodide, 730, 789
Methyl ketone, test for, 441, 446
Methyl methaerylate, 792
Methyl Orange, 564
Methyl phenylacetate, 792
Methyl *p*-hydroxybenzoate, 792
Methyl *p*-nitrobenzoate, 792
Methyl propionate, 792
Methyl salicylate, 487, 792
Methyl sulfoxide, solvent, 40
Methyl *t*-butyl ether, (*t*-butyl methyl ether),
solvent, 41
Methyl trimethylacetate, 792
Methyl valerate, 792
Methyl vinyl ketone, in Diels–Alder reaction, 590
2-Methyl-1,3-butadiene, (isoprene), 101
2-Methyl-1-butanol, 581–588
2-Methyl-1-butene, 187
2-Methyl-1-propanol, 492, 786
2-Methyl-2-butanol, 187
2-Methyl-2-butanol, 187
2-Methyl-2-butene, 187
5-Methyl-2-hexanone, 796
4-Methyl-2-nitroaniline, 790

5-Methyl-2-norbornene, 794
4-Methyl-2-pentanol, 786
4-Methyl-2-pentanone, 795
2-Methyl-2-propanol, as reactant, 379
2-Methyl-3-butyn-2-ol, 786
2-Methyl-3-butyn-2-ol, coupling, 335
Methyl-3-nitrobenzoate
  ^{13}C NMR, 370
  ^{1}H NMR, 370
  IR, 371
  synthesis of, 367
3-Methyl-3-pentanol, 786
2-Methyl-3-pentanol, NMR with shift
  reagent, 226
1-Methyl-4-isopropylbenzene, 102
2-Methyl-4-nitroaniline, 790
2-Methyl-5-nitroaniline, 790
N-Methylacetamide, 788
4-Methylacetophenone, 796
Methylamine, 516
Methylammonium ion, 516
N-Methylaniline, 789
3-Methylanisole, 793
4-Methylanisole, 793
3-Methylbutanal, 788
3-Methylbutyl acetate, 487
Methylcyclohexane, solvent, 484
2-Methylcyclohexanol
  synthesis of, 354
  ^{1}H NMR, 356
  IR 358
2-Methylcyclohexanone, 796
3-Methylcyclohexanone, 796
2-Methylcyclohexanone, borohydride reduction
  of, 354
N-Methylcyclohexylamine, 789
Methylene chloride
  as solvent, 40
  synthesis of, 277
N-Methylformanilide, 788
1-Methylnaphthalene, 795
2-Methylnaphthalene, 795
2-Methylpropene, 488
2-Methylpropyl formate, 487
2-Methylpropyl propionate, 487
α-Methylstyrene, 735, 795
2-Methylvaleric acid, 784
Mickey Finn, 436
Micro Büchner funnel, 10
Micrometer, IR measurement, 194
Micron, IR measurement, 194
Micropipette for TLC, 160
Microscale apparatus kit, 10
Microscale distillation, 86
Microscale experiments, advantages, 1
Midol, 502
Mifepristone, abortifacient, 361
Mineral oil, 309
Mint, 101
Mixed melting points, 67
Mixing, in reaction tube, 129
MM2 computer program, 251
MNDO (modified neglect of diatomic overlap)
  calculations, 737
Molecular distillation, apparatus, 119
Molecular ion peak, 242
Molecular mechanics calculations, 250–258
  benzophenone, 257
  butenes, 256

Compound X, 257
  dibenzalacetones, 257
  dichlorobutanes, 256
  hexaphenylethane, 257
  isopulegols, 257
  isopulegone, 257
  α-phenylcinnamic acid, 257
  pseudopellitierene, 257
  pulegone, 257
  stilbenes, 257
  p-terphenyl, 257
  tetraphenylcylcopentadienone, 257
  Wittig reaction, 257
Molecular modeling, dibenzalacetone, 457
Molecular orbital calculations, 737
Molecular sieves, drying agent, 137
Molecular sieves, 489
Molecular weight determination, by MS, 243
Molecular weight, determination, using mp
  depression, 72
Molisch test, 694
Monosaccharides, 691
Mordant dyes, 571
Morpholine, 789
Morse potential, 253
Mother liquor, 49
Mulls, for IR, 207
Multifiber Fabric, 562
Multistep synthesis, 628
Mundy and Ellerd, *Name Reactions in Organic
  Chemistry*, 802
Murex brandaris, 561
Mylar, 743, 754
Myrcene, 101
Myristic acid, 726, 784
Myrrh, 106

NAD+, 701
NADH, 699, 702
Nanometers, UV wavelength
  measurement, 235
1-Naphthaldehyde, 788
Naphthalene, 795
  crystallization of, 57
  extraction of, 135
  UV, 239
1,8-Naphthalic anhydride, 792
2-Naphthol, 564, 798
1-Naphthol, 581, 585, 798
  ^{1}H NMR, 587
  IR, 588,
α-Naphthyl isocyanate, 783
Naproxen, 502
Natta, Giulio, 741
Natural products synthesis, 727
Neoprene adapters, 12
Neral, 101
Nicotinamide adenine dinucleotide, 701
Nicotinamide, 788
Nicotinic acid, 785
Nitration, of aryl halides, 782
Nitration, of methyl benzoate, 367–371
Nitric acid
  as oxidizing agent, 302, 310
  oxidation of benzoin, 638
  safety, 29
Nitriles
  IR, 199
  test for, 771

Nitro compounds
  derivatives, 783
  test for, 774
Nitro group, IR, 200
3-Nitroacetophenone, 796
4-Nitroacetophenone, 796
4-Nitroaniline, 789
2-Nitroaniline, 790
3-Nitroaniline, 790
2-Nitroanisole, 793
4-Nitroanisole, 793
3-Nitrobenzaldehyde, 788
Nitrobenzene, 797
  ^{13}C NMR, 557
  reduction, 548
4-Nitrobenzenediazonium chloride, 573
3-Nitrobenzoic acid, 785
4-Nitrobenzoic acid, 785
4-Nitrobenzoyl chloride, 791
Nitrocellulose, 739
Nitrogen rule, MS, 245
Nitrogen, test for, 764
2-Nitro-m-xylene, 797
1-Nitronaphthalene, 797
Nitronium ion, 367
3-Nitro-o-xylene, 797
2-Nitrophenol, 798
4-Nitrophenol, 798
3-Nitrophthalic acid, 678
Nitroso group, as explosive, 27
2-Nitrotoluene, 797
3-Nitrotoluene, 797
4-Nitrotoluene, 797
Nitrous acid, 535
Nitrous oxide, gas phase IR, 212
NMR samples
  filtration of, 227
  preparation of, 227
NMR solvents, 228
NMR spectrometer, adjustment, 228
NMR spectrum, determination of, 228
NOESY, 2D NMR, 230
Nonanoic acid, 784
Nonbonded electrons, 684
Nonhazardous waste, 36
cis-Norbornene-5,6-endo-dicarboxylic acid
  ^{1}H NMR, 604
  hydrogenation, 347
  IR, 604
  synthesis, 597–598
cis-Norbornene-5,6-endo-dicarboxylic
  anhydride
  ^{13}C NMR, 586
  IR, 585
  synthesis, 595;^{1}H NMR, 603
Norethisterone, 361
Norit, 43
  use of, 59
Notebook, how to keep, 16–24
Nuclear magnetic resonance spectral analysis,
  216
Nuclear magnetic resonance spectroscopy,
  216–234
Nuclear Overhauser effect spectroscopy
  (NOESY), 230
Nucleophilic substitution reactions, 267
Nujol, for IR mulls, 207
Nuremburg trials, 502
Nutrasweet, 693

Nylon, 742
Nylon 6.6, 562, 743
Nylon 6.10, 744

Octadecanol, synthesis, 344
1-Octadecanol, 787
1-Octadecene, 794
1,8-Octanedicarboxylic acid, 744
Octanoic acid, 784
1-Octanol, 786
2-Octanol, 786
2-Octanone, 796
1-Octene, 794
Octyl acetate, 487
Oderiferous chemicals, deodorizing, 34–35
Odor, of organic compounds, 763
Oil pump, vacuum, 115
Oiling out, in crystallization, 62
Oils, in crystallization, 62
Oleomargarine, 349
Oleyl alcohol, hydrogenation, 344
Olive oil
    hydrogenation, 349, 496
    IR, 353
Optical brighteners, 580
Optical purity, 709
    determination of, 713
Optical rotation, 709
Optical yield, 709
Optically active shift reagent, 713
Oral contraceptive, 360
Orange II, 564
Orange odor, 487
Orange oil, 107
Organic Reactions, 803
Organic solvents, waste, 36
Organic Syntheses, 803
Orlon, 562
Osazones, 694
Out-of-plane bending energy, 253
Out-of-plane bending vibrations, for substituted
    benzenes, 383
Oxalic acid dihydrate, 784
Oxalyl chloride, 674
1,2-Oxetanedione, 675
Oxidation
    cyclohexanol to cyclohexanone, 313
    cyclohexanone to adipic acid, 311–324
    using hypochlorite, 317
    with pyridinium chlorochromate, 325
Oxidative coupling of alkynes, 335
Oxime, 439
Oxygen, as reactant, 336
Oxygen scavenger, 408
Oxygenation, balloon technique, 336
Ozonide group, as explosive, 28

Painkiller, 502
Palladium on carbon catalyst, 341
Palladium on charcoal catalyst, 341
Palmitic acid, 784
Paquette, ed., *Encyclopedia of Reagents for
    Organic Synthesis,* 802
Paracelsus, 106
Paraformaldehyde, as reactant, 389
Paraldehyde, as reactant, 389
Paraperiodic acid, 773
Parent ion peak, 242
Partial pressure, 81

Partition coefficient, 128
Pasteur pipette, 12, 15
    calibration marks, 15
    filtration technique, 456
    filtration with, 45
    for filtration, 45
Pasteur, Louis, 698
Pauson, P. L., 607
PCC (see pyridinium chlorochromate), 325, 329
PCC-alumina reagent, preparation, 328
PDC (see pyridinium dichromate), 326
Peach odor, 487
Pear odor, 487
Pellitized Norit, 43
Pennyroyal oil, 101
Pentamethylbenzene, 795
Pentane, solvent, 41
2,3-Pentanedione, 796
1-Pentanol, 786
2-Pentanol, 786
3-Pentanol, 786
2-Pentanone, 795
3-Pentanone, 795
Pentobarbital, 507
Perchlorates, safety, 30
Perchloric acid, safety, 30
Periodic acid test, for glycols, 773
Perkin reaction, 664
Perkin, William Henry, 561
Perkin's Mauve, 561
Peroxide group, as explosive, 28
Peroxides, detection, removal, safety, 29
PET (polyethyleneglycol tereph-thalate), 754
Petroleum ether, solvent, 41
Phase diagram, melting of mixed solids, 66
Phase transfer catalysis, 509
Phenanthrene, 795
2-Phenetidine, 789
Phenobarbital, 508
Phenols, 747, 798
    derivatives, 783
    extraction, 135
    IR, 195
    test for, 774
Phenyl benzoate, 792
Phenyl Grignard reagent, 465, 472
N-Phenyl-1-naphthylamine, 790
4-Phenyl-3-buten-2-one, 455, 796
Phenylacetaldehyde, 787
Phenylacetic acid, 664, 784
Phenylacetone, 796
N-Phenylbenzylamine, 731, 790
α-Phenylcinnamic acid
    synthesis, 664–668
    UV, 668
N-Phenyldiethanolamine, 576
1,2-Phenylenediamine, 639
o-Phenylenediamine, 639
1,2-Phenylenediamine, 790
1,3-Phenylenediamine, 790
1,4-Phenylenediamine, 790
1-Phenylethanol, 786
2-Phenylethanol, 786
trans-9-(2-Phenylethenyl)anthracene,
    synthesis, 479
trans-9-(2-Phenylethenyl)anthracene,
    fluorescer, 675
Phenylhydrazine, 697
Phenylmagnesium bromide, 464, 472

Phenylosazones, 696
Phenylurethanes, 780
Phosphoenolpyruvic acid, 700
Phosphoglucoisomerase, 701
2-Phosphoglyceric acid, 700
3-Phosphoglyceric acid, 700
Phosphoric acid, 504
    dehydration catalyst, 290
    Friedel–Crafts acylation catalyst, 420
Photochemistry, 683
Phthalic acid, 785
    crystallization of, 57
Phthalic anhydride, 578, 792
    as reactant, 407
2-Picoline, 791
3-Picoline, 791
4-Picoline, 791
Picrates, amine, 521
Picrates, preparation, 780
Picric acid, 521, 570
Pinacolone, 795
Pinacolone, rearrangement, 688
Pineapple odor, 487
DL-α-Pinene, 794
α-Pinene, 101
Piperidine, 789
Pipette pump, 12
    use of, 129
Plant pigments, TLC of, 163
Plasticizers, 740
Platinum(IV) chloride, 347
Pluro stopper, 10
PM3 (Parameterization method 3)
    calculations, 737
Polarimeter, 713
Polyamide, 743
Polyamino acids, 739
Polyester, 562
    fiberglass reinforced, 758
Polyethylene film, IR, 210
Polyethylene frit, 5, 46
Polyethylene glycol, 750
Polyethylene glycol terphthalate, 743
Polyethylene, high-density, 742
Polyethylene wash bottle, 13
Polyethyleneglycol terephthalate, 562, 754
Polyglucose, 739
Polymers, condensation, 739
    synthesis and recycling, 739
Polynucleotides, 739
Polypropylene, 562, 754
Polystyrene, 489, 742, 752
Polystyrene film, IR, 213
Polytetrafluoroethylene, 741
Polythene, 741
Polyurethane foam, 755
Polyvinyl acetate, 741
Polyvinyl chloride, 740
Polyvinyl chloride, PVC, 754
Polyvinylidene chloride, 741
Pomegranate, 727
Potassium antimonyl tartrate, 572
Potassium bromide disks for IR, 208
Potassium cyanide, 632
Potassium cyclopentadienide, 606
Potassium ferricyanide, 678
Potassium hydroxide, safety, 30
Potassium permanganate, 284
    test for unsaturation, 777

Potassium persulfate, 424
Powder funnel, 13
Pressure regulator, 34
Pressure-temperature boiling point
    nomograph, 119
Priestly, Joseph, 742
Primuline, 572
Progesterone, 361
Prontosil, 544
1,2-Propanediol, 786
Propanoic acid, 492
1-Propanol, 487, 786
2-Propanol, 786
2-Propanol, as reactant, 664, 667
Propargyl alcohol, 786
Propionaldehyde, 787
Propionic acid, 488
Propionic anhydride, 791
Propionitrile, 797
Propionyl chloride, 791
Propiophenone, 796
n-Propyl acetate, 487, 792
n-Propyl *p*-hydroxybenzoate, 792
n-Propylamine, 517, 788
Propylene glycol, 760
Prostaglandins, 502
Protein Data Bank, 804
Proteins, as polymers, 739
Prussian Blue, 764
Pseudopellitierene, synthesis, 727
Pulegone, 101
    from citronellal, 325–332
    UV, 238
Putrescine, 517
PVC, 740
Pyridine, 791
Pyridine, catalyst, 504
Pyridinium chlorochromate, 325, 329
Pyridinium dichromate, 326
Pyridinium hydrobromide perbromide, 659
Pyridinium hydrobromide perbromide, test for
    alkenes, 285
Pyrogallol, 798
Pyrrolidine, 789
Pyruvic acid, 699, 784

Quadrupole mass spectrometer, 241
Qualitative organic analysis, 762–798
Quinine, 106
Quinoline, 669, 791

Radiationless transition, 685
Radical chlorination, 274–282
Radical reactions, 274–282
Raoult's law, 81
Raspberry odor, 487
Rate of reaction, effect of temperature on, 2
Reaction tube, advantages of, 3
Reagents for Organic Synthesis, 800
Reciprocal centimeters, in IR, 194
Recycling plastics, 754
Red tetrazolium sugar test, 694
Reduced nicotinamide adenine dinucleotide,
    699, 702
Reduction of nitro compounds, 783
Reduction stereochemistry, 646
Reduction, of azo dyes, 569
Reflux apparatus, micro and macro, 4
Reflux apparatus, microscale, 262, 492, 512

Reflux ratio, in distillation, 83
Refluxing apparatus
    microscale, 342
    small scale, 343
Refluxing, 4
Refraction of light, 76
Refractive index
    definition, 76
    temperature correction of, 76
Refractometer, use of, 77
Regioselectivity, in Diels–Alder reaction, 591
Registry of Toxic Effects of Chemical Substances,
    (RTECS), 800
Relative reactivities of hydrogens, to
    chlorination, 275
Research project, 341
Resolution, enzymatic, of DL-Alanine, 715
Resorcinol, 578, 798
Retention of configuration, in Diels–Alder
    reaction, 590
Retention time, 185
Reverse Diels–Alder reaction, 592
Reyes syndrome, 502
Ring-opening polymerization, 750
Robinson, Sir Robert, 727
Rock candy, 692
Rodd, *Chemistry of Organic Compounds,* 800
p-Rosaniline hydrochloride, 441
Rosenblum, 607
Rotary evaporator, 179
RTECS, *Registry of Toxic Effects of Chemical
    Substances,* 800
RU-486, abortifacient, 361
Rubber, 742
Rum fragrance, 487

Saccharin, 691, 693
Safety, 25–37
Safety cans, 26
Safety glasses, 25, 30
Salicigen, 501
Salicyclic acid, 153, 503
Salicylaldehyde, 787
Salivary amylase, 785
Salt cell for IR, 204
Salting out, 316
Salvarsan, 544
Sand bath, 3
Sandmeyer reaction, 534–543
Santoprene connector, 4
Saponification, 496
Saran Wrap, 741
Saturated fat, 496
Saturated hydrocarbons, test for, 778
Saturated sodium chloride solution, as drying
    agent, 137
Sax, *Dangerous Properties of Industrial
    Materials,* 800
Saytzeff rule, 188
Schiff base, 439
Schiff's test, for aldehydes, 441, 446, 770
Schlenk-type filtration apparatus,
Schlesinger, H. I., 643
Science Citation Index, 801
SciFinder Scholar, 804
Scopolomine, 727
Sebacic acid, 744, 784
Sebacoyl chloride, 744
Sedatives, 436

Seliwanov test, 696
Semicarbazide, 439
Semicarbazide hydrochloride, 444
Semicarbazones, 439, 444, 780
Semiempirical MO calculations, 737
Separatory funnel, 141
    micro, 130
    micro and macro, 7
Septum, 12,
Sex hormones, 360
Shellac, 739
Shift reagent, NMR, 225
Shift reagent, optically active, 713
Short-necked flask, 5-mL, micro, 10
Sidechain oxidation products of aryl
    compounds, 782
Silica gel, 157, 171
    disposal of, 36
Silicon Graphics computer, 737
Silicone oil, as GC support, 184
Silicone oil, for melting point baths, 67
Silicone rubber, as GC support, 184
Silk, 562
Silver acetate, 488
Silver chloride IR cell, 204
Silver mirror, 441
Silver nitrate, ethanolic, test reagent, 272
Silver nitrate, 440, 445
Simple distillation, 82
    apparatus, microscale, 86–88
    microscale, 89
    macroscale, 92
Singlet excited state, 675, 685
Sintering of Teflon, 741
Sleeping pills, 508
Small-scale sublimation apparatus, 121
Smith and March, *Advanced Organic
    Chemistry,* 802
SmithKline Beecham, 502
S_N1 reaction, 269
S_N2 reaction, 269
    steric hindrance, 269
Soap, synthesis of, 496
Sodium, 513, 763
    disposal of, 35
Sodium acetate, 504
Sodium acetylsalicylate, 531
Sodium anthraquinone-2-sulfonate, 408
Sodium borohydride
    for hydrogenation, 347
    reducing agent, 354, 643, 643, 655
    reduction of benzil, 643
Sodium bromide, 260
Sodium chloride solution, as drying agent, 137
Sodium cyanide, 764
Sodium cyclamate, 691
Sodium dichromate, 311
Sodium ethoxide, 513
Sodium fluoride, 706
Sodium fusion test, 763
Sodium hydride, 750
Sodium hydrosulfite, reducing agent, 408, 414,
    581, 584, 678
Sodium hydroxide, safety, 30
Sodium hypochlorite, 317
Sodium iodide in acetone, test reagent, 272
Sodium methoxide, synthesis, 483
Sodium nitrite, 535, 563
Sodium nitroprusside, 765

Sodium pentothal, 508
Sodium phenoxide, extraction, 135
Sodium plumbite, 765
Sodium salicylate, 501
Sodium stearate, 496
Sodium sulfate, drying agent, 138
Sodium trichloroacetate, thermal
    decomposition, 302
Solubility tests, 56
    organic unknown, 766–767
Solutes for column chromatography, 172
Solvent correction, UV, 238
Solvent evaporation, micro, 50
Solvent pairs, for crystallization, table, 42
Solvents for crystallization, 39
Soxhlet extractors, 626
    operation of, 126
Soybean oil, 349
Spanish fly, 591
Spartan computer program, 737
Spatula, stainless steel, 13
Specific rotation, 713
Spilled solids, cleaning up, 35
Squalene, 364
Squalene oxide, 364
Standard-taper ground-glass apparatus, 11
Starch, 699
Starting material, 1
Stationary phase, for GLC, 185
Steam bath, 15
Steam distillation, (see distillation, steam), 98
    apparatus, microscale, 305
    experiment, 98–109
    of aniline, 549
    of cyclohexanone, 313
Stearic acid, 726, 784
Stearonitrile, 797
Stereochemistry of borohydride reduction, 646
Stereochemistry of ketone reduction, 355
Stereospecific polymerization, 742
Steric energy calculations, 255
Sterling drug, 502
Stilbene, 654
    UV, 653
Stilbene dibromide, 669–673
meso-Stilbene dibromide, synthesis, 658
1*R*,2*S*-Stilbene dibromide, synthesis, 658
Z-Stilbene, synthesis, 669-673
Stilbenediol diacetate, 650
    UV, 650
STN International, 803
Stolow, R. D., 381
Stopcock, polyethylene/nylon, 10
Strain energy, 251
Styrene, 742, 753, 760
Styrene/butadiene copolymer, 794
Sublimation
    apparatus, 5, 6
    apparatus, microscale, 121
    of caffeine, 532
    of ferrocene, 610
    of unknown, 123
Succinic acid, 785
Succinic anhydride, 792
Succinonitrile, 797
Sucrose, 692, 699
    ^{13}C NMR spectrum of, 224
    fermentation, 703
Suction filter assembly, macro, 6

Sugar substitutes, 691
Sugars, 692
Sulfa drugs, 545
Sulfanilamide, 544–560
    IR, 560
    mp standard, 70
Sulfanilic acid, 563
Sulfonamides, 520
    test for, 775
Sulfur, test for, 765
Sulfuric acid
    catalyst, 379
    dehydration catalyst, 188
    fuming, test for alkenes, 285
    safety, 29
Sulfuryl chloride, 277
Superheating, 41
Sweeteners, 691
Sweetness of sugars and sugar substitutes, 693
Swirling of a solution, 43
Synthetic rubber, 742
Syphilis, treatment of, 544
Syringe, polypropylene, 10

Tannic acid, 571
Tare, 5
    definition of, 17
Tartar emetic, 572
D-Tartaric acid, 785
Tea bags, 146
Teflon, 741
Teratogens, 31
Terelyene, 754
Terephthalic acid, 743, 754, 785
Ternary azeotrope, 84, 489
Terpenes, 101, 327
p-Terphenyl, synthesis, 596–599
Test Identification Stain, 577
Testosterone, 360
Tetrabromofluorescein, 578
Tetracene, UV, 239
1,1,2,2-Tetrachlorethane, 793
Tetrachlorobenzene, 1,2,4,5-, 794
Tetrachloroethylene, 793
Tetrachloromethane, synthesis, 277
Tetrachlorophthalic anhydride, 792
Tetrachlorotricyclo[7.1.0.0[4.6]]decane, *cis*- and
    trans, synthesis, 302
^{1}H NMR, 310
1-Tetradecanol, 787
1-Tetradecene, 794
Tetrahydrofuran, 793
    safety, 29
Tetrahydrofurfuryl alcohol, 786
Tetrahydronaphthalene,1,2,3,4-, 795
Tetramethylbenzene,1,2,4-, 795
Tetramethylbenzene,1,2,3,5-, 795
Tetramethylbenzene, 1,2,4,5-, 795
Tetramethylsilane, NMR reference, 218, 227
Tetraphenylcyclopentadienone, 624
    as reactant, 424
    synthesis of, 619–621,
1,2,3,4-Tetraphenylnaphthalene, 424
Theoretical plates, 83
Theoretical yield calculations, 260
    example, 22
Thermometer
    adapter, 7
    adapter, macro, 13

calibration, 69
calibration of, 85, 91
digital, for boiling points, 74
for melting points, 68
Thermoplastic polymers, 740
Thermosetting polymers, 740
Thermowell heater, 13
Thiamine hydrochloride, catalyst, 633
Thiamine pyrophosphate, 699
Thiamine, catalyst, 633
Thiele, Johannes, 649
Thin-layer chromatography, 156–170
    apparatus and visualization, 162
    uses of, 156
Thionyl chloride, 655, 744
Thiourea, inclusion complex, 373, 376
Thomas-Hoover melting point apparatus, 67
Thomson, J. J., 241
Threading Teflon tube through septum, 279
Threading tube through septum, 374
Thymol, 798
Tin(II) chloride reduction, 414
Tin, 548
TLC, (see thin-layer chromatography), 146–170
TMS, NMR reference, 227
Tollens' reagent, 445
Tollens' test, 440, 445
4-Tolualdehyde, 787
p-Toluene sulfonic acid, 486
Toluene, 784, 795
Toluene, solvent, 41
Toluene, steam distillation of, macroscale, 104
Toluene, vapor pressure of, 82
m-Toluic acid, 784
o-Toluic acid, 784
4-Toluic acid, 785
4-Toluic acid, mp standard, 70
p-Toluides, preparation, 779
p-Toluidine hydrochloride, 536
p-Toluidine, 518
2-Toluidine, 789
3-Toluidine, 789
4-Toluidine, 790
2-Tolunitrile, 797
4-Tolunitrile, 797
3-Tolunitrile, 797
Tolylene diisocyanate, 756
Tomato, TLC of pigments, 163
Toxic substances, working with, 30
Transesterification, 755
trans-Fatty acids, 349
Transfer hydrogenation, of olive oil, 349
Transfer of a solid, technique, 15
Trap, aspirator, 55
2,4,6-Tribromoaniline, 790
Tricaprylmethylammonium chloride, 509
Trichloracetic acid, 784
Trichloroacetaldehyde, 387
Trichloroacetonitrile, 797
1,2,3-Trichlorobenzene, 794
1,2,4-Trichlorobenzene, 794
1,1,1-Trichloroethane, 793
1,1,2-Trichloroethane, 793
2,2,2-Trichloroethanol 786
Trichloroethylene, 793
Trichloromethane, synthesis, 277
Trichloromethyl anion, 302
2,4,6-Trichlorophenol, 674
1,2,3-Trichloropropane, 793

Triethyl phosphite, as reactant, 479
Triethylamine picrate, 522
Triethylamine, 522, 664, 791
Triethylene glycol dimethyl ether, 2, 431, 615
Triethylene glycol, solvent, 618, 660, 678
Triglyme, solvent, 431, 615
Triiodomethyl carbanion, 442
Trimethyl phosphite, 485
  ¹H NMR, 485
Trimethylacetic acid, 785
2,4,5-Trimethylaniline, 790
1,2,4-Trimethylbenzene, 795
Trimethylcarbocation, 379
2,3,5-Trimethylphenol, 798
2,4,6-Trinitrophenol, 521
Triosphosphate isomerase, 701
2,3,5-Triphenyl-2H-tetrazolium chloride, 695
Triphenylacetic acid, 401
Triphenylmethane, 399
Triphenylmethane dyes, 572
Triphenylmethanol, 394
Triphenylmethanol, as reactant, 405
Triphenylmethyl bromide, 397
Triphenylmethyl carbocation, 394
Triphenylmethyl chloride, 403
Triphenylmethyl fluoborate, 399
Triphenylmethyl iodide, 398
Triphenylmethyl methyl ether, 394
  ¹H NMR, 397
Triphenylmethyl peroxide, 405
Triphenylphosphine oxide, 479
Triphenylphosphine, 479
Triplet excited state, 675
Triplet state, 685
Triptycene, synthesis, 430
Tris(dipivaloylmethanato)europiumIII, shift
  reagent, 225
Triton B, catalyst, 618
Trityl bromide, 397, 405
Trityl carbanion, 401
Trityl carbocation, 394
Trityl chloride, 405
Trityl fluoborate, 399
Trityl iodide, 398
Trityl methyl ether, 395
Trityl radical, 405
Tropilium fluoborate, 399
Tropilium iodide, 399
Tropilium ion, 399
Tropinone, 727

Truth serum, 508
Tse-Lok Ho, *Reagents for Organic
  Synthesis,* 802
Tswett, Michael, 162
Tubing, polyethylene, 10
Turkey Red, 571
Turpentine, 101, 731
Two-dimensional NMR, 228
Tylenol, 502
Tyrian Purple, 561

Ultraviolet spectroscopy, 235–240
2-Undecanonc, 796
Unimolecular nucleophilic substitution, 269
Unsaturated hydrocarbons, test for, 777
Urea
  mixed melting point, 71
  mp standard, 70
  reactant, 513
Urethane, 755

Vacuum distillation (see Distillation, vacuum,
  110–120)
Vacuum sublimator, large, 121
Valeric acid, 784
Van der Waals energy, 253
Van der Waals forces, and melting points, 65
Van Helmont, 698
Vanillin anion, UV, 240
Vanillin, 788
Vanillin, UV, 240
Vanquish, 502
Vapor phase chromatography, 184–192
Vapor pressure vs. temperature, 80
Vapor pressure, vs. temperature curves, for water
  and benzene, 99
Vat dyes, 574
Velox, 739
Vesicant, 592
Vibration modes, IR, 195
Vigreux column, 113
Vinyl acetate, 792
Vinyl chloride, 740
Vinyl halides, reactivity, 270
4-Vinyl-1-cyclobexene, 794
5-Vinyl-2-norbornene, 794
Viscose rayon, 562
Vitamin, D₃, 362
Viton connector, 10
Von Baeyer, Adolph, 507

Von Hohenheim, Theophrastus Bombastus, 101
Von Mering, August, 507

Wagner-Meerwein rearrangement, 731
Washing and drying lab equipment, 14
Washing laboratory equipment, 14
Waste treatment and disposal, 36
Waste, definition, 36
Water aspirator, 55
  for vacuum distillation, 114
Water, solvent, 40
Water, vapor pressure vs. temperature, 100
Web of Science, 802
Weissback, *The Beilstein Guide,* 800
Weissberger, *Techniques of Organic Chemistry,* 803
Whiting, 607
Wien, 241
Wilfilter, 6
  filtration apparatus, 7
  filtration with, 51–52
Wilkinson, 607
Williamson gas phase IR cell, 209
Willstätter, R., 163, 727
Wintergreen odor, 487
Wittig reagent, 479
Wittig-Horner reaction, 479
Woodward, R. B., 592, 607
Woodward's rules, for UV spectra, 236–237
Wool, 562

Xanthophylls, 163
m-Xylene, 795
o-Xylene, 795
p-Xylene, 795
m-Xylene, alkylation, 382, IR, 385
Xylose, 691

YAD, 701
Yeast alcohol dehydrogenase, 701
Yeast, 698, 708
Yield calculations, 260
  example, 22
Ylide, 479

Ziegler, Karl, 742
Zinc chloride, 578
Zinc dust, 416, 649
  debromination, 294
Zinc, for debromination, 294
Zinc, for hydrogen generation, 345